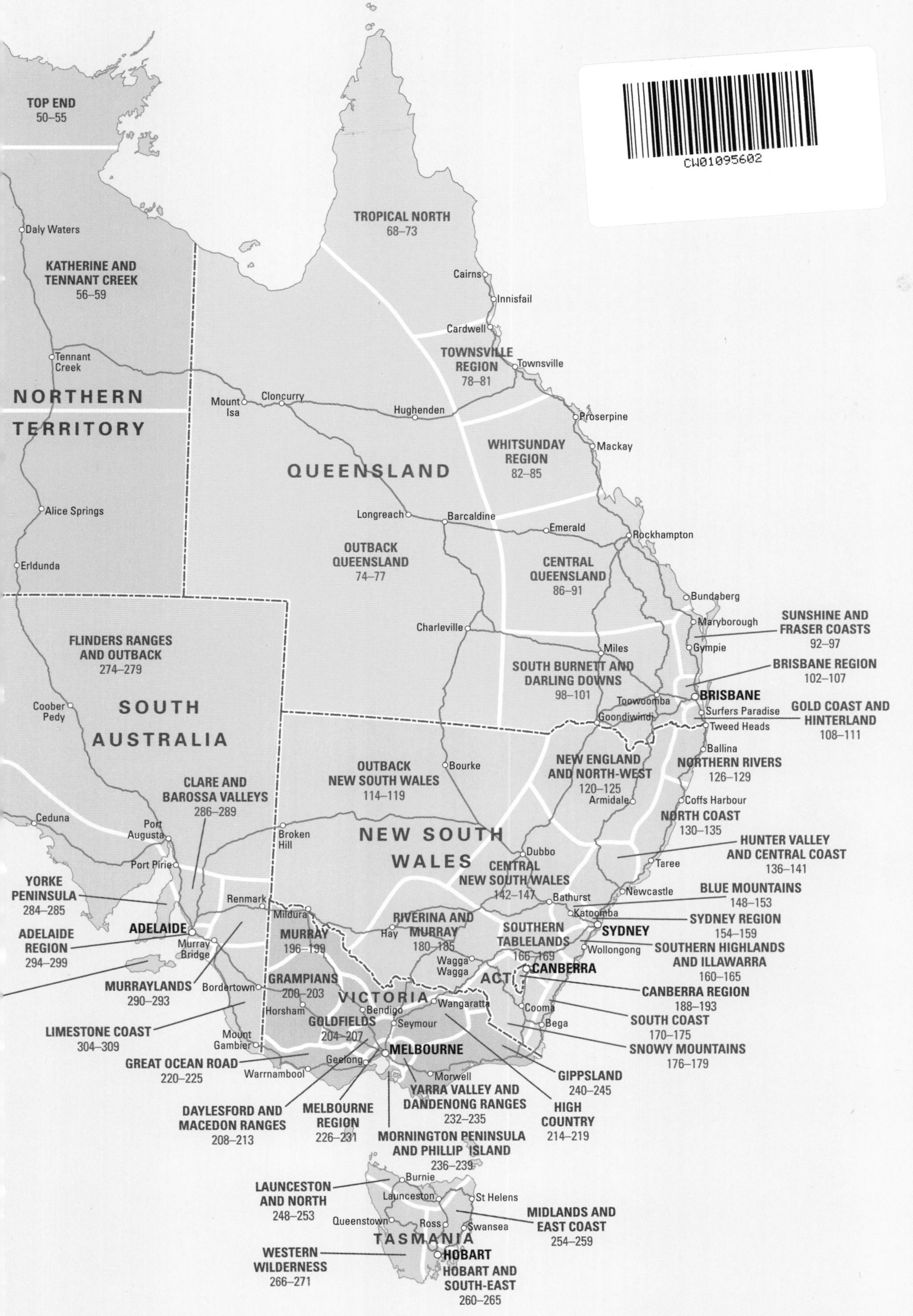
TOP END
50–55
Daly Waters
KATHERINE AND TENNANT CREEK
56–59
Tennant Creek
NORTHERN TERRITORY
Alice Springs
Erldunda
TROPICAL NORTH
68–73
Cairns
Innisfail
Cardwell
TOWNSVILLE REGION
78–81
Townsville
Mount Isa
Cloncurry
Hughenden
Proserpine
Mackay
WHITSUNDAY REGION
82–85
QUEENSLAND
Longreach
Barcaldine
Emerald
Rockhampton
OUTBACK QUEENSLAND
74–77
CENTRAL QUEENSLAND
86–91
Bundaberg
Maryborough
SUNSHINE AND FRASER COASTS
92–97
Gympie
Charleville
Miles
SOUTH BURNETT AND DARLING DOWNS
98–101
BRISBANE REGION
102–107
BRISBANE
Toowoomba
Surfers Paradise
GOLD COAST AND HINTERLAND
108–111
Goondiwindi
Tweed Heads
Ballina
FLINDERS RANGES AND OUTBACK
274–279
Coober Pedy
SOUTH AUSTRALIA
OUTBACK NEW SOUTH WALES
114–119
Bourke
NEW ENGLAND AND NORTH-WEST
120–125
Armidale
NORTHERN RIVERS
126–129
Coffs Harbour
NORTH COAST
130–135
CLARE AND BAROSSA VALLEYS
286–289
Ceduna
Port Augusta
Port Pirie
Broken Hill
NEW SOUTH WALES
Dubbo
CENTRAL NEW SOUTH WALES
142–147
HUNTER VALLEY AND CENTRAL COAST
136–141
Taree
Newcastle
BLUE MOUNTAINS
148–153
YORKE PENINSULA
284–285
Renmark
Mildura
Bathurst
Katoomba
SYDNEY REGION
154–159
ADELAIDE
ADELAIDE REGION
294–299
Murray Bridge
MURRAY
196–199
Hay
RIVERINA AND MURRAY
180–185
SOUTHERN TABLELANDS
166–169
SYDNEY
Wollongong
SOUTHERN HIGHLANDS AND ILLAWARRA
160–165
Wagga Wagga
ACT
CANBERRA
CANBERRA REGION
188–193
MURRAYLANDS
290–293
Bordertown
GRAMPIANS
200–203
VICTORIA
Wangaratta
Cooma
SOUTH COAST
170–175
Horsham
Bendigo
Seymour
Bega
GOLDFIELDS
204–207
LIMESTONE COAST
304–309
Mount Gambier
MELBOURNE
SNOWY MOUNTAINS
176–179
GREAT OCEAN ROAD
220–225
Geelong
Warrnambool
Morwell
GIPPSLAND
240–245
YARRA VALLEY AND DANDENONG RANGES
232–235
HIGH COUNTRY
214–219
DAYLESFORD AND MACEDON RANGES
208–213
MELBOURNE REGION
226–231
MORNINGTON PENINSULA AND PHILLIP ISLAND
236–239
LAUNCESTON AND NORTH
248–253
Burnie
Launceston
St Helens
MIDLANDS AND EAST COAST
254–259
Queenstown
Ross
Swansea
TASMANIA
WESTERN WILDERNESS
266–271
HOBART
HOBART AND SOUTH-EAST
260–265

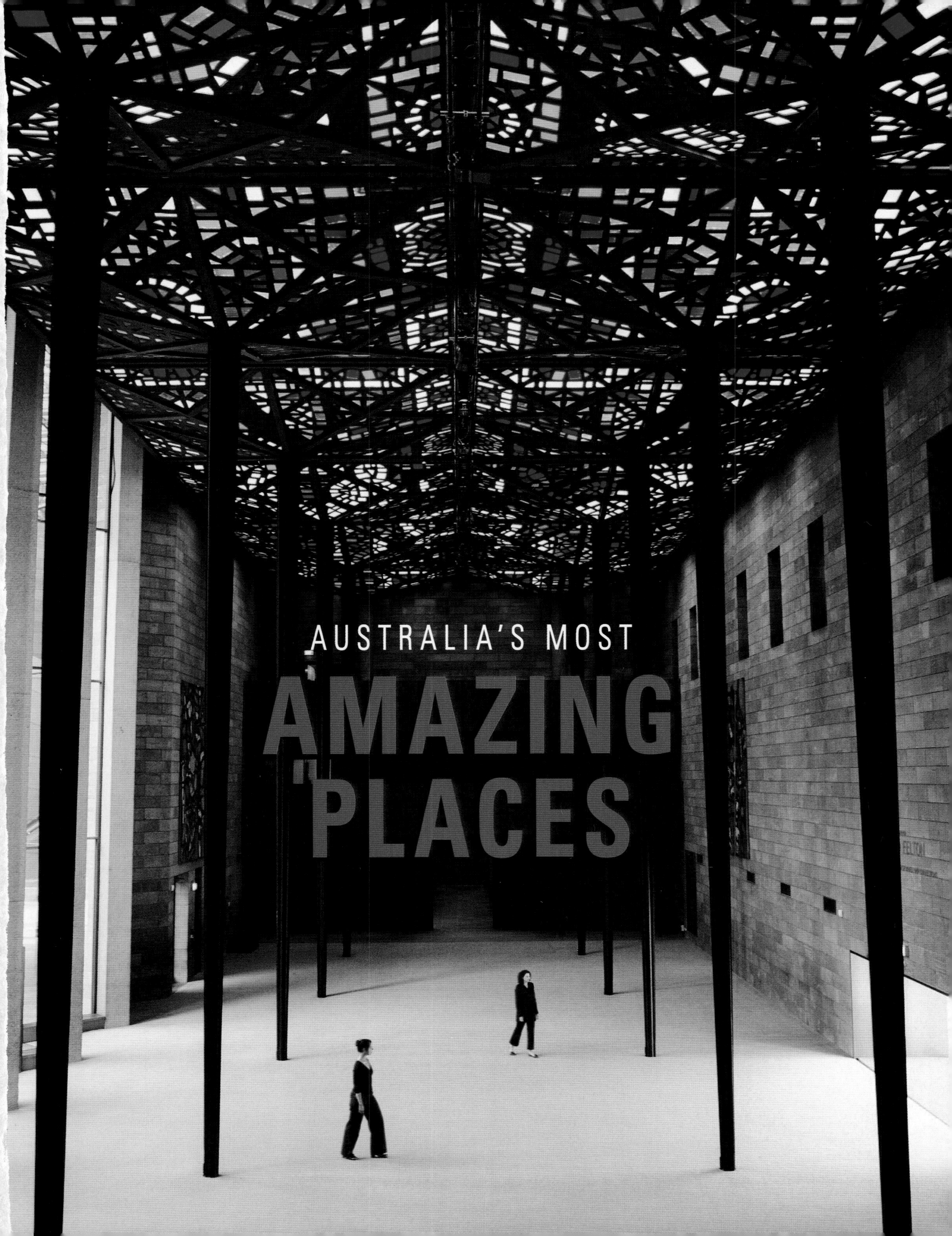

AUSTRALIA'S MOST AMAZING PLACES

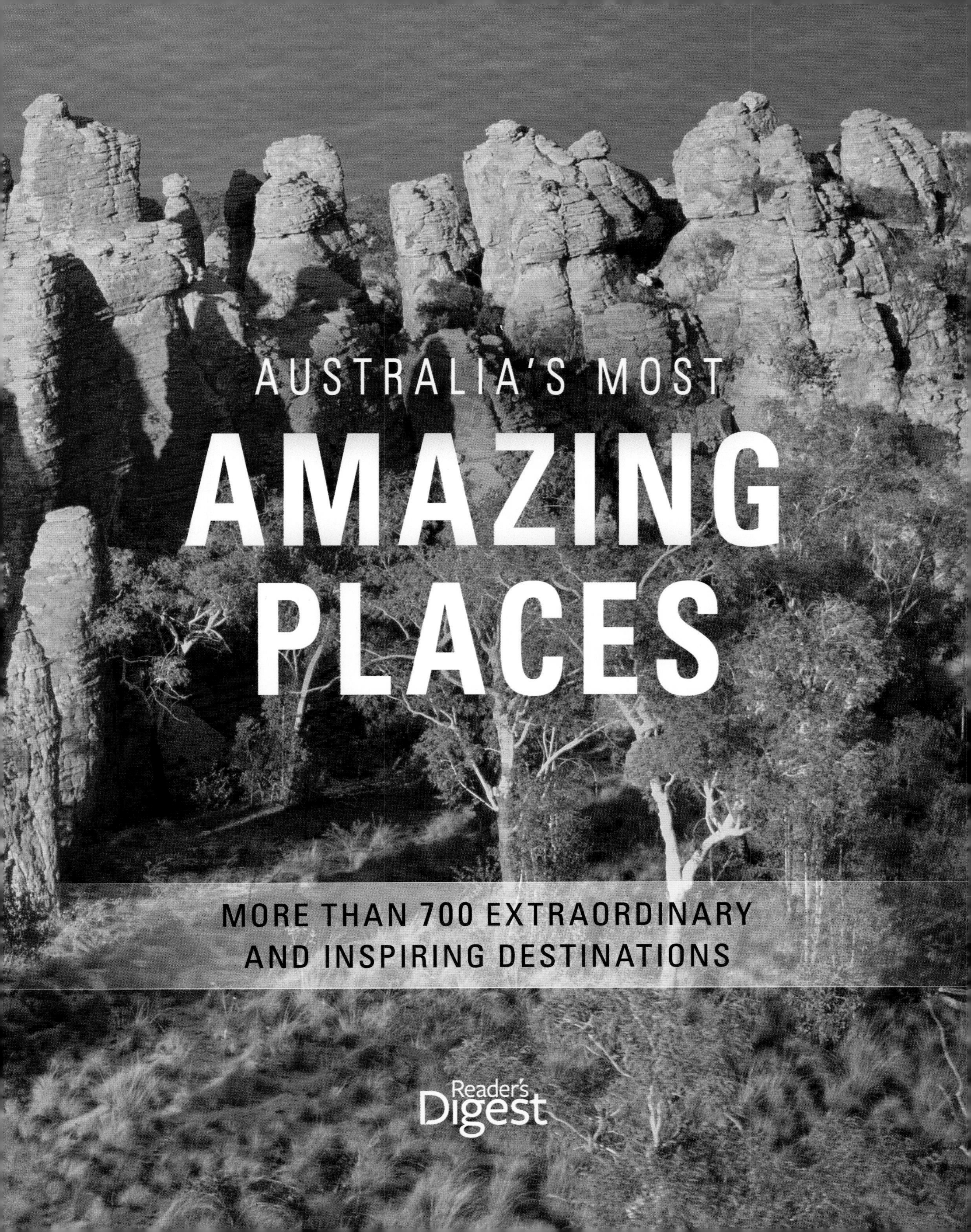

AUSTRALIA'S MOST

AMAZING PLACES

MORE THAN 700 EXTRAORDINARY AND INSPIRING DESTINATIONS

Reader's Digest

Contents

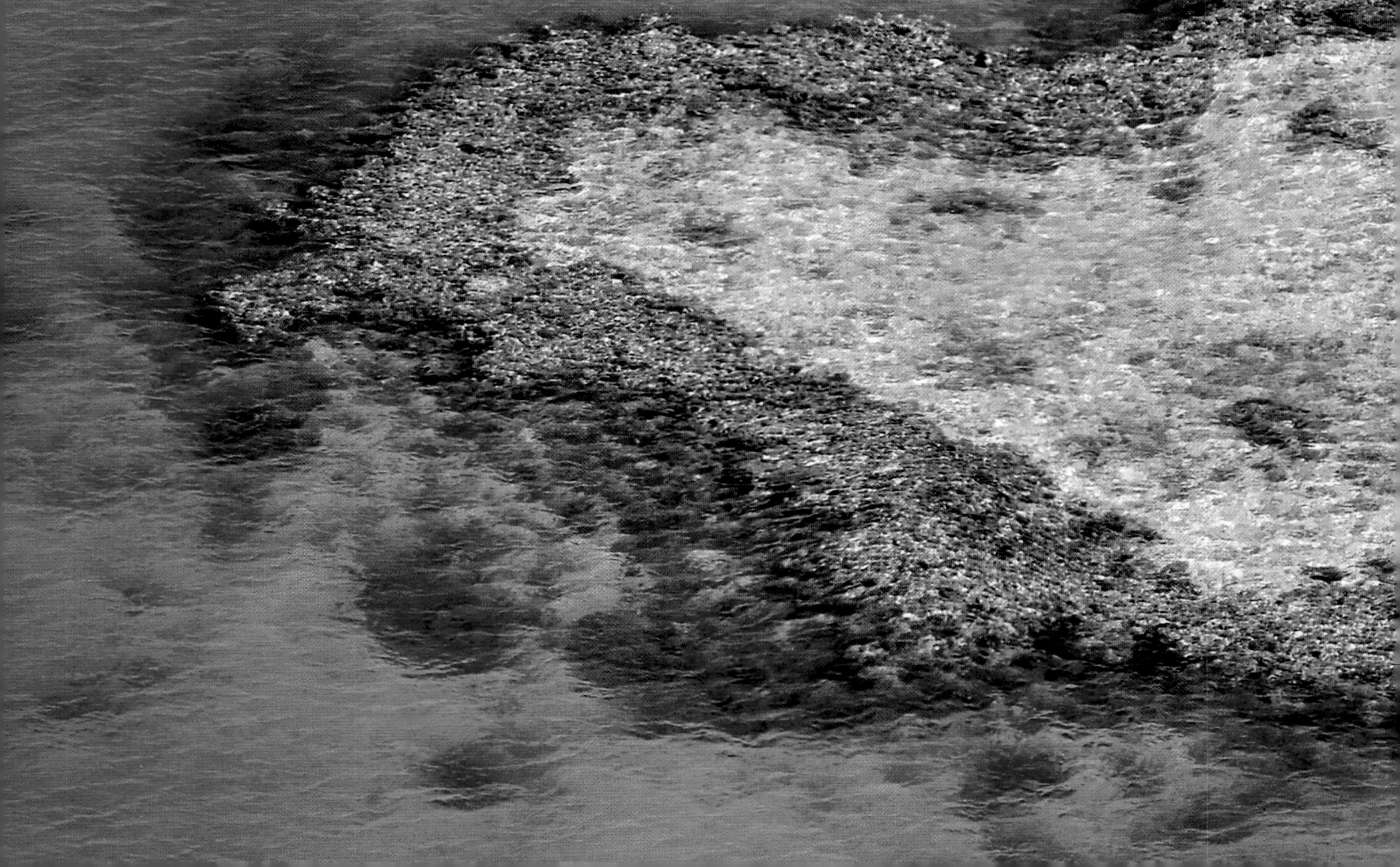

An amazing land

Australia is truly an extraordinary place. The sixth-biggest country in the world, it encompasses some of the most spectacular and diverse landscapes on the planet, abundant and unique wildlife, ancient remnants of one of the world's oldest societies, a rich colonial heritage, and diverse and vibrant cultures.

Though they are spread across a vast area, Australia's attractions are mostly accessible, safe to visit and well preserved. They're all out there, waiting to be discovered – with a little help from this guide.

The following pages will take you to more than 700 amazing places scattered across this remarkable continent, from the desert shores of Western Australia and the tropical rainforests of Queensland to the Victorian goldfields and the vineyards of South Australia, via every state and territory capital. These destinations span all kinds of attractions, from stunning scenery to historic towns and villages, from wineries to wildlife parks, and from rock art to railway museums.

You'll discover astonishing buildings, such as a Moorish castle in the Queensland rainforest, underground churches in the South Australian desert and the Southern Hemisphere's largest Buddhist temple; learn about unusual natural phenomena, including a mountain that has been on fire for 5500 years and waterfalls that flow sideways; see little-known landscapes such as the strangely eroded spires of a 'lost city' and the world's second-largest silt jetties; and explore unusual art and museum collections, from a sculpture gallery on a salt lake to a pharmacy museum and a cricket hall of fame.

Finding your way

The book is divided into eight chapters, one for each state and territory, beginning with Western Australia and moving clockwise around the country. Each chapter is divided into smaller regions. Within each region, the featured places are numbered, and presented in a logical geographical order, usually north to south. Interspersed with the entries are longer features on intriguing facets of each region's landscape, wildlife and human history.

All the states, territories and regions are shown on the map inside the front and back covers. Each chapter opens with a map that shows that state's or territory's regions, and the locations of the featured places. Each chapter also includes a map of the state or territory capital, showing places within the city area.

Further information

At the end of each entry are simple directions for finding the place. Opening hours are included only when they are out of the ordinary, such as when an attraction is open just a couple of days a week or only by appointment. In all cases, it is advisable to check road access and opening times before you set off. Telephone numbers of all the relevant accredited visitor information centres are included for each region.

Useful websites

Tourism Australia www.australia.com
National parks www.deh.gov.au/parks
National Trust www.nationaltrust.org.au

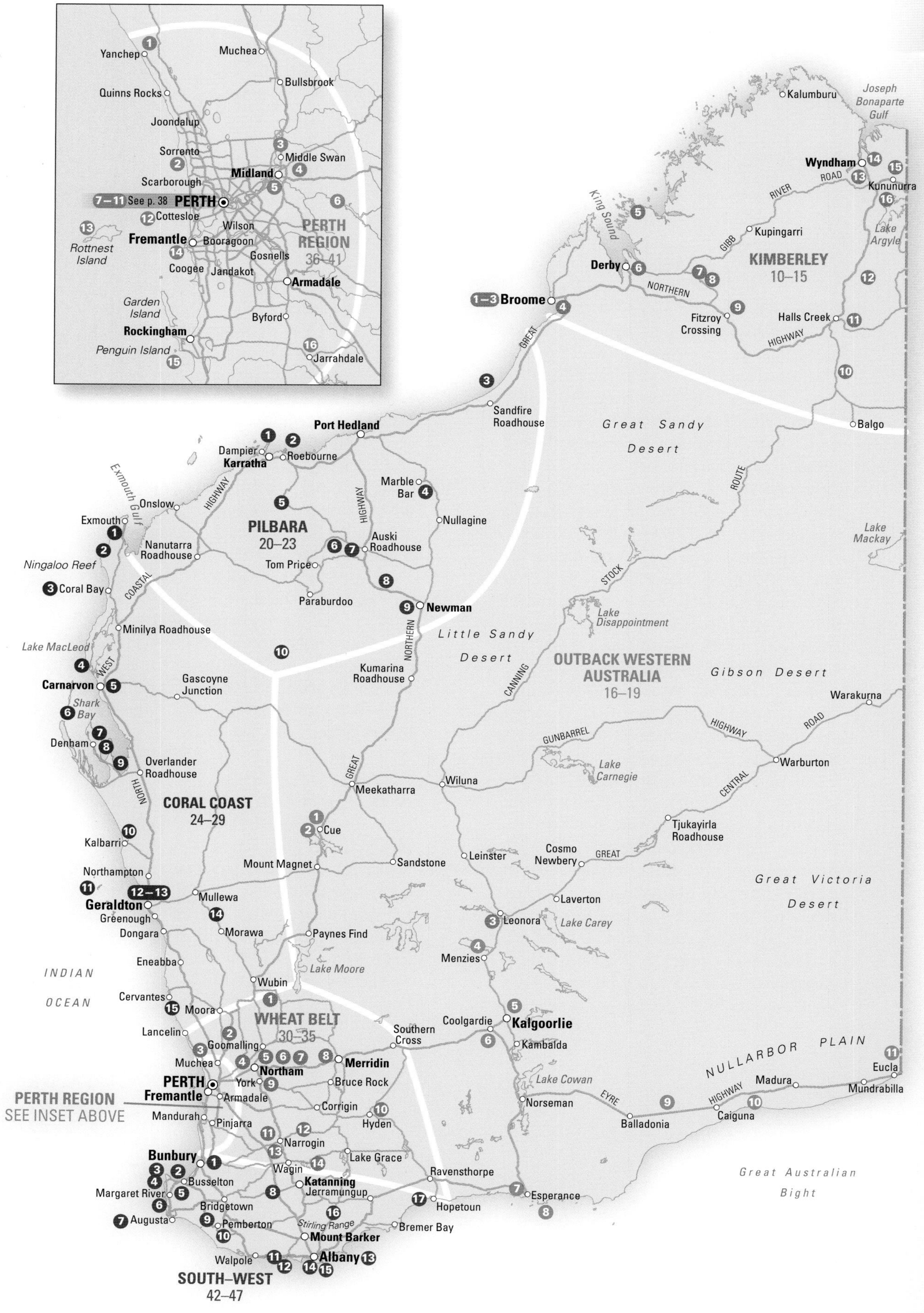

Yanchep
Muchea
Bullsbrook
Quinns Rocks
Joondalup
Sorrento
Middle Swan
Scarborough
Midland
7–11 See p. 38
PERTH
Cottesloe
Wilson
PERTH REGION
36–41
Fremantle
Booragoon
Rottnest Island
Gosnells
Coogee
Jandakot
Armadale
Garden Island
Byford
Rockingham
Penguin Island
Jarrahdale
Kalumburu
Joseph Bonaparte Gulf
Wyndham
Kununurra
ROAD
RIVER
King Sound
Kupingarri
GIBB
Lake Argyle
KIMBERLEY
10–15
Derby
NORTHERN
1–3 Broome
Fitzroy Crossing
Halls Creek
HIGHWAY
GREAT
Sandfire Roadhouse
Great Sandy Desert
Balgo
Port Hedland
Dampier
Karratha
Roebourne
Exmouth Gulf
HIGHWAY
Marble Bar
Onslow
Exmouth
Nullagine
ROUTE
PILBARA
20–23
Auski Roadhouse
Nanutarra Roadhouse
Lake Mackay
Ningaloo Reef
Tom Price
STOCK
Coral Bay
COASTAL
Paraburdoo
Newman
Lake Disappointment
Minilya Roadhouse
NORTHERN
Little Sandy Desert
Lake MacLeod
Kumarina Roadhouse
OUTBACK WESTERN AUSTRALIA
16–19
Gibson Desert
WEST
CANNING
Carnarvon
Gascoyne Junction
Shark Bay
Warakurna
HIGHWAY
ROAD
Denham
GUNBARREL
Overlander Roadhouse
Lake Carnegie
Warburton
NORTH
COASTAL CORAL COAST
24–29
GREAT
Meekatharra
Wiluna
CENTRAL
Cue
Tjukayirla Roadhouse
Kalbarri
Cosmo Newbery
GREAT
Mount Magnet
Sandstone
Leinster
Northampton
Great Victoria Desert
12–13
Mullewa
Laverton
Geraldton
Greenough
Dongara
Morawa
Paynes Find
Leonora
Lake Carey
Menzies
Eneabba
INDIAN OCEAN
Lake Moore
Wubin
Cervantes
Moora
WHEAT BELT
30–35
Coolgardie
Kalgoorlie
Lancelin
Southern Cross
Goomalling
Kambalda
NULLARBOR PLAIN
Muchea
Merridin
Northam
York
Bruce Rock
Eucla
PERTH
Fremantle
Armadale
Lake Cowan
Madura
Mundrabilla
PERTH REGION
SEE INSET ABOVE
Norseman
EYRE
HIGHWAY
Corrigin
Mandurah
Pinjarra
Hyden
Balladonia
Caiguna
Narrogin
Bunbury
Lake Grace
Wagin
Ravensthorpe
Great Australian Bight
Busselton
Katanning
Margaret River
Jerramungup
Esperance
Bridgetown
Hopetoun
Augusta
Pemberton
Stirling Range
Bremer Bay
Mount Barker
Walpole
Albany
SOUTH–WEST
42–47

Western Australia

Take time to roam Australia's largest state and you reap rich rewards: atmospheric ports and astounding marine life, rust-red chasms and gold-rush-era outposts. But even short outings from the capital pay dividends in the form of extraordinary buildings, fascinating maritime relics and awe-inspiring forests and coastline.

Useful websites

Visitor information www.westernaustralia.com
Parks and reserves www.dec.wa.gov.au
Motoring organisation www.rac.com.au

SAND DUNES NEAR EUCLA TELEGRAPH STATION

Kimberley

Fringed by desert and spectacular coastline, this is an untamed realm of rugged mountains and vast grasslands, huge cattle stations and atmospheric ports. Dramatic rock formations and bizarre bottle-shaped boab trees rise from the plains, and deep gorges harbour abundant fossils and rock art.

1 Cable Beach

One of the continent's most famous stretches of coastline

Broad and smooth, this breathtaking arc of immaculate white sand extends for 22 km, lapped along its length by turquoise waters, and backed by gentle dunes, patches of vivid green grass and outcrops of ochre rocks. It's easy to see why it is frequently rated one of the world's most beautiful beaches. Conditions for swimming are normally ideal (though stinger jellyfish are present from November to May) and whales and dolphins are often spotted offshore. At day's end, the sight of the sun sinking into the Indian Ocean is a majestic spectacle – one that many visitors enjoy on a sunset camel ride. The name of the beach derives from the telegraph cable that once came ashore here. Laid in 1889, it linked Broome and Australia to Java and, thereby, the rest of the world.

► *3 km west of Broome.*

2 Gantheaume Point

Trace the tracks of ancient creatures

Peer closely at the surface of the heavily weathered, deep-red rock platforms here and they soon come into view: clusters of animal prints, wide and webbed, three-toed and five-toed. These are no ordinary animal tracks, however, but the fossilised footprints of dinosaurs that roamed this region approximately 130 million years ago. The prints lie at the water's edge and must therefore be visited at low tide, but a plaster-cast replica can be viewed higher up the cliffs. Anastasia's Pool, on the north side of the point, is a basin chiselled out of the rock by one lighthouse keeper so that his arthritic wife could bathe safely in the ocean.

► *3 km south-west of Broome at southern end of Cable Beach.*

3 Japanese Cemetery

A poignant reminder of Broome's pearling heyday

Around 1900, Broome was the pearling capital of the world, berthing place of 400 luggers, and thronging with pearlers from across eastern Asia and the Pacific.

SUNSET CAMEL RIDE, CABLE BEACH

Stark and beautifully maintained, this graveyard is the last resting place of 919 Japanese, many of whom died from the bends or drowned while working locally as pearl divers. It is the largest Japanese cemetery in Australia. The first burial dates from 1896; most of the graves are marked by carved beach rocks bearing Japanese inscriptions.

▶ *Anne St, Broome.*

4 Broome Bird Observatory

Internationally renowned refuge for migratory shorebirds

From August onwards, Roebuck Bay teems with thousands of migratory shorebirds, many having come from as far away as eastern Asia. Some rest only briefly before continuing south, but many remain, forming enormous roosting flocks and foraging en masse on the mudflats at low tide: plovers, oystercatchers, godwits, sanderlings, stints – up to 150,000 birds at a time, of more than 50 kinds, one-third of the world's shorebird species. From March, they set off again, departing steadily in single-species groups, usually at dusk. Yet, even through winter, the seashores, woodlands and wetlands here are alive with other birds. The observatory monitors the birdlife while enabling visitors to view it up close. Marked trails lead through the diverse habitats, courses are available, and chalets, rooms and camp sites can be hired.

▶ *25 km east of Broome.*

5 Horizontal Waterfalls

Extraordinary phenomenon created by giant tides

It sounds unlikely and has to be seen to be believed: water cascading sideways through narrow, craggy, red-walled gorges. It's the result of enormous tides – up to 10 m – building on one side of two narrow sea-flanked ridges roughly 300 m apart. Midway along these ridges, almost facing each other, are two gaps. The water rises on one side of the ridges faster than it can escape through these outlets, so it is thrust through at high speed, churning white and falling at an almost imperceptible angle. With the opposite tide, the flow is reversed. Scenic flights and boat tours from Broome and Derby make the trip here (there is no road access) and explore the majestic coastline with its deep inlets and 800 or so islands.

▶ *Talbot Bay, Buccaneer Archipelago.*

Visitor information

Broome 08 9192 2222
Derby 08 9191 1426
Kununurra 08 9168 1177

6 Boab Prison Tree

Gnarled giant once used as a lockup

No-one knows who first had the idea, but you can see why they thought of it. This massive hollow boab tree has a girth of more than 14 m and a narrow, doorlike opening that would have been easy to block up. Sometime in the 1890s, the tree was used as an overnight holding pen for prisoners being taken to Derby, among them an Aboriginal resistance leader, Jandamarra.

▶ *8 km south of Derby via Derby Hwy.*

7 Windjana Gorge

Canyon reveals ancient and recent life

For most of the Devonian Period (416 to 360 million years ago), much of what is now the Kimberley lay under sea, and in places great barrier reefs formed, teeming with marine life. As the seas retreated, the reefs crumbled and sediments settled on top, compressing the layers below into limestone. Since then, rivers have cut deep into the rock, exposing the ancient reefs. One such place is Windjana Gorge, where cliffs rising up to 100 m high are encrusted with fossils of fish and shells. Walking tracks lead to fine examples, and to caves adorned with rock art. And wildlife still abounds, notably freshwater crocodiles, fruit bats and corellas.

▶ *150 km north-east of Derby via Gibb River Rd.*

8 Tunnel Creek

Explore a subterranean cavern that became a fugitive's last hide-out

Amid the limestone ranges here, the waterway now known as Tunnel Creek has carved a 750-m-long tunnel. Roughly 15 m wide and 12 m high, this formation can be explored by visitors willing to brave the darkness (a torch is essential) and occasional confined spaces and wade through shallow water (present even in the dry season). Shine a light around inside and you'll see stalactites, faint rock art, eels and fish in the pools, and bats roosting in niches. In 1897, Aboriginal resistance leader Jandamarra hid here but was cornered and killed by police at the entrance to the tunnel.

▶ *180 km north-east of Derby via Gibb River Rd.*

THE BOAB PRISON TREE IS THOUGHT TO BE 1500 YEARS OLD.

Across the plateau

Traversing the heart of the Kimberley, the Gibb River Road provides access to grand, unspoiled landscapes.

Stretching for roughly 650 km from Derby to the Great Northern Highway south of Wyndham, the Gibb River Road was constructed to transport cattle from remote stations to the ports at Derby and Wyndham. These days, it is one of the country's most popular 4WD routes – and with good reason.

Heading north from Derby, the road traverses wide plains then climbs through jagged rocky outcrops to the horseshoe-shaped King Leopold Ranges. Stunning views of Mount Ord, the ranges' highest summit, and the surrounding plateau are unveiled at many a turn. Tucked within these uplands are gorges concealing shady pools and groves frequented by parrots and budgerigars, including Bell, Adcock and Manning gorges. In the north-east, the ochre cliffs of the Cockburn and Saw ranges rim sweeping semiarid plains.

Travellers on the Gibb River Road must have a sturdy, high-clearance 4WD. Services are limited, though accommodation and camp sites are on offer at some pastoral stations. Travel outside the dry season is difficult.

9 Geikie Gorge

Cruise along a prehistoric coral reef

The cliffs of Geikie Gorge rise 30 m sheer from the dark, mirror-like surface of the Fitzroy River, their rocks banded with colour: chalk-white at the waterline, ochre above, and a deep grey-brown at the crest. On dry-season boat tours run by the Department of Environment and Conservation and the Darlngunaya Aboriginal Corporation, Indigenous guides recount local Dreaming stories and explain the formation of the gorge, which was once part of a huge coral reef formed in the Devonian period (see Windjana Gorge, opposite). Distinct rock layers and marine fossils are visible in the gorge walls. Fruit bats, bowerbirds and rare lilac-crowned wrens dwell in the dense river-gum and cadjeput forests, and freshwater crocodiles frequent waterways home to barramundi, sawfish and archerfish.

▶ *20 km north-east of Great Northern Hwy at Fitzroy Crossing.*

10 Wolfe Creek Crater

The legacy of a cataclysmic collision

Roughly 300,000 years ago, an iron meteorite thought to have weighed more than 50,000 tonnes plummeted to Earth here, exploding ferociously and forming a vast crater about 900 m in diameter and probably around 120 m deep. Since half-filled by drifting sand and now fringed with flowering shrubs, Wolfe Creek Crater is the second-largest rimmed meteorite crater in the world. Scenic flights (from Halls Creek) provide stunning views, but visitors can also drive to the rim – the site of a shelter with interpretive displays – and walk into the crater. Despite its imposing scale, the crater didn't appear on modern maps until 1947, when it was spotted during an aerial survey.

▶ *145 km south of Halls Creek via Great Northern Hwy and Tanami Rd.*

11 China Wall

Unusual and deceptive geological phenomenon

Not far off the road to the original gold-rush settlement of Halls Creek (now known as Old Halls Creek), what appears to be a pale constructed wall runs upwards from a river valley and over the crest of a hill, in the manner, as suggested by its name, of the Great Wall of China. On closer inspection it is revealed to be a natural formation, a vertical outcrop of white quartz that rises in places almost 6 m above the ground. Believed to run for as much as 120 km underground, it is claimed to be the largest formation of its kind in the world.

► *6 km east of Great Northern Hwy at Halls Creek via Duncan Rd.*

12 Bungle Bungle Range

A wonderland of outlandish sandstone formations

Given the scale of the Bungle Bungle Range – it covers 450 sq km – it's hard to believe that it was only discovered by Europeans in 1985, when a group of film-makers flew over it. From the air it is an extraordinary sight: a maze of towering, beehive-shaped domes, striped orange and black. The range formed over 360 million years, as water and wind eroded a sedimentary plateau; the colours derive from orange iron oxide and black cyanobacteria in different layers of rock. At ground level, creekbeds wind through the domes to caverns and canyons, including Echidna Chasm, a narrow, 100-m-deep cleft in the rock, and Cathedral Gorge, a tranquil pool hemmed by towering domes. Scenic flights depart from Halls Creek, Kununurra and Warmun. The access roads are 4WD only and visitors must bring all food and water.

► *Purnululu National Park, 53 km east of Great Northern Hwy.*

BUNGLE BUNGLE RANGE

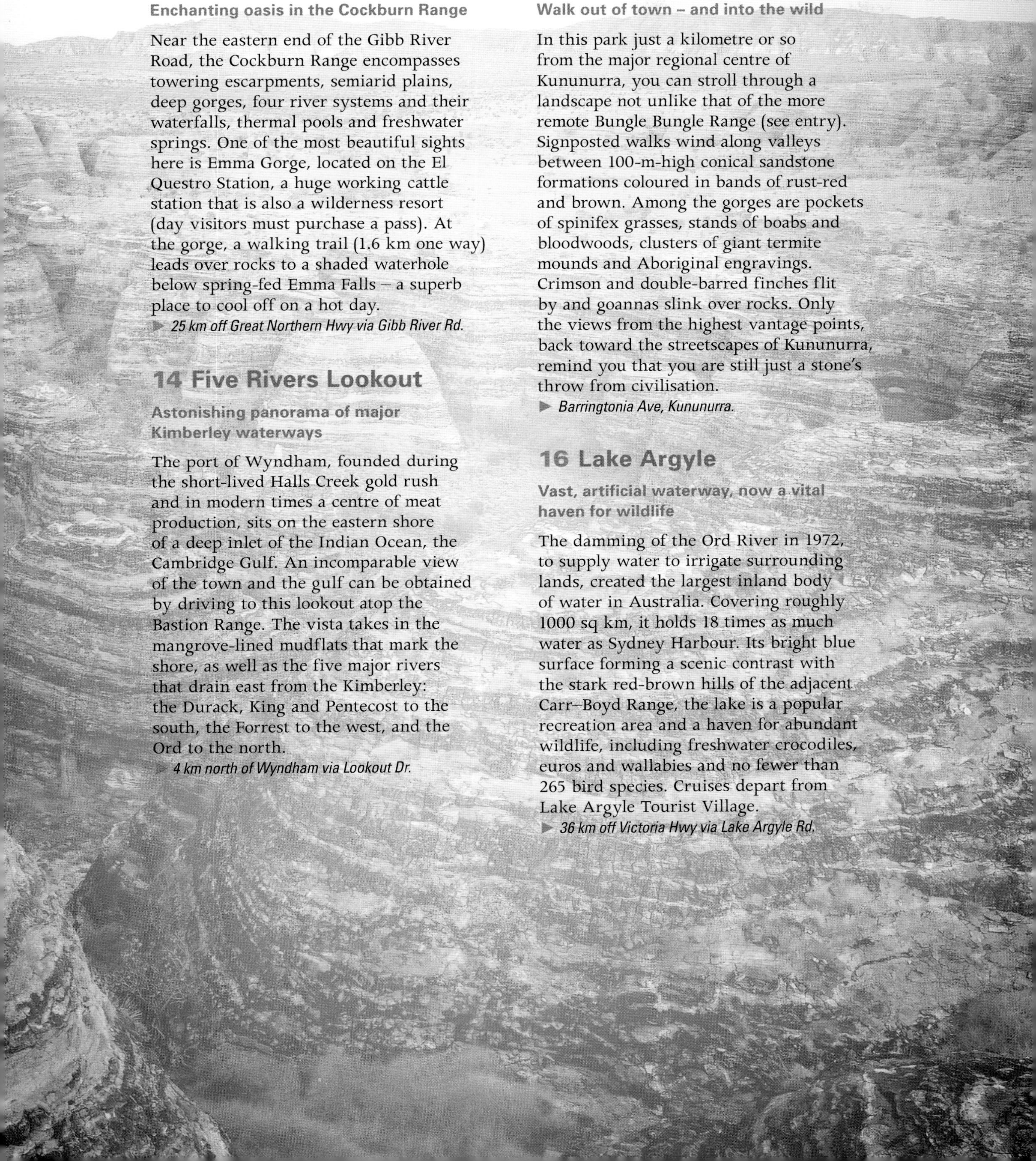

13 Emma Gorge

Enchanting oasis in the Cockburn Range

Near the eastern end of the Gibb River Road, the Cockburn Range encompasses towering escarpments, semiarid plains, deep gorges, four river systems and their waterfalls, thermal pools and freshwater springs. One of the most beautiful sights here is Emma Gorge, located on the El Questro Station, a huge working cattle station that is also a wilderness resort (day visitors must purchase a pass). At the gorge, a walking trail (1.6 km one way) leads over rocks to a shaded waterhole below spring-fed Emma Falls – a superb place to cool off on a hot day.

► *25 km off Great Northern Hwy via Gibb River Rd.*

14 Five Rivers Lookout

Astonishing panorama of major Kimberley waterways

The port of Wyndham, founded during the short-lived Halls Creek gold rush and in modern times a centre of meat production, sits on the eastern shore of a deep inlet of the Indian Ocean, the Cambridge Gulf. An incomparable view of the town and the gulf can be obtained by driving to this lookout atop the Bastion Range. The vista takes in the mangrove-lined mudflats that mark the shore, as well as the five major rivers that drain east from the Kimberley: the Durack, King and Pentecost to the south, the Forrest to the west, and the Ord to the north.

► *4 km north of Wyndham via Lookout Dr.*

15 Mirima National Park

Walk out of town – and into the wild

In this park just a kilometre or so from the major regional centre of Kununurra, you can stroll through a landscape not unlike that of the more remote Bungle Bungle Range (see entry). Signposted walks wind along valleys between 100-m-high conical sandstone formations coloured in bands of rust-red and brown. Among the gorges are pockets of spinifex grasses, stands of boabs and bloodwoods, clusters of giant termite mounds and Aboriginal engravings. Crimson and double-barred finches flit by and goannas slink over rocks. Only the views from the highest vantage points, back toward the streetscapes of Kununurra, remind you that you are still just a stone's throw from civilisation.

► *Barringtonia Ave, Kununurra.*

16 Lake Argyle

Vast, artificial waterway, now a vital haven for wildlife

The damming of the Ord River in 1972, to supply water to irrigate surrounding lands, created the largest inland body of water in Australia. Covering roughly 1000 sq km, it holds 18 times as much water as Sydney Harbour. Its bright blue surface forming a scenic contrast with the stark red-brown hills of the adjacent Carr–Boyd Range, the lake is a popular recreation area and a haven for abundant wildlife, including freshwater crocodiles, euros and wallabies and no fewer than 265 bird species. Cruises depart from Lake Argyle Tourist Village.

► *36 km off Victoria Hwy via Lake Argyle Rd.*

Outback Western Australia

The state's immense interior is an arid, sparsely inhabited yet awe-inspiring realm of desert, sparkling salt lakes, isolated rock outcrops harbouring Aboriginal art, and fascinating gold-rush towns, some now abandoned, some still thriving.

1 Cue

Echoes of the era of gold

At the height of the 1890s gold rush in the Murchison River region, Cue was one of the state's richest fields, referred to as 'the Queen of the Murchison', and had no fewer than 13 hotels. Just one remains and the population is small today, but the elegant main street and a scattering of National Trust–classified buildings summon up that affluent era. Notable among them are the Masonic Hall (1899), with its elegant ironwork veranda, the old jail (1896) and the Cue Shire Office (1895), former headquarters of the London and Western Investment Company, which now houses a display of historic photographs.

▶ *Great Northern Hwy.*

2 Walga Rock

Site of a ship in the desert

It seems incongruous to say the least, among an array of Aboriginal rock art, in the middle of the desert, 300 km from the sea: a drawing in white ochre of a European masted ship. Various theories surround its origins, including that it was drawn by a shipwrecked Dutch sailor; more likely, it seems, it is an image of a steamship made by a Malay pearl diver brought to Australia in the 1870s. What is certain is that it is part of one of the state's finest assemblages of rock art, located on the flanks of a spectacular monolith, Walga Rock, a place of great spiritual significance to Indigenous people.

▶ *48 km west of Cue via Cue–Dalgaranga Rd.*

A vast, forbidding realm

Despite the intrusions of explorers, pastoralists and miners, the deserts of western-central Australia remain steadfastly unconquerable.

From the Kimberley south to the Great Australian Bight stretches one of the most formidable expanses of arid country in the world, covering approximately two-thirds of Western Australia. Three major deserts make up this parched wilderness. In the north, the Great Sandy Desert is a vast sea of red sand dunes, as large as Great Britain and Italy combined. In the south is the Great Victoria Desert, a sea of lower dunes becalmed by stabilising scrub. Between lies a searing, desolate expanse of spinifex plains broken by sand ridges, the Gibson Desert.

To the east of the Great Northern and Goldfields highways, this extraordinary land can be explored via historic 4WD tracks, including the famous Gunbarrel Highway and the Canning Stock Route. Journeys along these routes require thorough preparation, plentiful supplies, a robust vehicle and expert guidance, but reveal a humbling, majestic world of great beauty.

3 Gwalia

Former home of a US president

Discovered in 1896, the 'Sons of Gwalia' mine was funded by Welsh prospectors – *Gwalia* is Welsh for 'Wales' – and became the centre of a go-ahead community that had the state's first electric trams and a double-decker bus service. In 1897, a certain Herbert Hoover arrived from the United States to become mine manager and built himself a grand residence above the mine. Now called Hoover House, it is part of the Gwalia Historic Site, which encompasses a fascinating array of relics of that era, ranging from buildings and trams to mining equipment and one of the nation's first twin-tub washing machines. Hoover moved on to greater things, of course, serving as the 31st US president from 1929 to 1933.

▶ *4 km south of Leonora.*

4 Lake Ballard

One of the largest art galleries on Earth

Walking across the lakebed, crunching through salt deposits, it seems like there is little to see. But then you notice thin, dark figures ranged at wide intervals along the horizon. Taking in one of the continent's biggest art installations requires quite a hike (at least 2 hours), but it's all part of an extraordinary experience. The figures are 51 sculptures by British artist Antony Gormley, together constituting a work called *Inside Australia*. Made of dark steel, each sculpture is a stylised shape based on a body scan of a local resident. For Gormley, visitors add to the work, their tracks forming a 'tracery or drawing of connecting lines' that never stays the same.

▶ *55 km north-west of Menzies.*

Visitor information

Esperance 08 9083 1555
Kalgoorlie 08 9021 1966
Laverton 08 9031 1361
Norseman 08 9039 1071

STEEL SCULPTURE, LAKE BALLARD

LUCKY BAY, CAPE LE GRAND NATIONAL PARK

5 The Super Pit

Heart of gold

Kalgoorlie's goldfields have been the most productive in Australia – indeed they are one of only four goldfields in the world to have yielded 50 million ounces. The hub of this extraordinary output has always been the so-called Golden Mile, and the modern beating heart of the Golden Mile is the mammoth Super Pit, the largest open-cut goldmine in the Southern Hemisphere. So large is this colossal scoop out of the Earth's crust that you could fit Uluru neatly inside. Viewed from the public lookout, its scale dwarfs the giant trucks that trundle along its terraces, and the workers seem like tiny ants.

► *Hainault Rd, Kalgoorlie.*

6 Coolgardie Pharmacy Museum

Medicinal paraphernalia, and more

Housed in Coolgardie's historic Drill Hall, this collection of early 1900s medical paraphernalia, one of the finest of its kind in Australia, usually surprises and amuses visitors while leaving them deeply thankful for more recent advances in medicine. Rows of vials, jars and bottles – fine examples of period glassware in themselves – are arrayed in antique cabinets; colourful advertisements for medicines – some familiar, some highly suspect – line the walls; and tables and glass cases are crowded with lotions, potions and somewhat alarming dental and surgical instruments.

► *Bayley St, Coolgardie.*

7 Pink Lake

An impressive splash of colour, most of the time

At its most vivid, this lake attains a hue not unlike that of strawberry ice cream. But its colour – due to the presence of salt-tolerant algae – constantly varies, depending on algae, water and salinity levels, and you could come upon it blue or even purple. The salt in the lake is especially pure, and about 14,000 tonnes a year are harvested and sent to Fremantle for processing. To view the lake and the glorious coastal landscapes that surround it, follow the Great Ocean Drive, a 38-km loop scenic route west of Esperance.

► *5 km north-west of Esperance on Pink Lake Rd.*

8 Cape Le Grand National Park

Granite headlands offer inspiring views

The imposing headlands here caught the attention of early European navigators. French Admiral Bruni d'Entrecasteaux, passing in 1792, named the highest peak and the cape below it Le Grand, after one of his ensigns; during a storm in 1802 Matthew Flinders took shelter in the lee of the cape in an inlet he gratefully named Lucky Bay. Today, protected by the national park, it is still much the same eye-catching landscape. Granite tors jut above mallee heathland hemmed by cliffs and white-sand beaches where large groups of kangaroos like to doze in the sun. Vantage points offer sweeping views across the park and out to the islands of the Archipelago of the Recherche, just offshore. There are two campgrounds and several walking tracks.

▶ *50 km south-east of Esperance via Merivale Rd and Cape Le Grand Rd.*

9 90 Mile Straight

The continent's longest stretch of straight road

Few roads convey as strong a sense of the vastness and emptiness of the interior as the Eyre Highway, and on the section between Caiguna and Balladonia Station that sense is heightened considerably. For 145 km – 90 miles in imperial terms – the bitumen kinks not an inch, running poker-straight toward the horizon. Not only that but it is virtually flat the whole way, and the surrounding country rolls past uniform and seemingly limitless (Rawlinna Station, on the northern side, covers 1.4 million ha). It's a drive not without its hazards – in a shimmering heat haze, distances and speeds can be hard to judge, and the unchanging scene can tip weary drivers into slumber. But for those alert to their surroundings it's an inspiring stage of an epic journey.

▶ *Eyre Hwy.*

10 Eyre Bird Observatory

Birdwatching hot spot at isolated, historic outpost

Struggling along coastal cliffs in March 1841, after making the first, harrowing crossing of the Nullarbor Plain by a European, Edward Eyre found a small soak that provided a lifesaving draught of water; Aboriginals then pointed him to a more substantial supply close by. In 1897 it became the site of the Eyre Telegraph Station, which in 1977 reopened as the country's first bird observatory. Researchers and amateur twitchers make the long trek here to tick off as many as they can of the more than 240 species recorded in the area, including 15 kinds of honeyeater and the endangered southern scrub robin. Visitors are welcome (4WD access only) and accommodation, food and highway pick-ups can be arranged.

▶ *36 km south of Eyre Hwy.*

11 Eucla Telegraph Station

Early colonial communications hub, slowly vanishing

Inexorably, the remains of Eucla Telegraph Station are being steadily entombed by the inland drift of this coastline's giant sandhills. Despite or perhaps because of this, the station is one of the most atmospheric historic sites in the country. Established in 1877, along the telegraph line that linked Perth with other colonial capitals, the complex consisted of the main repeater station and a cluster of buildings for the operators and their families. People and provisions arrived at the jetty still visible 1 km to the south, which was linked to the settlement by a tram line. The station was abandoned in 1929 when a new station was built inland along the transcontinental railway.

▶ *4 km south of Eyre Hwy via Eucla.*

Pilbara

The famously dramatic, iron-red gorges of the Hamersley Range are not to be missed, but the Pilbara offers much else besides: remote palm-fringed oases, an amazing array of Aboriginal art and extensive unspoiled beaches.

1 Burrup Peninsula

One of the world's richest rock-art sites

At least 10,000 and possibly up to a million carvings, made over thousands of years, are scattered among the cliffs, clefts, gorges, caves and boulders that line this rocky sea-flanked promontory north of Dampier. Thought to be mainly the work of people of the Yapurrara language group, they include images of thylacines (Tasmanian tigers) and other ancient creatures, some of which have been extinct for over 3000 years. The most accessible art site is Deep Gorge, near Hearson Cove, a popular swimming spot; guided tours depart from Karratha.

► *10 km north of Dampier via Burrup Rd.*

2 Cossack

Formerly vital port, frozen in time

It must have been demoralising for the people of the young and formerly thriving port of Cossack around 1900, watching as their harbour slowly silted up, shipping shifted to Point Samson, and residents steadily drifted away. The silver lining for subsequent generations is that the town remains much as it was in its late 1800s heyday, when it was the Pilbara's principal port: in the 1870s, 57 pearl luggers operated out of here and even after that industry shifted to Broome the 1880s brought a new influx of ships, people and wealth. Many elegantly restored bluestone buildings date from that era, including the Galbraith Store (1890), customs house (1895) and the old court house (1895) that now houses Cossack's excellent museum. There are fine views from local lookouts, including out to Jarman Island, site of the 1888 cast-iron lighthouse.

► *14 km north of North West Coastal Hwy via Roebourne.*

3 Eighty Mile Beach

One of Australia's longest unbroken stretches of sandy shore

Eighty miles (129 km) sounds impressive enough; but in fact the beach's beautiful white, shelly sands extend even further, for 220 km, or 140 miles, from Cape Keraudren in the south to Cape Missiessy in the north. Given the beach's length and beauty, it's surprising that there is limited access – by far the easiest vehicle route is the one to Eighty Mile Beach Caravan Park. This remoteness and tranquillity have helped make the beach a haven for migratory shorebirds, which arrive in summer from north-eastern Asia – some 15,000 km away – including Caspian terns, bar-tailed godwits, red knots and Oriental plovers. Total resident numbers at times exceed 400,000.

► *9 km north of North West Coastal Hwy at Eighty Mile Beach Caravan Park.*

Visitor information

Karratha 08 9144 4600
Newman 08 9175 2888
Port Hedland 08 9173 1711
Roebourne 08 9182 1060
Tom Price 08 9188 1112

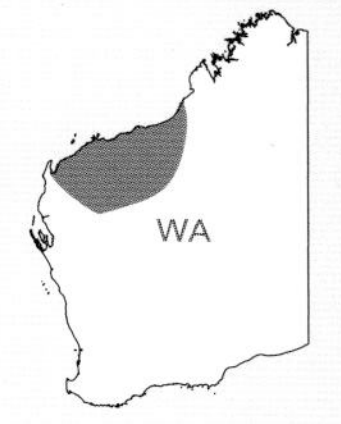

An ancient, iron-rich land

The rust-red cliffs of the Pilbara's gorges are among the oldest exposed rocks in Australia.

The Pilbara began to take shape some 2.5 billion years ago, as sediments deposited at the bottom of a sea. Layer upon layer built up and was steadily compressed into rock. Subsequently the rocks were tilted, folded and crumpled by tectonic forces, as is vividly apparent in many of the region's gorge walls. As the sea retreated, wind and rain fashioned mountains such as the Hamersley Range, and rivers cut deep into the bedrock. Elevated levels of iron in these rocks are responsible for their rust-red colour, and the Pilbara has yielded some of the richest iron-ore deposits in the world, mined on a massive scale at mining centres such as Tom Price and Newman (see Mount Whaleback Mine, p. 23).

4 Marble Bar

Brave the heat and head for the bar

In the 161 days prior to 20 April 1924, the mercury never once dropped below 100°F (37.8°C) at Marble Bar. On the basis of that record, which still stands, Marble Bar has come to be known as Australia's hottest town. But its claims to fame amount to more than that. For a start, there's the extraordinary geological feature that gave it its name: a huge exposed block of what was thought initially to be coloured marble, but is actually jasper. The Bar, as it is known, can be viewed on the Coongan River, 5 km out of town. Then there is the fascinating history of this mining town, which was home to 5000 people during the 1890s rush. Several buildings, notably the grand government buildings, remain from those times, and tours of the Comet Gold Mine provide insights into the lives and dreams of prospectors.

▶ *177 km south of North West Coastal Hwy via Marble Bar Rd.*

5 Millstream

Lush oasis in arid ranges

In the 19th century, Afghan camel drivers carrying goods between Cossack (see entry) and inland stations used to rest at the chain of cool, palm-shaded, spring-fed pools here. At Chinderwarriner Pool they planted date palms that give this spot the air of a classic Arabian oasis (though, as a non-native plant, the palms are now being removed). Centuries before, this oasis was a gathering place for Indigenous people. A loop road takes in the main pools – good for canoeing and swimming – and the Millstream Homestead Visitor Centre provides maps.

▶ *Millstream–Chichester National Park, 125 km south-east of Karratha via North West Coastal Hwy and Roebourne–Wittenoom Rd.*

6 Hamersley Gorge

Banded chasm amid rolling hills

The gorge is a deep gash in the rolling spinifex-clad country of the Hamersley Range. Follow the steps down from the lookout to the valley floor, where a cliff of crumpled orange, rust-red and cream rock layers rises above wide pools. Then scramble 1 km or so along the gorge to reach 'The Grotto', a sheer, fern-lined cleft.

▶ *Karijini National Park, 186 km west of Great Northern Hwy via Karijini Dr.*

RED GORGE VIEWED
FROM OXER LOOKOUT

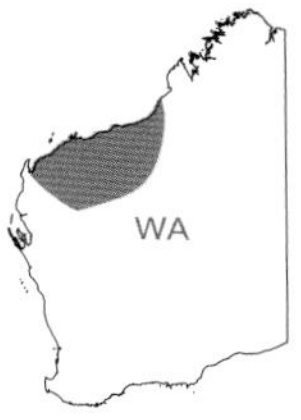

7 Oxer Lookout

You'll need a head for heights

As you approach the edge of the lookout, the ground drops away on either side somewhat disconcertingly, revealing precipitous, rust-red, layered cliffs. You realise you are now perched atop a sliver of land at the junction of four narrow, jagged chasms: Weano, Red, Hancock and Joffre gorges. The view is staggering, vertiginous. Walking tracks nearby lead down the cliffs to shaded pools far below, but should only be attempted by the fit and well prepared. And bizarre as it may seem in this parched landscape, the pools are so cold that hypothermia can be a risk – check the temperature first before diving in. Guided tours are recommended.

▶ *Karijini National Park, 100 km west of Great Northern Hwy via Karijini Dr.*

8 Wanna Munna

Small but delightful art site

In the shady gorge here on the upper reaches of Weeli Wolli Creek, detailed depictions of human figures, boomerangs and animals such as kangaroos and emus have been etched into flat rock faces among a jumble of large red boulders. These petroglyphs, as such carvings are known, are hugely impressive in their number, detail and craftsmanship; they are also sacred to Indigenous people and fragile, and should therefore not be touched. Further down the gorge are pools frequented by kangaroos, as well as some impressive rock formations.

▶ *2 km north of Great Northern Hwy, 77 km north of Newman. 4WD only.*

9 Mount Whaleback Mine

Visit the world's largest open-cut iron-ore mine

Guided tours of Newman's Mount Whaleback Mine provide a fascinating insight into the rich resources of the Pilbara and the challenge of extracting and refining them. The mine was built on a huge ore deposit discovered in 1957 and named for its resemblance to a humpback whale; the town was founded in 1960 to house workers. White House lookout provides a panoramic view of the gargantuan pit, where everything is on a giant scale: those puny-looking Haulpak trucks trundling around below weigh 200 tonnes and have tyres that measure 3.6 m in diameter! Extracted rocks pass through giant crushers, along conveyor belts and onto some of the world's longest freight trains. Book your tour at the handsome rammed-earth visitor centre, which also houses a gallery and museum.

▶ *Newman, Great Northern Hwy.*

10 Mount Augustus

Tour the biggest rock on Earth

Known to Aboriginals as Burringurrah, Mount Augustus is nowhere near being the highest mountain in the state. But it is 8 km long, occupies 4795 ha, can be seen from the air from 160 km away, and is more than twice the size of Uluru, which it resembles. That makes it the largest single rock, or monolith, in the world. Its lower granitic layers formed around 1.65 billion years ago; the upper sedimentary layers are a more youthful 1 billion years old. Spend a day on the Bowgada Drive, a 49-km circuit suitable for 2WD, and you'll get something of the measure of it. Viewpoints provide diverse perspectives, and turn-offs lead to gorges, pools and rock art. Walking tracks include two to the 717-m summit, but be warned: even the easier one requires six hours and thorough preparation.

▶ *490 km east of Carnarvon.*

Coral Coast

On this little-developed western coastline, the outback extends to the seashore, and wide bays and fringing reefs are home to some of the densest and most accessible colonies of marine life in the world.

1 Charles Knife Canyon

Ride the ridgetops for sublime views

Cape Range is a narrow spine of eroded limestone that runs down the centre of the North West Cape peninsula. Over millions of years, erosion by water and wind has formed dramatic gorges and ridges, cave systems, and sheer-sided sinkholes. Much of this rugged country is inaccessible, but to gain a sense of its grandeur follow the drive on the eastern side of the range into Charles Knife Canyon. Mostly gravel and usually suitable for 2WD (check conditions with the tourist or park office before you set off), it climbs into the range and twists along razorback ridges, revealing stunning panoramas across the peaks, back to Exmouth Gulf and into the yawning chasm of Charles Knife Canyon.

► *Cape Range National Park, 21 km south of Exmouth.*

Visitor information

Carnarvon 08 9941 1146
Exmouth 08 9949 1176
Geraldton 08 9921 3999
Kalbarri 08 9937 1104
Shark Bay 08 9948 1590

2 Yardie Creek

A cool refuge among arid ranges

On the western side of Cape Range, Yardie Creek, the range's only permanent watercourse, snakes through a series of high-sided, multicoloured gorges and spills into a small saltwater lagoon. High on the cliffs, rare black-footed rock wallabies forage along ledges and shelter under overhangs. Birds perch on ridges and flit among the lagoon's mangroves. It's an idyllic scene, best enjoyed from one of the daily boat tours, which provide an informative commentary on the environment and wildlife, though the gorge can also be explored on foot, via two walking tracks.

► *36 km south of Exmouth.*

3 Coral Bay

Short cut to the reef

This is one of very few places in Australia where a coral reef comes within a few hundred metres of the mainland. And it's not just any coral reef, but Ningaloo Reef, one of the longest and richest reefs on Earth (see opposite). Here, it extends across the bay forming, with the stunning white-sand beach, a magnificent natural lagoon, where even inexperienced snorkellers can catch a glimpse of the ocean's wonders. Those who prefer to stay dry can still participate, by joining a glass-bottom boat tour.

► *88 km north of North West Coastal Hwy at Minilya Roadhouse.*

Among the giants of the sea

Australia's longest continuous fringing coral reef, extending roughly 290 km, Ningaloo Reef teems with marine life ranging from the tiniest coral polyps to the biggest fish on Earth.

Imagine: you hang suspended in a cobalt sea, bedazzled by branching coral formations and hordes of tiny, colourful, jewel-like fish when all at once something the size of a bus comes careering out of the shadows. Fortunately, its steering is precise and the huge spotted fish glides past, tail fin swaying, as your heart resets to its normal beat. If you can cope with that kind of bolt from the blue and have mastered snorkelling, you're ready to enjoy one of the world's most extraordinary nature experiences: swimming with whale sharks on Ningaloo Reef.

Mass coral spawning is what draws whale sharks to the reef. They arrive in March and stay till about June, feeding on plankton. The world's largest fish, they can be up to 12 m long. However, they are filter feeders and therefore have no teeth; what's more they are docile, and they seem remarkably unfazed by the presence of human swimmers.

Comings and goings

Though whale sharks are the major drawcard at Ningaloo, the reef is home to at least 500 other kinds of fish, 250 species of reef-building corals and a range of marine mammals, so there is plenty to see year-round. Dugongs forage in seagrasses, turtles lay eggs in protected beach rookeries, dolphins roam the bays, and manta rays make for pretty impressive swimming companions in the absence of whale sharks. Humpback whales pass through between August and October.

In addition to Coral Bay (see entry) the 4000-sq-km reef can be accessed at various points, and in various ways, along its length. A wide range of whale-shark, snorkelling, coral-viewing and fishing tours depart from Exmouth; contact the tourist office for details.

SWIMMING WITH A WHALE SHARK

4 Point Quobba

Wave power on display

You develop a new appreciation for the forces of nature while taking in the action at the Point Quobba blowholes. Waves thundering under a rock platform are forced upwards through narrow channels, sending jets of spray soaring up to 20 m into the air. It's mesmerising, but don't tune out too much: sudden large waves have claimed lives here and care must be taken. The nearby point, with its red-capped lighthouse, provides superb coastal panoramas and is an excellent vantage point for spotting humpback whales during their August-to-October migration. There is also fine swimming off the sandy beach.

▶ *66 km north-west of Carnarvon via North West Coastal Hwy and Blowholes Rd.*

5 One Mile Jetty

Ride a train out over the sea

Built in 1889, the jetty is a vivid reminder of those late-1800s days when Carnarvon became the north-west coast's major port. Immense flocks of sheep were driven here from some of the country's largest stations to be exported, and camel trains hauled in huge loads of goods – the town's 40-m-wide streets were designed to allow camel teams to turn. The jetty stretches 1493 m out over the Indian Ocean. You can hike out the whole way, enjoying the unusual sensation of walking more than a kilometre offshore, or hop on the 'Coffee Pot' train, which runs its entire length. The jetty is part of the Heritage Precinct, which also encompasses the intriguing Railway Museum and Lighthouse Keeper's Cottage Museum.

▶ *Babbage Island, 2 km north-west of Carnarvon town centre.*

6 Shark Bay Marine Park

Expansive, transparent bay teems with marine life

It's a bit like an underwater Serengeti: vast grasslands roamed by countless creatures. But in this case the grasslands are immense meadows of seagrasses and the creatures are marine animals including turtles, sharks, rays and dugongs. The seagrasses, flowering plants that grow and pollinate in the ocean, cover more than 4000 sq km, including the largest single seagrass bed in the world, the Wooramel Seagrass Bank. Because the waters are relatively shallow and crystal clear, marine mammals and large fish are easily observed from cruise boats and scenic flights, which operate out of Carnarvon, Denham and Monkey Mia. Shark Bay was the site of some of the first-known landings by Europeans in Australia, including visits by Dirk Hartog in 1616 and William Dampier, who named the bay, in 1699.

▶ *Denham is 125 km north-west of North West Coastal Hwy.*

7 Monkey Mia

Dolphin rendezvous point

Daily, a small crowd gathers at the shore here, standing knee-deep in the bay, to witness a remarkable spectacle: wild bottlenose dolphins coming to take food from and interact with humans. Rigorously controlled by rangers, these extraordinary, humbling encounters have become world-famous and attract visitors from around the globe. They originated in the 1960s, when a local, Mrs Ninni Watts, started feeding the dolphins that followed her husband's fishing boat home. The excellent Dolphin Information Centre provides background on the dolphins and Shark Bay, and offers a range of tours.

▶ *25 km east of Denham via Monkey Mia Rd.*

SHELL BEACH EXTENDS FOR MORE THAN 100 KM ALONG SHARK BAY.

8 Shell Beach

Seashells here form the seashore

Dig as deep as you like, but you won't get down to sand. The whole of this stunning, dazzlingly white beach is a mass of tiny white shells – the casings of cardiid cockles – lying up to 10 m deep. The cockles have long thrived in the highly saline waters of the bay, and the shells have accumulated here for approximately 4000 years. Over time, their weight has compacted the lowest layers to form a type of rock called coquina limestone. It is quarried locally and has been used as a building material, notably in Denham.

▶ *78 km north-west of North West Coastal Hwy via Shark Bay Rd.*

9 Hamelin Pool

Home of the oldest living organisms on the planet

The bulbous formations spread across the shallow pools here don't exactly overwhelm the visitor with their size or grandeur. But when you learn a little about their age, growth and rarity, you realise you are in the presence of something truly remarkable. These are not rocks but mounds of living algal material, known as stromatolites, and they have been growing here for thousands of years, protected by the highly saline waters of the pool, which their predators cannot tolerate. They are found in very few other places in the world, and this is certainly the largest-known colony. And they have been on Earth for probably 3.5 billion years. That makes them the oldest known living organisms and a direct link to the first life forms on the planet.

▶ *30 km west of North West Coastal Hwy via Shark Bay Rd.*

10 Kalbarri National Park

Admire the majestic handiwork of the mighty Murchison River

Roughly 2 million years ago, great blocks of sandstone here were gradually thrust upward by tectonic shifting. As the land rose, the Murchison River gouged deep to maintain its course to the sea, creating a spectacular series of gorges extending for more than 80 km. Several walking trails and lookouts within Kalbarri National Park provide majestic views of this geological wonder. At The Loop, a natural rock arch known as Nature's Window frames river and gorge exquisitely, while at the Z Bend, the Murchison flows through a tight ravine where banded cliffs rise 150 m from its banks. The park is also famed for its coastal scenery and magnificent displays of wild flowers in spring.

► *18 km west of North West Coastal Hwy via Ajana–Kalbarri Rd.*

11 Houtman Abrolhos

Beautiful but perilous archipelago

Frederick Houtman was the first European to discover these reef-rimmed islands, in 1619, bestowing the name 'Abrolhos', a Portuguese word for a spiked war machine, in recognition of their hazards. The appropriateness of this comparison no doubt became abundantly clear to those on board the *Batavia*, which ten years later foundered on a reef here. Taking refuge on the islands, the ship's company famously fell to mutiny and murder. In later years, the rich marine life drew fishermen, who built jetties and shacks, still used as seasonal bases. Day tours are available from Geraldton, enabling visitors to savour the amazing scenery, marvel at the abundant wildlife, and snorkel over stunning reefs. Scenic flights are also available.

► *60 km west of Geraldton.*

12 Western Australian Museum – Geraldton

A treasure trove of shipwreck relics

This rugged, at times tempestuous coastline has accounted for many a shipwreck over centuries of European exploration, including that of the *Zuytdorp*, a Dutch cargo ship heading for the East Indies in 1712, and most famously, the *Batavia*, wrecked on the Houtman Abrolhos islands (see entry) in 1629. Artefacts from both ships and many others are on display in this fabulous museum, alongside mementoes of the recently rediscovered Second World War ship HMAS *Sydney* and displays outlining the natural and social history of this region.

► *Museum Pl, Geraldton.*

13 St Francis Xavier Cathedral

Opulent masterpiece of architect–priest

It was a chance meeting in Rome with the Bishop of Geraldton that brought English architect-turned-priest John Cyril Hawes to Australia in 1915. Taking up the dual role of missionary and church designer, he spent the next 24 years in Western Australia and left a remarkable legacy of churches and chapels in places such as Mullewa, Morawa, Perenjori and Yalgoo. Without doubt his masterpiece is Geraldton's cathedral, an attractive and unusual blend of Romanesque and Spanish mission styles, with a grand central dome and twin bell towers, and a striking grey-, white- and red-striped interior. Plagued by technical and financial difficulties, its construction took more than 20 years.

► *Cathedral Ave, Geraldton.*

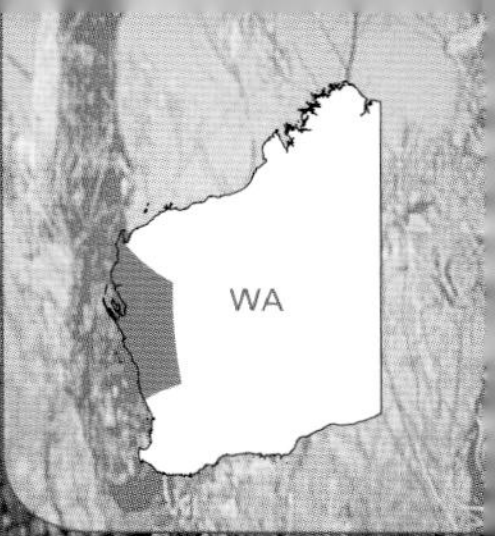

14 The Wildflower Way

Where nature puts on an astounding annual display

The driving route known as the Wildflower Way winds for 240 km from Mullewa in the north to Dalwallinu in the south, through rolling, picturesque country. Between July and October it is a riot of colour as flowering plants burst into bloom across the verges and fields. Rare ground-hugging wreath flowers and orange and scarlet wild pomegranates sprout around Mullewa; everlasting daisies paint the land between Perenjori and Wubin with hues of red, gold, pink, purple and white; and at Dalwallinu gorgeous wattles seize the limelight. Short strolls into the bush by the roadside reveal native foxgloves, cornflowers, ground orchids and clumps of bright red Sturt's desert peas.

► *State Highway 115 from Great Northern Hwy at Wubin.*

15 The Pinnacles

An enchanted forest of timeworn limestone columns

Some look like ancient standing stones, others resemble hunch-shouldered, hooded figures, and in the shifting sunlight they soon assume yet other forms. The columns appear to have sprouted from the sand, but in fact it was the departing ground that left them behind. They began as deposits of limestone capped with calcrete. Water seeping through cracks and the tunnelling of plant roots left tall blocks of hard stone surrounded by sand. Then, 6000 years ago, winds carried away the sand, exposing the blocks to wind and rain, which whittled them to the forms you see today. A loop drive and walking trail lead through the formations.

► *Nambung National Park, 54 km from Brand Hwy via Cervantes.*

EVERLASTING DAISIES ON THE WILDFLOWER WAY

Wheat Belt

Though given over mainly to expansive plantings of wheat, the plains of the south-western interior are dotted with islands of native vegetation abounding in wild flowers and encompass some of the state's oldest towns, as well as extraordinary geological formations.

1 Petrudor Rocks

Snapshots of eras long gone

In a vast sea of wheat sits a perfectly square island of fenced-off native bushland crowned by this imposing granite outcrop, an understandably popular local picnic spot. The rocks are a remnant of an ancient granite plateau that once capped the entire region, before most of it eroded to form sand plains, and the bush is a snapshot of the vegetation as it was when Europeans first arrived. Petrudor Rocks is thus a vital refuge for wildlife once abundant and now much less visible. Quandong trees, which produce bright red fruit, are plentiful. Flowering plants include wattles, pink everlastings, grevilleas and orchids, which splash the slopes with colour come spring. Lizards bask on the rocks, echidnas forage in nooks and clefts, and emus and kangaroos can be seen in open areas. Birdlife is also diverse and bountiful.

▶ *33 km east of Great Northern Hwy at Pithara.*

Visitor information

Merredin 08 9041 1668
Narrogin 08 9881 2064
Northam 08 9622 2100
York 08 9641 1301

2 New Norcia

Australia's only monastic community

Turn off the highway into this sprawling settlement and you suddenly find yourself in southern Europe: grand cream-and-ochre buildings in Gothic, Classical and Byzantine styles flank lawns and pathways; church spires rise above the trees. New Norcia was founded as a mission in 1846 by a Benedictine monk, Dom Rosendo Salvado, and named after St Benedict's birthplace, Norcia, in Umbria, Italy. In the mission's early days, the Benedictines worked to aid and support the local Yuart Aboriginal people. Land was set aside for cultivation and sheep and horse breeding, and instruction provided, resulting in a self-sufficient community. The flour mill, which started operating in 1879, is the state's oldest and still functions. In the 20th century, several ornate boarding colleges were constructed. Benedictine monks continue to run the community and visitors still come to experience monastic life. Others are drawn by the remarkable buildings, 27 of which are classified by the National Trust, and the impressive New Norcia Museum and Art Gallery, which houses a collection of religious art including works by Italian and Spanish masters. Guided tours of the museum and gallery are available and a heritage trail runs through the township.

▶ *Great Northern Hwy.*

3 Gravity Discovery Centre

Gateway to the outer solar system – and beyond

Here you can stroll the length of our solar system and back – and it will take you less than an hour. The Walk to the End of the Solar System is one of several interactive exhibits at this excellent science education centre, where hands-on activities teach visitors about cosmology, gravity and breakthroughs in science and how these relate to their lives and experience. Highlights include the space observatory, with displays on the origins of the universe, and the extraordinary Leaning Tower of Gingin, a 45-m-high metal tower tilted at an angle of 15 degrees, which is used to demonstrate the principles of gravity – and also offers stunning views.

► *20 km west of Brand Hwy at Gingin.*

4 Toodyay

One of WA's best-preserved townships

You can view an extraordinary array of 1860s buildings here, no fewer than 25 of which are classified by the National Trust. The name of the town (pronounced 'Too-jay') comes from an Aboriginal word said to mean 'place of plenty'. The first settlement, on flood-prone flats downstream, was abandoned in 1860 in favour of the present site. The new town was called Newcastle, but given its present name in 1910. Among the most notable buildings are the three-storey steam flour mill and the old Newcastle jail, from which the state's most famous bushranger, Moondyne Joe (Joseph Bolitho Johns), escaped three times.

► *66 km north-west of Great Northern Hwy at Middle Swan via Toodyay Rd.*

SPIRES AND CRENELLATIONS CROWN MANY OF THE BUILDINGS AT NEW NORCIA.

A lifeline to the goldfields

The creation of the Goldfields Water Supply Scheme, a pipeline to carry water from Mundaring near Perth to Kalgoorlie, was an extraordinary feat of engineering.

The discovery of gold in Kalgoorlie in the 1890s resulted in a sudden surge in the region's population, as thousands of miners rushed to stake their claims. Just as quickly another natural resource became almost as valuable as the gold: water. Without it, the future of the mining communities appeared uncertain.

In 1895, Charles Yelverton O'Connor, the state's engineer-in-chief, proposed a solution that involved capturing water in a reservoir in the Darling Range near Perth and then pumping it, by means of eight purpose-built pump stations, all the way – roughly 560 km – to Kalgoorlie. This ambitious scheme got the go-ahead and soon construction began.

However, constant criticism of the project took its toll on its architect, and one month before the opening of the pipeline in March 1902, O'Connor shot himself. Nevertheless, his vision was vindicated and the project more successful than anyone had anticipated. Water from the pipeline now supplies more than 100,000 people and 6 million sheep spread over 44,000 square km – an area two-thirds the size of Tasmania.

A 650-km driving route, the Golden Pipeline Heritage Trail, follows the pipeline across the state, taking in the original pump stations, as well as their modern replacements. For details, see www.goldenpipeline.com.au.

5 Northam

Handsome historic town with unusual inhabitants

It's the riverside setting that makes Northam so splendid, and it's here, on the grassy banks of the graceful Avon (upper Swan), that you will find the town's most famous attraction, a colony of white swans. The descendants of a group of birds brought to Australia in the early 1900s by a Russian settler, Oscar Bernard, later mayor of Northam, they form Western Australia's only breeding colony. Nearby, a pedestrian suspension bridge across the river is said to be the longest of its kind in Australia. Sprawling on either side of the Avon, Northam has more than 180 historic buildings. The oldest, mudbrick Morby Cottage, was built in 1836 by the first settler, John Morrell, and had the previously unheard-of luxury of glass windows; the cottage is now a museum devoted to the history of early European settlement. Also of interest is the old railway station. Now a folk museum, it was built following the 1892 decision to make Northam the terminus for the goldfields railway. Until the line was extended to the goldfields, the station was the railhead from where thousands of hopeful prospectors began their arduous 450-km trek east to the goldfields, pushing their meagre belongings in wheelbarrows.

▶ *Great Eastern Hwy.*

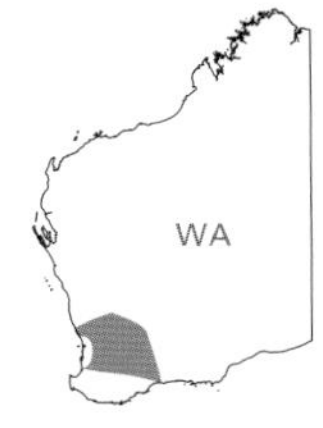

6 Meckering

Vivid evidence of tectonic forces

At 10.59 am on 14 October 1968, an earthquake measuring 6.9 on the Richter Scale – one of the largest ever recorded in Australia – all but destroyed this small town. Interpretive panels at the Meckering Earthquake Gazebo display photographs of the event; nearby are twisted rail lines and a telescoped piece of pipeline. Fifty homes were crushed in the quake – the ruins of one, Salisbury, a large homestead, can be seen on Goomalling Road, north of town. At the same time a fissure 32 km long and up to 2 m deep opened up; a 1-km section can be viewed on Quellington Road, 12 km south of town.

▶ *Great Eastern Hwy.*

7 Number 3 Pump Station

Grand remnant of an ambitious scheme

Cunderdin was chosen as a site for one of the eight pump stations required to support the Goldfields Water Supply Scheme (see opposite). This grand brick structure, built to house the Number 3 pump, was completed in 1902 and the huge brick tower outside dates from 1919. Today, the station is home to the Cunderdin Museum, but the pump can still be viewed inside. Originally powered by a triple-expansion steam engine, it weighs more than 80 tonnes and is one of only six such pumps left in the world. Other exhibits in the museum include an Interactive Earthquake House designed to replicate the sensation of an earthquake like the one that struck nearby Meckering (see entry) in 1968.

▶ *Forrest St, Cunderdin, off Great Eastern Hwy.*

8 Merredin Peak

A natural water catchment that gave rise to a town

Surveying the area in 1889, Henry King noted the substantial run-off from this prominent granite outcrop. When the railway arrived four years later, it was this water supply – ideal for replenishing steam locomotives – that led to the development of a town, now a major regional service centre. A 100-m wall was built on the side of the peak to channel the water into a dam, from where it was pumped into a water tower. Today a picnic area borders the dam and from there two walking trails, lined with informative plaques, climb the granite peak, revealing superb views over the town and salmon-gum woodlands.

▶ *Great Eastern Hwy.*

9 York

Learn about early colonial life in the state's oldest inland town

The Swan River Colony had been in existence only a few years when Ensign Dale of the 63rd Regiment led a series of expeditions over the Darling Range to explore the interior. His third trip resulted in the founding of York in 1831. Wool became the mainstay of the community, but growth was hindered by isolation – initially, freight costs from York to Fremantle were higher than those from Fremantle to London! Among the early buildings are the National Trust–listed Courthouse Complex, begun in 1852; the Holy Trinity Church, dating from 1856; and the Residency, built in 1843, originally the convict depot, later the official residence of York's magistrates, and now a museum of colonial life. Redolent of a later era, York Motor Museum has a magnificent collection of vintage vehicles.

▶ *33 km south of Great Eastern Hwy via Northam–York Rd.*

10 Wave Rock

Deceptive 2.7-billion-year-old formation

It looks for all the world like a wave frozen just as it's about to break, its crest poised high above your head. It is in fact the north wall of Hyden Rock, an isolated granite hill, or inselberg, one of many that stud this region and rise up to 30 m high. The 110-m-long wave shape is the result of millions of years of weathering of the lower slope. The vertical bands of colour that streak its face, caused by mineral-laden water running down the rock, accentuate the effect. Visible in places along the top of the rock is a low retaining wall; this diverts rainwater into a dam that supplies the nearby town of Hyden.

► *5 km east of Hyden.*

11 Dryandra Woodland

Night tours spotlight rare wildlife

Open woodlands of wandoo and paperbark here protect some of the state's most endangered animals, including its emblem, the elusive numbat, a termite-eating, cat-sized marsupial. Guided nocturnal tours from Barna Mia sanctuary, in the heart of the woodlands, allow visitors to see it and other threatened species, such as bilbies, bettongs and barred bandicoots, at close range. During daylight hours, kangaroos, wallabies and echidnas may be spotted from the range of walking and cycle trails. You can also follow a 25-km radio drive trail called Sounds of the Dryandra Woodland (100 FM), with commentary at marked sites along the route.

► *17 km north-west of Narrogin via Wandering–Narrogin Rd.*

12 Wickepin

Isolated town with intriguing literary heritage

Albert Facey, author of the classic autobiography *A Fortunate Life*, grew up in the Wickepin area in the early 1900s and after serving in the First World War was granted a property there under the soldier-settlement scheme. His house, built in 1924, has since been moved to the centre of town and turned into a fascinating museum; it retains original Facey family furniture and displays other artefacts from the pioneer days. It is also the starting point for the Albert Facey Trail, a half-day drive through lovely country taking in places mentioned in Facey's book. Another native of Wickepin was Dorothy Hewett, who chose the town as the setting for her play *The Man from Mukinupin*.

► *40 km north-east of Narrogin via Williams–Kondinin Rd.*

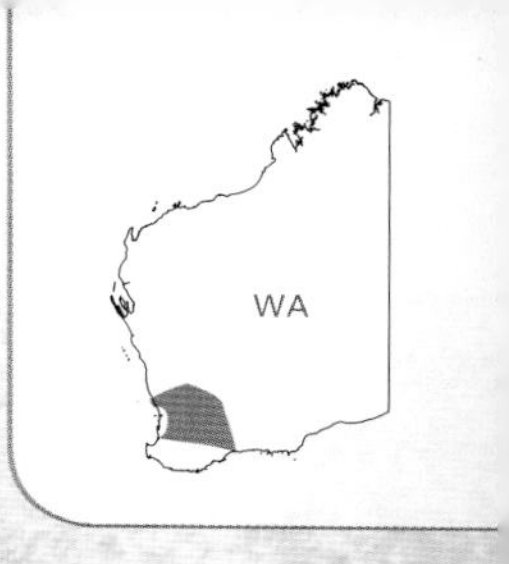

13 Narrogin

Where walking trails wind through history

Follow the 100 black granite tiles of Narrogin's Centenary Pathway and take a trip back through more than a century of local history, from the formation of the town in the 1890s, following the arrival of the Great Southern Railway, to its modern status as the commercial hub of the Central–South region. Elsewhere, interpretive signs along the Noongar Dreaming Path beside Narrogin Brook revive knowledge of local Indigenous peoples and the Newton House Barbecue, built on the site of a pioneer home and enveloped by lush gardens, tells the story of the region's earliest European settlers.

► *Great Southern Hwy, 30 km north-east of Williams.*

14 Dumbleyung Lake

Empty or full, a venue for speedsters

When full, this is the largest natural inland lake in the state, covering 5200 ha. Water levels vary dramatically, however. In the early 1900s, the lake was so dry it was used as a racetrack. In contrast, record rainfall in 1946 filled it to overflowing, and in 1964 the British racing driver Donald Campbell set a world water speed record here – a monument on Pussy Cat Hill honours his achievement. As well as being popular for watersports, the lake is one of the most important wetlands in the south-west, providing habitat for myriad bird species.

► *30 km east of Wagin via Wagin–Dumbleyung Rd.*

FROZEN IN TIME, WAVE ROCK WAS 2700 MILLION YEARS IN THE MAKING.

Perth Region

The gleaming towers of central Perth overlook the broad estuary of the Swan River. Sandy beaches fringe the city to the west and the forested slopes of the Darling Range lie to the east. From Fremantle, the city's port, a string of settlements facing the Indian Ocean stretches north.

1 Yanchep Caves

Former subterranean nightspot

The caves number more than 600, and most are small and close to the surface. In the 1930s, one of the larger caves was converted, with the addition of a concrete floor and wall seating, into an underground nightspot. It was named the 'Ballroom Cave', and later the 'Silver Stocking Cabaret Cave'. Today, called just Cabaret Cave, it is used as a function centre. In contrast, Crystal Cave remains in its natural state. Delicate limestone formations hang from the ceiling and ripple its walls, and its underground streams are home to tiny shrimp-like creatures called amphipods.

► *Yanchep National Park, 50 km north of Perth via Mitchell Fwy and Wanneroo Rd.*

2 Aquarium of Western Australia

Enjoy an underwater stroll with sharks, stingrays and turtles

Walking through the aquarium's tunnel beneath the Indian Ocean is about as close as you can get to diving without actually donning scuba gear, and almost certainly as close as most of us will ever get to the locals that glide and weave around you: 4-metre sharks, turtles, stingrays and hundreds of fish of all shapes and sizes. Other displays showcase the diverse marine habitats of Western Australia's 12,000-km coastline, ranging from icy southern waters to tropical coral reefs.

► *Sorrento, 20 km north of Perth via Mitchell Fwy.*

3 Swan Valley

Cruise upriver to sip fine vintages at historic wineries

In 1830, English botanist Thomas Waters planted vines and olive trees brought from South Africa in the loamy red soil of the Swan Valley, thereby establishing Western Australia's first vineyard. Known today as Olive Farm Winery, it is one of several stops for the river ferries that cruise up the Swan River from Perth. Others include Houghtons, which produced its first vintage in 1859 and has fine heritage buildings and gardens, and Sandalford, where the first vines were planted in the 1840s by John Septimus Roe, the west's first surveyor-general, on land granted to him on his retirement. Full- and half-day cruises depart daily from Barrack Street Wharf, and you can, of course, reach these and other wineries in the Swan Valley by road.

► *Middle Swan, 20 km north of Perth via the Great Northern Hwy.*

Visitor information

Fremantle 08 9431 7878
Guildford 08 9379 9400
Mundaring 08 9295 0202
Perth 08 9483 1111
Rockingham 08 9592 3464
Rottnest Island 08 9372 9732

4 Swan View Tunnel

Follow a bushland trail through an accident-prone railway tunnel

This is the only railway tunnel ever built in Western Australia. It opened in 1896 and was used for only a relatively short time, for it became clear that the crews of steam trains were at risk of asphyxiation due to inadequate ventilation in tunnels. Several accidents occurred. In the worst incident, in 1942, fumes from an engine caused the entire crew of a freight train to pass out; the train then rushed uncontrolled downhill through the tunnel to pile up in a mighty wreck at the other end. A bypass was completed three years later. Today the 340-m-long tunnel and four associated railway bridges are part of the John Forrest Heritage Trail. Walking through is perfectly safe.

▶ *John Forrest National Park, 26 km east of Perth via the Great Eastern Hwy.*

5 Guildford

Old river port, full of colonial charm

Guildford was established in 1829 on a loop of the Swan River. Its colonial charm is best appreciated on foot by following the Heritage Walk that begins at the visitor centre. Historic buildings include the still-operating 1841 Rose and Crown Hotel, where in the 1890s travellers on the dusty road to the Kalgoorlie goldfields stopped for refreshment; Baker and Gull's Warehouse, a reminder of the businesses that boomed during Guildford's peak years as a port and market town; and St Matthews Church, located within the village green in the exact centre of town.

▶ *12 km north-east of Perth via the Canning Hwy.*

6 Number 1 Pump Station

Museum honours the world's longest freshwater pipeline

Mundaring Weir was a key part of CY O'Connor's visionary Goldfield's Water Supply Scheme (see p. 32). Inside its historic Number 1 Pump Station you will find the original boilers and one of the steam engines that in 1903 sent the first water off on its 560-km journey east to Kalgoorlie. Interactive exhibits provide insights into the engineering genius of the scheme and tell the stories of the people who built it.

▶ *Mundaring Weir, 43 km east of Perth via the Great Eastern Hwy.*

7 Scitech

Take off on a journey through space

In Scitech's planetarium, the largest in the country, you sit under a tilted, 18-m domed screen onto which six projectors beam an accurate image of the Perth night sky. Then, via the images on the screen, you zoom into space and on through the solar system and beyond. The images are so realistic that many experience a feeling of motion or flight.

▶ *Sutherland St, West Perth.*

8 Western Australian Museum

A full-size dinosaur model looms large amid an extraordinary collection

Exhibits here reach back millions of years and include diamonds that predate our solar system, as well as fossils of extinct life. Other displays focus on Western Australia, tracing the story from the time when dinosaurs – such as the Carnotaurus, shown full-size – roamed the land, up to the arrival of the first humans and on to the present day. A replica of an Aboriginal camp site is contrasted with the hardships faced by Europeans as they settled and reshaped the land.

▶ *James St, Perth.*

9 Perth Mint

Watch a traditional gold pour

This is where gold from the Kalgoorlie diggings was made into sovereigns for use throughout the British Empire and visitors today can watch the same process. As well as exhibits of bullion bars, nuggets and coins and a reconstruction of an old miner's camp, the Mint also has special scales for those curious to know what their weight is worth in gold.

► *Hay St, East Perth.*

10 Kings Park

Bushland haven in the heart of the city

Mount Eliza was once regarded as an obstacle that blocked the westward expansion of Perth. Today, as Kings Park, it is one of the city's greatest assets. Within its 400 ha of native bush, possums, euros, parrots and black swans carry on their existence as they have done for thousands of years, and in spring wild flowers turn the park into a blaze of colour. Within the park are numerous memorials and statues, bushland trails, picnic grounds, a treetop walk and the state's Botanic Gardens.

► *Vehicle entry from Thomas St, Kings Park Rd and Poole St, Perth.*

11 Swan Bells

Historic bells relocated from London

For more than five centuries, the bells of St-Martin-in-the-Fields church have rung out to celebrate historic events, from victory over the Spanish Armada in 1588 to the safe return of James Cook in 1771; they now peal in Perth. Recast between 1725 and 1726, the 12 bells were presented to Western Australia as a gift to mark the Australian Bicentenary. Today, the old bells, along with a further five cast in 1988 and one made in 1999, are housed in a tower topped by a glass spire at the river's edge – a massive musical instrument that is played daily. You can watch the bell-ringers at work, protected by glass panels from the potentially ear-damaging volume of the chiming bells.

► *Barrack Sq, Perth.*

PERTH CITY CENTRE

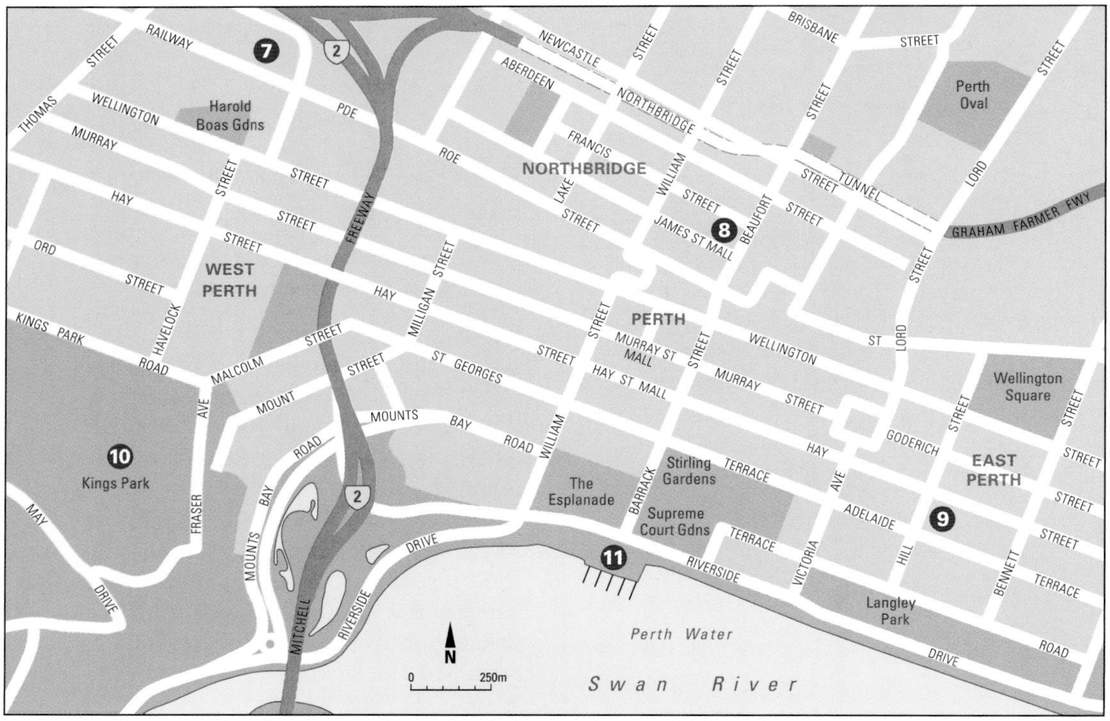

THE SWAN BELLS HAVE BEEN
RINGING FOR FIVE CENTURIES.

12 Cottesloe Beach

A fine place to be at the end of the day

It's a Perth tradition: fish and chips or a picnic on the terraced lawns that edge Cottesloe Beach while watching the sun slip below the waves. This is the closest beach to the city, and with its clear waters, regular swell and wide arc of pale sand, one of its most popular. Bobbing offshore is the Cottlesloe Bell, a floating pylon dating from the 1930s that some swimmers use as a diving platform.

► *10 km south-west of Perth via Stirling Hwy.*

13 Rottnest Island

A car-free, care-free retreat

Bicycles (available for hire) are the main mode of transport here, a factor that contributes much to Rottnest's relaxed atmosphere. The island is washed by the warm Leeuwin Current; just offshore in crystal waters perfect for snorkelling are some of the world's southernmost coral reefs. Also on offer are pristine beaches for swimming, sparkling bays for wind-surfing and a network of paths for walking and cycling. But perhaps the main attraction is the island's sizeable population of quokkas, the small, solidly built wallabies that Dutch explorer Willem de Vlamingh in 1696 mistook for rats, leading him to call the island 'rat's nest'. These friendly creatures spend most of the day resting in the shade, then emerge at dusk to graze.

► *18 km west of Fremantle; ferry services from Fremantle, Perth and Hillary's Boat Harbour.*

14 Round House

The oldest public building in the west

Despite its name, this still-forbidding former jail is not round at all, but is in fact a 12-sided structure. It opened in 1831 and, in a rather surprising challenge to its security, a tunnel was built under it soon after to provide a route out for whalers operating from Bathers Beach in front. By the 1850s the eight cells, with up to 15 unfortunates crowded together in each, were proving increasingly inadequate and the prison closed in 1886. For a time the building was used as accommodation for the chief constable, his wife and their ten children. Arrive just before 1 pm to see the time ball drop and the time gun fired.

► *Arthur Head Reserve, Fremantle.*

ROTTNEST ISLAND IS A HAVEN FOR QUOKKAS.

Fremantle's maritime heritage

Historic docks, maritime museums, warehouses and modern wharves, busy with commercial, fishing and pleasure craft, vividly evoke the early days of Perth's port.

The thousands of miners who passed through Fremantle during the Western Australian gold rushes of the 1890s landed at Long Jetty, which then jutted into the open sea from Bathers Beach, in front of the Round House (see entry). However, it was not until 1897, when a rocky bar was blasted from the mouth of the Swan River to create an inner harbour accessible to larger ships – a scheme devised by engineer-in-chief CY O'Connor – that Fremantle came to the fore as a shipping hub. Although since deepened, extended and modernised, the port remains much as it was then. The original cargo sheds on Victoria Quay house a market and artists' studios. Nearby, the Western Australian Museum – Maritime tells of Fremantle's role in whaling, trade, naval defence and migration; the decommissioned submarine HMAS *Ovens*, on the slipway outside, can be explored on guided tours.

15 Penguin Island

Cruise to a pristine island abounding with seabirds

Just offshore from Rockingham, Penguin Island is home to the largest colony of little penguins on the west coast. The birds breed in limestone caves and in hollows under the dense vegetation. The island also has significant nesting and feeding sites for seabirds seldom seen on the mainland. Injured penguins and chicks rejected by their mothers are given shelter in the Penguin Experience – Island Discovery Centre, where visitors can see the birds up close in an environment similar to their natural habitat. The island is closed to the public during the penguin breeding season, June to September.

▶ *Shoalwater Islands Marine Park; regular ferry service from Mersey Point.*

16 Jarrahdale

The state's first timber town conjures up the past and looks to the future

Established in the 1880s, picturesque Jarrahdale was the first major timber milling operation in the state and, through the export of jarrah from here around the world, played an important role in the development of the economy of Western Australia. Jarrahdale's last mill closed in 1997 and in the same year, in recognition of the town's historic and architectural significance, it was classified by the National Trust. Today, Jarrahdale Heritage Park tells the stories of the region's unique jarrah forest and the logging communities that depended on it for their livelihood. Meanwhile, Heritage Sawmillers continues the tradition by operating a mill on the site, but one with a difference: it processes salvage logs and recycled timber, leaving the forest untouched.

▶ *45 km south-east of Perth via South Western Hwy.*

South-West

The scenic south-western corner of the continent is washed by two oceans and scalloped with white-sand beaches where dolphins and whales are frequently seen. Inland are towering forests, deep limestone caves, picturesque townships and vine-covered slopes that yield some of the country's finest wines.

1 Dolphin Discovery Centre

Rendezvous with friendly dolphins

The 'beach interaction zone' in front of this research centre on the shores of Koombana Bay is a regular stop for local dolphins, which drop in to swim close to people waiting in waist-deep water. There are no set times – the dolphins are wild animals and call the tune – so encounters can happen at any time of the day and last from between a few minutes to an hour. However, visits are most frequent between October and May, and most occur in the morning.

▶ *Bunbury, South Western Hwy.*

Visitor information

Albany 08 9841 9290
Augusta 08 9758 0166
Bunbury 08 9792 7205
Busselton 08 9752 1288
Denmark 08 9848 2055
Dunsborough 08 9729 1122
Kojonup 08 9831 0500
Margaret River 08 9780 5911
Pemberton 08 9776 1133
Walpole–Nornalup 08 9840 1111

2 Busselton Jetty

Walk – or ride – nearly 2 km out over sparkling waters

Holiday-makers in the early 1900s claimed that walking the length of Busselton's iconic jetty was as good as taking an ocean cruise, and with good reason: it arcs nearly 2 km into beautiful Geographe Bay and is the longest timber jetty in the land. It was constructed in stages from 1865, with extensions added over the years as ships became larger and the silting bay shallower. The jetty was closed to shipping in 1972 and after surviving cyclone and fire, has been restored for public use. Its historic train, now carrying visitors instead of hauling cargo, once again chugs to the end of the jetty. There, an underwater observatory 8 m below provides a fish-eye look at the corals, sponges and sea creatures that flourish on and flit between the wooden piers.

▶ *53 km south of Bunbury via Bussell Hwy.*

3 Cape Naturaliste

Lighthouse views of a rugged, treacherous coastline

Reefs and currents off this rugged point had claimed at least 12 ships before 1903, when this lighthouse sent out its first beams. Built of local limestone, it is now fully automated, but until 1978 three lighthouse-keepers worked in shifts to wind the mechanism that turned the light. They and their families occupied the nearby stone cottages, living in extreme isolation; today an intriguing maritime museum is housed in one of the buildings. You can join a tour of the lighthouse and enjoy sweeping views over the Indian Ocean from the top balcony, 120 m above sea level. The tower itself is only 20 m, but it sits atop a 100-m-high cliff.

▶ *27 km west of Busselton via Caves Rd.*

4 Canal Rocks

Watch waves race through an ocean-carved channel

Here a rocky point jutting well into the ocean has been gouged out by the force of the waves to form a granite-sided channel. This is a dangerous part of the coast where 'king' waves can sweep onto the shore at any time, but visitors are still drawn here to see the powerful ebb and flow of the Indian Ocean as its foaming waters rush into the main 'canal'. The spectacle can be viewed from a walkway built across a smaller canal to the side. Keep a lookout also for the bottlenose dolphins that often appear off the nearby beach.

▶ *35 km west of Busselton via Caves Rd.*

5 Vasse Felix Winery

Sumptuous wines – and an international art collection

This is where the Margaret River wine story began. Established in 1967, Vasse Felix was the first commercial vineyard in the region. The original plantings flank the streamside 'old winery', where the underground barrel hall serves as a cellar door for tastings and sales. Above is a performing-arts facility and impressive art gallery space, which hosts changing exhibitions of national and international works from the Holmes à Court Collection and live performances.

▶ *20 km south of Busselton via Bussell Hwy.*

6 Jewel Cave

Vast subterranean caverns decorated with majestic formations

Water dripping constantly over countless centuries has leached calcium carbonate from the limestone rock here to form and adorn the grand chambers of Jewel Cave. The largest publicly accessible cave system west of the Nullarbor, its caverns sink to a depth of 42 m and extend for nearly 2 km. Within is an impressive array of stalagmites, stalactites and shawls, including a 5.4-m straw stalactite and an unusual suspended table formation. The cave was also the last resting place, 25,000 years ago, of a thylacine, or Tasmanian tiger. Its fossilised remains are now stored in the Western Australian Museum.

▶ *7 km north-west of Augusta via Bussell Hwy and Caves Rd.*

BUSSELTON JETTY IS AUSTRALIA'S LONGEST TIMBER JETTY.

7 Cape Leeuwin

Where the swells of two oceans crash together

For sea-weary passengers on the long sailing voyage from Europe, the rocky finger of Cape Leeuwin was usually the first sight of land since leaving the Cape of Good Hope. It is the most south-westerly point in Australia, and is also the place where the Southern and Indian oceans come together – the Southern washes east to west, the Indian west to east. The line of white water that marks the meeting point can be identified from the clifftop, but is best seen from the top of the 39-m-high lighthouse tower. Opened in 1896, this is the tallest lighthouse on the Australian mainland and its piercing beam reaches nearly 50 km out to sea.

► *8 km south of Augusta via Bussell Hwy.*

8 The Kodja Place

An Indigenous perspective on the south-west's history and landscape

Kodja, a Noongar Aboriginal word meaning 'stone axe', gave the township of Kojonup its name (stone for axe-heads came from a freshwater spring here) and is also the name of its excellent interpretive centre. Built around the theme of 'One Story, Many Voices', The Kodja Place uses the traditional Noongar style of story-telling to trace the many influences that shaped this rural community. Sit beside a campfire to hear Noongar stories about the land and learn about the experiences of the early European settlers through interactive displays. The theme continues in the adjacent Rose Maze, where the linked stories of three women – Yoondi, a Noongar woman; Elizabeth, an English woman; and an Italian woman, Maria – are told as you walk through.

► *Kojonup, Albany Hwy.*

9 Pemberton

Delightful timber town in the woods

Restored wooden cottages and well-tended gardens are a feature of this forest-encircled timber town. Logging here dates from the late 19th century, and the town grew around three sawmills. Displays in the Pioneer Museum recall those days, but visitors can get an updated perspective by touring the still-operating Pemberton Mill. A novel way of exploring the towering forest is on the Pemberton Tramway, which trundles out daily. The region is also known for its wines and fine foods, including trout and marron from the nearby streams and rivers, berries in season, and even truffles.

► *30 km off South Western Hwy via Vasse Hwy.*

10 Gloucester Tree

Fire lookout rewards intrepid climbers with unrivalled treetop views

This enormous tree towers above its fellow karris, which is the reason it was chosen, in 1947, as a fire lookout. Foresters kept a regular watch for smoke from a cabin built in its lofty crown. Today the climb is open to the public, but the ascent of the 153 simple metal rungs that spiral 60 m up the trunk are not for the fainthearted. However, if you take up the challenge, the view from the top is magnificent. The tree was named after the then governor-general, the Duke of Gloucester, who was visiting nearby Pemberton at the time of the tower's construction.

► *33 km off South Western Hwy via Vasse Hwy and Pemberton.*

11 Valley of the Giants Treetop Walk

Walkway loops through the leafy canopy of forest giants

Venturing onto this slightly swaying, 600-m-long steel walkway is a thrilling experience in itself, quite apart from the bird's-eye view it provides of life in the tops of a stand of mighty tingle trees. Some 40 m below, the Ancient Empire walk, a wheelchair-accessible boardwalk, winds between their massive trunks. Tingle trees are towering rough-barked eucalypts that grow only in this area; some of these veterans are more than 400 years old.

▶ *95 km west of Albany via South Coast Hwy.*

12 Greens Pool

Turquoise-green waters sheltered by colossal boulders

Giant, waterworn granite boulders edging pristine white sands and rocky shelves extending 100 m out to sea together temper the wild waves of the Southern Ocean to create Greens Pool, a large area of calm water that is a perfect spot for swimming and snorkelling. Across the headland to the east is Elephant Rocks, where a cluster of smooth-shouldered boulders, named for their resemblance to a herd of elephants, form a barrier protecting another magical swimming spot.

▶ *William Bay National Park, 66 km west of Albany via South Coast Hwy.*

VALLEY OF THE GIANTS TREETOP WALK

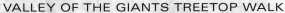

A botanist's delight

The Stirling Range is famed for the staggering concentration, beauty and variety of the wild flowers that flourish on its slopes.

Rising abruptly up to 1000 m from the surrounding plains, the Stirling Range consists of a string of craggy and often mist-shrouded peaks that stretch 65 km from east to west, creating a cool and moist 'ecological island' with climate and conditions markedly different to the lowlands. This is one of the most outstanding botanical environments on the planet, with some 1500 species of flowering plants, including 87 that occur nowhere else.

Blooms can be seen at any time of the year, but are most prolific between August and November, when tourists by the thousands arrive here to witness the annual display. Unique species include the Stirling Range banksia (one of 18 banksia species in the range) and several types of mountain bells, and there are more than 120 different orchids. Another highlight is the southern cross, whose lovely white flowers resemble the four stars of the Southern Cross constellation.

13 Albany

The west's first European settlement

Albany was founded in 1826, three years before Perth, so it is not surprising that the oldest intact dwelling in the state – Patrick Taylor Cottage, dating from 1832 – is located here. The 11-room wattle-and-daub building is furnished with period artefacts and is open to the public. The Albany Convict Gaol, in the nearby historic precinct, is a complex of cell blocks and warders' quarters built between 1852 and 1875, while the Western Australian Museum – Albany is housed in the former commissariat and stores building, later used as the home of the resident magistrate. A short walk away is a scale replica of the brig *Amity*, which stands just 200 m from where the original vessel landed Albany's first settlers (convict tradesmen and their soldier guards) on Christmas Day, 1826.

▶ *South Coast Hwy/Albany Hwy.*

VIEW ACROSS THE STIRLING RANGE FROM BLUFF KNOLL

14 The Gap

Watch mighty waves pound massive granite formations

Here the titanic power of the Southern Ocean has carved out a series of dramatic rock formations – cracklines that 'blow' ocean spray, natural bridges high above the swirling waters, and The Gap, an awesome opening where thundering waves rush in to dash against the base of a 24-m-high cliff then at once retreat seawards. Follow the walkway from the car park to the lookouts.

▶ *Torndirrup National Park, 16 km west of Albany via Frenchman Bay Rd.*

15 Whale World

Australia's last whaling station, now a fascinating museum

Hunting whales was the earliest industry in this area, and until 1978 the whales' carcasses were processed in this complex of buildings, now home to an impressive museum of whaling history. Audiovisual displays bring the sounds of the former whaling station to life, and the original machinery is still in place and in working order. Beached nearby and open for inspection is the *Cheynes IV*, the last of the whale-chasing ships.

▶ *20 km south of Albany via Frenchman Bay Rd.*

16 Bluff Knoll

High point of the south-west

Bluff Knoll, at 1095 m above sea level, is the highest peak in the region and its near-vertical main face is one of the most impressive cliffs on the Australian mainland. Walkers on the steep 6-km, 4-hour return walk pass through alpine meadows en route to the summit. Mists permitting, the views pan across the ranges to glimmering salt lakes in the north and south to the coast.

▶ *Stirling Range National Park, 80 km north of Albany.*

17 Hamersley Drive Heritage Trail

Sublime seaboard touring route

The 70-km-long, unsealed Hamersley Drive Heritage Trail heads south from the highway through a flora-rich wilderness to the ocean, then continues east along the coast to the tiny and historic outpost of Hopetoun. Along the way, there are sweeping vistas over the wild heart of the park, and spur roads detour to pristine beaches. In winter (July to October), southern right whales calve in sheltered bays. Allow a full day to complete the drive or camp overnight in the park; the road is not suitable for caravans.

▶ *Fitzgerald River National Park, South Coast Hwy.*

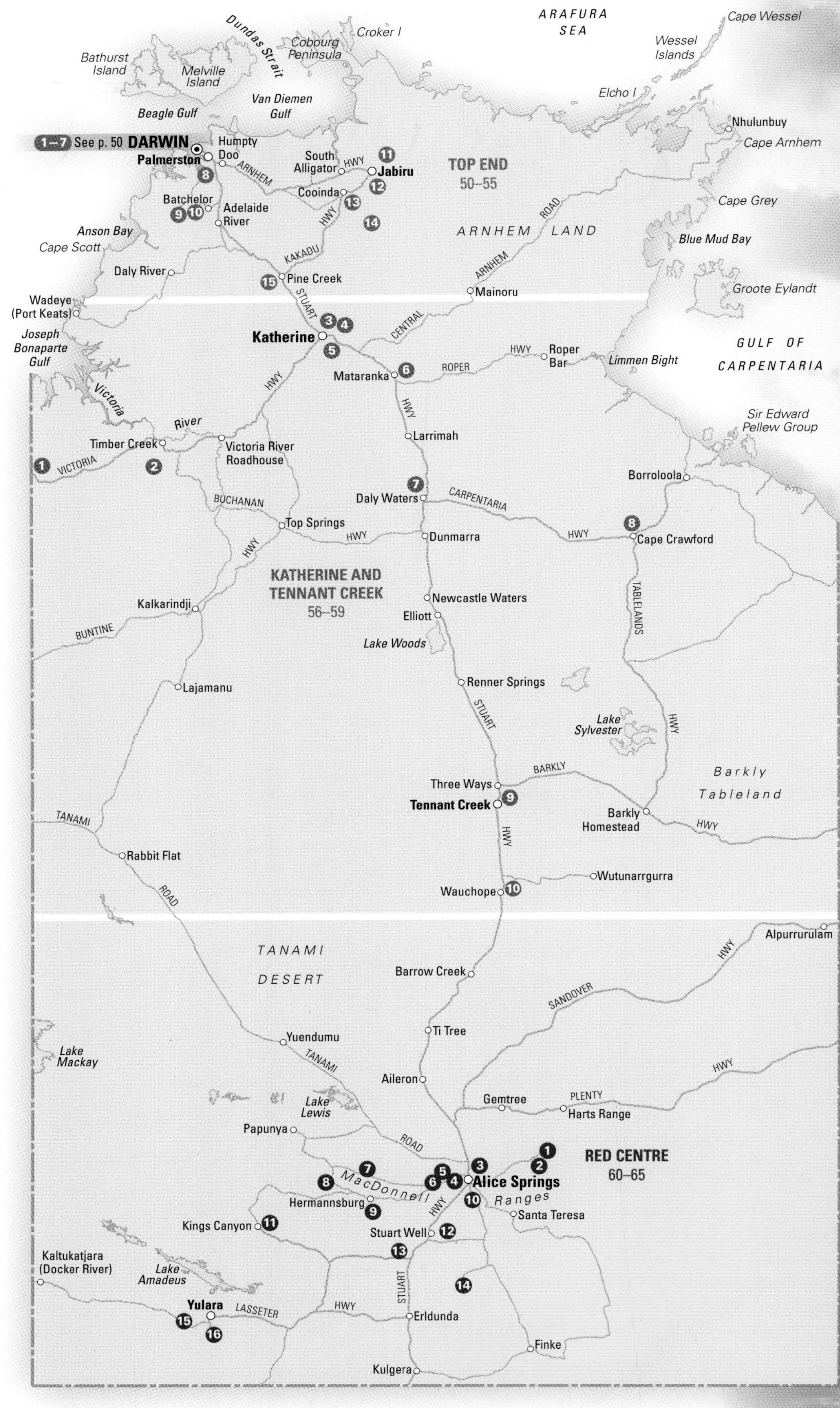
ARAFURA SEA
Cape Wessel
Dundas Strait
Croker I
Cobourg Peninsula
Wessel Islands
Bathurst Island
Melville Island
Elcho I
Van Diemen Gulf
Beagle Gulf
Nhulunbuy
1–7 See p. 50
DARWIN
Humpty Doo
Palmerston
South Alligator
HWY
Jabiru
TOP END
50–55
Cape Arnhem
ARNHEM
Cooinda
Batchelor
Adelaide River
Cape Grey
HWY
ARNHEM LAND
ROAD
Anson Bay
Cape Scott
Blue Mud Bay
KAKADU
ARNHEM
Daly River
Pine Creek
Groote Eylandt
Mainoru
Wadeye (Port Keats)
STUART
Joseph Bonaparte Gulf
Katherine
CENTRAL
GULF OF CARPENTARIA
HWY
Roper Bar
Limmen Bight
Mataranka
ROPER
HWY
Victoria
HWY
River
Sir Edward Pellew Group
Timber Creek
Victoria River Roadhouse
Larrimah
VICTORIA
Borroloola
BUCHANAN
Daly Waters
CARPENTARIA
Top Springs
HWY
Dunmarra
HWY
Cape Crawford
HWY
KATHERINE AND TENNANT CREEK
56–59
TABLELANDS
Newcastle Waters
Kalkarindji
Elliott
BUNTINE
Lake Woods
Lajamanu
Renner Springs
STUART
Lake Sylvester
HWY
Three Ways
BARKLY
Barkly Tableland
Tennant Creek
Barkly Homestead
TANAMI
HWY
HWY
Rabbit Flat
Wutunarrgurra
ROAD
Wauchope
Alpurrurulam
TANAMI DESERT
HWY
Barrow Creek
SANDOVER
Ti Tree
Yuendumu
TANAMI
Lake Mackay
HWY
Aileron
PLENTY
Gemtree
Harts Range
Lake Lewis
Papunya
ROAD
RED CENTRE
60–65
Alice Springs
MacDonnell Ranges
Hermannsburg
HWY
Santa Teresa
Kings Canyon
Stuart Well
Kaltukatjara (Docker River)
Lake Amadeus
STUART
Yulara
LASSETER
HWY
Erldunda
Finke
Kulgera

Northern Territory

From the Top End to the Red Centre, the Territory enthralls. It offers majestic outback scenery, remarkable Indigenous culture and art, isolated pioneer settlements and highly visible wildlife, ranging from Kakadu's massed flocks of waterbirds to desert-dwelling reptiles and marsupials.

YELLOW WATER, KAKADU NATIONAL PARK

Useful websites

Visitor information en.travelnt.com
Parks and reserves www.nt.gov.au/nreta/parks
Motoring organisation www.aant.com.au

Top End

Once a frontier town, tropical Darwin is now Australia's most modern capital – the result of rebuilding after wartime bombings and Cyclone Tracy. Inland, two magnificent national parks, Kakadu and Litchfield, protect ancient and majestic landscapes crowded with wildlife and rich with Indigenous heritage.

1 Darwin Military Museum

Relive the dark days of wartime Darwin

At the start of the Second World War, Darwin, as the largest city in the north, became both a vital military base and a key defensive post. It was therefore considered vulnerable to attack and its existing fortifications were quickly strengthened. The gun emplacements on East Point date from that time, as does the nearby concrete army command bunker, which now houses wartime memorabilia. Its collection includes weapons and equipment and, particularly chilling, dramatic footage of the February 1942 bombing of Darwin Harbour, then packed with Allied ships, which cost 240 lives. On a brighter note, Lake Alexander, close by, is one of the few places where Top Enders can swim year-round safe from the attentions of stingers (including potentially deadly box jellyfish) and crocodiles.

► *East Point, Darwin.*

DARWIN CITY CENTRE

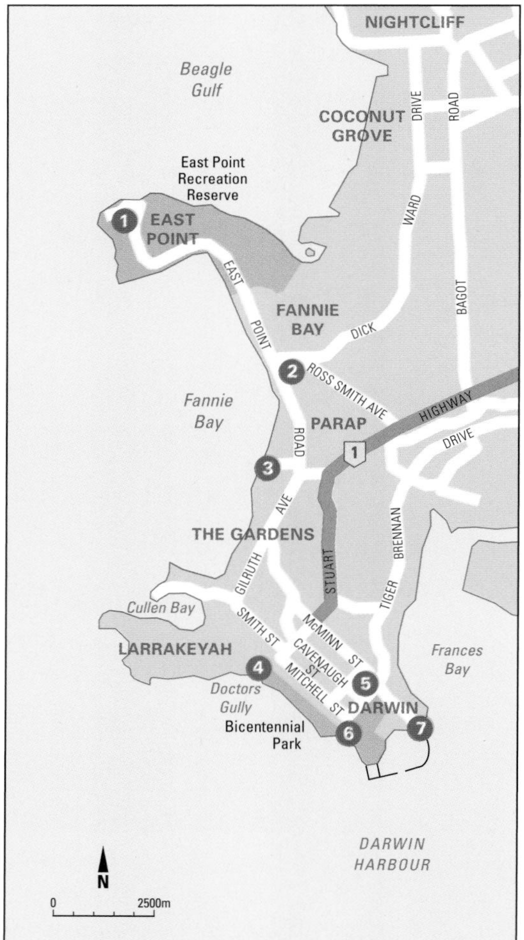

2 Fannie Bay Gaol Museum

Grim reminders of prison life

From 1883 to 1979, this was Her Majesty's Gaol and Labour Prison. The restored complex includes the original square stone cells dating from the 1880s, corrugated iron cells and 1970s steel-clad structures. Visiting is a fascinating but sobering experience: the interiors are spartan and forbidding, and displays include the gallows mechanism constructed for the Territory's last hangings in 1952. In 1942, following the bombing raids on Darwin, prisoners here were released in a general amnesty; in 1975 fate dealt the same 'lucky' hand to short-term prisoners, who were freed because of damage to the buildings by Cyclone Tracy.

► *East Point Rd, Fannie Bay, Darwin.*

Visitor information

Darwin 08 8936 2499

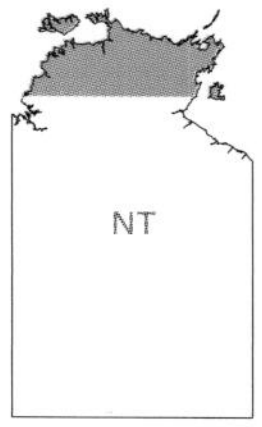

3 Museum and Art Gallery of the Northern Territory

Art, history and a famous croc

Here you can investigate almost every historical aspect of the Top End. The Gallery of Indigenous Art displays examples of the region's different stylistic traditions including Arnhem Land art and carvings from Bathurst and Melville islands. Another gallery is devoted to Tracy, the cyclone that took 71 lives and virtually destroyed Darwin in the early hours of Christmas Day, 1974. And you can also come face to face with the stuffed hide of Sweetheart, a 5-m-long saltwater crocodile infamous in the 1970s for menacing fisherfolk in dinghies, who drowned during an operation to remove him from a popular angling spot.

▶ *Conacher St, Fannie Bay, Darwin.*

4 Aquascene

Provoke a feeding frenzy

Every day at high tide, hundreds of wild fish, including barramundi, catfish, bream and metre-long milkfish, mass in the waters here to snatch bread from the hands of those bold enough to venture down the sloping ramp into the shallows. It's a ritual that began in the 1950s, when a local regularly tossed scraps to mullet that arrived with the tide. Today, bags of stale bread can be purchased to hand-feed the milling throng.

▶ *Doctors Gully Rd, Darwin.*

5 Chinese Temple

Historic place of worship reflects the city's long association with Chinese settlers

A Chinese temple has stood on this site since 1887 – the date on the original ceremonial bell. At this time the Chinese population of the Top End, many of whom arrived as labourers during the Territory gold rushes of the 1880s, outnumbered Europeans. The first temple building was badly damaged by cyclones in 1897 and 1937 and by bombing raids during the Second World War, then obliterated by Cyclone Tracy in 1974. The current temple is known as Chung Wah Temple or Darwin's Temple and is a place of worship for Confucians, Taoists and Buddhists. Artefacts and photographs in the adjacent museum chronicle the way of life and the struggles faced by those early Chinese settlers.

▶ *Woods St, Darwin.*

6 Northern Territory Parliament House

Stylish setting for political stoushes

One of Darwin's most prominent buildings, Parliament House opened in 1994 and is a gleaming example of modern tropical architecture and post-Tracy renewal. A façade across the columned exterior screens sunlight from the granite-and-timber interior, which is filled with Indigenous artworks and contains the Northern Territory Library, a comprehensive collection of historical and contemporary documentary material. The library and other parts of the building are open daily to the public and tours are available on Wednesday (dry season only) and Saturday. Visitors can also watch the Legislative Assembly when in session.

▶ *State Sq, Darwin.*

7 Indo-Pacific Marine

Tropical ocean displays in full kaleidoscopic colour

This is no ordinary aquarium. Flourishing within its tanks is an entire live coral reef system, complete with fragile corals and other reef inhabitants from the Timor Sea, north of Darwin. Here box jellyfish and venomous spined stonefish can be viewed safely behind glass, alongside more appealing starfish, seahorses and clown and butterfly fish. Each display is self-supporting, requiring no feeding, filtration or water changing.

▶ *Stokes Hill Wharf, Darwin.*

X-RAY STYLE ROCK
ART AT UBIRR

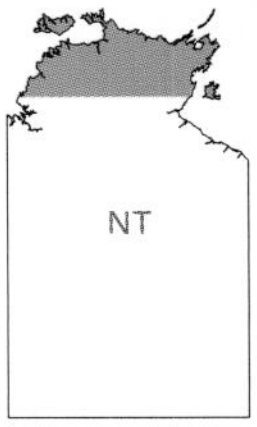

8 Territory Wildlife Park

Catch a train to meet the locals

This is wildlife watching made easy, where trackless 'trains' take you to the main attractions and activities. These include a walk beside the billabongs and lagoons of a Top End freshwater river system, complete with abundant birdlife (viewed from discreetly placed hides) as well as freshwater crocs and turtles; strolling past the treetops of a monsoon vine forest in a giant aviary; and spying on seldom-seen bats and owls in the nocturnal house. Hop on and off the train as you please. Particularly popular are the freshwater aquarium, where barramundi, whip rays and other freshwater species glide above and beside the walk-through tunnel and a 3.4-metre saltwater crocodile awaits at the end, and the 'flight deck', where white-bellied sea eagles and other free-flying birds of prey go through their paces.

▶ *12 km west of Stuart Hwy via Cox Peninsula Rd.*

9 Wangi Falls

Dramatic tumble to plunge pool

From the heights of Tabletop Range, Wangi Falls cascade down the rust-red escarpment to fill a deep waterhole shaded by paperbark trees. This sandy-bottomed pool is a popular swimming spot, with a grassed picnic area nearby; it may be closed to swimmers after heavy rain when surging waters cause dangerous currents. A 2-km loop walking track from the pool takes in a viewing platform at the base of the falls, then climbs through a monsoon forest to a second viewing platform that allows you to peer into the forest canopy.

▶ *Litchfield National Park, 80 km west of Stuart Hwy.*

10 Magnetic Termite Mounds

Precision-built, temperature-controlled towers

Thin, wedge-shaped slabs, up to 2 m high, standing like tombstones on the wet plains here, are the work of toiling armies of tiny and sightless termites. Their building material, a mixture of mud, saliva and excreta, dries rock-hard and weatherproof. The intricate architecture of the interior includes arches, tunnels, air vents, nursery chambers and larders (termites feed on dead grass harvested at night and chewed into fine pellets for storage). All towers are identically aligned with their thin edges pointing to the North and South magnetic poles – hence their name. This minimises their exposure to the full force of the noonday sun, and maintains an even temperature within. A boardwalk leads to a viewing point.

▶ *Litchfield National Park, 50 km west of Stuart Hwy.*

11 Ubirr

Inspect magnificent rock art then climb on to enjoy panoramic views

The rock shelters around Ubirr, close to the food-rich waters and flood plains of the East Alligator River, were a favoured wet-season camp site for countless generations of Aboriginal people, and the rock art galleries here are a window onto their world. Ochre murals and distinctive X-ray paintings depict the animals they hunted – barramundi, turtles, snakes, magpie geese and wallabies – and show a thylacine (long-extinct on the mainland) and human figures. An easy 1-km (1-hour) track loops through the site; take another 30 minutes to climb to the lookout and you'll be rewarded with a 360-degree view of the surrounding countryside and the dramatic Arnhem Land escarpment.

▶ *Kakadu National Park, 46 km north-east of Jabiru.*

12 Nourlangie Rock

Layered record of life, culture and changing times

The large rock overhang of Anbangbang, at Nourlangie Rock, shelters occupants from both sun and rain. Here protected dry ground has preserved evidence of people using this site as a base camp for as long as 20,000 years: stone implements from the lower levels and, in the higher layers, remains of past meals, string from games, and spear points of bone and wood. Painted and repainted on the walls are hundreds of images, often superimposed one over the other. They include depictions of important creation ancestors, such as Namarrgon, the Lightning Man, and range in style from the older hand stencils, large drawings of humans and animals and smaller, stick-like figures to more recent X-ray paintings, which show the skeleton and internal organs, and art depicting axes and firearms. You can view the art on a 1.5-km circuit track, there are information boards and, in the dry season, rangers give talks several times a day.

▶ *Kakadu National Park, 33 km south of Jabiru.*

13 Yellow Water

Wildlife hub teeming with wetland birdlife – and crocs

Kakadu is home to 290 bird species (that's more than one-third of Australia's birds) and during the Dry, when they flee diminishing water sources elsewhere, you'll find most taking refuge here, massed in mixed groups waiting for the next rains. The brolgas, jabirus, whistling ducks, egrets, kingfishers and stilt-legged jacanas that crowd the Yellow Water wetlands can be viewed from a boardwalk across the waterlily-covered billabong, but for the full experience, join a cruise. Ducks and honking magpie geese rise in noisy flapping flocks as watercraft pass by and you'll also spot more than a few crocodiles. Cruises operate year-round; early morning or late afternoon is best.

▶ *Kakadu National Park, 45 km south-west of Jabiru.*

Sandstone stronghold

Vast, little developed and spectacularly scenic, the enormous sandstone plateau of Arnhem Land is one of Australia's last bastions of traditional Indigenous culture.

Aboriginal people have been living in Arnhem Land for more than 40,000 years. Rock paintings in the 1500 'galleries' found across the plateau are thought to represent the longest continuous record of human culture anywhere in the world. They illustrate the relationship of the people to the land and its plants and animals, and also record contact with visitors from across the sea to the north – Macassans – who, from the 17th century onward, fished along the coast here for bêche de mer (sea cucumbers).

Apart from Kakadu and the Gove Peninsula outpost of Nhulunbuy, the sprawling 90,000 sq km of Arnhem Land is Aboriginal-owned and permission to enter must be obtained from the Northern Land Council. Equipped with a permit and 4WD, you can explore by yourself. However, a wide range of guided tours is also on offer – contact Darwin tourist office for details.

14 Jim Jim Falls

Colossal wet-season cascade

Jim Jim Falls flow at furious full volume in the late wet season (March to May) when swollen by summer rains, but at this time it's impossible to reach them by road; in the Dry, the waters dwindle to the merest trickle. So to experience one of Kakadu's most majestic offerings, you'll need to take to the air with a sightseeing flight from Jabiru. It's an astonishing spectacle – churning waters thunder over the Arnhem Land escarpment into a deep pool 150 m below, sending a flurry of mist and spray swirling upwards. Road access requires a 4WD and is dry season only.

▶ *Kakadu National Park, 100 km south of Jabiru.*

AERIAL VIEW OF JIM JIM FALLS IN THE WET SEASON

15 Pine Creek

Reminders of a golden past

Pine Creek was named in 1870 by a surveyor on the Overland Telegraph Line after the small creek that was 'remarkable for the pines growing there'. Even more remarkable were the traces of gold the team discovered while digging post holes, leading to a frantic rush of miners, many of them Chinese, who trekked south from Darwin. After exhausting the alluvial gold, the miners turned their attention, in the 1880s, to the more difficult-to-recover reef gold. Machinery from these times is on display at Miners Park. Standing beside the nearby 1888 railway station, the one-time southern terminus of the North Australian Railway and now a museum, is the 1877 Beyer Peacock locomotive which chugged between Darwin and Pine Creek from 1915 to 1945. Also of interest is a corrugated-iron bakery, complete with an antbed oven (made out of a termite mound).

▶ *Junction of Stuart Hwy and Kakadu Hwy.*

Katherine and Tennant Creek

The standout attraction of this vast and ancient region is grand Katherine Gorge, but here you will also find hot springs and cool waterholes, time-worn formations of sandstone and limestone, and links to a rich Indigenous and European past.

1 Keep River National Park

Meander through sandstone domes to ancient rock art and occupation sites

This tiny park straddles the meeting place of the Kimberley sandstone country, to the west, and the Victoria River escarpment, to the east. Over thousands of years the Keep River has carved out a 4-km-long sandstone gorge. Along its length are shelters and occupations sites used by the Miriwoong people (with middens showing the remains of long-ago meals), and rock art on the red gorge walls. In the dry season, you can follow the Jinumum walk along the riverbed to take in these sights.

▶ *Victoria Hwy.*

2 Limestone Gorge

Invigorating hikes to spectacular vistas

At Limestone Gorge, a moderately arduous loop track (1.8 km) winds up from the campground through bizarrely shaped limestone formations and clusters of boab trees to reveal a breathtaking panorama over the East Baines River valley. A short distance back down the access track, the easier Calcite Flow Walk (600 m) presents more fine views of the limestone landscape as well as examples of stromatolites – one of the earliest life forms on earth. The road to the campground is closed in the wet season (November to May) and not suitable for caravans; a 4WD is recommended.

▶ *Gregory National Park, 42 km south of Victoria Hwy via Bullita Access Rd.*

3 Leliyn (Edith Falls)

Majestic cascade flanked by ochre cliffs

This broad cascade tumbles year-round over a rugged rock face into a wide, forest-fringed waterhole, the lowest of three pools. Swimming is safe, although you may spot small freshwater crocodiles. Grassy areas close by are the location of a camp site, picnic area and kiosk. The Leliyn Trail (2.6 km loop) follows the escarpment to the Upper Pool, then returns along the opposite side of the gorge. Tours led by the traditional owners, the Jawoyn people, explain the significance of the area.

▶ *Nitmiluk National Park, 18 km east of Stuart Hwy.*

4 Katherine Gorge

Cruise or canoe through a grand, extraordinary gorge system

This is not one gorge, but an 11-km-long chain of 13 individual gorges gouged out of the 1.65-billion-year-old sandstone plateau by waters running to the Timor Sea. During the Wet, the river surges uninterrupted through the channel, but in the Dry water levels drop, forming tranquil pools. This is when tour boats cruise the deep, still waters of the lower gorges, nosing beneath soaring red walls where pockets of rainforest crowd giant cracks, and stop to visit a rock-art site. To venture further, you'll need to hire a canoe and be prepared to carry it around the rocks and rapids that separate the upper gorges. Scenic helicopter flights are also available.

▶ *Nitmiluk National Park, 30 km north-east of Katherine.*

KATHERINE GORGE – AN 11-KM-LONG CHAIN OF THIRTEEN GORGES

5 Cutta Cutta Caves

Five-hundred-million-year-old chambers home to rare bats

According to the beliefs of the Jawoyn Aboriginal people, this cave system was where the stars sheltered during the day – *cutta cutta* means 'many stars'. For today's visitors the stars are two species of endangered bat, the ghost bat and the orange horseshoe bat, and two species of blind and colourless shrimp. These can be seen on guided tours. Don't be alarmed by the brown tree snakes often seen coiled on ledges, they feed on the bats and are harmless to humans.

▶ *Stuart Hwy, 27 km south of Katherine.*

6 Mataranka Thermal Pool

Natural hot springs fringed by lush tropical forest

For thousands of years the warm, mineral-rich waters that gush from Rainbow Spring have filled waterholes that were a meeting point and place of relaxation for local people. Now flowing through a landscaped pool surrounded by rainforest palms at a rate of 30.5 million litres a day, they are as popular as ever. The temperature is a constant 34°C. The pool can be reached via a short boardwalk from Mataranka Homestead.

▶ *Elsey National Park, 7 km east of Stuart Hwy at Mataranka.*

Visitor information

Katherine 08 8972 2650

Desert defences

During the Second World War, the Stuart Highway and the string of air force bases along its route were crucial to the defence of Australia.

In 1940, air attacks on coastal shipping prevented the movement of troops and materials by sea, prompting the upgrading of the Stuart Highway – then a dirt track – into an all-weather sealed road for the transport of personnel and materials between Darwin and points south. Most particularly, it served a string of airstrips located out of the flying range of enemy planes and the bases built to house the influx of Allied personnel and to tend and refuel their bombers and fighter aircraft.

Gorrie Airfield, just south of Katherine, was the largest – and one of the largest in the entire Pacific region – accommodating 6000 RAAF personnel responsible for aircraft and vehicle maintenance; the remains of its runway and other structures can still be seen. Nearby Larrimah, then a railhead, became the largest military staging post in Australia, able to host up to 3000 servicemen as they passed through on their way to Darwin; its history is told in the Larrimah Museum.

7 Daly Waters Aviation Complex

Visited by legendary flyers and once a vital Allied base

A landing strip was built here in 1928 in association with the ill-fated Alice Springs–Darwin rail link, which was planned to terminate at Daly Waters. Although the line did not eventuate, within two years the extreme remoteness of the airfield had become a boon, giving it a vital role as a stopover point for aircraft on international flights. Pioneer aviators Amy Johnston, Bert Hinkler and Charles Kingsford Smith all touched down here. In the 1930s, the airfield was a refuelling stop for Qantas planes between Sydney and Singapore, and during the Second World War it was a base for US and Australian bombers on their way to the combat zone. In the 1950s, the aerodrome reverted to civilian use. The complex on view today includes the restored 1930 hangar, accommodation buildings, an oil store and the foundations of the radio and navigational buildings.

▶ *Kalala Rd, Daly Waters.*

8 Lost City

Eerie forest of sandstone spires

In the Abner Range on remote McArthur River Station, hundreds of narrow stone spires rise up to 25 m from the plains, forming what looks like a maze of densely clustered, rocky skyscrapers. These are the spectacularly eroded remnants of bedrock laid down under an ancient sea more than 1.4 billion years ago. Helicopter tours depart from Cape Crawford, flying over the 'city' to reveal astonishing views and landing in a wide natural amphitheatre so that visitors can study the formations up close, view Aboriginal rock art and learn about the plants and animals that flourish in the vegetated corridors between the rocks. Those who prefer to keep their feet on the ground at all times can view similar formations in Caranbirini Conservation Reserve, 64 km north-east of Cape Crawford, where the Barrawulla Loop Walk (2 km, 2 hours) winds through majestic sandstone columns.

▶ *Cape Crawford is 273 km east of Stuart Hwy via Carpentaria Hwy.*

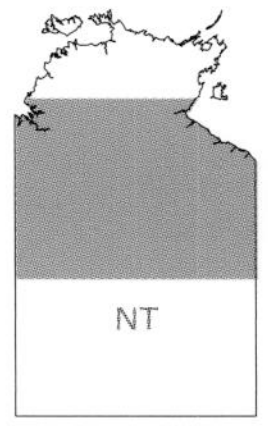

9 Tennant Creek Telegraph Station

Handsome outpost highlights hard life of first European residents

Consider the life of operators on the Overland Telegraph Line: they were crucial in linking Australia with the rest of the world yet, apart from the tapped messages they relayed, lived in the most extreme isolation. Here, their world was confined to this cluster of thick-walled buildings, dating from 1875 and made of locally quarried stone in contemporary English style. Supplies of flour, sugar and salt arrived every six months via camel train; stock was slaughtered every week and meat preserved by smoking or salting; bread was baked in an antbed oven (made out of a termite mound); and a garden provided vegetables. The telegraph office, the hub of the complex, was manned 24 hours a day. The station closed in 1935, when a post office was built 10 km to the south at Tennant Creek township, founded after the discovery of gold in the area.

▶ *Stuart Hwy, 10 km north of Tennant Creek.*

10 Karlu Karlu – Devils Marbles

Massive rock formations perch precariously atop sandstone ledges

Scattered in piles over a wide shallow valley, these gigantic 'marbles' seem poised to roll away at any moment. For their traditional owners, the Warumungu people, the weathered granite boulders represent the eggs of the rainbow serpent creative being, and the site is of great spiritual significance. Geologically, the formations were formed from molten rock which fractured into regular blocks as it cooled; water widened the cracks and rounded the edges. The boulders are a place of refuge for wildlife including fairy martins, whose bottle-shaped mud nests hang from the rocks, and small black-headed goannas, sometimes seen peeping from crevices.

▶ *2 km east of Stuart Hwy, 9 km north of Wauchope.*

GIANT BOULDERS AT KARLU KARLU – DEVILS MARBLES

Red Centre

This is a landscape of extraordinary age and scale. Looming large from the spinifex plains are the massive rock formations of Uluru and Kata Tjuta. To the north lie the MacDonnell Ranges, the weathered remains of a once mighty mountain chain, cut by pool-filled chasms that for millennia have been oases for humans and wildlife.

1 Arltunga Historical Reserve

Atmospheric ruins of remote 1887 mining settlement

Reports of rubies to be had by the handful set hopeful miners off on a fearsome 600-km desert trek from Oodnadatta, the closest railhead, north to the Arltunga area. The rubies turned out to be garnets, but a keen-eyed prospector instead discovered gold in the dry creekbed and soon 300 diggers were trying their luck here. When the alluvial gold ran out, a battery was established to crush gold-bearing quartzite; this too came to an end, in 1913. Arltunga was the centre's first township – Alice Springs at that time was just a telegraph station. Its rough dwellings were stone-walled and often canvas-roofed. They now stand in ruins, together with the renovated police station, abandoned mining equipment and old workings.

▶ *110 km north-east of Alice Springs via Ross Hwy.*

Visitor information

Alice Springs 1800 645 199

2 N'Dhala Gorge

Treasure house of ancient engravings

The walls of shady N'Dhala Gorge are covered with nearly 6000 individual rock carvings, or petroglyphs. They record the art and stories of the Arrernte people and are of two styles, pecked and pounded. The earliest are as old as 10,000 years, but most date from about 2000 years ago, and are a connection across the millennia to a still-living culture. The last 11 km of access road, beyond Ross River Homestead, is 4WD only and impassable after heavy rain.

▶ *100 km north-east of Alice Springs via Ross Hwy.*

3 Alice Springs Telegraph Station

Lonely link on the Overland Telegraph Line

Sited close to the original 'Alice Springs' – a waterhole in the sandy bed of the Todd River – this was the first permanent European structure in the Centre and is the best preserved of the 12 stations on the Overland Telegraph Line. From 1872 its telegraph operator received messages in Morse code – world, business and personal news, births and deaths – then relayed them on to the next station along the line. By 1900, in addition to the stationmaster and his family, the remote outpost was home to a cook, blacksmith–stockman, a governess and four linesmen–operators. The solid stone buildings, complete with period furnishings, provide intriguing insights into pioneer life.

▶ *4 km north of Alice Springs via Stuart Hwy.*

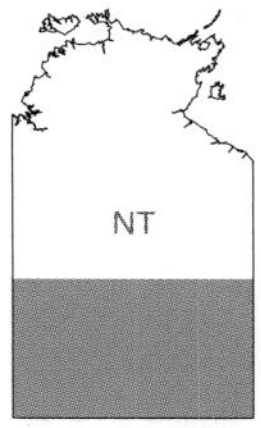

4 Alice Springs Desert Park

Perfect introduction to the flora, fauna and culture of Central Australia

Set in the foothills of the MacDonnell Ranges, the three re-created desert habitats here – sand country, desert rivers and woodland – provide a fascinating introduction to the natural and cultural environment of the arid inland. Visitors encounter a range of desert creatures, including birds of prey, unusual reptiles and rare desert mammals such as the stick-nest rat, extinct on the mainland but breeding successfully here, and can also, in the nocturnal house, see creatures of the night that are near impossible to see in the wild. Indigenous guides share traditional stories and knowledge of bush foods and medicines.

▶ *6 km west of Alice Springs via Larapinta Dr.*

5 Simpsons Gap

Red cliffs and rare wallabies

So well do they blend with their surroundings, that often it is not until one moves that you realise just how many of Simpsons Gap's population of rare black-footed rock wallabies have emerged to bask in the late afternoon sun. One by one, they lope onto the tumble of red rocks that rises steeply from the sandy creekbed. Its proximity to Alice Springs makes Simpsons Gap, a deep cleft cut through the quartzite cliffs by the once mighty waters of Roe Creek, a popular destination with daytrippers. The easy 15-minute Ghost Gum Walk offers a fine introduction to the plant life of the gorge, while the climb to Cassia Hill (1.5 km, 1 hour return) rewards with terrific views over the gorge and ranges. Simpsons Gap can also be reached via the 17-km-long cycle path starting from Flynns Grave, west of Alice Springs.

▶ *West MacDonnell National Park, 25 km west of Alice Springs via Larapinta Dr.*

6 Standley Chasm

Join the midday crowd to watch cool walls blaze

This sheer-sided cleft in the MacDonnell Ranges is most spectacular at noon when for a few minutes the rays from the overhead sun shine directly into the narrow passage. The effect is electric, causing the 80-m-high cliff face on one side to blaze with such fiery intensity that the opposite wall also glows with reflected colour. Not surprisingly, this is when most people time their visit. Allow at least 20 minutes for the walk along a ferny gully from the car park to the chasm.

▶ *50 km west of Alice Springs via Larapinta Dr.*

7 Ormiston Gorge

Imposing gorge with lake-like waterhole and fern-studded walls

Ormiston Gorge was carved out by the ancient floodwaters of the now sluggish Ormiston Creek. Its ochre-coloured walls rise to 300 m and at the southern end is a long, deep, mirror-surfaced waterhole shaded by old river red gums – its chilly waters are popular for a quick summer dip. Beyond, ferns thrive in a moist microenvironment and niches in the cliff walls are home to rare, slow-growing cycads. At dusk, noisy flocks of zebra finches, pied butcher birds, spinifex pigeons and cockatoos congregate here. Rare mammals including the long-tailed dunnart and central rock rat have recently been rediscovered in this remote refuge. Follow the Larapinta Trail up the iron-stained ridge for sweeping views west across mulga- and spinifex-dotted hills.

▶ *West MacDonnell National Park, 135 km west of Alice Springs via Larapinta Dr and Namatjira Dr.*

8 Tnorala (Gosse Bluff)

Massive meteor crater and sacred site

According to the beliefs of the Arrernte Aboriginal people, the circular rock walls here were formed during the creation time, when one of a group of women dancing across the sky dropped a wooden baby carrier; it crashed to earth to become the ramparts of Tnorala. Scientists cite a celestial origin – a meteor or comet that slammed into the ground 140 million years ago. The outer crater rim, with a diameter of 22 km, has long since eroded away and is today distinguishable only by a greyish circular drainage system. An inner ring of 250-m-high hills has a diameter of 5 km. The site is of great cultural significance to the Arrernte people.

▶ *Tnorala (Gosse Bluff) Conservation Reserve, 175 km west of Alice Springs via Larapinta Dr and Namatjira Dr.*

9 Palm Valley

Gorge walls shelter a lush oasis of rare cabbage palms

Walkers on the Arakaia Track (2 km, 1 hour), which loops along the edge of the valley's rust-red bluff, can first gaze into the rock-floored gorge cut by the Finke River between the James and Krichauff ranges, then descend into the valley to explore the remarkable oasis it shelters. Here, in a moist microclimate flanking a string of pools, a pocket of slender red cabbage palms has continued to flourish 10,000 years after the surrounding land dried to desert. They are found nowhere else. The last 16 km of the access road follows the sandy bed of the Finke River and is restricted to 4WD vehicles only.

▶ *Finke Gorge National Park, 138 km west of Alice Springs via Larapinta Dr, 22 km south of Hermannsburg.*

10 Ewaninga Rock Carvings

Artistic legacy of Arrernte culture

The claypan here acts as a natural bowl, trapping and holding scant rain, and drawing people and animals to the waters. For the generations who camped along its edge, the surrounding outcrops of soft red sandstone provided natural galleries for engraving symbols and motifs recording important beliefs. These pecked images are called petroglyphs and their age is unknown, although weathering and the range of styles suggest that some may be very ancient indeed. A 680-m loop trail leads visitors to the best sites. The Arrernte custodians ask that you do not climb over the rocks or touch the fragile carvings in any way. The unsealed access road may be impassable after rain.

▶ *Ewaninga Rock Carvings Conservation Reserve, 24 km south of Stuart Hwy via Old South Rd.*

11 Kings Canyon

Towering sandstone walls frame a creek-carved canyon

The steep climb from the valley floor to the canyon rim requires a reasonable level of fitness, but those who tackle the 6-km Rim Walk loop can get their breath back while taking in spectacular views over the gorge that slices through the sandstone plateau of the George Gill Range. Along the way walkers pass through the weathered maze of 'The Lost City' and descend to the sunken waterholes of 'The Garden of Eden' where palms, ferns and ancient cycads grow. Shorter and less strenuous is the 2-km-return walk along Kings Creek, whose waters, over the eons, have sculpted this landscape, to a viewing platform at the foot of the 100-m-high canyon walls.

▶ *Watarrka National Park, 270 km from Stuart Hwy via Lasseter Hwy and Luritja Rd.*

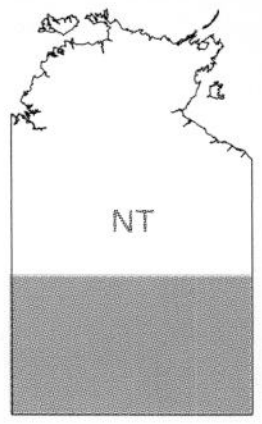

Rocks of ages

The MacDonnell Ranges curve 400 km across the heart of the continent and are the timeworn remnants of some of the oldest mountains on Earth.

Running east and west of Alice Springs, the MacDonnells consist of rocks laid down 850 million years ago as layers of sand on the bed of a shallow sea. Over millions of years, these layers were compressed, folded, buckled and uplifted by tectonic forces into a mighty range, now long-since worn by wind and rain into a series of sparsely vegetated ridges. Along the ranges' length, ancient waters slowly widened natural weaknesses into a series of clefts and canyons. Many still shelter plants, such as cycads, that are relics from a tropical past, and hide the permanent waterholes that support a rich variety of birds and animals and have sustained human life here for 30,000 years.

The highest peaks and deepest gorges lie to the west of Alice: Simpsons Gap and Standley Chasm (see p. 61), the icy waters of Ellery Creek Big Hole, steep-sided Serpentine Gorge, Ormiston Gorge (see p. 61) and Glen Helen Gorge, where the ancient Finke River pools beneath red cliffs. Of the peaks, Mount Zeil, at 1530 m, is the highest, but perhaps more impressive is Mount Sonder, with its stark profile and mauve colouring – a favourite subject of artist Albert Namatjira.

The Larapinta Trail

Winding along the MacDonnells' time-worn spine, from Alice Springs west to Mount Sonder, is the 223-km-long Larapinta Trail. To walk its entire length takes two weeks, so it has great appeal to serious trekkers, but, because it is made up of 12 vehicle-accessible, one- and two-day sections (each graded for difficulty), it also attracts novice walkers. One of the easier sections meanders for 10 km between the Ormiston Gorge campground and the outpost of Glen Helen Resort, on the way climbing to a hilltop lookout and crossing the sandy bed of the Finke River – *lara pinta* in the local Arrernte language.

THE MACDONNELL RANGES – BACKBONE OF AN ANCIENT LAND

SHADOW AND LIGHT CREATE AN EVERCHANGING SCENE AT ULURU.

12 Rainbow Valley

Multihued sandstone formations rise sheer from desert claypans

These towering sandstone cliffs, part of the James Range, are particularly spectacular at sunrise and sunset, when the low rays of the sun shine directly onto the cliff faces, making them appear to glow from within. Their rainbow-like coloured bands are the result of water-borne minerals, particularly iron. Aboriginal paintings, engravings and artefacts are found throughout the valley and surrounding hills. The unsealed access road is sandy in places and recommended for 4WD vehicles only.

▶ *Rainbow Valley Conservation Reserve, 97 km south of Alice Springs, 22 km east of Stuart Hwy.*

13 Henbury Meteorites

Strange lunar landscape formed by cataclysmic collision

When the plummeting Henbury Meteorite disintegrated with a thunderous roar in the skies above here 4700 years ago, it scattered the land with colossal lumps of metal-heavy rock. These blasted out 12 craters ranging in size from 180 m wide and 15 m deep to 6 m wide and only a few centimetres deep. A self-guided walk takes about 40 minutes to loop across the site. The craters stand out most clearly in low sun, so visit early or late in the day for the best views.

▶ *Henbury Meteorites Conservation Reserve, 13 km west of Stuart Hwy.*

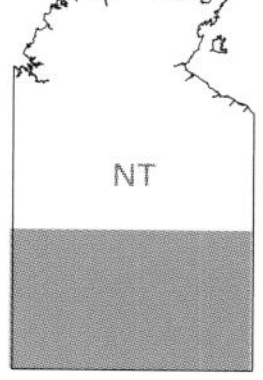

14 Chambers Pillar

Solitary remnant of an ancient mountain

Wind and rain have whittled away the softer surrounds of a tabletop mountain here, leaving a single column of pebbly sandstone rising from a mound of rubble to tower 50 m above the surrounding plain. For early European travellers in the days before the railway, the pillar was a landmark on the long trek from Adelaide to Alice Springs, and many carved their initials on its walls including, in 1870, the explorer Ernest Giles. A walking track winds round the base of the pillar and to a sunset viewing platform. The access road is rough, rocky and sandy, and may be closed after rain; a 4WD is essential.

▶ *Chambers Pillar Historical Reserve, 160 km south of Alice Springs via Old South Rd.*

15 Kata Tjuta

Magical walks wind through giant domes to hidden gorges and groves

Rising across the plains 30 km to the west of Uluru are the 36 steep-sided domes of Kata Tjuta ('many heads'). They cover an area of 3500 ha, and may once have been a single dome, like Uluru, but many times its size. The highest dome soars 546 m above the sands. The plants and animals that flourish in the sheltered valleys can be seen on the 2.6-km-return walk between the domes into moisture-rich Walpa Gorge; the more challenging 7.4-km-return Valley of the Winds walk climbs through stony country to a lookout. Kata Tjuta is of great significance to its traditional owners, the Anangu people.

▶ *Uluru–Kata Tjuta National Park, 290 km west of Erldunda via Lasseter Hwy.*

16 Uluru

The continent's most iconic and dramatic landform

The soaring sandstone red bulk of 'the Rock' is but the visible tip of a huge and folded slab of sedimentary rock laid down some 500 to 600 million years ago. It looms 348 m above the plain and extends perhaps as much as 5 km beneath it. In Aboriginal belief, Uluru was created by the activities of ancestral beings, and each feature has cultural and religious significance to its traditional owners, the Anangu people. For the visitors who come here each year, it is the rock's sheer size – best appreciated on the 9.4-km circuit walk around its base – and its changing colours that fascinate. The monolith's content of iron oxide renders it rusty red during much of the day, but at sunset it blazes bright red, then fades to orange, terracotta and purple; at sunrise the reverse occurs. There are special viewing areas for each spectacle.

▶ *Uluru–Kata Tjuta National Park, 260 km west of Erldunda via Lasseter Hwy.*

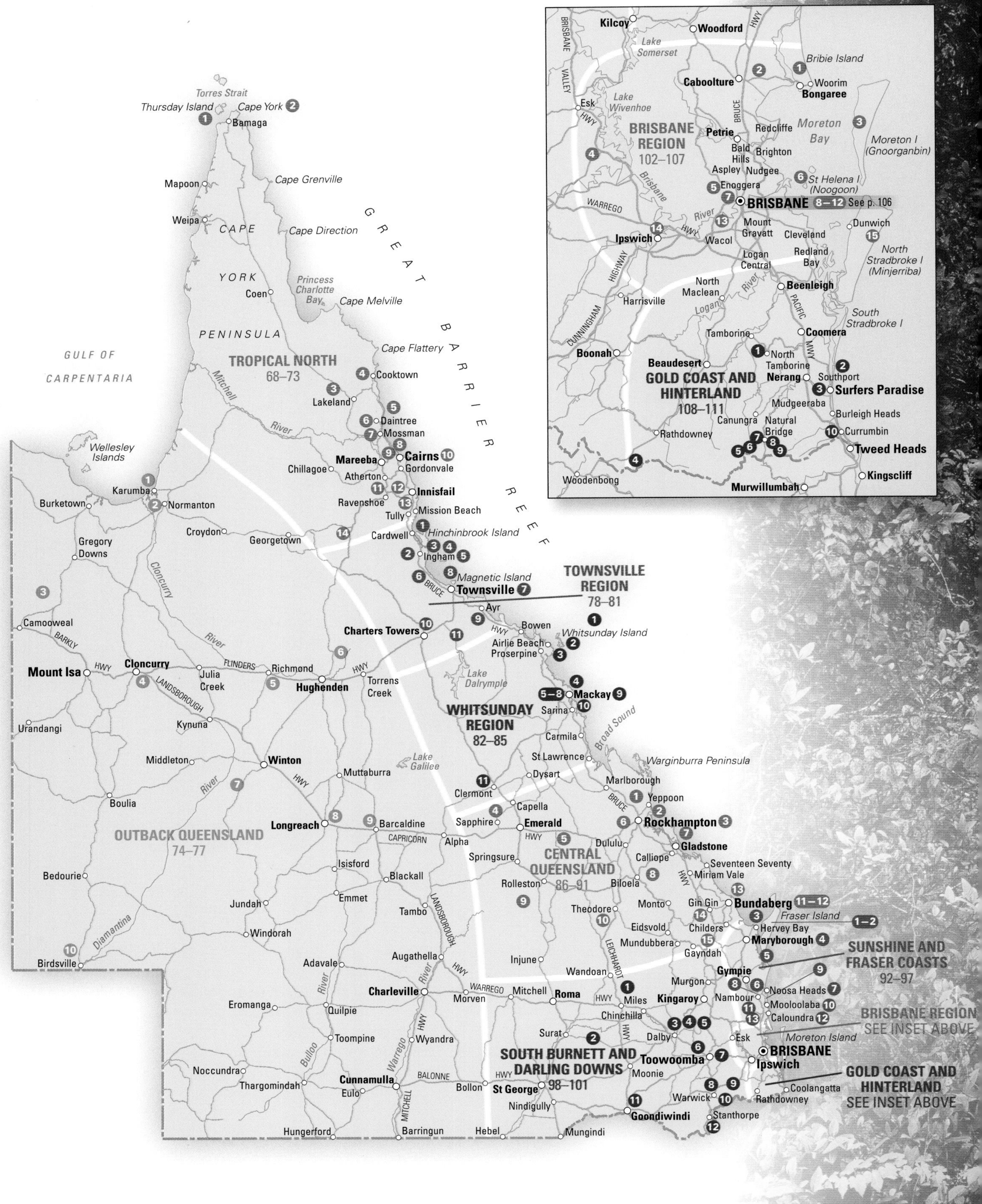
Kilcoy
Woodford
Lake Somerset
Bribie Island
BRISBANE VALLEY HWY
Caboolture
Woorim
Bongaree
Esk
Lake Wivenhoe
BRUCE HWY
BRISBANE REGION
102–107
Petrie
Redcliffe
Moreton Bay
Moreton I (Gnoorganbin)
Bald Hills
Brighton
Aspley
Nudgee
Brisbane River
St Helena I (Noogoon)
Enoggera
WARREGO HWY
BRISBANE 8–12 See p. 106
Mount Gravatt
Dunwich
Ipswich
Wacol
Cleveland
North Stradbroke I (Minjerriba)
CUNNINGHAM HIGHWAY
Logan Central
Redland Bay
North Maclean
Beenleigh
Harrisville
Logan River
PACIFIC MWY
South Stradbroke I
Tamborine
Coomera
Boonah
North Tamborine
Beaudesert
GOLD COAST AND HINTERLAND
108–111
Nerang
Southport
Surfers Paradise
Mudgeeraba
Canungra
Natural Bridge
Burleigh Heads
Rathdowney
Currumbin
Tweed Heads
Woodenbong
Murwillumbah
Kingscliff
Torres Strait
Thursday Island
Cape York
Bamaga
Mapoon
Cape Grenville
Weipa
CAPE YORK PENINSULA
Cape Direction
GREAT BARRIER REEF
Coen
Princess Charlotte Bay
Cape Melville
GULF OF CARPENTARIA
TROPICAL NORTH
68–73
Cape Flattery
Mitchell River
Cooktown
Lakeland
Daintree
Mossman
Wellesley Islands
Mareeba
Cairns
Gordonvale
Chillagoe
Atherton
Karumba
Innisfail
Normanton
Burketown
Ravenshoe
Mission Beach
Tully
Croydon
Georgetown
Cardwell
Hinchinbrook Island
Gregory Downs
Ingham
Cloncurry River
Magnetic Island
BRUCE
Townsville
TOWNSVILLE REGION
78–81
Ayr
Camooweal
Charters Towers
Bowen
Whitsunday Island
BARKLY HWY
Flinders River
Airlie Beach
Proserpine
Mount Isa
Cloncurry
Julia Creek
FLINDERS HWY
Richmond
Hughenden
Torrens Creek
Lake Dalrymple
LANDSBOROUGH
Mackay
Sarina
Kynuna
WHITSUNDAY REGION
82–85
Urandangi
Broad Sound
Carmila
Middleton
Winton
Lake Galilee
St Lawrence
Warginburra Peninsula
Muttaburra
Dysart
Marlborough
Boulia
River
Clermont
Yeppoon
Capella
Longreach
Barcaldine
Sapphire
Emerald
Rockhampton
OUTBACK QUEENSLAND
74–77
CAPRICORN HWY
Alpha
Dululu
Gladstone
Springsure
CENTRAL QUEENSLAND
86–91
Calliope
Seventeen Seventy
Isisford
Miriam Vale
Bedourie
Blackall
Rolleston
Biloela
Emmet
Jundah
Tambo
Theodore
Monto
Gin Gin
Bundaberg
Fraser Island
Hervey Bay
Eidsvold
Childers
Diamantina
Windorah
LEICHHARDT
Mundubbera
Maryborough
Gayndah
SUNSHINE AND FRASER COASTS
92–97
Birdsville
Adavale
Augathella
Injune
Wandoan
Gympie
Noosa Heads
Charleville
WARREGO HWY
Mitchell
Roma
Murgon
Morven
Miles
Kingaroy
Nambour
Mooloolaba
Eromanga
Quilpie
Chinchilla
Caloundra
BRISBANE REGION SEE INSET ABOVE
Surat
Dalby
Moreton Island
Toompine
Wyandra
Esk
BRISBANE
Bulloo
Warrego
SOUTH BURNETT AND DARLING DOWNS
98–101
Toowoomba
Ipswich
Noccundra
Moonie
GOLD COAST AND HINTERLAND SEE INSET ABOVE
Thargomindah
Cunnamulla
BALONNE HWY
Bollon
St George
Coolangatta
Eulo
Warwick
Rathdowney
MITCHELL
Nindigully
Goondiwindi
Stanthorpe
Hungerford
Barringun
Hebel
Mungindi

Queensland

Queensland's 3000-km-long, island- and reef-fringed eastern shore is its star attraction. Yet almost as enticing are the rainforest-swathed ranges and the wide, rolling plains of the interior, dotted with towns that still embody the adventurous spirit of the first European settlers.

MILLAA MILLAA FALLS, ATHERTON TABLELAND

Useful websites

Visitor information www.queenslandholidays.com.au
Parks and reserves www.derm.qld.gov.au/parks_and_forests
Motoring organisation www.racq.com.au

Tropical North

The great triangle of Cape York is edged on its eastern side by steep, rainforested slopes that run down to pristine beaches and tropical seas. Inland are ancient rock-art galleries. Close offshore lie the cays and islands of the northern Great Barrier Reef.

1 Thursday Island

Multicultural island with rich heritage

Much of the history of this small (3-sq-km), hilly island can be learned in its cemetery. From the 1870s to the 1930s, the island was a pearling centre and buried here are 700 Japanese who died diving for mother-of-pearl shells; also here lie sailors and passengers drowned at sea, generations of Thursday Islanders, and even a former premier of Queensland. Elsewhere on the island are an 1892 fort built to guard against a feared Russian invasion and the Quetta Memorial Chapel, location of the bell from the SS *Quetta*, which in 1890 struck a rock off the island and sank with the loss of 133 lives. Thursday Island was named by Captain Bligh; Wednesday and Friday islands are close by.

▶ *Ferry from Seisia, Cape York; air services to nearby Horn Island.*

2 Cape York

It's a long way to the top, but getting there is a major milestone for many

The tapering tip of Cape York terminates in a series of scrub-covered hills and sandstone ridges. From the most northerly point on the Australian mainland, marked by a small sign, you look out across the sparkling waters of Torres Strait, dotted with islands running north to New Guinea, just 150 km away. There are fine walks in the rainforest of the nearby Lockerbie Scrub and excellent fishing. Camping and cabins are available at Punsand Bay and Seisia. The roads require a 4WD and may be closed in the Wet.

▶ *864 km north of Cooktown via Peninsular Development Rd.*

3 Split Rock Galleries

Where Quinkans wait in the shadows

The extraordinary concentration of prehistoric paintings in the sandstone country around the tiny township of Laura comprises one of the richest bodies of rock art in the world. The galleries here are at least 15,000 years old and the paintings display a range of styles and techniques. Most are large colourful representations of humans and wildlife and include post-European arrival subjects such as pigs, horses and guns (the last paintings probably date from the 1920s). Unique to the region are depictions of the tall, distinctive figures of Quinkans – spirit creatures, both good and bad, who dwelled in crevices and lurked in the shadows ready to punish those who broke tribal law. Their dramatic images, roughly human in shape, but with distorted features and huge eyes, stare down from the walls of Split Rock, the most accessible site. Visit the Quinkan Cultural Centre, in Laura, before taking a self-guided tour.

▶ *Laura, 140 km west of Cooktown via the Cooktown Development Rd and Peninsular Development Rd.*

Visitor information

Atherton 07 4091 4222
Babinda 07 4067 1008
Cairns 07 4051 3588
Cooktown 07 4069 6004
Innisfail 07 4061 2655
Kuranda 07 4093 9311
Mission Beach 07 4068 7099

4 Cooktown

Laid-back town with a frontier feel

Cooktown came into existence in the early 1870s as the rowdy port for the Palmer River goldfields. More than 30,000 miners landed here on their way inland, justifying the 60-odd hotels that soon sprang up. You can soak up the outpost atmosphere on a walk along the foreshore. You'll pass the statue of James Cook, who in the winter of 1770 spent seven weeks here with his crew repairing the damaged *Endeavour,* and the imposing 1880s former convent, now the James Cook Museum, where the anchor and cannon Cook jettisoned are on display. Further along is the memorial to tragic Mary Watson, who perished at sea with her baby son while fleeing Lizard Island in a container used to boil bêche-de-mer. Then climb Grassy Hill for sweeping views over the town, wharf and croc-infested Endeavour River.

▶ *325 km north of Cairns via Captain Cook Hwy and Peninsular Development Rd.*

5 Cape Tribulation

Where rainforest meets the sea

As you gaze from the headland over sparkling waters and tangled rainforest tumbling from dark green ranges to pristine sands, spare a thought for James Cook. It was he who gave the cape its unfortunate name 'because here began all our troubles'. Offshore, just before midnight on 10 June 1770, Cook's ship was holed on what is now called Endeavour Reef. Today, the headland lookout, with its stunning views, is reached by an easy, 400-m paved path. On the southern side of the point the Dubuji ('place of spirits') Boardwalk loops for 1.2 km through lowland rainforest and mangrove swamps. There are information boards on both.

▶ *Daintree National Park, 140 km north of Cairns via Captain Cook Hwy and Cape Tribulation Rd.*

CAPE TRIBULATION

6 Daintree National Park

Immense swathe of ancient, World Heritage–listed rainforest

Tropical rainforest and coral reef – two of the world's richest ecosystems – lie side by side in this park, which is part of the Wet Tropics World Heritage Area. The rainforest has been in continuous existence for at least 110 million years, long before the Australian continent broke away from its parent continent, Gondwana, and harbours an astonishingly rich variety of flora, including a high concentration of the most ancient plants on Earth. It is also home to the greatest diversity of wildlife on the continent. The Daintree Discovery Centre, in the northern section of the park, provides an excellent introduction, including walkways and a canopy tower.

▶ *Daintree Discovery Centre, 115 km north of Cairns via Captain Cook Hwy.*

7 Mossman Gorge

Deep, forest-flanked valley carved by fast-flowing river

The cool, crystal-clear waters of Mossman River rush through this steep-sided gorge, on the way cascading over and surging around granite boulders long ago washed down from the tablelands. Sandy pools tempt swimmers, but take note of signs warning of swift currents, flash flooding and slippery rocks. A 2.4-km rainforest circuit walk crosses slower Rex Creek via a 40-m-long steel suspension bridge; here the sharp-eyed may spot freshwater turtles surfacing to breathe. Guided bushwalks conducted by the traditional owners of the area, the Kuku Yalanji people, introduce visitors to the gorge's rainforest fauna and flora, identify bush tucker sources, visit traditional bark shelters and take in cave paintings and culturally significant sites.

▶ *Daintree National Park, 5 km west of Mossman.*

8 Rex Lookout

Stop here for sweeping views of a stunning coastline

The drive between Cairns and Port Douglas is spectacular at almost every turn, but this roadside lookout has perhaps the best view of all and one you can take time to savour. Vegetated slopes drop steeply to meet the long gleaming curve of Wangetti Beach; beyond are the northern beaches of Cairns; inland, a string of jutting headlands rise to blue-smudged ranges; and to the east are the turquoise waters of the Coral Sea. Hang-gliders launching from here often add a splash of extra colour to the scene.

▶ *Captain Cook Hwy, 35 km north of Cairns.*

9 Kuranda

Getting here is half the fun

Rainforest-framed views punctuate the pleasant drive from the coastal strip to this cool tableland retreat, but by far the best way to visit Kuranda is via the unbeatable combination of scenic railway and cable car. Pulled by a diesel locomotive, vintage carriages zigzag up past Barron Falls to a fern-bedecked, 1915 railway station. After investigating the town's craft and produce markets, passengers can return the fast way – an exhilarating 7.5-km treetop-skimming descent to Caravonica, on one of the longest cableways in the world.

▶ *28 km north-west of Cairns via Captain Cook Hwy and Kennedy Hwy.*

10 Tjapukai Aboriginal Cultural Park

Throw a boomerang, listen to the didgeridoo and watch a corroboree

Through theatre, dance and technology, the Tjapukai ('rainforest') people immerse you in their traditional culture. Performers interact with giant holograms to tell creation stories, and in a natural bush amphitheatre present traditional corroboree dances and songs. You can also discover how tools and weapons were used (and see ancient artefacts once used by Tjapukai people and recently returned to them by the Queensland Museum), find out how toxic foods were treated to prepare them for consumption, taste local bush tucker, and learn about bush medicines.

▶ *Captain Cook Hwy, Caravonica, Cairns.*

11 Mount Hypipamee Crater

Deep and unnerving lake-filled chasm

At the summit of Mount Hypipamee thick rainforest suddenly gives way to sheer walls of granite that plunge into a motionless lake 60 m below. Volcanic in origin, this gaping hole was formed when the mounting pressure of gases, having found no point of weakness through which to escape, instead blasted away the rock. A platform perched on the rim edge provides a view into the lake – 80 m deep, 70 m across and covered with a vivid green layer of native waterweed.

▶ *Mount Hypipamee National Park, Kennedy Hwy, 110 km south-west of Cairns.*

WATER-SCOURED BOULDERS STUD MOSSMAN GORGE.

TROPICAL FOREST ENFOLDS EUROPEAN GRANDEUR AT PARONELLA PARK.

12 Millaa Millaa Falls

Cascading rainforest waters

A number of Atherton Tableland streams fall in spectacular fashion over basalt columns, but none quite as daintily as the lacy, single-drop curtain of Millaa Millaa Falls. The pool at its base is a popular swimming spot and home to platypuses (keep an eye out in the late afternoon) and the bright blue and more easily seen Ulysses butterfly. Millaa Millaa Lookout, about 5 km to the west and high on the Cardwell Range, offers sweeping views over the tableland, across to the coast at Innisfail and away to the north as far as the granite dome of Bartle Frere, Queensland's highest mountain.

▶ *70 km west of Innisfail via Palmerston Hwy.*

13 Paronella Park

Tropical pleasure gardens and turret-topped Moorish castle

In 1929, Spanish immigrants José and Margarita Paronella bought a 13-ha pocket of rainforest here and began work on their life's dream. The pair built terraces and pathways out of hand-plastered reinforced concrete, spanned a creek with footbridges, dug ponds, plumbed fountains and even installed a hydroelectric generating plant. The centrepiece was a castle-like structure, flanked by grand staircases, with a ballroom and teahouse. The park opened to the public in 1935, and became the focus of a thriving social scene. Although flood, fire and cyclone wrought great damage over the years, the buildings have been restored and the park is back in business – the admission price includes a guided tour and Indigenous culture talk.

▶ *14 km west of Bruce Hwy.*

14 Undara Lava Tubes

Cool legacy of a fiery past

This snaking network of lava tubes was created 190,000 years ago when a volcanic eruption sent great flows of molten rock across the land. The outer layers of the lava flows cooled rapidly and solidified but the molten cores flowed on, eventually draining to leave tunnel-shaped cavities. These still stretch intact for 35 km underground and, where their ceilings have collapsed, as narrow, tree-filled gullies. The tubes range in size from soaring caverns to low tunnels and are home to a variety of wildlife, including bats and owls. They can be visited only on guided tours.

▶ *Undara Volcanic National Park, 30 km west of Kennedy Hwy via Gulf Developmental Rd.*

Undersea wonderland

The seemingly endless chain of reefs that guards the eastern coast of Queensland is the world's largest coral reef system, a submerged skein of fragile structures studded with white sandbars and inviting islands and home to astonishingly varied marine life.

The Great Barrier Reef is a work in progress and its architects are coral polyps – tiny soft-bodied creatures related to jellyfish – that produce as a protective skeleton the cement-like material that forms the reef's fabric. When a polyp dies, another builds atop its stony skeleton.

An outer line of ribbon reefs lies along the edge of the continental shelf like an underwater wall, in places up to 80 km wide and dotted with low-lying cay islands. Closer to the coast are 'high islands' (peaks of a submerged range), fringing reefs and coral outcrops called patch reefs. The entire structure is approximately 2300 km long.

Teeming with life

The coral passageways created are home to a myriad of fish in an estimated 1500 variations of shape, size and colour, as well as clams, stingrays and other creatures. Seabirds find refuge on the cays and islands, as do female turtles, which lumber ashore to lay eggs. The beauty of the reef can be seen from either a glass-bottomed boat or by snorkelling. In far northern Queensland, cruises and dive excursions depart daily from Cairns and Port Douglas. Green Island, just 40 minutes by charter boat from Cairns, is the closest and most accessible coral cay. Scenic flights provide a jawdropping overview of the scale of the reef, and opportunities for spotting rays, sharks and other large marine life.

FISH OF ALL HUES THRONG BARRIER REEF CORALS.

Outback Queensland

This vast realm of rolling plains is washed on its northern shores by the waters of the Gulf of Carpentaria and extends south to the edge of the inland deserts. It is rich in minerals and fossils, and features dramatic basalt landforms that originated during long-ago volcanic eruptions.

1 Karumba

Morning Glory and vivid Gulf sunsets

The southern Gulf country is the only place in Australia where you can see the weather phenomenon of roll clouds – low, narrow, rolling bands of cloud that can stretch up to 1000 km and resemble giant white ropes. Known locally as Morning Glory clouds, they appear during the Dry (September to mid-November), early on mornings when the air humidity is high. Gulf-edge Karumba is a prime viewing spot for both the Morning Glory and also, from the nearby beach, dazzling sunsets over Gulf waters.

▶ *450 km north of Cloncurry via the Burke Developmental Rd.*

2 Normanton

Home of the historic Gulflander train

Gulf country settlements are few and far between. Normanton, founded in the 1870s as a cattle centre, is the largest of them. In the 1880s, the discovery of gold, and later silver, saw an influx of miners; the town's grand historic buildings date from that time, as does the railway built to cart ore to the coast from inland mines. Known as the Gulflander, it still runs once a week through the majestic landscapes between Normanton and Croydon (150 km), a journey its operators happily describe as being 'from nowhere to nowhere'.

▶ *380 km north of Cloncurry via Burke Developmental Rd.*

MORNING GLORY CLOUDS OVER THE SOUTHERN GULF OF CARPENTARIA

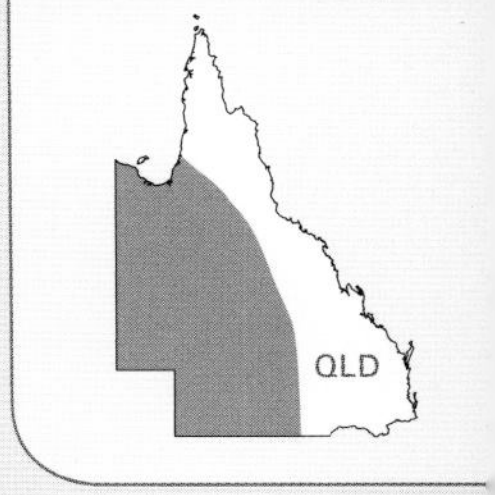

By air and airwaves

Outback clergyman John Flynn's inspired use of new technologies brought a mantle of safety to the outback.

The Reverend John Flynn recognised the great need in remote regions for access to medical help, but realised that, to make feasible his dream of 'flying' doctors, he needed a low-cost, reliable and easy-to-operate method of communication so isolated farms and outlying stations could contact the service. This was provided by Alfred Traeger who, at Flynn's instigation, developed the pedal wireless. Sets were installed in every remote homestead and Cloncurry was chosen as the first base for the service because it had a hospital and a Qantas aerodrome.

As a result, it became possible to diagnose many ailments and injuries and prescribe treatments over the airwaves. If further assistance was required, emergency doctors flew in to land on improvised runways. The first call was to an injured stockman at Julia Creek, east of Cloncurry, in 1928. Today the service has 21 bases delivering both 24-hour emergency services and everyday health care.

3 Riversleigh Fossil Field

Huge treasure trove of fossilised bones

The fossil deposits at Riversleigh lie along what was once a rainforest-flanked string of lakes where animals came to drink. The water here had, and still has, a high concentration of calcium, dissolved from the surrounding limestone. When it came into contact with the skeletons of animals that died here, it turned their bones into rock-hard fossils. Dating from 25 to 15 million years ago, Riversleigh's fossils reveal key stages in the evolution of Australian mammals. Unique and now extinct animals found here include marsupial lions, carnivorous kangaroos, the forebears of the thylacine, and huge pythons, platypuses, crocodiles and bats. A loop trail at the Riversleigh D site offers visitors an opportunity to view many fossilised mammals and reptiles first-hand.

▶ *Boodjamulla (Lawn Hill) National Park, 130 km north of Barkly Hwy.*

4 Cloncurry

List of firsts for pioneer copper town

Cloncurry came into existence following the 1865 discovery of copper here and mining continues today. The town can lay claim to some important firsts, having been the arrival point in 1922 for the first Qantas service (from Charleville via Longreach), the first operational base of the Royal Flying Doctor Service in 1928, and, in 1960, the base of the Queensland School of the Air. The fascinating John Flynn Place museum pays tribute to the Royal Flying Doctor Service founder; exhibits include the first pedal radio, early medical equipment and photographs.

▶ *Barkly Hwy.*

Visitor information

Barcaldine 07 4651 1724
Birdsville 07 4656 3300
Charleville 07 4654 7771
Mount Isa 07 4749 1555
Normanton 07 4745 1065
Richmond 07 4741 3429
Winton 07 4657 1466

5 Kronosaurus Korner

Ancient creatures unearthed from watery graves

Richmond claims to be the fossil capital of Australia, and with good reason. Graziers here sometimes unearth fossilised turtles, fish, shark's teeth and other creatures dating from the time a vast shallow sea covered this area, and fossicking visitors, too, stand a good chance of turning up a piece of the prehistoric past. Around 500 specimens, including some of the world's most significant vertebrate and marine fossils, are on display at Kronosaurus Korner. Highlights are the 'Richmond Pliosaur', a 4.25-m-long vertebrate fossil, and 'Minmi', a small armoured dinosaur with much of its fossilised skin intact, both 100 million years old. A life-size model of a kronosaurus, a 12-m-long, flippered, crocodile-like creature that once swam here, guards the entrance.

► *Richmond, Flinders Hwy.*

6 Porcupine Gorge

Lush vine forest lines a deep gash in the sprawling, arid plains

With an average depth of 120 m and approximately 27 km long, Porcupine Gorge is sometimes likened to a mini Grand Canyon. A lookout atop its towering cliffs provides a view over the vibrantly coloured sandstone walls and the thick vine forest fringing Porcupine Creek – a striking contrast with the surrounding sparsely wooded, dry plains. The gorge's cool depths and deep permanent waterholes are an oasis for wildlife. Further north, in a wider section of the gorge, the eroding action of the creek has carved out the multicoloured monolith of the Pyramid; a walking track from the nearby campground descends to the bottom of the gorge. The gorge access road is unsealed and may not be accessible to conventional vehicles after heavy rain.

► *Porcupine Gorge National Park, 60 km north-east of Hughenden via Kennedy Developmental Rd.*

7 Lark Quarry Dinosaur Trackways

Startling evidence of a dinosaur stampede

Located here are the only traces in the world of a dinosaur stampede. It took place 93 million years ago when up to 200 small, bird-footed dinosaurs – two herds, ranging in size from small chickens to emus – were disturbed beside a lake by a large, sharp-clawed dinosaur. The chaotic footprints of panicked prey and pursuing predator were imprinted in mud, later turned to stone. Entry to the trackways is by guided tour only.

► *122 km south-west of Winton via Winton–Jundah Rd.*

8 Longreach

Outback hub honours pioneers of exploration, settlement and aviation

Longreach played a pivotal role in the development of outback commerce, communications and aviation so it is a fitting location for two major museums that tell the story. In the Stockman's Hall of Fame, five themed galleries – Discovery, Pioneers, Outback Properties, Life in the Outback, and Stockworkers – pay tribute to the men and women who developed the inland, through a fascinating collection of archival material, photographs and audiovisual presentations. The Qantas Founders' Museum is housed in the company's original hangar, now restored, at the airport that became its operational base in 1922. The museum's collection of aircraft includes a decommissioned but fully equipped ex-Qantas 747 Jumbo Jet; tours take in the cockpit and cargo bay and even allow visitors to walk out onto the jumbo's wing.

► *Landsborough Hwy.*

TOURING THE 747 AT THE QANTAS FOUNDERS' MUSEUM, LONGREACH

9 Tree of Knowledge Memorial

A famous dead tree – and a whodunit

Barcaldine was a rallying point for shearers during the great strike of 1891. Their main meeting place was beneath a 10-m-high ghost gum, which stood near the railway station and came to be known as the Tree of Knowledge. For more than a century the tree was venerated as the birthplace of the Australian labour movement. Then, in 2006, it was poisoned. Today its preserved remains take centre stage in the Tree of Knowledge Memorial, an 18-m-high timber-and-steel structure; planks of recycled wood dangle from the ceiling above the dead trunk to create the impression of looking up into the canopy of a live tree. Just who poisoned the tree remains a mystery.

▶ *Capricorn Hwy, Barcaldine.*

10 Birdsville

Iconic outback town, venue for a famous and riotous annual race meeting

This remote town on the banks of the Diamantina River, between the sands of the Simpson Desert and the gibbers of Sturts Stony Desert, took its present name in 1885, apparently in deference to the district's abundant birdlife. In the days before Federation, Birdsville was a customs collection point for stock and supplies entering South Australia from Queensland. The Birdsville Working Museum looks back to that time, when the town had a population of 400, a blacksmith, a coach builder, three pubs and numerous shops. Displays include wagons, farm machinery, photos and antiques. Today, Birdsville is best known for its annual race meeting, held on a claypan course beside the dunes in September, when up to 6000 punters and spectators pour into the town by road and light plane.

▶ *690 km south of Mount Isa via the Diamantina Developmental Rd.*

Townsville Region

Australia's largest tropical city is the major centre on an otherwise sparsely populated and scenic coastline. A backdrop of verdant, rainforest-covered slopes separates the magnificent tropical beaches and coastal sugarcane fields from the historic goldmining towns of the interior.

1 Hinchinbrook Island

Take a walk on the wild side

Hinchinbrook looms just 8 km offshore, separated from the mainland by a labyrinth of mangrove-fringed tidal waterways that are home to dugong that feed on its seagrass beds. The largest island in the Great Barrier Reef and the largest island national park in Australia, it is dominated by the formidable, cloud-topped peaks of a precipitous, jagged mountain range. Along its eastern shore is a string of headlands and sandy beaches, traced by the famous 32-km Thorsborne Trail. For experienced and well-prepared walkers, this demanding multiday hike (it can be covered in four days, but allow a week to take time for swimming and relaxing) winds through rainforest ideal for birdwatching, crosses tidal and freshwater creeks, skirts waterfalls, and climbs to ocean-edge lookouts.

► *Hinchinbrook Island National Park, by charter or private boat from Lucinda, 19 km east of Bruce Hwy.*

Visitor information

Ayr 07 4783 5988
Cardwell 07 4066 8601
Charters Towers 07 4761 5533
Home Hill 07 4782 8241
Ingham 07 4776 5211
Townsville 07 4721 3660

2 Wallaman Falls

The highest waterfall in Australia

At Wallaman Falls, the waters of Stony Creek – a tributary of the Herbert River system which drains much of the Atherton Tableland – plunges abruptly for 268 m into a deep canyon. If the cascades above and below this single drop are included, the full height of the waterfall is 305 m, making it the tallest in the country. Snaking east is the sheer-sided gorge cut by the creek over millions of years. The falls lookout is reached by 10 km of winding, unsealed road that is not suitable for caravans.

► *Girringun National Park, Abergowrie Rd, then signposted roads, 51 km west of Bruce Hwy.*

3 Lucinda Jetty

The world's longest sugar-loading jetty

Its holiday-village atmosphere belies the fact that Lucinda is also a working port serving the local sugar industry. Its Bulk Sugar Loading Facility operates from one of the longest jetties in Australia. It is supported by more than 660 concrete-and-steel pylons and at 5.8 km is so long that its designers had to allow for the curvature of the earth – the jetty dips 1.2 m over its length as it spears seaward. Sugar takes more than 20 minutes to travel along the conveyor from the onshore storage sheds out to the shiploader. There is no public access but you can view the jetty from the adjacent but considerably shorter service jetty, which is also a popular fishing spot.

► *19 km east of Bruce Hwy.*

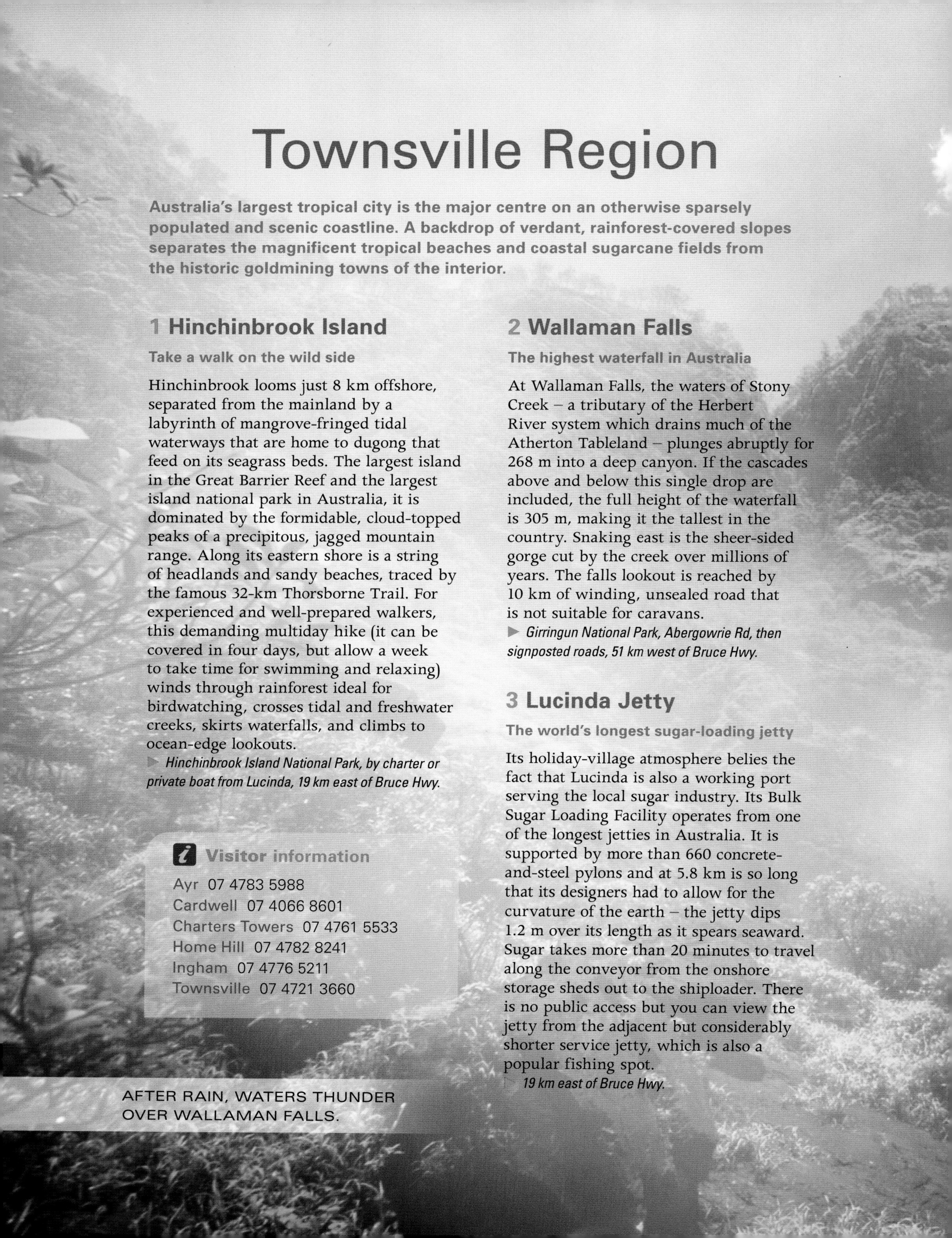

AFTER RAIN, WATERS THUNDER OVER WALLAMAN FALLS.

4 Orpheus Island

Coral-fringed Barrier Reef island with kaleidoscopic marine life

Lying 24 km offshore, Orpheus is one peak of a drowned coastal range. It bears scars of past volcanic activity in the eroded spiderweb patterns of ring dykes (where molten rock intruded into granite) seen in caves and crevices around its headlands. The surrounding shallow blue waters are a snorkelling paradise – a colourful maze of coral, made up of 340 of the 350 known species, and home to an extraordinary diversity of other sea creatures; in winter humpback whales even cruise through on their annual migration. Apart from a resort and a research station, the island is uninhabited national park.

▶ *By charter from Lucinda, 19 km east of Bruce Hwy, or private boat from Taylors Beach, 22 km east of Bruce Hwy.*

5 New Ingham Cemetery

Miniature city of marble mausoleums reflects sugar town's Italian heritage

Ingham's distinctive Mediterranean feel derives from its large Italian community – the first settlers from Italy arrived in 1891 to work in the sugarcane fields of the Herbert Valley and arrivals increased steadily, particularly between 1920 and 1939. The Italian influence is especially evident in the number of southern-European-style mausoleums – chapel-like structures where several family members are buried together – that characterise this 'new' cemetery, in use since 1949. The oldest were constructed in white stucco and marble and feature Gothic-style windows and doors; more recent mausoleums are flat-roofed and finished with terrazzo and tiles.

▶ *Cemetery Rd, Ingham.*

A little bit of sugar ...

Climate and soil perfectly suited to high yields have made the Ingham district one of the most prolific sugar-producing areas in the world.

Sugar cane has been grown in the Herbert Valley since the 1870s, and the two main local mills – Victoria and Macknade – now crush up to 6 million tonnes a year. Victoria Mill in Ingham is the largest crushing plant in Australia; Macknade Mill, north-east of Ingham, is the oldest continually operating mill in northern Queensland. From these mills, raw sugar is taken by rail to the Lucinda Jetty (see p. 78) to be shipped south for refining. Harvesting takes place between June and November. The famous preharvest burn-off no longer occurs; instead the cane is cut green and the leaves and other residue left in the field to assist regrowth. Sugar mill tours are available during the crushing season at Tully, in the far north of this region, and at Farleigh Sugar Mill near Mackay.

6 Paluma Range

Rainforest-clad hills, swimming holes and superb walking trails

The arched stone bridge spanning the tumbling waters of Little Crystal Creek was built during the Great Depression as an unemployment relief project; deep pools here are ideal for swimming. Paluma Road, carved into the mountainside, was part of the same scheme; as you drive up it, you'll enjoy magnificent views across deeply dissected valleys, and at McClellands Lookout, a panoramic vista over coastal rainforest to the blue-green waters of Halifax Bay. This is also the starting point for two short, lovely walks.

▶ *Paluma Range National Park, Mount Spec section, 3 km west of Bruce Hwy.*

7 Museum of Tropical Queensland

A look at the weird and wonderful, above and below the water

Exhibits here focus on tropical and marine themes and include a collection of diving helmets, a re-created rainforest and, in the museum's Great Gallery, a life-size replica of the bow of the ill-fated HMS *Pandora*, a British naval ship sent to the Pacific to capture the mutineers from the *Bounty*. After reasonable success in its mission – 14 mutineers were captured in Tahiti – in 1791 the homeward-bound *Pandora* came to grief on the Great Barrier Reef, 120 km east of Cape York, with the loss of 35 lives. The survivors, 89 crew and 10 prisoners, eventually reached Java in open boats, but the wreck lay undetected until 1977. Significant objects from the more than 7000 items recovered from the ship (ranging from inkwells to olive oil jars) are on display here and provide surprising insights into life on board an 18th-century British naval ship.

▶ *Flinders Street, Townsville.*

8 Magnetic Island

Wildlife abounds on this picturesque, easily accessed island

More than half of Magnetic Island is national park. Mountainous, strewn with mighty granite boulders and fringed by sheltered, sandy beaches (some enclosed by coral reefs), it was named in 1770 by James Cook, in the mistaken belief that it had affected his compass. A network of walking tracks threads through eucalypt woodland, stands of hoop pine and patches of rainforest that are home to koalas, rock wallabies, goannas and over 100 species of birds. The Forts, the remains of army installations built during the Second World War to protect Townsville, is the vantage point for spectacular 360-degree views. Regular bus services explore the island and cars, mokes, scooters and bicycles are available for hire.

▶ *Passenger or vehicle ferry from Townsville.*

9 Silver Link Bridge

Kilometre-long bridge built on sand

The 1.1-km bridge spanning the Burdekin River between Ayr and Home Hill is not only one of the longest bridges in the country, but is also said to be the only Australian bridge to be built without firm footings. There is no rock under the river to anchor its foundations, just sand, so the bridge instead rests on massive pieces of concrete sunk deep into its soft bed. To learn more, drop into the Silver Link Interpretive Centre in Home Hill.

▶ *Bruce Hwy.*

10 Charters Towers

A town that once had it all

In the 1890s, Charters Towers had a population of 30,000 and was so fabulously wealthy that it had its own stock exchange which, hooked to the rest of the world by telegraph, operated around the clock, six days a week. To its proud and newly rich inhabitants, their town was 'The World' – there was no need to go anywhere else. By 1916, the boom was over, but the superb heritage buildings clustered in the town centre are a lasting monument to those glorious days. Easily explored on foot, they include the elegant, glass-roofed Royal Arcade, which housed the stock exchange; the grandiose 1891 former Australian Joint Stock Bank (now part of the World Theatre Cultural Centre); and the former Excelsior Hotel. On the outskirts of town, visitors can also take a guided tour of the once furiously busy Venus Battery, where hologram 'ghosts' explain how the ore was crushed and the gold extracted.

▶ *Flinders Hwy.*

11 Ravenswood

Ghost town recalls boom times

The rush to Ravenswood began with the discovery of alluvial gold here in 1868, and continued with the shaft mining of reef gold until 1872, when the easily extractable ore ran out. Many residents then moved on to the fresh fields of Charters Towers, hauling their homes with them. However, in the early 1900s a second boom followed the installation of special separating equipment; deep mining began and Ravenswood reached a peak population of more than 4000, served by 42 hotels. Today, the town is virtually a ghost town, but its remaining buildings (including just two hotels, but both grand) are still a drawcard and classified by the National Trust. Exhibits in the Mining and Historical Museum, housed in the restored court house, tell the town's full story.

▶ *40 km south of Flinders Hwy.*

Whitsunday Region

The crowning glory of this region is undoubtedly the stunning archipelago that lies just offshore: the Whitsunday Islands. However, extraordinary sights are also to be found inland, ranging from extensive rainforests and dramatic gorges to early homesteads and the state's biggest and most productive coalmines.

1 Heart Reef

A romantic natural construction

If you sailed past it, you'd pay it no heed. For at just 17 m across this little coral bombora is dwarfed by other, much more imposing formations on the surrounding reef. But approached from the air, and from the right angle, its unusual and entirely natural form – an almost perfectly heart-shaped arrangement of coral – is virtually guaranteed to prompt a gasp, a sigh, or at very least a smile from even the most cynical of visitors. Flights to Heart Reef will also provide breathtaking views of islands and extensive coral atolls, and some tours land at beaches and floating pontoons for snorkelling.

▶ *Hardy Reef; flights from Airlie Beach.*

2 Whitehaven Beach

Prime candidate for Australia's most beautiful beach

Pristine, dazzlingly white silica sand stretches into the distance, bordered by brilliantly blue sea. There are no crowds, deckchairs or cars; no houses or resorts break the cover of forest climbing the hillsides. The sand is as soft and pure as any you will ever step in, and the water transparent and inviting. It's about as idyllic as it gets. At the northern end of the beach, at Hill Inlet, advancing and retreating tides create a network of channels that paint the white sands with sinuous patterns of blue. For a fine view of this natural artistry, climb the short track to Tongue Point. Access to Whitehaven Beach and Hill Inlet is by boat only, but cruises and tours land here, and scenic flights are also available.

▶ *Whitsunday Island; charter and cruise boats from Airlie Beach and Shute Harbour.*

3 Conway National Park

The coastal ranges as they used to be

Largely undeveloped, the park preserves a stretch of this glorious coastline in its original state. Walking tracks around Airlie Beach and Shute Harbour allow visitors to explore lowland tropical rainforest, mangroves, and paperbark and pandanus woodlands. Birdlife is prolific and includes waders and honeyeaters, scrubfowl and brush turkeys. For a spectacular seaward view, follow the track that climbs from Shute Harbour Road to the summit of Mount Rooper, passing through hoop-pine forest and grass trees to reveal a breath-taking panorama of emerald islands.

▶ *30 km east of Bruce Hwy at Proserpine.*

Visitor information

Bowen 07 4786 4222
Mackay 07 4944 5888
Marian 07 4954 4299
Proserpine 07 4945 3711
Sarina 07 4956 2251

Tropical paradise

This maze of islands and channels is rightly regarded as one of the country's most scenic realms and a paradise for sailors.

The Whitsunday Islands are the summits of a coastal mountain range that was submerged at the end of the last ice age. Consequently known as continental islands, they are still covered with the kind of forest that once cloaked most of the coastal ranges. Home to the Ngaro people for at least 9000 years, the archipelago was given its current name by James Cook, who spotted it on Whit Sunday, 1770.

All but a handful of the islands were designated national park in the 1930s and 1940s, so most remain undeveloped and uninhabited but dotted with camp sites allowing visitors to experience true 'desert-island' wilderness. If that doesn't appeal, there are resorts on several of the islands, ranging from backpacker lodges to five-star hotels. Walking tracks wind along unspoiled shores and climb through forest to peaks and headlands, and innumerable guided tours can be booked – undoubtedly one of the best ways to experience the islands is on a multiday sailing cruise. Contact Proserpine tourist office for details.

WHITEHAVEN BEACH AND HILL INLET

4 Cape Hillsborough National Park

Rugged, unspoiled coastal scenery

James Cook named this coastal promontory, as he sailed past in 1770, after the Earl of Hillsborough, then secretary of state for the colonies. Beautiful and tranquil, it's little changed today. Below steep-walled headlands, rhyolite boulders – evidence of ancient volcanic activity – lie scattered along deserted beaches. Mangroves, palms, and heaths border the sands and eucalypt and hoop-pine forests climb the slopes. Kangaroos roam widely, brush turkeys forage around picnic areas and sugar gliders can be spotted in the treetops at dusk. The 2-hour-return Andrews Point Track leads along the shore to Andrews Point, from where, at low tide, it's possible to walk out to Wedge Island via a causeway.

▶ *50 km north of Mackay via Bruce Hwy, Seaforth Rd and Cape Hillsborough Rd.*

5 Finch Hatton Gorge

Walk, swim or fly through one of the country's largest subtropical rainforests

Waters cascading out of the Clarke Range have created a deep fissure here, enveloped by lowland rainforest and studded with still pools. Wind your way through granite boulders on the fairly easy 2.8-km-return Araluen Cascades Track and you will come to a lookout above the falls. An extension of this trail, the Wheel of Fire Track, continues to a beautiful plunge pool at the foot of Wheel of Fire Falls (allow 2 hours return). Near the gorge, Forest Flying offers an entirely different perspective on the rainforest, by way of flying fox rides across the canopy, 25 m off the ground (book ahead).

▶ *70 km west of Mackay via Mackay–Eungella Rd.*

6 Broken River

Platypus central

From the viewing platform here, especially early or late in the day between June and August, you've got more chance of seeing a platypus than at virtually any other spot on the continent. Watch for clusters of bubbles, a good sign a platypus is about to surface, and have your camera ready. The surrounding forest is a delight and there are several superb walking tracks, ranging from the easy 700-m Rainforest Discovery Circuit, which loops through glossy elk and crowsnest ferns and towering trees festooned with vines, to the more demanding 5.5-km (one way) Clarke Range Track, which climbs over the Clarke Range to lookouts with stunning views into the Pioneer Valley.

▶ *80 km west of Mackay via Mackay–Eungella Rd.*

7 Melba House

Opera diva's one-time dwelling

The daughter of a local sugar-mill owner, Helen Porter Mitchell spent just a few unhappy months in this house, when it occupied its original location by the Pioneer River. Of her time here she wrote, 'My piano was mildewed; my clothes were damp; the furniture fell to pieces ... to say nothing of the snakes.' Now situated in Edward Lloyd Park, the house stands nevertheless as a fascinating monument to the internationally famous opera singer we know better as Dame Nellie Melba. Memorabilia and souvenirs are on display. The building also houses the Marian visitor centre and a display of local crafts.

▶ *Marian, 18 km west of Mackay via Bruce Hwy and Mackay–Eungella Rd.*

8 Greenmount Homestead

Birthplace of modern Mackay

The first squatters reached this district in late 1850s. Not far behind them, in 1860, came an organised expedition, funded by pastoralists and headed by Captain John Mackay. Having surveyed the Pioneer Valley, Mackay returned the following year with 1200 head of cattle and took up a run at Greenmount, which became the focus of a cattle industry and prompted the establishment of a port, subsequently named Mackay. In 1912, the property was sold to the Cook family, who built this elegant homestead. Maintained as a museum, it preserves furnishings and farm equipment from that time, and provides fascinating insights into pioneer life.

▶ *18 km west of Mackay via Bruce Hwy and Peak Downs Hwy.*

9 Mackay Regional Botanic Gardens

Stylish showcase for regional flora

Ranged along the scenic banks of a lagoon here are dozens of themed gardens representing particular districts of the Central Queensland Coast Bioregion, including the Sarina–Proserpine Lowlands and the Eungella Cloud Garden, and more widespread environments, such as the Hoop Pine Lawn and the Brigalow Belt. Overseas flora is represented too, in settings such as the Japan Precinct and Malta Garden. Pathways radiate out from the striking visitor centre, which houses a gallery and a cafe. Birds are everywhere: red-whiskered bulbuls chirrup from treetops, sunbirds sip nectar from flowers, and waterbirds including magpie geese, ducks and herons crowd the lagoon.

▶ *Mangrove Rd, Mackay.*

10 Port of Hay Point Lookout

Watch the workings of one of the world's largest coal-export facilities

The view from the public gallery in the Port Administration building, spanning the two massive coal terminals at Hay Point and Dalrymple Bay, is at once awe-inspiring and mesmerising. The wharves stretch off toward the horizon, extending 1.5 km over the ocean from Hay Point and a whopping 3.8 km seaward from Dalrymple Bay. A steady stream of colossal cargo ships sails in and out, loading up with coking coal for all corners of the globe. From inland, 2-km-long coal trains roll in carrying loads of up to 8500 tonnes. It's hard to tear yourself away, but you'd better: all this goes on 24 hours a day, 365 days a year.

▶ *36 km south-east of Mackay via Bruce Hwy and Hay Point Rd.*

11 Blair Athol Mine

Take a tour of one of Australia's most productive coalfields

Measuring up to 30 m thick, the 'Big Seam' at Blair Athol is the largest seam of steaming high-grade coal in the world. It was discovered in 1864, but its remote location made it uneconomical for another 26 years. Today, up to 12 million tonnes of thermal coal are shifted from here each year, much of it to customers in Asia and Europe. Daily tours departing from nearby Clermont, the oldest inland settlement in tropical Queensland, include viewing the vast open-cut seam and seeing how the coal is retrieved and processed. Don't delay, though: the Big Seam is expected to be exhausted by 2016.

▶ *22 km north of Clermont via Gregory Developmental Rd.*

Central Queensland

Subterranean marvels, including caves, tunnels and mines, honeycomb the hinterland of this region, while its towns testify to the economic heft of precious metals and minerals, as well as beef and sugar. Offshore, exquisite coral atolls provide entry points to the myriad marvels of the southern Great Barrier Reef.

1 Capricorn Caves

Wondrous subterranean world

It was a Norwegian immigrant, John Olsen, who stumbled upon this cave system, in 1882. Visiting today, one can begin to imagine his amazement at the sights he found. At the entrance to the caves, tree roots hang from and cling to the roof and walls. Beyond, stalactites, stalagmites, shawls and cave corals line a series of smaller chambers leading to the system's pièce de resistance, Cathedral Cave. Its ceiling soars more than 30 m above your head and the acoustics are so good that the cave is used for concerts. In midsummer, there's an annual highlight – literally – when the sun shines through a narrow opening, illuminating Cathedral Cave.

► *27 km north of Rockhampton via Bruce Hwy.*

2 Singing Ship

Unusual musical commemoration of a pioneering 1700s voyage

Sailing up the east coast of Australia aboard the *Endeavour* in 1770, James Cook named a string of features along this coastline, now known as the Capricorn Coast. Most are encompassed by the wonderful panorama from this memorial. A 12-m-high structure designed in the form of a large sail, the memorial is quirky and ingenious: a ship-shaped musical sculpture that produces a range of sounds as the wind passes through pipes inside. It was designed by Mrs Peggy Westmoreland in 1969 and built by SW Kele, a concrete contractor, with input from engineering specialists.

► *Kele Park, Emu Park, 40 km east of Rockhampton.*

THE HERITAGE HOTEL ON QUAY STREET, ROCKHAMPTON, DATES FROM 1897.

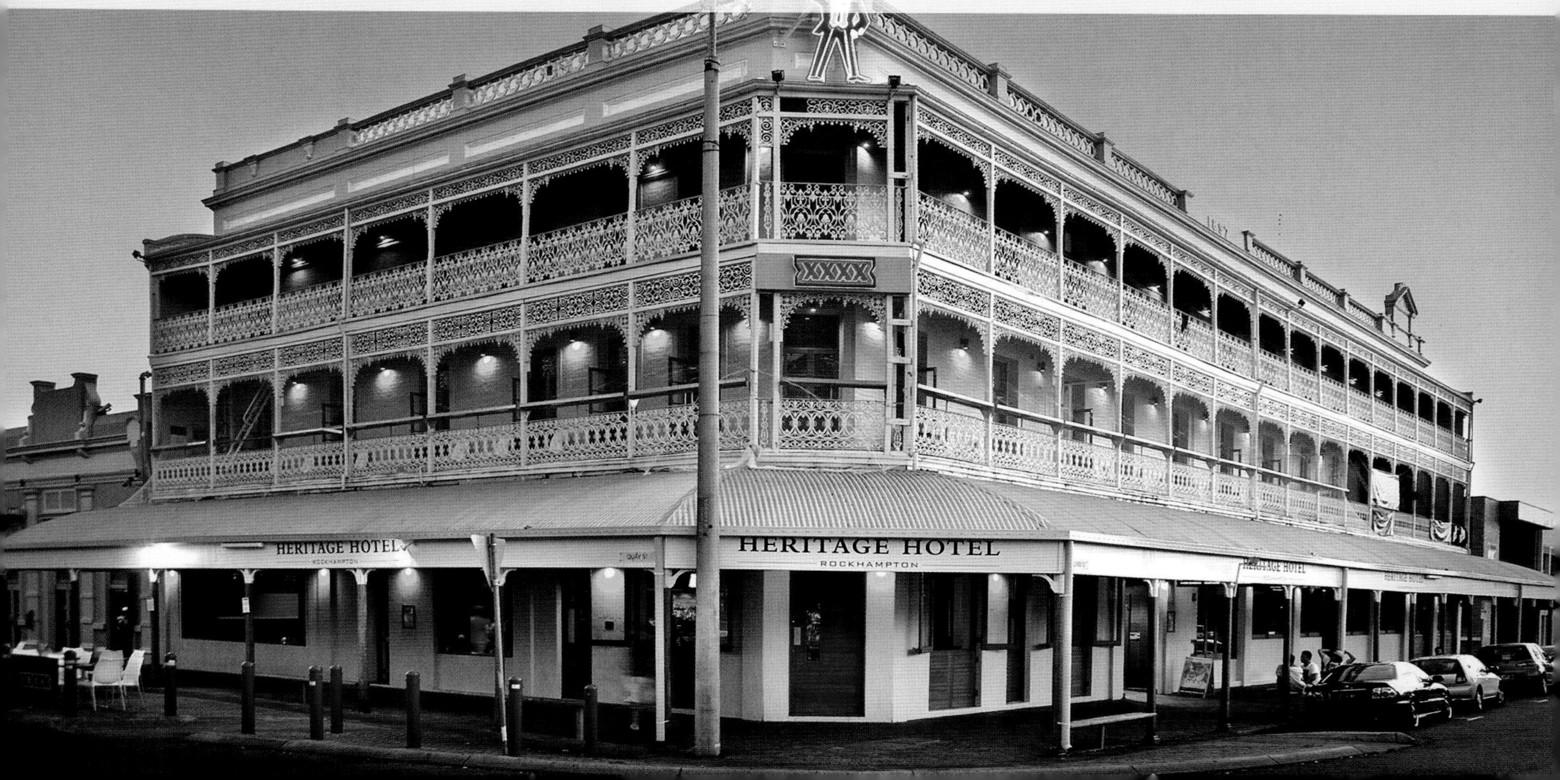

Sapphire fields

Around the towns of Rubyvale, Sapphire and Anakie spreads the Southern Hemisphere's largest sapphire field.

Aboriginal people were aware of the preponderance of gems in this region and traded stones with Europeans from the 1870s on. But it was not until the 1890s, when economic quantities were discovered, that the gemfield became commercially viable. Today it covers 900 sq km. Large-scale open-cut mining still takes place, and adventurers still arrive seeking fortunes.

One of the most remarkable discoveries occurred in the 1930s at Anakie, when 14-year-old Roy Spencer stumbled across a large black star sapphire. After using it as a doorstop for a while, his father sold it for $18,000. Later cut to a 733-carat stone and named the Black Star of Queensland, it is thought to be the biggest sapphire of its type ever found and was valued at $100 million in 2002.

Visitors can explore mines, see polished gems and try their luck fossicking at parks in Anakie, Sapphire and Willows.

3 Quay Street

Echoes of an affluent era

Central Queensland's capital, Rockhampton was founded in 1853 as a port serving sheep farmers, but it was beef, gold and copper that soon boosted its rapid development. The grand buildings along Quay Street, the longest National Trust–listed street in the state, evoke that affluent era. Prominent among them are the striking Customs House (1898–1901), with its copper dome, which now houses the visitor centre; the former headquarters of the Mount Morgan Gold Mining Company (1897), today home to the ABC, which uses the old gold vault as a sound-proof studio; the old Queensland National Bank Building (1880) and the former Union Bank of Australia Building (1886), both boldly neoclassical in style; and the French-Classical Criterion Hotel (1889), which occupies the site of the city's first hotel, the Bush Inn, built in 1858.

▶ *Central Rockhampton.*

4 Rubyvale

Enter the world of the sapphire miner

A range of attractions in this small settlement at the heart of the gemfields provides a fine overview of the gem-mining process, from prospecting to final polishing. The Miners' Heritage Park has exhibits explaining local geology and fine examples of cut and polished stones, and tours lead visitors down real mining tunnels. Guided tours of an underground mine are also available at the Bobby Dazzler Mine, which has stones and jewellery for sale. At the Rubyvale Gem Gallery, you can watch gem-cutters at work.

▶ *56 km west of Emerald via Capricorn Hwy and Rubyvale–Anakie Rd.*

Visitor information

Biloela 07 4992 2405
Bundaberg 07 4153 8888
Eidsvold 07 4165 7233
Emerald 07 4982 4142
Gin Gin 07 4153 8888
Gladstone 07 4972 9000
Rockhampton 07 4922 5625
Yeppoon 07 4939 4888

5 Blackdown Tableland National Park

There be monsters in this 'Lost World'

Three mountain ranges converge at Blackdown Tableland – the Dawson, Expedition and Shotover ranges – forming a towering escarpment that rises more than 600 m from the valley in places. Reminiscent of Conan Doyle's 'Lost World', the plateau encompasses hidden valleys, gorges concealing waterfalls, pools, groves of ferns, and plants and animals found nowhere else on Earth. One is even known as the Blackdown monster; but don't worry, it's just a rather bizarre-looking subterranean cricket. Most roads are fine for 2WD (but check conditions before you head off) and walking tracks take in waterfalls and lookouts with magnificent views, as well as impressive rock art of the Ghungalu people.

> *126 km east of Emerald via Capricorn Hwy and Charlevue Rd.*

6 Mount Hay

Eggs laid, and cooked, by a volcano

The site of an ancient volcano, this is one of the best places in the world to stock up on so-called thunder eggs – not something for your packed lunch but solid balls of volcanic rock that, when cut open, frequently reveal a core of colourful agate, sometimes surrounding crystals of amethyst, jasper or quartz. The eggs formed when molten lava cooled and crystals grew inside gas bubbles. The Mount Hay Gemstone Tourist Park provides advice and equipment for fossicking, and can have any serendipitous discoveries cut and polished.

▶ *36 km west of Rockhampton via Capricorn Hwy.*

SEABOUND GREEN TURTLE HATCHLINGS, HERON ISLAND

7 Heron Island

Wildlife-crammed coral cay

Don a snorkel, stroll off the shore here and peer beneath the waves and you immediately enter an astonishing world, where kaleidoscopic clouds of colourful fish drift over coral gardens, and turtles, wide flippers outstretched, seem to be flying through the transparent waters. Heron Island is a coral cay, made up of crumbled coral and snow-white sands, in a remote part of the southern Great Barrier Reef. Densely forested, it hosts abundant birdlife, including noddy terns and wedge-tailed shearwaters, as well as a cornucopia of sea creatures. This draws not only tourists, who stay at the former turtle-canning factory turned resort, but also biologists, who hole up at the island's research station. Green and loggerhead turtles nest here from November until January, when hatchlings can be seen making a desperate dash to the sea.

▶ *Capricornia Cays National Park, 2 hours by catamaran from Gladstone.*

8 Beautiful Betsy

A Second World War bomber entombed in the wilderness

On 26 February 1945, an Allied Liberator bomber disappeared while carrying eight men and supplies from Darwin to Brisbane. Not until almost 50 years later were its remains discovered in this densely forested tableland in the Calliope Range, now part of Kroombit Tops National Park. Today a short walking track leads from the access road, past signs recounting the sombre story, to the remains of the bomber itself, still stranded amid the trees. It's an intriguing but sobering sight. There is much else uplifting about Kroombit Tops, however: rainforest and eucalypts fill gorges and cap cliffs, and the park has some of the state's finest stands of hoop pine. Walks explore rainforest and skirt escarpments. A 4WD is recommended.

▶ *Kroombit Tops National Park, 85 km west of Gladstone via Dawson Hwy.*

9 Carnarvon Gorge

Magnificent rock art in majestic chasm

For 30 km, towering walls of sandstone, rising up to 200 m high, flank the Carnarvon River here, where it has cut deep into the Great Dividing Range. Cabbage tree palms, eucalypts, rainforest and ferns line the main chasm, narrow side gorges and hanging valleys. Swamp wallabies and kangaroos browse in the undergrowth, platypuses and turtles swim the streams and more than 170 species of birds can be seen. Visitors can explore via 21 km of walking tracks, taking in waterfalls, lookouts and spectacular rock art. Overhangs covered with stencils can be viewed on the easy 1-km-return Baloon Cave Aboriginal Cultural Trail. The much longer hike to the Art Gallery (10.8 km, 3–4 hours) repays with more than 2000 engravings, stencils and paintings covering a 62-m-long sandstone wall.

► *196 km south of Emerald via Gregory and Dawson hwys and Carnarvon Developmental Rd.*

10 Isla Gorge

Deep cleft amid a bewildering maze of sandstone formations

Water and wind have worked their magic on the sandstone tableland at the southern end of the Dawson Range, fashioning an intricate arrangement of stone structures, including cliffs, canyons, spires and peaks. The centrepiece is dramatic Isla Gorge, which can be viewed from a lookout off the highway. There are no walking tracks and the descent into the gorge should not be attempted due to loose rock on the slopes.

► *30 km south of Theodore via Leichhardt Hwy.*

11 Bundaberg Distilling Company Bondstore

The spirit of Bundy

Heady aromas of alcohol and molasses; giant pot stills, fermenters and oak vats; tastebud-tingling samples of rums, mixers and liqueurs – just some of the smells, sights and flavours that tantalise the senses during tours of this iconic distillery. Situated in a major sugar-producing area, it rolled out its first barrel of rum in 1888 and now produces half a million cases of the spirit every year. Tours take in the production process, from cane harvesting to bottling, and there's a museum in the visitor centre, Springhill House, once a sugar plantation manager's home.

► *Whittred St, Bundaberg.*

ROCK ART IN BALOON CAVE, CARNARVON GORGE

12 Hinkler Hall of Aviation

Celebrating the achievements of the pioneer flyer

It was while observing the apparently effortless flights of ibises at lagoons around Bundaberg in the early 1900s that local boy Bert Hinkler first set a course for the skies. He built his own glider and made his maiden (unpowered) flight at Mon Repos (see entry). After perfecting his skills in the British Royal Air Force during the First World War and subsequently as a test pilot, he undertook numerous pioneering flights, including the first solo flight from England to Australia, in 1928, before dying in a crash in 1933 while chasing another record. This state-of-the-art museum honours and explains his achievements. Exhibits include aircraft and flight simulators, as well as Hinkler House, Bert's English home, brought to Bundaberg in 1983, and elegant Fairymead House (1890), which now contains a museum chronicling the local sugar industry.

▶ *Botanic Gardens, cnr of Mount Perry Rd and Young St, Bundaberg.*

13 Mon Repos Conservation Park

Productive turtle nursery

Between November and February, female leatherback, loggerhead and flatback turtles lumber out of the surf here to lay their eggs in the dunes, and from January to March hatchlings emerge en masse and make their frantic dash to the sea and safety, running the gauntlet of predators including seagulls. Such scenes unfold at sites along the coastline, but this is one of the best and most accessible places to witness them, and has the largest concentration of nesting turtles on the eastern seaboard. Visitors must join ranger-led evening tours during the breeding season; bookings are essential.

▶ *14 km east of Bundaberg via Bargara Rd.*

14 Boolboonda Tunnel

The longest unsupported tunnel in the Southern Hemisphere

Cutting this 192-m tunnel through the granite of the Boolboonda Range took two teams of workers (one starting at each end) two years of backbreaking labour, and was finally completed in November 1883. The incentive was to create a rail link between the recently opened Mount Perry copper mine and the port at Bundaberg. Trains ran through the tunnel until the early 1960s, when the line was dismantled. Today the track-free route is negotiable by car and provides an interesting, occasionally spooky experience – there's little light in there, but a host of bats.

▶ *35 km west of Bruce Hwy at Gin Gin.*

15 Coalstoun Lakes

Twin volcanic craters

The lakes themselves are hardly impressive – they have water only after heavy rains – but the hollows they occupy are something to ponder, once you realise they are the vents of a major volcano, Mount Le Brun, active until 600,000 years ago. Scan the shoreline (or dry lakebed) and you might spot evidence of ancient, ferocious activity: basalt fragments, pumice stones and lava bombs – solidified lumps of ejected lava. The climb to the rim takes half an hour and reveals splendid views; inside the craters, bottle and ash trees sprout from vine scrub and sedges carpet the lakebeds when they are dry.

▶ *17 km east of Burnett Hwy at Ban Ban Springs.*

Sunshine and Fraser Coasts

Off the northern part of this region, the sandmass of Fraser Island conceals clear lakes and towering rainforest and shelters Hervey Bay, home to turtles, dolphins and dugongs. On the mainland shore, exquisite beaches, wetlands and resorts stretch south, while inland pretty hill towns nestle in volcanic ranges.

1 Wanggoolba Creek

Transparent stream flanked by rare and beautiful ferns

On sandy Fraser Island, springs bubbling from a vast aquifer below the dunes send pristine, sand-filtered streams east and west to the coast. One such is eastward-flowing Wanggoolba Creek. Its silent, barely moving water is so clear that it seems like you are looking through glass to its rippled bed of impossibly white sand. Boardwalks along its banks protect a fragile forest of rare and ancient king ferns, which have the largest fronds in the world. It may surprise, but logging of rainforest timber was once the major industry here; nearby Central Station, now a popular camping and picnic spot, was the operational headquarters. Driving on the island requires a 4WD.

► *Great Sandy National Park, Fraser Island; ferries from Hervey Bay, River Heads and Inskip Point.*

2 Lake Wabby

Serene lake bordered by a wall of sand

Technically, Lake Wabby is a 'barrage' lake. It was formed when the moving sands of Hammerstone Sandblow – the dune that rears up on its eastern side – blocked a watercourse. Wabby is the deepest lake on Fraser Island, and with its green waters and semicircle of forest edging its western shores, is a popular swimming spot. It is reached by a 3-km-return walk from the eastern beach. The sandblow is made up of loose grains liberated when strong winds broke through the vegetation cover of an old dune, and swept them westward. It is moving inexorably across the island and will one day engulf not only Wabby but also the forest beyond. Climb to the top of the 'blow' for an illustration of the processes that are shaping and reshaping the island. You'll find both the stumps of an ancient forest once buried but now laid bare by the winds, and the tentative shoots of grasses that in time will stabilise the sands and replace the cover.

► *Great Sandy National Park, Fraser Island; ferries from Hervey Bay, River Heads and Inskip Point.*

Visitor information

Caloundra 07 5420 6240
Glass House Mountains 07 5438 7220
Gympie 07 5483 6656
Hervey Bay 07 4125 9855
Maroochydore 07 5448 9088
Maryborough 07 4190 5742
Montville 07 5478 5544
Mooloolaba 07 5478 2233
Noosa Heads 07 5430 5020

Behind the dunes

At 120 km long and 14 km wide, Fraser Island is the largest sand island in the world. Despite its lack of soil, it is covered with an extraordinary variety of sand-adapted vegetation and dotted with lakes.

The high dunes that line the island's eastern, ocean-facing shore hide a surprising hinterland of towering rainforests of satinay, kauri and hoop pines; a cool, dense understorey of shady ferns and palms; and open banksia heathlands brimming with wild flowers and bristling with birdlife. Plants here cope with the poor and sandy soil in a number of ways: some store nutrients in bulbous lumps on their trunks, others have aerial roots to accommodate sand movement, while 'sundew' plants catch insects to obtain the nitrogen they cannot get from the soil.

Hinterland lakes

Surprising, too, are the island's numerous freshwater lakes. More than 40 are so-called perched lakes, held high above the water table in an impermeable saucer-shaped skin formed of hardened organic matter. With a surface area of 200 ha, Lake Boomanjin, its waters tea-coloured by tannins from fringing melaleuca trees, is the largest such lake in the world; the popular swimming lakes of Birrabeen and McKenzie are also perched.

The lakes' clear waters are low in nutrients and so support only isolated populations of tiny fish. Far more common are freshwater turtles, which range from hatchlings hardly bigger than a fingernail to old females the size of dinner plates; watch for their heads breaking the surface to breathe. Birds are abundant, with more than 350 species recorded, ranging from honeyeaters and fairy wrens to migratory wading birds, and including the rare ground parrot.

WHITE SANDS OUTLINE LAKE MCKENZIE.

3 Hervey Bay Marine Park

Where humpbacks hang out in winter

From late June to early November, an estimated 2000 humpback whales break their long journey from their northern breeding grounds back to their Antarctic feeding grounds to rest and play in the calm waters of Platypus Bay, close to the sheltered western shore of Fraser Island. Whale-watching cruise boats depart from Urangan wharf to sail among families of frolicking humpbacks; usually several pods are in the bay at any one time, so sightings are virtually guaranteed. The park is also visited by southern right, melon-headed and Bryde whales, and is home to dugong, turtles and four species of dolphin.

▶ *Cruises from Urangan, 4 km east of Hervey Bay.*

4 Maryborough

Historic river port with stately architecture

In the 1860s, Maryborough was a thriving port and second only to Sydney as an entry point for immigrants, including the thousands who passed through heading to the Gympie goldfields. An impressive number of restored colonial buildings remain in its well-preserved wharf precinct; today many serve as museums and can be visited on a short walking trail. They include the 1864 Bond Store, now a museum with liquor barrels left over from that time; the 1868 Graham and Gataker wine and spirits warehouse, housing an art gallery; the 1879 JE Brown warehouse, home of the Military and Colonial Museum; and the iron-lace-decorated, former Bank of New South Wales (1878), now the Maryborough Heritage Centre. A few doors away, in front of another former bank, is a statue of Mary Poppins – her creator, Pamela Travers, was born in the building when her father was its bank manager.

▶ *4 km north-east of Bruce Hwy.*

5 Rainbow Beach

Multihued cliffs fringe stunning beach

The cliffs that give Rainbow Beach its name are the remnants of an ancient dune. Bound with clay and stained by iron-rich minerals and leached vegetable dyes into shades of reds, browns and yellows, its sands hardened over millennia. Rising up to 200 m high along the long white beach, these imposing ramparts are about 2 km from Rainbow Beach township; access is along the beach by foot or 4WD.

▶ *Great Sandy National Park, Cooloola Section, 75 km north-east of Bruce Hwy at Gympie.*

HUMPBACK WHALE, HERVEY BAY

6 Majestic Cinema

Where Rudolph Valentino still shines on the silver screen

Pomona's cinema has never really left the 1920s – the decade of its construction. The first films shown came courtesy of the travelling picture showman, and the cinema has operated continuously ever since. It was particularly busy during the years of the Second World War, when troops from a nearby army base provided full houses seven nights a week. Then, in the 1980s, when its competition was turning to multiscreen cinemas, the Majestic reverted to showing silent movies, first in an annual film festival and then in occasional matinees. Since 2006, the cinema has been community owned. Its regular screenings of silent-era classics starring the likes of Buster Keaton and Rudolph Valentino are accompanied by rousing music from a theatre organ.

▶ *Pomona, 40 km south of Gympie via Bruce Hwy.*

7 Noosa National Park

Ditch the glitz for a wilderness walk

A short stroll east along the beach from the chic boutiques and eating places of Noosa's lively Hastings Street delivers you to the small but beautiful world of Noosa National Park. Here walking tracks offer the choice of continuing around the shore (5.4 km, one way) for views along the coast, dolphin-spotting and, in winter, whale-watching, or taking a rainforest path to the wild and ragged headland. The Palm Grove circuit (1 km) passes under a shady canopy of palms, ferns and hoop pines, providing a cool alternative to the beach on hot days, while the longer Noosa Hill circuit (3.4 km) winds across the tops through eucalypt woodlands and shrublands where you have a chance of encountering some of the park's rare and threatened wildlife, which includes glossy black cockatoos and a small and dwindling number of koalas.

▶ *Noosa Heads, 25 km east of Bruce Hwy.*

8 Yandina Ginger Factory

Sample the wares of the world's largest sugar-processed ginger supplier

Yandina's claim to be the 'Ginger Capital of the World' is supported by the fact that about 40 per cent of the global sugar-processed ginger comes from this factory. The combination of volcanic soils, high rainfall and humidity makes the district perfect for growing ginger, a rainforest plant. The first crops were planted a century ago in nearby Buderim, and commercial processing began in the 1940s, using two vats in an old blacksmith's shop. The factory re-located to Yandina in 1979 and today, as well as turning out ginger in an amazing variety of sweetened forms – you can smell and taste samples – offers tours of the production line, a 'cane-train' ride through its tropical gardens, a cafe, ice-creamery and the old-style shops of 'Gingertown'.

▶ *8 km north of Nambour via Bruce Hwy.*

9 Maroochy Wetlands Sanctuary

Life on the edge in an estuarine waterway

This wetland is an extreme environment. Freshwater one minute and then, with the turn of the tide, saltwater the next. Yet life thrives. When the tidewaters retreat, fiddler crabs – the crab is the sanctuary's logo – scamper across the mudflats waving large orange claws, and swamp wallabies creep from the shadows to graze on meadows of marine couch. More than 200 species of birds are resident, ranging from waterbirds such as ibises, herons, grebes and snipe to honeyeaters, satin bowerbirds and button quail in the wetland forests and, wheeling in the skies, goshawks and wedge-tailed eagles. Boardwalks thread through casuarina and melaleuca (with the region's largest remaining stands of mangrove fern), salt marsh and mangroves down to a floating jetty on the Maroochy River.

▶ *10 km east of Nambour via Bli Bli.*

10 HMAS *Brisbane*

Swim with fish through a coral-encrusted former missile destroyer

Scuttled in 2005, the ex-HMAS *Brisbane* now lies 9 km offshore in 28 metres of water (although the smoke stack starts 3 m below the surface), a purpose-designed dive wreck that offers excellent habitats for marine life and ideal conditions for certified divers. The ship itself is eight stories high and as long as seven cricket pitches. Wide access holes allow divers into its interior to view living and sleeping quarters in natural light, and inside the engine and boiler rooms. Several local operators offer dive tours.

► *Ex-HMAS Brisbane Conservation Park, off Mooloolaba, 8 km east of Bruce Hwy.*

11 Montville

Views and bygone charm in a ridgetop timber town

Montville was settled by timber-getters in the 1880s, and has many of the traditional trappings of a European village – a water-wheel, quaint cottages fronting a village green, and tearooms in the main street. It also has a most spectacular and panoramic view east to the coast from its location high in the Blackall Range. Browse the galleries and craft shops here (where items handmade from local timber are on sale), take tea in a heritage building, then set off for another local offering, Kondalilla National Park, 5 km to the north. An easy 1.7-km circuit walk from a clifftop picnic area reaches a vantage point with valley views, while a more demanding 4.7-km circuit descends through rainforest to the base of 90-m-high Kondalilla (meaning 'rushing waters') Falls.

► *19 km south-west of Nambour.*

12 Queensland Air Museum

Fine museum of flight with more than 40 vintage aircraft

In 1973 a group of aviation enthusiasts bought a Canberra bomber. One plane led to another and by 1987, with four aircraft to display, this museum opened its hangar doors at Caloundra Aerodrome. Only one of its planes, the Wirraway (an Australian-designed aircraft from the Second World War), arrived by air; the rest, including a Fokker Friendship, the largest aircraft in the collection, were transported by road. Today the collection numbers nearly 50 and includes a Tiger Moth, Spitfires, planes used by the Royal Flying Doctor Service, and a Douglas DC-3. Adding a musical note is a ukulele autographed and played by Charles Kingsford Smith.

▶ *Caloundra, 11 km east of Bruce Hwy.*

13 Glass House Mountains

Jagged chain of towering volcanic plugs

Dark and looming, these rocky spires may not fit everyone's idea of a glasshouse. In 1770, though, when James Cook spied them from the sea, they evoked the conical glass furnaces of his native Yorkshire, and so he called them the 'Glass Houses'. The peaks are the remnants of giant cores of lava that 25 million years ago formed in the vents of now-extinct volcanoes, then solidified to hard rock. Subsequent weathering removed the volcanic slopes, leaving the distinctive plugs standing proud. Challenging walking tracks to the summits of three of the peaks – Mounts Beerwah, Ngungun and Tibrogargan – reward the energetic with sweeping views.

▶ *Glass House Mountains National Park, 68 km north of Brisbane via Bruce Hwy and Steve Irwin Way.*

GLASS HOUSE MOUNTAINS, VIEWED FROM BRIBIE ISLAND

South Burnett and Darling Downs

Taken up eagerly by European settlers, the fertile western slopes of the Dividing Range are now a sea of farmland dotted with intriguing islands of unusual native vegetation. Well-preserved towns and homesteads powerfully evoke the settler era.

1 Miles Historical Village

Turn a corner and turn back time

The main street in this reconstruction of a late-19th-century settlement is so authentic and spick and span that you feel you have indeed wandered back in time, or perhaps onto a film set. Weatherboard shops with awnings line one side of the appropriately dusty street. Nearby are an old slab hut, a tiny jail and antique farm machinery and vehicles, including a steam locomotive. There are re-creations of an early school room and hospital, and the museum has impressive collections of shells, rocks and fossils, medicines and more.

▶ *Murilla St, Miles.*

2 Myall Park Botanic Garden

Startling legacy of amateur botanist

Not only is Myall Park one of the most significant collections of semiarid plants in Australia, but it also plays a vital role in biodiversity preservation at a global level. Many plant species cultivated here have since become extinct in the wild, and the garden is also working to attract and protect threatened butterfly species and other invertebrates. Myall Park was set up by David Gordon, who in the 1940s and 1950s collected plants and cuttings from all over Australia and propagated them here. Fascinated by the concept of hybridisation, he created three popular grevillea hybrids, named after his daughters Robyn, Sandra and Merinda. Visitors can explore the floral displays via a network of paths.

▶ *141 km south-west of Miles via Leichhardt Hwy and Surat Developmental Rd.*

3 Jimbour House

Beautifully preserved pastoral homestead

In October 1844, when explorer Ludwig Leichhardt was planning his expedition from the Moreton Bay area to Port Essington near present-day Darwin, he chose as his departure point Jimbour Station, a large pastoral property then on the fringe of European settlement. Established two years earlier, it had recently been bought by Thomas Bell, an affluent squatter. Bell developed the property and constructed the magnificent two-storey bluestone homestead, endowing it with lighting and the state's first windmills. The house is still a private residence, but visitors can view the exterior and magnificent gardens and follow a 'Living History Walk' around the property, taking in its outbuildings, summer houses and chapel. Particularly impressive is the water tower, built in the 1870s and still part of the estate's water-supply system. At different times, it has also been used as station staff accommodation, a visitor centre and a winery cellar door.

▶ *20 km north of Dalby.*

i Visitor information

Dalby 07 4662 1066
Goondiwindi 07 4671 2653
Kingaroy 07 4162 6272
Miles 07 4627 1492
Stanthorpe 1800 762 665
Toowoomba 1800 33 11 55
Warwick 1800 060 877

WATER TOWER, JIMBOUR HOUSE

4 Bunya Mountains National Park

Isolated upland refuge for rare and threatened species

The Bunya Mountains formed around 30 million years ago, when massive lava flows cooled to form basalt blocks, and are a western spur of the Great Dividing Range. Swathed in forest, they were plundered by timber-cutters for their red cedar in the late 1800s, but in 1908 part of the range was declared national park, only the second in Queensland. Walking tracks explore rainforest, grassland, eucalypt forest and clifftops providing expansive views. Among the more than 30 endangered and threatened species the park protects are the sooty owl, powerful owl and black-breasted button quail. The major drawcard, however, is the world's largest stand of bunya pine, a huge native conifer of the genus *Araucaria*, which produces pineapple-shaped cones holding egg-sized edible nuts. Aboriginal peoples considered the nuts a delicacy and often gathered here to feast on them.

► *55 km north-east of Dalby, 56 km south-west of Kingaroy.*

5 The Palms National Park

Pocket of native bush in a sea of paddocks

This tiny park protects a remnant of once-widespread palm-vine forest and subtropical rainforest. An 800-m circuit walk loops past bunya and hoop pines, Moreton Bay figs, tree ferns and piccabeen palms, with their tall, slender trunks and distinctive flower clusters like intricate filigree necklaces. Sharp-eyed visitors might spot grey-headed flying foxes roosting in the canopy in summer, and black-breasted button quails scurrying through the undergrowth.

► *16 km south-west of Yarraman via New England Hwy and Upper Yarraman.*

6 Museum of Australian Army Flying

Superb display of historic aircraft and aviation memorabilia

The town of Oakey's links with aviation date back to the Second World War, when an aircraft depot and training facility was established here, now the Oakey Army Aviation Centre, a major training establishment. The museum chronicles these developments, as well as the broader history of flight. Exhibits include numerous aircraft, such as a Bristol Boxkite, first flown in Australia in 1912; a Fokker DR1 triplane, made famous by the 'Red Baron', Manfred von Richthofen; and a Bell 47 Sioux helicopter, the first helicopter used by the Australian Army service. A wide range of memorabilia is also on show, and visitors can at times watch volunteers restoring aircraft.

► *Oakey, 29 km north-west of Toowoomba via Warrego Hwy.*

7 Cobb + Co Museum

Australia's finest collection of horsedrawn vehicles

The Victorian gold rush of the 1850s created a sudden demand for transport services in south-eastern Australia, an opportunity seized by a group of four Americans, headed by Freeman Cobb, who in 1854 initiated a stagecoach service that eventually expanded all over Australia (see p. 210). The museum commemorates the service and displays fine examples of its coaches, alongside an array of other horsedrawn vehicles including farm wagons, delivery carts and carriages. Its excellent Heritage Workshops program includes classes on blacksmithing, silversmithing, leadlighting and leatherwork.

► *Lindsay St, Toowoomba.*

8 Glengallan Homestead

Abandoned mansion frozen in time

John Deuchar was a man with a grand vision. Having established himself as a station manager following his immigration from Scotland in 1839, he acquired the Glengallan estate, commenced a lavish lifestyle and began planning a huge complex of stone buildings as his family residence. Construction began in 1867, but only one wing was completed before drought and an economic downturn brought abrupt ruin. The property changed hands over the decades, but the stone house was abandoned, until 2002, when a restoration project brought it back to its former glory. Now filled with period furnishings and flanked by formal gardens, it reveals much about the early European settlement of this district.

► *14 km north of Warwick via New England Hwy.*

9 Cunninghams Gap

Historic gateway to the Darling Downs

English botanist Allan Cunningham became the first European to reach the Darling Downs, in 1827, having journeyed inland and north from New South Wales. Aware that the Great Dividing Range constituted a barrier to settlement of the fertile Downs from the colony at Moreton Bay, he scoured the ranges for crossings and found this pass in 1828. A road was built across it in 1927 and is now part of the Cunningham Highway. From the car park at the crest of the pass, walking tracks head into Main Range National Park, leading to lookouts with magnificent views.

▶ *80 km south-west of Ipswich via Cunningham Hwy.*

10 Queen Mary Falls

Imposing forest-fringed cascade

After tumbling down a series of basalt ledges, Spring Creek, a tributary of the Condamine River, here plummets 40 m into a deep gorge. An easy circuit walk (allow an hour, and follow a clockwise route from the picnic area) leads to the base of the falls through open forest of red gum and brushbox, and subtropical rainforest. Pools harbour platypuses and red spiny crayfish, waterdragons sunbathe on boulders, and on either side of the waterfall staghorns and orchids, nourished by constant spray, cling to branches and ledges.

▶ *Main Range National Park, 40 km south-east of Warwick via Warwick–Killarney Rd.*

11 Customs House

Where travellers paid their dues

Completed in 1859, the Customs House testifies to a time when Goondiwindi was a vital, well-policed crossing point between the colonies of Queensland and New South Wales. A ferry across the Macintyre River here was a major interstate route, and a team of customs officers based at the house patrolled the crossing and collected excise duties on goods. Handsomely preserved, the Customs House is now home to a museum of local history.

▶ *McLean St, Goondiwindi.*

12 Girraween National Park

Dramatic plateau studded with grand granite formations

Across the hillsides here, massive streaked rock faces bulge out of the woodlands, narrow tors sprout above the forest canopy, and boulders balance precariously on cliff edges. The easy 1.4-km Granite Arch Circuit leads to a natural stone arch, while a 3.4-km-return track climbs the enormous granite dome known as the Pyramid, revealing majestic vistas. Yet more demanding trails take in the flanks and summit of Mount Norman.

▶ *36 km south of Stanthorpe via New England Hwy.*

LOOKING INLAND FROM CUNNINGHAMS GAP

Brisbane Region

Queensland's vibrant capital not only has an abundance of diverse and intriguing urban attractions but also provides easy access to the sand islands of Moreton Bay and the glorious forested hills of the D'Aguilar Range.

1 Bribie Island

Ideal for a fast getaway

It's a mere kilometre or so across Pumicestone Passage, and easily reached by bridge, but much of Bribie feels like a far more remote realm. Outside of the small towns at the southern end of the island, most of the coastline is national park and the waters offshore are part of the Moreton Bay Marine Park. White-sand beaches stretch for kilometres, dolphins and dugongs swim by, and wild flowers bloom in profusion in spring. Walking and cycling tracks crisscross the island, there is fine surfing on the east coast, and conditions are ideal for boating and waterskiing. Buckley's Hole Conservation Park, in the south, is a highly-rated bird-watching spot – more than 190 species have been spotted here.

▶ *18 km east of Bruce Hwy via Caboolture–Bribie Island Rd.*

2 Abbey Museum of Art and Archaeology

Extraordinary collection spanning thousands of years

Prehistoric stone carvings, an ancient Egyptian death mask, illuminated manuscripts and magnificent stained glass – the artefacts on show here reflect the history of art and culture from the earliest times. Although the exhibits encompass ancient Egypt and Mesopotamia, the Americas and the Far East, there's a particularly strong focus on artworks from medieval Europe, including ceramics, glassware, woodwork, sculpture, rare books and frescoes. The museum is also renowned for its annual medieval festival, held in July over two days, and featuring jousting tournaments, markets, banquets and music from the Middle Ages.

▶ *5 km east of Bruce Hwy via Caboolture–Bribie Island Rd.*

The bountiful bay

Muddy Moreton Bay has been a rich food source for thousands of years.

Around 6000 years ago, rising sea levels flooded the valley of the lower Brisbane River, creating a fantastically rich source of marine foods. Still visible today along the coast are huge Aboriginal middens containing the discarded remains of countless meals of fish, shellfish, turtles and dugongs. Fish were caught by various means. At present-day Toorbul Point are the remains of a large fish trap, a wall that trapped fish as the tide receded between its loosely packed stones. Most extraordinarily, Aboriginal people are known to have trained dolphins to drive schools of fish toward the shore, where they could be caught. Early European visitors reported the bay to be thronging with thousands of dugongs, and Matthew Flinders described nets up to 30 m long that the Aboriginals used to catch these large creatures. Dugongs and other marine mammals are now protected, but the bay remains a top fishing spot and is renowned for its blue swimmer and mud crabs.

3 Tangalooma

Sunset meet-and-greet with the dolphins

Every evening, after a long day's hunting around Moreton Bay, a small group of bottlenose dolphins – usually 11 members of two close-knit families – heads for the western shore of Moreton Island to play, relax and socialise with ... a bunch of humans. From the foreshore at the Tangalooma Island Resort, the humans wade into the water, wide-eyed with amazement, and hand out fish. The dolphins gulp them down, or, occasionally, flip them back and forth to each other. One gets the feeling that it's an intriguing encounter for both groups. The feeding sessions are open to Tangalooma Island Resort guests and passengers arriving on daily dolphin tours from Brisbane.

▶ *Tangalooma Island Resort, Tangalooma, Moreton Island; by ferry or helicopter from Brisbane.*

4 Bellevue Homestead

Superbly preserved late-Victorian abode

In the early 1840s, the first European squatters, mainly English aristocrats, began taking up land in the Brisbane Valley and establishing pastoral holdings. Originally part of the huge Wivenhoe run, Bellevue Station became a separate property in 1858. Refurbished in the late 1800s by the Taylor family, the homestead was the social hub of an affluent district. The original 1870s farmhouse and a grand guesthouse completed in 1904 are replete with period furniture, fittings and decor, all beautifully maintained and on view at weekends and on public holidays. Guided tours, food and lodging are available.

▶ *48 km north-west of Ipswich via Brisbane Valley Hwy.*

Visitor information

Bribie Island 07 3408 9026
Brisbane 07 3006 6290
Caboolture 1800 833 100
Fernvale 07 5427 0200

MEDIEVAL FESTIVAL AT ABBEY MUSEUM

5 Walkabout Creek

Accessible wilderness in the Brisbane hinterland

Just 15 minutes drive from the state's largest city, in D'Aguilar National Park, you can explore 35,000 ha of mountain wilderness including eucalypt woodland and subtropical rainforest, deep gorges and mountaintop lookouts. The excellent Walkabout Wildlife Centre provides the perfect introduction to the park's diverse environments. You can familiarise yourself with local flora and fauna by wandering through the aviary, peering at nocturnal creatures in the night-house and watching the resident platypus and wallabies, then make a short foray into the surrounding sclerophyll forest via the 1.5-km Corymbia Circuit. And if that whets your appetite for further exploration, set off along Mount Nebo Road to access spectacular lookouts and superb bushland walking trails.

▶ *12 km north-west of Brisbane.*

6 St Helena Island

Atmospheric ruins of 'Brisbane's Alcatraz'

Following the transformation of the Moreton Bay penal colony into the free settlement of Brisbane, local prisons, somewhat ironically, became full to overflowing. In 1867, it was decided to turn the quarantine station on this tiny island into a maximum-security jail for the settlement's worst felons. The convicts themselves constructed new buildings, cleared the surrounding dry vine forest and planted crops. Today, guided tours take in the remains of the buildings, including the prison stockade, wardens' housing, a sugar mill and what was, in 1884, Queensland's first tramway. The prison closed in 1932; following a short period in which it was used for grazing, the island became a national park in 1979.

▶ *Guided tour only, departing by ferry from Brisbane.*

7 Mount Coot-tha

Look down at the city and up at the stars

The twisting ascent to Mount Coot-tha, which rises to a height of 287 m, is a delight, revealing ever-changing views of Brisbane, the coastline and the forested hinterland at every turn. The magnificent lookout at the top allows you to savour those panoramas longer, perhaps most impressively the stunning bird's-eye view of the capital. The slopes beneath are part of a bushland reserve threaded by excellent walking trails leading to picturesque picnic spots including Simpson Falls and JC Slaughter Falls. At the foot of the mountain are the fabulous Brisbane Botanic Gardens and the Sir Thomas Brisbane Planetarium, which has an observatory, interactive displays and by means of its Cosmic Skydome shows takes visitors on mind-bending trips through the solar system and beyond.

▶ *6 km west of Brisbane via Sir Samuel Griffith Dr.*

8 Old Windmill

The state's oldest and possibly most versatile building

One of only two buildings in the city remaining from the convict era (the other is the Commissariat Store in William Street), the windmill was built in 1828 and fitted with large canvas sails and wheels to grind flour. However, it failed to function efficiently as a windmill and instead a convict-powered treadmill was installed to turn the grinding wheels and provide an 'effective' form of punishment for the most troublesome prisoners. Following the closure of the penal settlement, the mill became a signal station for shipping; a gallows; a natural history museum (1862–68); a timepiece that signalled 1 pm by dropping a timeball (still in place) and firing a gun; and a radio and television transmission tower at which TV was demonstrated for the first time in the state, in 1934. There is no access to the interior.

▶ *Wickham Tce, Spring Hill.*

9 Story Bridge

Masterpiece of engineering and iconic city landmark

Perhaps the prettiest of Brisbane's bridges and easily its most distinctive, Story Bridge, which links Fortitude Valley and Kangaroo Point, was the brainchild of John Bradfield, designer of Sydney Harbour Bridge. As with the Sydney bridge, the Story Bridge was constructed in two halves, projecting from the north and south banks. The joining of the two halves had to be carried out at a time when wind and temperature were just right. That occurred in the early hours of 23 October 1939. You can enjoy close-up views of the bridge from Captain Burke Park, and guided climbs are available.

▶ *Bradfield Hwy, Brisbane.*

STORY BRIDGE AND THE BRISBANE SKYLINE

BRISBANE CITY CENTRE

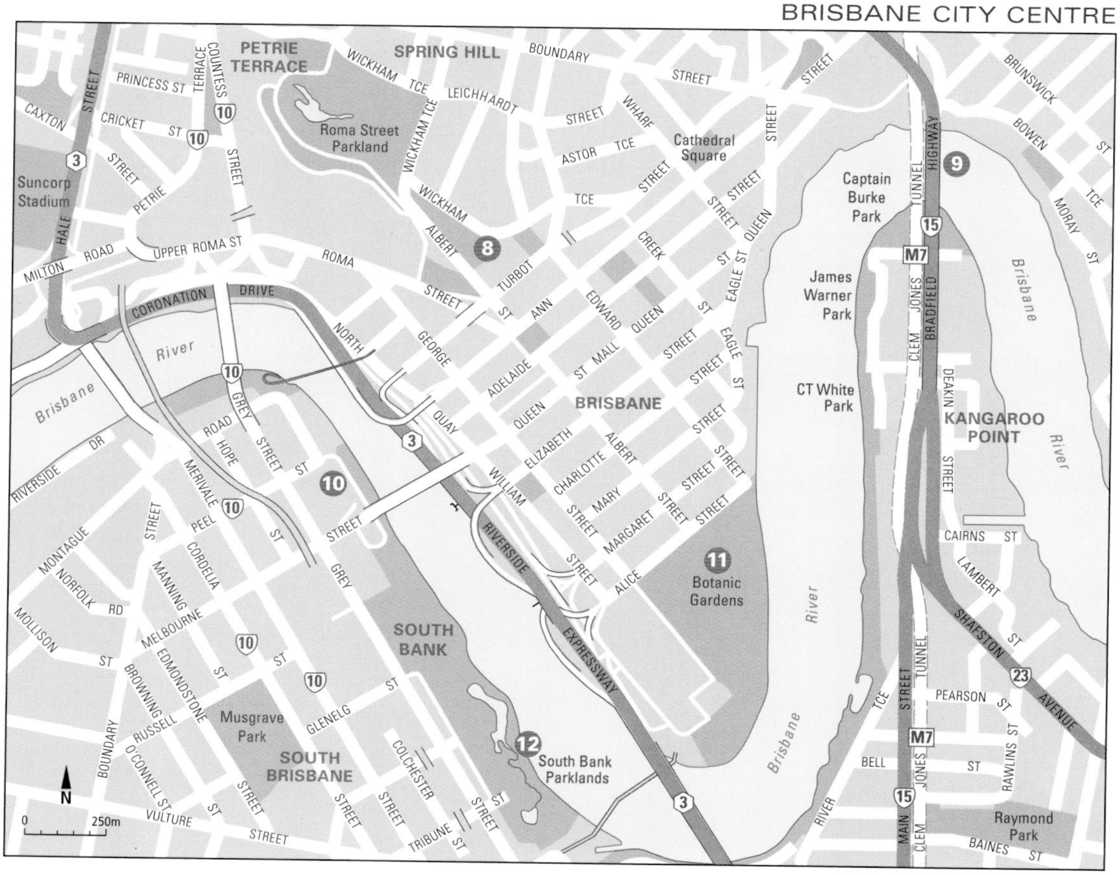

10 Queensland Art Gallery

A magnificent survey of Australian and international art

The collection occupies two striking buildings situated on the Brisbane River frontage: the Queensland Art Gallery, dating from 1982, and the Gallery of Modern Art (GoMA), opened in 2006. Australian painting and sculpture are chronicled from colonial times to the present day and there is a superb collection of Indigenous art. The International Collection surveys medieval religious art, portraiture, ceramics and modernist painting. GoMA focuses on 21st-century art, highlighting the works of leading international artists working in a variety of media, including drawing, painting, video, photography and digital design.

▶ *Stanley Place, South Bank, Brisbane.*

11 City Botanic Gardens

Gateway to the state for exotic flora

With their towering palms, rainforest garden and thickets of bamboo, these lush city-centre riverside gardens do much to accentuate Brisbane's sultry tropical atmosphere. Established in 1855 on a site earlier set aside for growing food for the penal colony, the gardens were planned for recreational but also highly practical, indeed vital, purposes. Most notably, they were used for trialling crops and plants from around the world to assess their suitability for cultivation in Queensland – mangoes, pineapples, sugar cane, coffee and grapes (to name but a few) were first introduced here, as well as Australia's first jacaranda tree. Today's visitors can explore a range of themed areas linked by several self-guided walking trails.

▶ *Access via Parliament House, Alice St or Goodwill Bridge.*

12 Streets Beach

Head for the beach – in the city centre

There aren't many places in the world where you can tuck your toes into the pale sand of a tropical, palm-lined beach while enjoying a close-up view of a city centre skyline, but this is one of them. Streets Beach is an artificial lagoon in the heart of the South Bank Parklands. Bordered by sand, trees, creeks, landscaped gardens and playgrounds, it even has its own lifeguards. The sand comes from Moreton Bay and is replenished every year.

▶ *South Bank Parklands, Brisbane.*

13 Lone Pine Koala Sanctuary

The world's largest koala sanctuary

Opened in 1927, this is also the oldest koala sanctuary in the world. Around 130 of these sleepy creatures dwell here and opportunities for hugs and photos abound. A wide range of other native wildlife is also well represented: regular shows include bird-of-prey displays, kangaroo-feeding sessions, snake holding and sheepdog round-ups.

▶ *11 km south-west of Brisbane via M5 Motorway.*

14 Workshops Rail Museum

Celebrating Queensland's railway heritage

On 31 July 1865, four steam locomotives departed from the railway workshops at Ipswich and trundled 35 km or so west to Bigges Camp, now Grandchester. It was the first railway journey ever undertaken in Queensland and the beginning of a remarkable endeavour: the creation of a statewide narrow-gauge rail network. The Ipswich Railway Workshops continued to play a leading role in building and maintaining rollingstock and still operate to this day. In addition, it hosts this splendid museum featuring a hugely impressive and enjoyable collection of vintage locomotives, wagons and carriages as well as informative displays on the history of Queensland rail. Highlights include the state's oldest locomotive, a diesel-cab simulator, and the sumptuous Vice-Regal Car, built at great expense in 1903 for the use of the governor of Queensland and visiting royalty.

▶ *North St, North Ipswich.*

15 Blue Lake National Park

Vivid, vital waterway perched atop giant sand island

Choose a calm, sunny day for your visit and you'll realise at once why the lake is so named. Its still, tannin-stained waters form a perfect mirror reflecting the intense colour of a clear sky. Fringed by eucalypt forest, banksias, sedges and ferns, Blue Lake is a haven for wildlife. Visit early or late in the day and you'll see ducks and grebes on the lake, honeyeaters and lorikeets zooming through the trees and, with luck, golden wallabies, members of a species found only on North and South Stradbroke islands. The lake is a sacred site for the Quandamooka people; for that reason and due to dangerous underwater snags, swimming is discouraged. The walk to the lake and back via the 5.2-km Karboora Track, through lovely wallum woodlands, takes up to 2 hours but is easy going. A more challenging hike (6 km, up to 2.5 hours) leads from the car park to Nemeeba Lookout, which reveals stunning views south to the Gold Coast.

▶ *North Stradbroke Island; ferries to Dunwich from Cleveland and Redland Bay.*

Gold Coast and Hinterland

Two contrasting worlds sit side by side here: the bustling glitzy city of the Gold Coast, with its unrivalled theme parks, golden beaches and vibrant nightlife; and the mountainous, verdant, little-developed interior, where bounteous wildlife roams volcanic peaks and ancient forests.

1 Tamborine Mountain

Enchanting waterfalls and sublime views from summit to coast

An outlying peak of the McPherson Range, which straddles the Queensland–New South Wales border, Tamborine Mountain was once cloaked with rainforest, but much of it has been cleared for farms, vineyards and horse studs. The upside of this is spectacular views: at Eagle Heights, for example, the panorama extends across hills and valleys to the ocean, as far as North and South Stradbroke islands and the islands of Moreton Bay in the north and Point Danger in the south. Tracts of the original vegetation have, however, been preserved in the various enclaves of Tamborine Mountain National Park, which has some superb walks. In the Joalah section, a short track winds through rainforest and down steps to lovely views of Curtis Falls and adjacent cliffs. In the Cedar Creek Falls section, a 900-m-return walk leads to a lookout above the picturesque cascade. For a breathtaking view westward, head for Rotary Lookout, south of North Tamborine.

► *24 km west of Pacific Mwy at Oxenford via Tamborine–Oxenford Rd.*

Fun at every turn

The Gold Coast's diverse theme parks contribute hugely to its fun-loving, family-friendly atmosphere.

Opened in 1981, Dreamworld, near Coomera, is the country's largest theme park. It has some of the most exhilarating rides in the country, including the 13-storey Cyclone rollercoaster and the Giant Drop, a 120-m, 39-storey freefall in a gondola. Wildlife exhibits and an IMAX cinema are also part of the complex. Next door is White Water World, where you can whirl, spin and bounce your way down a bewildering array of water slides.

You'll spot a few familiar faces spruiking the movie-themed shows and rides at Warner Bros Movie World, down the highway near Oxenford, among them Batman, Sylvester the Cat and Austin Powers. If you can't get enough of the water, you can launch yourself into it in any number of different ways – via slides, tubes and tunnels, on floats and rubber rings – at nearby Wet'n'Wild. Also here is the Australian Outback Spectacular, where expert riders display riding, mustering and whipcracking skills in a venue resembling an outback homestead. Further south at Main Beach, Seaworld is a marine theme park offering rides, activities and enthralling shows starring dolphins and seals. Discount and multipark tickets are sold at the Gold Coast tourist offices.

2 The Spit

Head for the dunes to escape the crowds

Follow the Federation Walk (6 km return) north from the entrance to Seaworld and soon the ostentatious high-rise developments dwindle, the throngs of sunbathers and surfers peter out, and you find yourself in a relatively unspoiled landscape of beach, sand dunes and coastal scrub. The walk winds through she-oaks and littoral rainforest, home to numerous bird species, including friarbirds and honey-eaters; side-routes lead down to the shore. At the north end, the track runs under the Sandpump Jetty, a popular fishing spot, then out along the southern training wall of the Gold Coast Seaway, providing fine views over the entrance to the Broadwater.

► *4 km north of Surfers Paradise via Gold Coast Hwy and Sea World Dr.*

3 SkyPoint

Shoot to the top of the highest of the Gold Coast high-rises

Australia's only beachside observation deck, SkyPoint occupies the 77th floor of the Q1 building, at 322.5 m (including its spire) one of the world's tallest residential buildings and higher than the Eiffel Tower and New York's Chrysler Building. The superfast lift whisks you up 77 levels in 43 seconds. From the SkyPoint deck, the astounding view stretches, on a clear day, 80 km in all directions, to Brisbane in the north, Byron Bay in the south, and the hills of the hinterland to the west.

► *Surfers Paradise Blvd, Surfers Paradise.*

Visitor information

Beaudesert 07 5541 4495
Canungra 07 5543 5156
Coolangatta 1300 309 440
Mount Tamborine 07 5545 3200
Rathdowney 07 5544 1222
Surfers Paradise 1300 309 440

4 Mount Barney National Park

Challenging walks reward with stunning mountain scenery

Several imposing mountains sprout precipitously here, forming some of the most dramatic upland scenery in southern Queensland. They include Mount Barney's two peaks, the East Peak, which reaches 1351 m, and the West Peak, which tops 1359 m and is Queensland's third-highest mountain. The 7.4-km-return Lower Portals track climbs moderate-to-steep gradients to a beautiful pool on Barney Creek between sheer cliffs, while the 13-km Cronan Creek trail leads around the base of the mountains through wildlife-rich rainforest. There are no marked trails leading to the top of Mount Barney and the ascent should be attempted only by experienced, well-equipped bushwalkers.

► *20 km south-west of Rathdowney via Lindesay Hwy.*

5 Green Mountains

Ideal introduction to rainforest realm

High up a mountain in dense rainforest, you would hardly expect to be stopped in your tracks by a large blue-and-white crustacean, waving its claws and hissing menacingly. But that could just happen in Lamington National Park, for among its many outlandish residents is the spiny crayfish, which regularly ventures out of streams to feed on rotting plant and animal matter. Other exotic locals range from the rare Albert's lyrebird and the pouched frog to the magnificent black-and-green Richmond birdwing, Australia's third-largest butterfly. Along the lovely Rainforest Circuit at Green Mountains you might also spy red-necked pademelons, and from atop the Tree Top Walk at O'Reilly's Guesthouse, a walkway 30 m above the forest floor, you might come face to face with wonga and topknot pigeons, bellbirds and rosellas.

► *Lamington National Park, 62 km south-west of Nerang via Canungra.*

6 Binna Burra

Portal to a primeval world

To enter Lamington National Park is to travel back 70 million years, to the time when Australia was still part of the supercontinent of Gondwana. Then, much of the continent was swathed in dense, moist forest, dominated by ferns, conifers and beech trees. As Australia detached itself from Gondwana and drifted, its climate became drier and most of the forests disappeared. But at Binna Burra, several walking trails enable visitors to re-enter this prehistoric landscape. The 5-km (1.5-hour) Tullawalla Circuit climbs to a stand of mossy, gnarled Antarctic beech trees. Widespread in Gondwanan times, they have changed little since. Among the oldest-known conifers are hoop pines; what may be one of the largest intact stands of this species can be seen on the Caves Circuit (5 km, 1.5 hours).

► *Lamington National Park, 33 km south-west of Nerang via Beechmont Rd.*

7 Egg Rock

Eye-catching volcanic formation

Just as the road begins to climb into the Binna Burra section of Lamington National Park from Beechmont, this colossal lump of rock looms from the forested slopes of Nixon's Creek valley. Egg Rock is a rhyolite plug that formed when lava cooled and hardened inside one of the many vents of the vast volcano that once centred on Mount Warning (see p. 127) and last erupted 22 million years ago.

► *Lamington National Park, 25 km south of Canungra via Beechmont.*

8 Natural Bridge

A cave full of surprises

Follow the 1-hour circuit trail here through rainforest and across Cave Creek, and you will come upon an extraordinary sight: a waterfall cascading through a hole in the roof of a cave into a deep pool. Return at night for another magical scene: a colony of glow-worms lights up the cave ceiling after dark. You'll need a torch to get there at night, but don't shine it on the glow-worms or disturb them in any other way, as they are easily harmed.

▶ *Springbrook National Park, 30 km south of Nerang via Nerang–Murwillumbah Rd.*

9 Best of All Lookout

Get the measure of a colossal caldera

It's initially hard to comprehend, but what you see from here, perched on the New South Wales border and peering south towards Murwillumbah, is the outline or collapsed form – the caldera, in other words – of what was once a vast volcano measuring 80 km in diameter and rising to a height of 2000 m. The most prominent peak is Mount Warning (see p. 127), which was the central vent of the volcano, through which huge quantities of lava rose and spilled across the land. It, like many other features in the area, formed when lava cooled and hardened in the vent and the softer cone of the volcano wore away.

▶ *Springbrook National Park, 42 km south of Nerang via Nerang–Murwillumbah Rd and Pine Creek Rd.*

10 Currumbin Wildlife Sanctuary

Friendly encounters with natives

Daily, the delighted shrieks of visitors echo around this park as they are assailed – in a friendly manner – by hordes of rainbow lorikeets descending on their hands, arms and heads to feed. Close encounters of this kind are much encouraged at Currumbin: you can pat a friendly dingo, hold a wedge-tailed eagle and have your photo taken with a barking owl. Run on a not-for-profit basis by National Trust Queensland, the sanctuary is home to around 1400 animals and plays a role in wildlife rescue and conservation.

▶ *Tomewin St, Currumbin.*

AT NATURAL BRIDGE, CAVE CREEK PLUMMETS INTO A BROAD CHAMBER.

MANLY BEACH AND
SYDNEY HARBOUR

Useful websites

Visitor information www.visitnsw.com

Parks and reserves www.environment.nsw.gov.au/nationalparks

New South Wales

You'll be spoilt for choice in Australia's most populous state. Head west to historic river ports and colourful mining towns. Crisscross the Great Dividing Range via volcanic peaks, rainforests and alpine heathlands. Or follow coastal highways to tranquil lagoons and beaches, and headlands with astonishing views.

Outback New South Wales

These wide brown lands hold great riches – ragged ridges threaded with seams of gold, silver and opal, precious galleries of Aboriginal rock art, and expansive grazing lands. Winding diagonally across the region is the Darling River, which has been a lifeline for the region's human inhabitants for more than 40,000 years.

1 Corner Country

Starkly beautiful arid lands surround remote junction

Marching straight as a die across rippled red dunes is a 1.8-m-high wire-netting fence built to keep dingoes out of the sheep flocks and cattle herds of the southern part of the continent. In the north-west corner of New South Wales, it follows the border between Queensland and South Australia and turns at a right angle where the three states meet – Camerons Corner, named for the surveyor who left his mark here in 1880. Today, those who make their way by 4WD from Tibooburra to this isolated intersection pass through the dramatic gibber and grass-covered plains of what is now Sturt National Park. They teem with wildlife, from chattering flocks of tiny finches to mobs of huge red kangaroos. At the Corner is a stone cairn with a visitors' book.

► *Sturt National Park, 3 km north of Tibooburra.*

2 Tibooburra

Heat and art in NSW's most isolated town

Tibooburra's main claim to fame is its location in the hottest, driest and most remote corner of the state. Its name means 'heaps of boulders', a reference to the local rocky outcrops that early Europeans called the Granites, and where gold was discovered in the 1880s. The rush was short-lived; the hardy and hopeful who trudged here were defeated by lack of water and poor returns. The settlement that grew to supply their needs became a service town for the surrounding pastoral stations. A surprise awaits those who step inside its 1880s Family Hotel – bar walls covered with a startling mural by Clifton Pugh. And in Pioneer Park is a full-size replica of the whaleboat that in 1845 explorer Charles Sturt and his party dragged through this parched region in their search for an inland sea.

► *332 km north of Broken Hill via the Silver City Hwy.*

3 Milparinka

Fine architectural heritage, and volunteers, keep this ghost town going

Like nearby Tibooburra, Milparinka sprang from a short, sharp gold rush. By the 1880s, its population of 600 was served by four hotels and a cluster of impressive public buildings, including a school, post office, police station and court house, all built of locally cut sandstone. But in less than a generation most of its residents had drifted away and by the end of the 20th century only one building, the 1882 Albert Hotel, was occupied – and, amazingly, still trading. Recent years have seen a remarkable rebirth as the town is being slowly reconstructed with the help of visiting volunteers. The solid 1886 court house now houses exhibits on local Indigenous and European history, there is an information centre and gallery in the adjacent former police station, and the cells behind are occupied by a mining interpretative centre.

► *294 km north of Broken Hill via Silver City Hwy.*

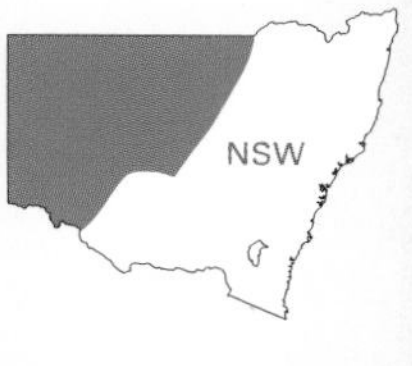

Slow and steady

Life-giving artery of the outback, the Darling follows a long, lazy 2700-km route from sources in southern Queensland to the Victorian border.

Despite their meandering routes across the eastern Australian interior, the Darling River and its tributaries drain a region of more than 650,000 sq km. Near Menindee, the Darling opens into a series of shallow overflow lakes, now kept permanently full by a dam (see Menindee Lakes, p. 119). But for most of its unhurried course, the river snakes through a blue-grey blur of saltbush and clumps of mallee scrub.

Aboriginal people have camped on its banks for more than 40,000 years, relying on its resources of fish, mussels and waterbirds. For early Europeans, the river was a ready highway that allowed the spread of settlement – at the peak of the river trade, in the 1870s, about 100 paddle-steamers and barges plied its waters, carrying everything from kettles to kerosene upstream and returning, low in the water, bearing huge bales of wool.

4 North Bourke Bridge

Historic lift bridge, a reminder of the Darling's glory days

This grand iron-and-timber bridge dates from the days when Bourke was an inland port, wool was king and the Darling was the main means of transporting the clip to southern centres. Built in England, the bridge was brought up the river in sections, reassembled on the site, and opened in 1883. It carried traffic until 1997, when it was replaced by a new bridge, and has since been restored as a footbridge – particularly popular for a sunset stroll. Easily seen are the remains of two huge pulley chains at the western end, and weights at both ends, which raised the central section to allow river traffic to pass beneath.

▶ *5 km north of Bourke via Mitchell Hwy.*

Visitor information

Bourke 02 6872 1222
Broken Hill 08 8080 3560
Lightning Ridge 02 6829 1670
Mildura 03 5018 8380
Silverton 08 8088 7566
Wentworth 03 5027 3624

5 Brewarrina Fish Traps

Ancient and ingenious riverbed construction

In the Barwon River, just downstream from Brewarrina Weir, is an elaborate complex of circular and diamond-shaped pens built of carefully placed rocks, which follows the contours of the riverbed. Possibly as much as 40,000 years old, it was designed by the local Aboriginal people to corral the fish migrating upstream after seasonal rains. The open mouths of the enclosures point downstream, and were closed off once the fish had swum in. The resulting catch is believed to have fed thousands of people at ceremonial gatherings. Maintained for millennia, the traps originally stood 1 m high and stretched like a stone net for 1.5 km along the river. Following European settlement, sections were removed to allow paddle-steamers to pass. About 500 m remains, and is still in use. Indigenous guides lead tours to the site.

▶ *Brewarrina, 95 km east of Bourke.*

CUSTOMISED CARS OUTSIDE
A SILVERTON GALLERY

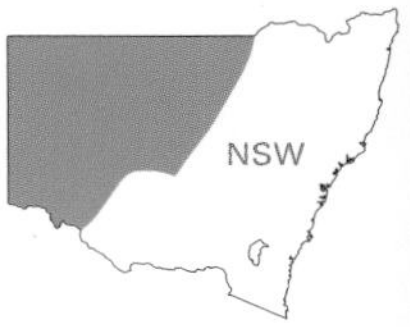

6 Lightning Ridge

'Speck' and 'noodle', then follow a trail of coloured car doors

Lightning Ridge is the world's major supplier of prized black opal. For more than a century, a multinational force of strong-headed individuals has been gouging it from the grey claystone here in hand-dug shafts. The tents of the early days have given way to homes made of corrugated iron, conglomerate boulders, and mud; there is even one made entirely of bottles. Each year, the permanent population of 1000 or so is swollen by thousands of tourists who come to look for 'colour' in the discarded mining dirt (mullock) by either simply scratching at the surface (specking) or picking through it (noodling) – the luckless can look to the town's vast array of commercial opal outlets for treasures. Colour is more easily found in the car doors placed along the roadsides; these mark four driving tours around the fields, each identified by a different-coloured door.

▶ *60 km north of Walgett via the Castlereagh Hwy.*

7 Mutawintji National Park

Crumpled red ridges conceal the secrets of an ancient culture

For thousands of years, the deep gorges, hidden gullies and reliable waterholes of the Byngnano Range have been a haven for animals and a meeting place and ceremonial centre for people. The caves and overhangs here shelter a rich collection of rock art – paintings, stencils and engravings – now protected within the park in Mutawintji Historic Site; entry is by guided tour, led by a traditional owner. Access roads are impassable after rain.

▶ *130 km north-east of Broken Hill via Silver City Hwy and signposted access roads.*

8 Day Dream Mine

Don a miner's hat to descend tunnels hand-hewn more than a century ago

It's hard to imagine 10-year-old boys hauling boxes of ore through these dark and narrow passageways, or to think of their bone-weary fathers working 12-hour shifts 6 days a week, even eating in the gloomy depths. Life here was desperately hard. Families lived in cramped stone huts – the ruins of the town that once sheltered 500 people remain – and the men died young, usually of respiratory disease. Day Dream is the only historic mine open to the public and a visit here is a thought-provoking experience.

▶ *33 km north of Broken Hill via Broken Hill–Silverton Rd.*

9 Silverton

Ghost town immortalised by movies

Just about the first thing you'll see as you pull into Silverton is a replica of Mad Max's V8 Interceptor parked outside the pub. Look in the bar and you'll find an extensive photographic collection that chronicles the many movies and television commercials shot in this very busy ghost town. Silverton's clear light and desert backdrop have also attracted another group keen to record its character – a community of artists – and many of the town's ochre-coloured buildings now serve as studios and galleries. In the 1880s, in the town's booming lead-, silver- and zinc-mining days, Miss Mary Jane Cameron, later and better known as the poet Mary Gilmore, taught in the high-ceilinged stone schoolhouse that still stands on the hill.

▶ *25 km north-west of Broken Hill via Broken Hill–Silverton Rd.*

10 Sculpture Symposium

Modern sculpture park crowns flora and fauna sanctuary

Most people time their visit to this sculpture-crowned hill for dusk, when the setting sun sets the sculptures aglow; some settle in with picnics, others wander the short loop that links the 12 artworks. Carved from local sandstone by artists from regions as diverse as Bathurst Island and Mexico, each stands dramatically against the skyline and each has a story to tell. To drive up, you'll need to pick up a key from the visitor information centre in Broken Hill, or you can hike to the top of the hill (about 20 minutes) from the Living Desert Reserve below; you'll need to take a torch for the downhill return if you plan to stay for sunset.

► *11 km north of Broken Hill via Nine Mile Rd.*

11 Mount Grenfell Historic Site

Richly coloured frieze of figures

A semi-permanent waterhole and the natural shelter of the rock ridge here made this an ideal meeting place for Aboriginal groups. Among the rocky outcrops are magnificent examples of ancient Aboriginal art painted with red and yellow ochres, black ash and white pipeclay; the images include a multicoloured panel of dancing figures, animals and hand stencils. The three main art sites are within an easy 500-m walk from the car park. The site is accessible in dry weather only.

► *72 km north-west of Cobar via Barrier Hwy.*

SUNSET OVER MENINDEE LAKES

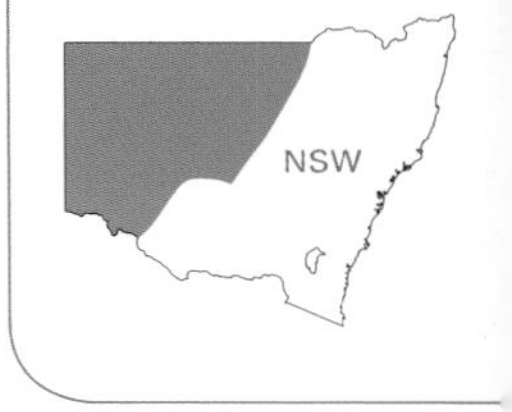

12 Menindee Lakes

Captive waters provide a haven for birdlife

Before the completion in 1960 of a water storage scheme, these saucer-shaped lakes filled in flood times, then drained into the falling river. Now they not only supply Broken Hill with water, but also provide plentiful food and ideal nesting places for a wide variety of waterbirds – from brolgas high-stepping in the shallows to pelicans enjoying a spa in the spillway below the Main Weir and cormorants drying their wings in the skeletons of trees drowned by permanent high water levels. Humans, too, flock to the lakes, to fish, sail and swim.

► *100 km south-east of Broken Hill via Menindee Rd.*

13 Kinchega Woolshed

Impressive symbol of pastoral past

The faint smell of greasy wool still lingers, marks where the blades were sharpened and freed of burrs scar the tar-stained walls, and if you close your eyes you can almost hear the clicking of the shears. Built in 1875, the Kinchega woolshed was the largest in the region. It rests on mighty upright trunks of river red gum and its floors and pens are built of slabs of the same durable timber. There are stands on the board for 62 blade shearers, each of whom could shear a tally of 60 sheep a day. In turn, every method of shearing was employed from hand blades to the electric machines in use when the shed closed in 1967. The steam traction engine which provided power for the first mechanical handpieces still stands beside the shed.

► *Kinchega National Park, 115 km south-east of Broken Hill via Menindee Rd.*

14 Walls of China

Ancient lakeside dune holding a 50,000-year record of Aboriginal life

Once there was a lake here, brimming with fresh water and edged with dunes. Families lived and fished along its sandy shores and hunted the giant marsupials that grazed adjacent fertile grasslands. When the lakes dried 20,000 years ago, the people stayed on, camping near soaks. The Walls of China are the weathered remains of a 30-km-long crescent of dunes that once fringed the lake's north-eastern shore. Within its eroded ramparts are the ashes of ancient camp fires, cooking hearths and the bones and shells from long-ago meals. At day's end, the pinnacles of the walls, glowing red in the setting sun, are a spectacular sight.

► *Mungo National Park, 150 km north-east of Wentworth via Pooncarie Rd.*

New England and North-West

A tumultuous geological evolution has bequeathed this region spectacular landforms, thermal springs and priceless gem deposits. Grand homesteads and towns reflect the wealth derived from grazing and mining, and celebrate the diverse heritage and accomplishments of their inhabitants.

1 Moree Hot Artesian Pool Complex

Enjoy a soothing dip in mineral-rich waters

Two Canadians, Crawford and McCray, were the first to sink a bore here, in 1895, tapping into the naturally hot waters of the Great Artesian Basin, almost 1 km below ground. When they struck water on 9 November, so much gushed out that the town was immediately flooded; the rapid construction of a pool, using railway sleepers, helped stem the flow and allowed locals to enjoy the waters' benefits. Since then, thousands of people have come here to seek relief from a variety of nervous, rheumatic and arthritic complaints. The modern spa complex has two large therapeutic pools into which the natural spring water is pumped at a steamy 41°C.

► *Cnr Anne St and Gosport St, Moree.*

2 CSIRO Australia Telescope Compact Array

Celestial listening post

Day in, day out, this facility trains its 'ears' – six gleaming dish antennas – on distant realms of the universe. Each dish can record individually, or they can all be brought into position, using 3 km of broad-gauge rail track, to function together as one 6-km-wide telescope. When operating in conjunction with the Parkes radio telescope, they form, effectively, an observation device measuring more than 300 km in diameter. You can view the antennas from the visitor centre, which also has interpretive boards and a video explaining the facility's operations.

► *25 km west of Narrabri via Yarrie Lake Rd.*

3 Sawn Rocks

Majestic volcanic outcrop

A classic 'organ-pipe' basalt formation, Sawn Rocks rises 40 m above Bobbiwaa Creek and is thought to extend at least another 60 m underground. It is the legacy of a series of eruptions that occurred between 17 and 21 million years ago. The almost perfectly symmetrical five-sided columns formed as a basalt lava flow cooled very slowly, permitting crystals in the rock to align consistently. Sections of the rock face have detached and tumbled into the creek below, forming a spiky jumble of columns, reminiscent of a ruined temple. The easy, pleasant walk to the viewing platform (1.5 km) leads through forest, rich in lilly pilly, native fig and native peach.

► *Mount Kaputar National Park, 38 km north-east of Narrabri.*

Visitor information

Armidale 02 6770 3888
Glen Innes 02 6730 2400
Inverell 02 6728 8161
Moree 02 6757 3350
Narrabri 02 6799 6760
Tamworth 02 6767 5300
Tenterfield 02 6736 1082
Uralla 02 6778 4496

ORGAN-PIPE FORMATIONS
AT SAWN ROCKS

4 Gunnedah

Self-styled koala capital of Australia

This is one place you are virtually guaranteed a sighting of koalas in the wild – you might even see one or two strolling along footpaths, wandering across streets or watching golfers from treetop vantage points on the local course. Careful creation and conservation of tree corridors in and around the town saw the already sizeable koala population burgeon in the 1970s and 1980s, and Gunndedah now has one of the country's largest and healthiest colonies. Ask at the visitor centre about the best places for sightings. If all else fails, visit the Waterways Wildlife Park, just out of town, where you can not only wander in an open koala enclosure but also get up close to kangaroos, possums, wombats, echidnas, dingoes and lizards.

► *71 km north-west of Tamworth via Oxley Hwy.*

5 Bald Rock

Sweeping 360-degree views from colossal granite dome

Hiking across the face of this vast mound of exposed, smooth, water-streaked rock – at 750 m by 500 m, the largest exposed granite formation in Australia – is not only an unusual and invigorating experience, but also yields astonishing panoramas, particularly at the 1277-m-high summit, where the views stretch unobstructed to the horizon on all sides. The trail to the top, the 3-km Bungoona Walk, is of medium difficulty and requires at least 2.5 hours. Along the way, you'll see deep gorges, stone arches and precariously balanced boulders. Echidnas snuffle around in pockets of flowering heath, and kangaroos and wallabies can occasionally be seen bounding over the rock. The park's more than 100 species of birds include rosellas, bowerbirds and fantails.

► *Bald Rock National Park, 29 km north of Tenterfield via New England Hwy and Mount Lindesay Rd.*

6 Tenterfield

Birthplace of the nation

In 1899, Sir Henry Parkes, who from 1882 to 1884 had been Member of the NSW Legislative Assembly for Tenterfield, returned to the town to deliver a speech supporting the federation of the Australian colonies. So persuasive and far-sighted was Parkes that, in the words of another architect of Federation, Sir Robert Garran, the meeting 'turned a vague ideal into a practical working program'; moreover, it would gain Parkes the title of 'Father of Federation'. The venue of the meeting, the elegant Sir Henry Parkes Memorial School of the Arts, houses displays recounting the event and following its outcome. Other intriguing Tenterfield sights include the grand Victorian Gothic railway station, dating from 1886, and the saddler's store operated by singer Peter Allen's grandfather and immortalised in his famous ballad 'Tenterfield Saddler'.

▶ *New England Hwy.*

7 Australian Standing Stones

Prehistoric-style circle celebrates Celtic connections

Prior to this stone circle's construction in 1992, it was probably a good few thousand years since anyone had built anything similar, and it's possibly the only structure of its kind in the Southern Hemisphere. The idea came from a group of locals who wanted to commemorate Glen Innes's Celtic origins – the majority of those who settled the area in 1838 were Scots. Modelled on the Ring of Brodgar, a Neolithic henge in the Orkney Islands, the circle consists of 40 stones, with some indicating compass points and others marking the summer and winter solstices. Each stone had to be 5.5 m high so that it would stand 3.7 m clear of the ground when embedded, and on average each weighs 17 tonnes. At the edge of the circle stands a reconstruction of a traditional crofter's cottage.

▶ *1.3 km east of Glen Innes via Gwydir Hwy.*

8 Inverell

Try your luck in the 'Sapphire City'

Source of half of Australia's sapphires and most of the world's blue sapphires, Inverell has an array of galleries and fossicking sites where visitors can admire the beauty of these gems, learn about their retrieval, sorting and grading, and hunt for their own potentially valuable specimens. The visitor centre has a mining museum and display of gems. You can watch stones being cut and polished at the Gem Centre and at the Dejon Sapphire Centre, then go fossicking at a range of sites, including 7 Oaks Sapphires, which provides all the equipment and instruction you'll need. Inverell also has fine heritage architecture, on display in the city and at Pioneer Village, a collection of historic buildings.

▶ *68 km west of Glen Innes via Gwydir Hwy.*

9 Balancing Rock

Ready to roll?

You'd think one good strong puff of wind would be enough to send this huge granite boulder tumbling off its base and across the surrounding paddock till it thumped to rest against some adjacent formation. Yet it has perched thus, atop a smaller, rounded, half-buried rock, for hundreds, maybe thousands, of years. Of course, way back it would have sat more firmly and securely, but eons of weathering have whittled the point of contact between the two rocks to a precarious 30 cm or so today. As the formation sits on private property, it must be viewed from the highway or the adjacent Stonehenge Recreation Reserve and cannot be approached or scaled – fortunately!

▶ *New England Hwy, 13 km south of Glen Innes.*

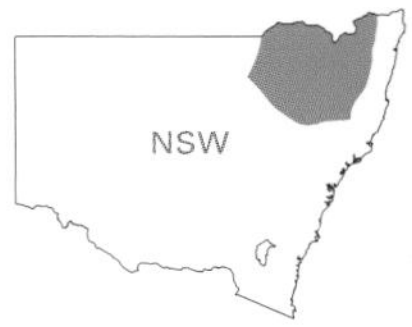

10 Booloominbah

Historic heart of Armidale's university

Booloominbah was built as the family home of Frederick White, a prominent grazier. He employed Canadian John Horbury Hunt, then Australia's most fashionable architect, to design the 45-room mansion in Queen Anne style. With its imposing staircase, stained glass, elaborate carvings, and warren of rooms, it rivals many English country mansions in its grandeur. The White family donated the building to the University of Sydney in 1933 and five years later it became the New England University College. University offices still occupy most rooms, but visitors can view the entrance hall – which features a striking stained-glass window depicting the life of General Gordon of Khartoum – former dining room and gardens, and sample the fare at the cafe, restaurant and bar in the west wing.

► *Booloominbah Dr, University of New England, Armidale.*

11 Wollomombi Falls

The highest waterfall in the state

One of the tallest cascades in Australia, Wollomombi Falls plummets a total of 220 metres – including a sheer drop of 100 m – from an undulating tableland over an imposing escarpment into rugged, precipitous Wollomombi Gorge. Adjacent to it is the almost equally impressive Chandler Falls. There is a lookout near the visitor area and the fairly easy (4-km) Wollomombi Track leads across the river and around the rim of the gorge to Chandler Lookout. To see the falls at their best, try to visit soon after heavy rain.

► *Oxley Wild Rivers National Park, 38 km east of Armidale via Waterfall Way.*

BOOLOOMINBAH WAS BEGUN IN 1882 AND COMPLETED IN 1888.

12 Cathedral Rock National Park

A rock-hopper's delight

The formation that gives this park its name is one of several huge freestanding granite boulders, or tors, that are scattered around the area. Like huge toys abandoned by giants, they stand surreally isolated, some perched precariously atop exposed stone platforms, others jutting out of the forest. They are the result of 230 million years or so of erosion of much larger granite deposits. From the picnic areas at Native Dog Creek and Barokee, walking trails fan out and ascend the tors. Gentler tracks lead through forests of peppermint, stringy-bark and mountain gum dotted with clumps of orchids and inhabited by robins, thornbills and parrots, as well as swamps and heaths. Climbing the tors requires a degree of agility, particularly on the ascent of Cathedral Rock itself, where climbers have to haul themselves up a chain near the summit.

► *70 km east of Armidale via Waterfall Way.*

13 Saumarez Homestead

Elegant Edwardian country home

Built between 1888 and 1906, Saumarez Homestead is a magnificently restored homestead that reveals much about early colonial history. Owned in its heyday by the White family, who also established Booloominbah (see p. 123), it became one of New England's grandest properties. A large staff served the house and tended the gardens, resulting in a self-sufficient community. Visit is by guided tour, on weekends and public holidays only.

► *New England Hwy, 5 km south of Armidale.*

14 Thunderbolt's Rock

Legendary bushranger's lookout

Perched atop the rocks, you can imagine the roguish Frederick Ward (see below) lurking behind the boulders, watching the highway for his next victim. The pile of giant granite stones, typical of many outcrops in the wider region but alone in an otherwise flat landscape here, would certainly have been a perfect eyrie. Also known as Split Rock, it makes a fine picnic spot, and those agile enough to climb the stones will enjoy sweeping views.

► *New England Hwy, 5 km south-west of Uralla.*

The robber's realm

The legend of 'Captain Thunderbolt' looms large over much of New England.

Several intriguing sites in this region recall the exploits of bushranger Frederick Ward, also known as Captain Thunderbolt. As well as his lookout at Thunderbolt's Rock (see entry), there's the cave north of Tenterfield that was his hideout, as well as what may be his grave in Uralla's Pioneer Cemetery, and a grand equestrian statue that graces Uralla's main street. In folklore, Ward is something of a blend of Ned Kelly and Robin Hood. But, while he is known to have shown compassion for some of his victims, there is no evidence that he had any altruistic motives for his crimes. In a rampage lasting seven years in the 1860s, he notched up 25 mail-coach robberies, more than 30 raids on homes, hotels and shops, and no fewer than 80 horse thefts. He outran the authorities until 1870, when a hawker who had been robbed at Uralla alerted the police in time for them to trap Ward near a creek; he was shot dead in a struggle with a constable.

MASSED RANKS OF GUITARISTS AT THE TAMWORTH COUNTRY MUSIC FESTIVAL

15 Tamworth

Australian capital of country music – all year-round

For ten days in January every year, Tamworth's population balloons as about 55,000 visitors from across Australia and beyond flock to town for the annual Country Music Festival, a national institution since 1973. Singers, fiddlers, banjo pickers, guitarists and line dancers perform all over town at an astounding 2,500 individual events. Even if you don't make it to the big bash, you can get a feel for the festival and investigate its history and most famous acts at a range of local attractions, at any time of year. The Big Golden Guitar Tourist Centre, dwarfed by the 12-m guitar outside, has displays and wax figures of country legends. More exhibits and memorabilia are on show at the Walk a Country Mile Interactive Centre, and at the Hands of Fame you can peruse the handprints of famous acts who have performed in town.

▶ *New England Hwy.*

16 First Fleet Memorial Gardens

Affecting tribute to Australia's first European settlers

In a picturesque garden alongside Quirindi Creek, hand-carved tablets, made by master stonemason Ray Collins, list the names of all the convicts, civilians, crew and commanders who arrived at Sydney Cove aboard the ships of the First Fleet in 1788. Extracts from logs and other historic records recount their stories, as well as the experience of the voyage and the early history of Sydney's penal colony. A second, more recently constructed garden covering the arrival of the Second Fleet is adjacent.

▶ *New England Hwy, Wallabadah.*

Northern Rivers

From the ranges that line the northern New South Wales border, volcanic peaks and ridges fall east to verdant, rolling hills, dotted with alternative-lifestyle communities, and busy beach and surfing centres. In the south, the Clarence River links former inland ports with unspoiled coastline.

1 Point Danger

Unusual lighthouse marking the state border

Sailing north along this coastline on 16 May 1770, James Cook was forced to veer offshore to avoid a series of reefs, leading him to name this, the most prominent headland, Point Danger. Today a memorial commemorates Cook's journey while an adjacent lighthouse warns modern sailors off the reefs. Built of concrete in a modernist style in 1971, the lighthouse was the first in the world to use lasers to create its beam – though the experiment was subsequently adjudged unsuccessful and the lasers replaced with conventional lamps and mirrors. The lighthouse memorial straddles the Queensland–New South Wales border, and splendid views stretch north to Surfers Paradise and south to Byron Bay.

▶ *Tweed Tce, Tweed Heads.*

2 Tweed Range Scenic Drive

Rollercoaster ride through magnificent subtropical rainforest

One of the most dramatic drives in the country, this 90-km, mostly gravel road (suitable for 2WD in dry weather) climbs, dips, twists and turns along the rainforest-shrouded rim of the Tweed Caldera, the vast bowl that is a remnant of an ancient volcano centred on Mount Warning (see entry). From the Antarctic Beech picnic area you can look north to the Lamington Plateau, while Blackbutts Picnic Area reveals a stunning panorama of the entire caldera, with Mount Warning at its centre. It's best to start the drive at Wiangaree, north of Kyogle; allow at least four hours.

▶ *Wiangaree, 78 km south-west of Murwillumbah via Kyogle–Murwillumbah Rd and Summerland Way.*

Visitor information

Ballina 02 6686 3484
Byron Bay 02 6680 8588
Lismore 02 6626 0100
Maclean 02 6645 4121
Murwillumbah 02 6672 1340
Nimbin 02 6689 1388
Tweed Heads 07 5536 6737

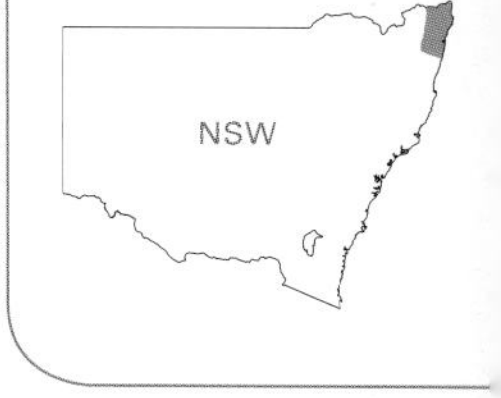

3 Mount Warning

The Tweed's volcanic core

Roughly 23 million years ago, a massive eruption took place here, forming a volcano 40 km in diameter. Since then the cone has been whittled away by the elements, leaving a bowl-shaped range of peaks, known as the Tweed Caldera, and, at its centre, this dramatic peak, formed from the lava that solidified in the volcano's central vent. Aboriginal people knew the mountain as Wollumbin, and it remains a sacred site for Bundjalung people (who would prefer that visitors do not climb to the summit). James Cook gave it its European name, recommending that sailors steer clear of the reef-fringed coast as soon as they saw it on the horizon. For a close-up view, follow the road to Breakfast Creek, where the Lyrebird Track leads through the mountain's mantle of rainforest, home to scrub turkeys, lyrebirds and red-necked pademelons.

▶ *Wollumbin National Park, 12 km south-west of Murwillumbah.*

4 Cape Byron

The Australian mainland's most easterly point

From the exquisite beaches north and south of Byron Bay, the coastline climbs to this steep-sided promontory jutting out into the ocean. At its highest point, atop precipitous slopes dropping almost 100 m to the sea, stands the Cape Byron Lighthouse, constructed in 1901 and renowned for the power of its lamp, which can be seen up to 43 km out to sea. A 5-km walking trail leads around the summit of the headland, taking in coastal heath, littoral rainforest and banksia forest, as well as the lighthouse, and providing panoramic views, inland to the Border Ranges and up and down the coast. James Cook named the cape in May 1770, after John Byron, explorer and grandfather of the poet.

▶ *3 km east of Byron Bay.*

5 New Italy Museum

Intriguing Italian outpost chronicles a remarkable saga

Replica Renaissance sculptures, pergolas draped with grape vines, and a cafe with superb espresso all add to the Mediterranean atmosphere of this museum complex. It chronicles the extraordinary journey of a group of 50 Italian families, who, in the 1880s, migrated to New Ireland (now part of Papua New Guinea) to take up what had been advertised as fertile, freely available land. Finding it anything but, they decamped, disillusioned, to Australia, where they eventually found their own settlement here on the Richmond River, establishing orchards, vineyards and a small silk industry.

▶ *Pacific Hwy, 51 km south of Ballina.*

CAPE BYRON LIGHTHOUSE

6 Iluka Nature Reserve

World Heritage–listed rainforest reserve

From the eastern fringe of Iluka, a tranquil port renowned for its fishing, this little reserve runs down to the shoreline. What it lacks in size it makes up for in diversity and ecological significance, for this is the state's largest remaining beachfront rainforest. Follow the 2.5-km walk through thick stands of riberry and lilly pilly draped with vines, orchids and ferns. Listen for the crack of the eastern whipbird and the noisy chatter of the multicoloured noisy pitta; you might even spot a regent bowerbird or a rare barred cuckoo-shrike.

▶ *17 km east of Pacific Hwy via Iluka Rd.*

7 Angourie Walk

One of the country's best coastal hikes

Yuraygir National Park protects one of the most extensive tracts of undeveloped coastline in New South Wales, and one of the finest experiences it offers is the Angourie Walk (10 km, 3 hours). Departing from Marra Creek, just south of Angourie, it heads south through bird-rich heathlands and along sandy shores, taking in view-points with breathtaking panoramas – notably at Point Dirrigan, from where dolphins are often spotted – and coastal caves. The southern end of the walk reveals impressive views of conical Clarence Peak before reaching delightful Lake Arragan. You can camp here and, if the walk has whetted your appetite, continue all the way to Red Rock on the four-day, 65-km Yuraygir Coastal Walk.

▶ *Yuraygir National Park; Angourie is 17 km east of Pacific Hwy via Yamba Rd.*

From convict hell-hole to tourist haven

Once a much-dreaded penal colony, Norfolk Island is now an affluent outpost with a fascinating historical and ecological heritage.

A speck in the Pacific Ocean measuring just 34 sq km, Norfolk Island is volcanic in origin and rises from a submerged ocean ridge. James Cook found the island uninhabited in 1774, though it seems to have been earlier occupied by Polynesians. Settlers and convicts lived here following the founding of Sydney, but departed in 1814.

In 1825, another settlement was founded, as an earthly Hell for troublesome convicts. That colony closed in 1855 and a year later the descendants of the *Bounty* mutineers were resettled here from Pitcairn, bringing with them their own language: a mixture of 18th-century English and Tahitian still spoken and today called Norfolk.

On the trail of the Norfolk pine

The World Heritage–listed site of Kingston encompasses several superbly well preserved buildings from the convict era, including the ruins of a prison and a convict cemetery, as well as a clutch of museums. Plentiful rainfall and volcanic soil have endowed the island with lush native vegetation, notably the famous Norfolk Island pine, which belongs to the widespread genus *Araucaria*.

Bushwalks in Norfolk Island National Park wind through forest to coastal lookouts, and to the summits of Mounts Pitt and Bates, the island's highest points. Flights to the island depart from several east coast cities.

8 Ulmarra

Delightfully intact former river port

The whole of this tiny settlement, one of the country's finest examples of a 19th-century river port, is classified by the National Trust. Once a major loading point for farm and dairy produce, it is now mainly a tourist and craft centre and, occasionally, a location for film and television period dramas. The Commercial Hotel by the river has fine latticework verandas and most of the main street's old shops, many with elegant awnings, are beautifully preserved; several house excellent antique and craft shops.

▶ *Pacific Hwy, 12 km north of Grafton.*

9 Grafton

Wander through the history of this gracious riverside city

Grafton's jacaranda-lined avenues, elegant buildings and pleasant parks invite leisurely, low-speed exploration and there's no better way to get a feel for the city, founded as a river port in 1839, than by just ambling around. Stroll down Victoria Street to take in fine examples of Victorian architecture, including salmon-coloured Christ Church Cathedral (completed in 1884), designed by John Horbury Hunt, and the post office, court house and police station, then backtrack along Fitzroy St to admire grand private residences with their shady verandas and timber shutters. A visit to the Clarence River Historical Society Museum will fill out the historical background. Flowering jacarandas make an October visit especially delightful.

▶ *Pacific Hwy.*

STATELY JACARANDA TREES LINE THE BROAD STREETS OF GRAFTON.

North Coast

A chain of tranquil, attractive seaside towns, divided by estuaries, lagoons and heath, lines this long stretch of shoreline. In the hinterland, picturesque timber towns and dairy farms nestle in valleys beneath volcanic slopes swathed with extensive temperate rainforests.

1 Guru Nanak Sikh Temple

Ornate place of worship for thriving Sikh community

As the gleaming white onion-domed temple comes into view atop the green hills above Woolgoolga, you feel you've been transported to the Subcontinent. The structure looks exotic, incongruous even, but it is in fact the principal place of worship for a sizeable proportion of long-time local residents. Opened in 1970, the Guru Nanak Temple was constructed by descendants of Sikhs from the Punjab who first arrived in eastern Australia in the late 19th century. Sikhs settled in Woolgoolga in the 1940s, first working on, then acquiring, banana plantations. Visitors are welcome outside of hours of worship, but must cover their heads and remove their shoes before they enter.

► *River St, Woolgoolga.*

2 Muttonbird Island

Summer breeding ground of world-travelling seabirds

Somehow, after passing the winter feeding adrift on Northern-Hemisphere seas, tens of thousands of shearwaters belonging to three species – sooty, wedge-tailed and short-tailed – manage to find their way back each summer to this tiny speck of land on the other side of the world. Arriving at nightfall, they creep through the shrubbery to the burrows of the previous season and commence breeding. Walk out over the breakwater and follow the paved walkway to view the nesting birds, but don't stray from the path or you may disturb or destroy their burrows.

► *Marina Dr, Coffs Harbour.*

3 Dorrigo National Park

Check out the rainforest high life

This World Heritage–listed national park protects some of the country's largest remaining tracts of subtropical and warm-temperate rainforest, and its superb and accessible walking tracks allow visitors to view this magical, wildlife-rich environment from a variety of perspectives. Make your first stop the Rainforest Centre, to learn about the park's environments, then stroll out along the Skywalk, a canopy boardwalk 70 m above the ground, for a breathtaking overview: the panorama stretches from the upland peaks across the forested plateau and down to the sea. The short (800-m, 20-minute) Lyrebird Link is an easy stroll into the forest at ground level. For a more in-depth investigation, continue along the Wonga Walk (6.6 km circuit, 2–3 hours), through giant 300-year-old trees and strangler figs, to the short Walk with the Birds boardwalk, which climbs to the mid-levels of the forest, where birds and canopy flowers are easily observed.

► *42 km west of Pacific Hwy via Waterfall Way.*

Visitor information

Bellingen 02 6655 1522
Bulahdelah 02 4997 4981
Coffs Harbour 02 6648 4990
Nambucca Heads 02 6568 6954
Nelson Bay 02 4980 6900
Port Macquarie 02 6581 8000
South West Rocks 02 6566 7099
Taree 02 6592 5444

4 Bellingen

Sophisticated, beautifully preserved country town

For many residents and regular visitors, Bellingen has achieved an ideal blend of town and country, old and new, traditional and alternative. The surrounding picture-book-pretty farmland is hemmed by tracts of unspoiled forest; platypuses swim in the river, flying foxes roost in the trees above. In town, stylish cafes serving fine cuisine and boutiques offering the latest fashions occupy late-19th-century buildings, such as the Hammond and Wheatley Emporium in Hyde St. Local farms produce quality dairy produce and fruit as they have done for a century and more, while more recent arrivals, including artists and alternative-lifestylers, run galleries and craft outlets, notably the Old Butter Factory.

► *12 km west of Pacific Hwy via Waterfall Way.*

5 Bowraville

Admire the fine streetscapes of the 'Veranda Post Town'

Founded in 1870 as a timber town, Bowraville entered a period of economic stagnation after the Second World War as the demand for timber waned. The silver lining to this temporary cloud was that the town centre remained unspoiled by postwar modernisation and its main streets are today a time capsule of late-19th-century architecture, distinguished by their handsome verandas and awnings. Don't miss the 1899 St James Anglican Church and the Folk Museum, a treasure trove of memorabilia, trinkets and gadgets.

11 km north-west of Princes Hwy at Macksville.

RAINFOREST IN DORRIGO NATIONAL PARK

TRIAL BAY GAOL CROWNS A SCENIC HEADLAND AFFORDING SUBLIME VIEWS.

6 Trial Bay Gaol

Intriguing, short-lived 1880s prison in a picturesque location

Wandering around the outside of this jail, admiring the elegant buildings of pink and grey granite, and enjoying the magnificent coastal views and (usually) the district's fine, sunny weather, you have to keep reminding yourself that this was a place of punishment. Opened in 1886, the jail was built to house convicts assigned to build a breakwater at the mouth of the Macleay River; it closed in 1903, though it was also briefly an internment camp during the First World War. Inside, the sombre purpose of the building is somewhat clearer: bars line every window and the exhibits in the small museum describe the prison regime. Guided tours are available and there is an excellent restaurant.

► *Arakoon State Conservation Area, 40 km north-east of Kempsey.*

7 Timbertown

Faithful reconstruction of pioneer logging settlement

The enveloping forest and the perfectly preserved shopfronts; the thundering hooves of passing bullock teams and the clang of the hammer on the blacksmith's anvil; the ever-present odours of freshly cut logs and wood fires – every sight, sound and smell here enhances the convincing re-creation of the life of an early logging community. There are displays of wood-cutting and furniture-making, and you can ride a horsedrawn wagon or a vintage steam train and buy souvenirs, food and wines.

► *Wauchope, 12 km west of Pacific Hwy via Oxley Hwy.*

8 Ellenborough Falls

The second-longest single-drop waterfall in the Southern Hemisphere

According to local legend, these falls have never run dry, pouring relentlessly over a sheer 200-metre drop at the eastern edge of the New England tableland. They are thus always a dramatic sight, and yet more impressive after heavy rains. A 30-minute walk (including 641 steps) leads to the base of the falls, while another path (10 minutes) climbs to The Knoll, offering a marvellous view of the plummeting waters and cliffs.

▶ *85 km south-west of Port Macquarie via Oxley Hwy and Conboyne Rd.*

9 Diamond Head

Spectacularly scoured promontory with awe-inspiring views

Erosion of this headland's quartz-rich rocks (which gave it its name) has shaped dramatic cliffs, stone arches and narrow chasms, best viewed from the 4.8-km (2-hour) Diamond Head Loop Walk between Diamond Head and Indian Head. From the summit of Diamond Head, stupendous views open out across the sea and north across Dunbogan Beach towards distant North Brother Mountain. This is also an excellent vantage point for observing whales during their May-to-July and August-to-October migrations. South of Indian Head is Kylie's Beach, named after writer Kylie Tennant, who lived for a time at the hut now called Kylie's Hut, just a short walk away.

▶ *13 km east of Pacific Hwy at Kew via Ocean Dr and Diamond Head Rd.*

10 Wingham

The English-style village with a wild heart

Established as a timber port, this was the first official settlement to be laid out in the Manning Valley, in 1843. Named after a 7th-century village in Kent, England, it was designed in English style around a grassy common. Many of the buildings that still line the common, Central Park, are heritage-listed. By the river in the heart of town is Wingham Brush, a remarkable 10-ha tract of bushland that is one of the state's last surviving areas of subtropical flood-plain rainforest. Dense with Moreton Bay figs, vines, ferns and orchids and threaded by boardwalks, it is home to flying foxes and more than 100 species of birds.

▶ *14 km north-west of Taree via Wingham Rd.*

11 National Motorcycle Museum

Fabulous range of bikes and memorabilia

A report in 1988 that many classic Australian motorbikes were being snapped up by overseas collectors prompted Brian and Margaret Kelleher, former motorcyle retailers, to step in, start acquiring pre-loved two-wheelers and, eventually, display them at this purpose-built complex. The more than 700 bikes on show range from a 1914 Iver Johnson and a 1919 Kenilworth scooter to classic BSAs and modern superbikes.

▶ *Clarkson St, Nabiac.*

12 Green Cathedral

Open-air lakeside church

There are no walls or roof, just lines of towering cabbage palms, their wide fronds forming a glorious canopy. A gap through the trees leads to rows of rough wooden pews; just behind the simple stone altar, the waters of Wallis Lake lap the shore. It's an appropriate spot to ponder the wonders of creation. The church was built, or one might say planted, in 1922 by the members of the Reorganized Church of Jesus Christ of the Latter-day Saints. It is still used for services and for private wedding ceremonies. At the boatshed next door, you can hire canoes to paddle out over the expansive, picturesque lake.

▶ *13 km south of Forster on The Lakes Way.*

A place to escape the world

Bounded by reefs and capped by craggy peaks, Lord Howe Island remains remarkably and charmingly undeveloped.

Situated 500 km or so due east of Port Macquarie, World Heritage–listed Lord Howe is a little arc of volcanic land uplifted from the seafloor some 7 million years ago. In the early days of South-Sea whaling and penal colonies, it was ignored as a potential settlement due to an apparent lack of fresh water. This helped preserve its unusual flora and abundant wildlife and minimise development. Even today, while it has become a popular holiday destination, it seldom seems crowded or its pace of life in any way hurried.

The island's relatively few houses, shops and guest lodgings – no large, flashy resorts here – are concentrated in the northern half of the island. Walking tracks climb the hills from here to clifftop lookouts where acrobatic red-tailed tropicbirds soar and swoop, and green turtles can sometimes be spotted in clear waters far below.

Wildlife abounds

Within the island's arc lies The Lagoon, bounded by the world's southernmost coral reef, home to an astonishing array of colourful fish. The mountainous southern half of the island is dominated by the bulky volcanic peaks of 765-m Mount Ligbird and 875-m Mount Gower. The day hike to the top of the latter is an enthralling trek, revealing dizzying views and a magical, primeval-looking cloud forest at the summit.

Wherever you go, the most visible of the island's creatures are its birds, which include huge breeding colonies of sooty terns, red-tailed tropicbirds and flesh-footed shearwaters, as well as a small population of the flightless woodhen, rescued from the brink of extinction in the 1980s. Flights to the island (taking approximately 2 hours) depart from east-coast cities.

VIEW FROM MALABAR HILL, LORD HOWE ISLAND

13 The Grandis

The tallest tree in the state

This colossal flooded gum stands 76 m high and measures nearly 3 metres in circumference at its widest point. Believed to have been already two centuries old when Europeans first saw it, it somehow escaped the axe and is now protected. A boardwalk leads up to the tree and there is a pleasant picnic area.

▶ *Myall Lakes National Park, 13 km south of Bulahdelah via Old Pacific Hwy and Stoney Creek Rd.*

14 Sugarloaf Point

Historic lighthouse commanding majestic coastline

Beyond the isolated former fishing village and newly fashionable seaside retreat of Seal Rocks, the road ends at a car park beneath this steep-sided headland, and a walking track curves upward past dramatic cliffs and blowholes to a grand lighthouse rising 15 m above the surrounding vegetation. Waves crash and pound on the rocks far below and the views stretch endlessly past beaches and headlands north and south. The lighthouse dates from 1875, and below it are quaint keepers' quarters and well-preserved outbuildings of a similar vintage.

▶ *34 km east of Bulahdelah via The Lakes Way and Seal Rocks Rd.*

15 Mungo Brush

From lakeside over dunes to the sea

Myall Lakes National Park protects the state's largest fresh–brackish lake system, made up of four large lakes – Myall, Two Mile, Boolambyte and The Broadwater – as well as surrounding swamp-oak, paperbark and red-gum forests, coastal heaths and dunes. The Mungo Brush area, on the eastern side of the park, provides a fine introduction to this environment, taking in both lake and ocean. From the lakeside picnic area on The Broadwater, the easy, half-hour Mungo Brush Rainforest Walk loops through a pocket of littoral (coastal) rainforest, winding through native olive, coogera, brush bloodwood and strangler figs. Keep an eye out for koalas and birds including white-headed pigeons, satin and regent bowerbirds and rufous fantails. Across Mungo Brush Road, tracks thread through towering quartzite dunes to stunning stretches of deserted white-sand beach.

▶ *Myall Lakes National Park, 22 km north of Hawks Nest via Mungo Brush Rd.*

16 Tanilba House

Early colonial homestead incorporating its own jail and temple

Though its original owners, the family of naval lieutenant William Caswell, sold up and left this 14-room dwelling more than a century ago, it feels like they have only just departed: family letters lie open on desktops, antique crockery and books line the shelves, and in winter a roaring fire burns in the hearth. Dating from 1831, the house was constructed by convicts using locally mined porphyry stone. Built into the cellars is a small jail, and a friendly ghost is said to roam the corridors. From the airy veranda, a delightful view extends across the lawn and Tanilba Bay to Snapper Island. The charming gardens incorporate a small temple, designed and installed by a later resident, Henry F. Halloran. The present owner offers guided tours and Devonshire teas.

▶ *Admiralty Ave, Tanilba Bay, 28 km east of Raymond Tce via Richardson Rd and Lemon Tree Passage Rd.*

Hunter Valley and Central Coast

One of the first regions outside Sydney to be settled by Europeans, the Hunter Valley retains fine colonial homesteads and towns, as well as its long-established vineyards. Tracts of wilderness border the valley north and south, while to the east attractive beach resorts, lakes and inlets line the populous Central Coast.

1 Burning Mountain

Fire down below

Understandably, early European visitors to Mount Wingen, as this peak is more formally known, assumed the smoke rising from its summit was seeping out of volcanic vents. In fact, it rises from a seam of coal that has been burning underground for more than 5500 years, and is one of just a few such naturally burning coal seams in the world. The initial spontaneous combustion has been fed by oxygen filtering down from the surface through cracks and fissures, and the fire continues to move south at a rate of about 1 m per year. A walking track lined with interpretive panels leads up the hill to a viewing platform overlooking the burning head of the seam.

► *Burning Mountain Nature Reserve, New England Hwy, 21 km north of Scone.*

Visitor information

Central Coast 02 4343 4400
Dungog 02 4992 2212
Gloucester 02 6558 1408
Maitland 02 4931 2800
Newcastle 02 4929 2588
Pokolbin 02 4990 0900
Scone 02 6545 1526

2 Barrington Tops National Park

Diverse forest communities scale wild, rugged plateau

Rising from near sea level up the flanks of an extinct volcano to a height of 1500 m, this magnificent park protects a huge range of vegetation and, consequently, a vast array of wildlife. At lower levels lie pockets of subtropical rainforest, festooned with vines, orchids and ferns, and home to koalas, gliders and pademelons. Higher up are some of mainland Australia's largest tracts of temperate rainforest – warm temperate and cool temperate – roamed by kangaroos and red-necked wallabies. Explore the lower forests at Gloucester River and Williams River – the 1-hour Blue Gum Loop Track, which crosses two bridges over the river, is delightful. The Barrington Tops State Forest Road, which is partly gravel but generally suitable for 2WD vehicles, crosses the high plateau, taking in walks through stunning Antarctic beech forest and wonderful lookouts such as Devils Hole, whose views stretch 90 km to the coast.

► *37 km north of Dungog, 42 km west of Gloucester.*

Fortunes on the vine

The Lower Hunter Valley is the oldest commercial winemaking centre in Australia and one of its most visited.

No one is quite sure who planted the Hunter's first commercially productive crop, but the prime mover was unquestionably a public-spirited Scotsman called James Busby. In 1830, after studying viticulture in France, Busby published an instruction manual on growing grapes in Australian conditions, and in 1832 he imported hundreds of vine cuttings from Spain and France. A year later, Busby left to become British resident administrator in New Zealand, but in his absence he authorised the distribution, over the next few seasons, of more than 20,000 cuttings to other landowners.

Around the same time, George Wyndham founded his Dalwood Winery (now Wyndham Estate, see p. 138) and in the late 1800s and early 1900s other future Hunter dynasties were established, including Tyrrell's and McWilliam's. In those early days, fortified wines were most in demand, but, following the Second World War, varietals came to the fore, such as shiraz and, in particular, semillon, for which the Hunter is these days internationally famous.

Wine touring

The Lower Hunter wine region is centred on the settlement of Pokolbin, south of the river, and encompasses more than 120 wineries, many of which offer cellar-door tastings and sales, as well as cafes and restaurants; some also host major cultural events such as the October Opera in the Vineyards and Jazz in the Vineyards festivals. Scattered among the vineyards are gourmet-produce outlets and a range of accommodation. Call in at the Hunter Valley Wine Country visitor centre in Pokolbin for maps and help with planning an itinerary.

VINEYARDS IN THE LOWER HUNTER VALLEY

3 Stroud

Lovely colonial town with convict-constructed architecture

One of three towns planned from scratch in the early 1800s by the Australian Agricultural Company (AAC), which had been granted more than 400,000 ha west of Port Stephens, Stroud is believed to have been the first company town in Australia. Named after Stroud near Gloucester in England, it was chosen as the headquarters of the AAC and was, for a time, the region's most important settlement. When the head office moved to Sydney in 1856, development halted – preserving the historic sandstone buildings and village atmosphere. Take a walk around and look in particular for the handsome convict-built St John's Anglican Church (1833), the attractive post office (1834) and stately Stroud House (1834), originally a guest-house for visiting company commissioners.

▶ *28 km east of Dungog via Stroud Hill Rd and Bucketts Way.*

4 Wyndham Estate

Historic winery, location of an architectural gem

This is one of the Hunter Valley's most famous and oldest wineries; indeed, it is the oldest continuously operating winery in the country and was the birthplace of shiraz in Australia – pioneer winemaker George Wyndham planted the first commercial shiraz vineyard here in 1830 and his wines later won major awards at international competitions. Tour the winery and gardens, sample the wares and make sure you take a look at Dalwood House, the magnificent residence designed by Wyndham in Greek Revival style. Built in the early 1830s, it fell into disrepair in the 20th century and is being restored by the National Trust.

▶ *2 km north-east of New England Hwy at Branxton.*

HAVE A PICNIC WITH ALICE AND FRIENDS IN THE HUNTER VALLEY GARDENS.

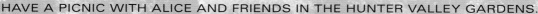

5 Tocal Homestead

Early farm complex, long a hub of agricultural innovation

Established in 1822 using convict labour, Tocal was one of the Paterson Valley's first farms and became the site of the district's grandest homestead in 1834. It was then leased to Charles Reynolds as a base for a thoroughbred horse and Hereford cattle stud. In the 1960s, it was bequeathed to the Presbyterian Church, which turned it into an agricultural college, now run by the Department of Agriculture. On weekends in summer (and by appointment), visitors can tour the grand Colonial Georgian homestead, which retains furnishings and artefacts from all periods of its history, and the remarkable outbuildings, which include an imposing barn designed by famed architect Edmund Blacket – and referred to by Philip Cox as the 'cathedral of barns' – and a cottage said to have been used by bushranger Captain Thunderbolt (see The Robber's Realm, p. 124).

▶ *14 km north of Maitland via Paterson–Dungog Rd.*

6 Walka Water Works

Remarkable and ornate industrial complex

This unusual, atmospheric attraction is a fine example of Victorian industrial architecture, engineering – and ingenuity. Constructed in handsome two-tone brickwork, the complex supplied the Lower Hunter region with a hygienic water supply from 1887 to 1925. Aside from a period as a temporary power station, it then remained empty until 1984, when restoration began. Particularly attractive is the Italianate pumphouse in what is now the picnic area, with its elegant chimney, boiler house, and settling tanks and filter beds used to clean the water pumped from the Hunter River. In the adjacent recreational area are a lake, walking trails and a model railway. All in all, a grand day out.

▶ *Scobies La, Oakhampton, 3 km north of Maitland.*

7 Hunter Valley Gardens

The largest display gardens in the Southern Hemisphere

You can follow 8 km of walking trails here through more than 25 ha of gardens, divided into various themed plantings. More than 8000 individual bushes throng the Rose Garden; the Sunken Garden encloses a dramatic 10-m waterfall; and the Indian Mosaic Garden features antique Indian elephant gates and a stunning mosaic made from pebbles and ground-cover plants, including richly fragrant Indian spices. You can also visit a magnificent two-storey Japanese pagoda in the Oriental Garden, and wander among topiary animals and statues of nursery-rhyme characters in the Storybook Garden. Shops and eateries are on site.

▶ *12 km south of New England Hwy at Pokolbin.*

8 Wollombi

Staging post preserved in its prime

In the 1830s, Wollombi seemed set to prosper, ideally placed as it was to serve the steady stream of travellers along the newly completed Great Northern Road (see Devines Hill, p. 140) from Sydney to the Hunter Valley. But by the 1880s, road transport had been superseded by rail and ship, and the inland route became a backroad and its towns backwaters. Today's visitor reaps the benefit. Situated on a rise with fine views over the river valley, Wollombi's honey-coloured sandstone buildings are little changed since those early days. Prominent among them are the two-storey former post office, the elegantly simple St John's Anglican Church (1846–49), and the nearby police station (1846) and court house (1866). The charming Endeavour Museum, inside the court house, offers an intriguing collection of artefacts, as well as guides and maps.

▶ *50 km south of Singleton via Broke Rd and Wollombi Rd.*

9 Fort Scratchley

Bulwark against an attack that never came

Bizarre as it might sound now, in the late 1800s there was a widespread fear that Russia might invade Australia. A series of conflicts between Britain and Russia, starting with the Crimean War of 1853–56, led the British government to believe that its foe might seize some of its colonies; so outposts all over the world were ordered to strengthen defences, especially at ports. In response, Fort Scratchley was built atop Signal Hill in 1882 to guard the entrance to Newcastle Harbour, and equipped with massive walls, a moat and large guns. It was another 60 years before its guns were fired in conflict, however, and then it was at a quite different target: a Japanese submarine, quickly repelled. Today the fort is an engaging military and maritime history museum – guided tours of its warren of tunnels are recommended.

► *Nobbys Rd, Newcastle.*

10 Dobell House

Controversial portrait painter's retreat

It was in a state of some distress that artist William Dobell first came to live at Wangi Wangi. The award of the 1943 Archibald Prize for portraiture should have brought him satisfaction and security, but had delivered anything but. Two artists had brought a court case against the judges' decision, claiming Dobell's winning painting of Joshua Smith was a caricature, not a portrait, and although the case had been thrown out it had left Dobell a nervous wreck. This house, which had belonged to his father and which Dobell would share with his sister, subsequently became a refuge, and the shores of Lake Macquarie an inspiration, helping Dobell recover his gifts. Though he later travelled widely, he always returned home to paint. Open at weekends, the house and studio are preserved much as they were when Dobell died, in 1970.

► *Dobell Drive, Wangi Wangi, 18 km east of Pacific Hwy.*

11 Devines Hill

Civil engineering feat of the colonial era

Between 1826 and 1836, the hills north of Wisemans Ferry rang with the sound of pick on rock and were the scene of backbreaking toil. Up to 700 convicts laboured here to complete the 240-km Great Northern Road from Sydney to the Hunter Valley, clearing trees, hewing rock, building bridges and levelling ground. Just north of the Hawkesbury River they faced one of their greatest challenges: the steep climb up the escarpments. Walk the 3.6-km-return track up Devines Hill today and you get some idea of what they faced: walls and buttresses rise more than 10 m high; pick marks can be seen in the rocks. Despite its solid construction, the road was abandoned by travellers in the 1880s, in favour of steamship services.

► *Dharug National Park, 68 km west of Pacific Hwy via Peats Ridge Rd and Wisemans Ferry Rd.*

12 Wisemans Ferry

Site of Australia's oldest ferry service

A boatman on the River Thames, Solomon Wiseman was convicted in 1805 of stealing wood and transported to Australia. Pardoned in 1812, he became an innkeeper on the Hawkesbury River and in the mid-1820s began operating a ferry service. It turned out to be a prescient choice of location: soon the ferry was linked to the main Sydney–Hunter Valley road. Today, a cable-operated punt operates at the same scenic location on a bend in the river, beneath a forested escarpment, and the settlement that bears Wiseman's name is still a sleepy scattering of sandstone buildings, including Wiseman's former home, now the Wisemans Ferry Hotel.

► *67 km west of Pacific Hwy via Peats Ridge Rd and Wisemans Ferry Rd.*

13 Brooklyn

Gateway to the Hawkesbury River

Established as a fishing village, Brooklyn is an attractive residential and boating centre with a marina and seafood cafes. But it's the wide waterway it borders that makes it such an enticing destination. Join a commercial cruise or hire a boat to explore the broad reaches, placid inlets and forest-shrouded shores of the beautifully scenic and still little-developed Hawkesbury River. One of the best ways to view the sublime scenery and get a sense of life among its widely scattered, often isolated communities is to hop aboard the Riverboat Postman, which spends a leisurely 4 hours each morning on weekdays delivering mail and supplies to homes upriver.

► *3 km east of Pacific Hwy.*

HAWKESBURY RIVER
AT WISEMANS FERRY

Central New South Wales

The rolling plains here hold fascinating pointers to the distant past – layers of fossils and peaks of lava from volcanic turmoil of long ago. In its historic towns are echoes of gold rushes and bushrangers, while the domes and dishes of its observatories peer through clear skies, seeking to unlock the mysteries of space.

1 Siding Spring Observatory

Gleaming domes atop volcanic peaks

Perched high in the Warrumbungle Range are the great white dome and cluster of smaller domes that comprise Siding Spring Observatory. Together they house 11 telescopes, including the Anglo-Australian Telescope (AAT), the largest optical telescope in Australia. Though you can't look through it, as it is reserved for research purposes, you can observe its enormity from the viewing gallery then visit the Siding Spring Exploratory, a small museum of astronomy. Billboards along the roads to Siding Spring are part of the Virtual Solar System Drive, and display planets in their relative position to the sun.

▶ *26 km west of Coonabarabran via John Renshaw Pkwy and Timor Rd.*

2 Warrumbungle National Park

Spires of solidified lava guard a unique mingling of wildlife

The jagged profile of the Warrumbungle Range rises abruptly from the plains and is visible for 100 km in some directions. This is a landscape born 13 million years ago in the turmoil of bubbling magma and blinding ash. The bare pinnacles and peaks that jut skywards from forested slopes are the weathered cores of a single but multi-throated volcano. These extraordinary mountains shelter a rich bioregion where the plants and animals from the semiarid interior and the humid coast and tablelands meet. Wildlife is prolific and frequently seen along the 43 km of walking tracks. Most popular, but with some strenuous climbs and requiring the best part of a day, is the Grand High Tops track (12.5 km, 5 hours) which skirts the rock sliver of the Breadknife and offers panoramic views.

▶ *41 km west of Coonabarabran via John Renshaw Pkwy.*

3 Taronga Western Plains Zoo

Roam free in a zoo without bars

It's not often you get the chance to cycle leafy tracks past giraffes and elephants, meet a meerkat troop, picnic in an Asian wetland and feed a lion. Set in more than 300 ha of bushland, Dubbo's open range zoo is home to more than 1000 endangered and exotic animals; visitors can drive, walk or cycle (bikes can be hired) around the zoo's 6-km loop road; there are also 15 km of bush trails. Along the way are opportunities to see animals being fed and to listen to keeper talks. Stay overnight in the on-site accommodation and you'll likely wake to shrieks of howler monkeys and the not-so-distant roar of lions.

▶ *3 km south of Dubbo via Newell Hwy.*

Visitor information

Bathurst 02 6332 1444
Coonabarabran 02 6849 2144
Cowra 02 6342 4333
Dubbo 02 6801 4450
Gulgong 02 6374 2691
Mudgee 02 6372 1020
Orange 02 6393 8226
Wellington 02 6845 1770

4 CSIRO Parkes Radio Telescope

Local link to a giant leap

In 1969 the observatory here played an important part in relaying images of the first moonwalk, a story later told in a whimsical movie *The Dish*. Three tracking stations received the signals simultaneously, but the Parkes pictures were of a superior quality, so NASA used this footage for most of the 2.5-hour telecast. The 64-m diameter dish began scanning the heavens in 1961, and since then has discovered a large proportion of the known pulsars (small stars that produce 'flashes' of radio waves). The visitor centre, built in the shadow of the telescope, has displays and exhibits, the 3D Theatre which takes you on a trip to Mars, and the Invisible Universe presentation on the Parkes telescope.

▶ *20 km north of Parkes via Newell Hwy and Telescope Rd.*

CSIRO PARKES RADIO TELESCOPE

Strike one

News of the first payable gold find in Australia, in 1851, at Summer Hill Creek, Ophir, fuelled a gold-rush frenzy that transformed the country.

Although the major gold deposit at Ophir was exhausted within a year, the massive social changes triggered by this find, and those that followed at nearby Lucknow, Sofala, Forbes, Hill End and Gulgong, continued for decades. Thousands flocked across the mountains to the diggings, merchants as well as miners, almost emptying Sydney of its able-bodied workforce. Many were new immigrants who stayed on, taking up other jobs when the gold ran out. Today nothing is left of Ophir, Australia's first gold-rush town, apart from still-visible shafts more than a century old. The furrowed slopes are still a popular fossicking area, but visitors should not venture too close to the old mines, which are dangerous.

5 Wellington Caves and Phosphate Mine

Hidden world of fossils and limestone formations

Here you can take a guided tour of two very different caves. Cathedral Cave features a massive stalagmite 15 m high and 32 m around the base, while the smaller Gaden Cave is known for its delicate limestone formations. Then don a hard hat and tour the historic phosphate mine, with its restored equipment, and nearby Bone Cave, where fossils and ancient bone fragments stud the walls.

▶ *10 km south of Wellington via Mitchell Hwy.*

6 Gulgong

Rich heritage at every turn

Gulgong's crooked streets were laid down in the frantic days of the 1870s gold rush, and their winding ways echo the narrow lanes that snaked through a canvas town of tents pitched beside claims. Later buildings followed suit, hence the kink in the street line of the Commercial Hotel. Riches from the diggings enabled the town's music hall (the grandly named Prince of Wales Opera House, still standing in Mayne Street) to engage some of the best performers of the era, including singer Nellie Melba, and the poet Henry Lawson spent his childhood on the outskirts – the Henry Lawson Centre in the former Salvation Army Hall houses a fine collection of memorabilia. The iron lace and clapboard of the numerous original buildings, the horse troughs and hitching posts still to be seen in Mayne Street and, around the corner, the superb collection in the Pioneers Museum all bring it vividly to life.

▶ *29 km north of Mudgee via Castlereagh Hwy.*

7 Mudgee

Elegant hub of a thriving wine and food region

Mudgee's wide and leafy grid-plan streets graced with solid civic buildings and grand sandstone houses, some dating from the 1850s, have been described as 'one of the finest groups of townscape in a country area'. Although it benefited from the influx of the gold rushes, Mudgee's wealth has always been based on its fertile countryside. Today it is the centre of a wine district and noted also for fine food, with lamb, venison, olives, nuts and honey all regional specialties.

▶ *Castlereagh Hwy.*

8 Hill End

Tantalising glimpses into a boom town's golden past

Hill End flared into existence in 1871, with fantastically rich returns from the mining of reef gold. Major finds included the monstrous Beyers and Holtermann specimen, the largest-known single mass of gold-bearing rock. At its peak, in 1874, the town's boom-swollen population rivalled those of Melbourne and Sydney. Residents lived mainly in neat cottages in orderly laid-out streets, and were served by a busy commercial district with 28 hotels (one remains in business), stores (several still operate), stone churches and, on the hill, a fine hospital, now the visitor centre. By the end of the decade, it was all over. Almost a century later, in 1967, the entire village was declared a historic site in recognition of its national significance and the serendipitous fact that, when the miners moved on, the streetscapes they left behind survived largely intact.

▶ *75 km north of Great Western Hwy at Bathurst via Turondale.*

HILL END IS A LIVING MUSEUM OF GOLD-RUSH ARCHITECTURE.

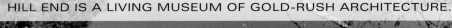

EXQUISITE LIMESTONE FORMATIONS ADORN ABERCROMBIE CAVES.

9 Mount Canobolas

It's all downhill west of this old volcano

At 1395 m above sea level, the volcanic crown of Mount Canobolas is the highest peak between here and Perth. The summit, often snow-capped in winter, offers 360-degree views over the gracious city of Orange and east to the Blue Mountains. The winding road up passes through one of the most diverse vegetation zones in the region, which ranges from stringy-bark forests to snow gums and is home to an array of fauna, including grey kangaroos, wombats, koalas and lorikeets. Walking tracks lead to intriguing geological formations, the result of past volcanic activity, and impressive Federal Falls.

► *17 km south-west of Orange via Grenfell Rd, Lake Canobolas Rd and Pinnacle Rd.*

10 Somerville Collection

A lifelong passion, now Bathurst's greatest treasure

Warren Somerville found his first fossil at the age of nine. Over the following 60 years he amassed one of the world's finest private collections of fossils and minerals, and then he gave it to the nation. Housed in Bathurst's 1876 former public school building, now the Australian Fossil and Mineral Museum, it includes a 10-m-long skeleton of *Tyrannosaurus rex*, fossil dinosaur eggs, opalised fossils and a 40-million-year-old lizard caught in amber, as well as crystals from more than 100 Australian mine sites and diamonds, sapphires, rubies and emeralds from around the world.

► *Howick St, Bathurst.*

11 Age of Fishes Museum

Chance discovery of treasure trove of fish fossils

It could so easily have ended in rubble; instead, an observant roadworker in 1955 decided to bulldoze to one side the strangely marked rock slab he had turned over. Later expert examination revealed the detailed impressions of over 100 ancient and bizarre freshwater fish. All had perished, trapped in shrinking waters as a large lake teeming with fish dried up during a severe drought 360 million years ago. Further excavations unearthed more than 3500 fossils – some with armoured shells, others with crocodile-like jaws and many new to science. Their massed remains constitute one of the world's greatest finds of fish fossils in one area. The original slab and many other exhibits are on display in the museum.

► *Gaskill St, Canowindra.*

12 Carcoar

Atmospheric mid-19th-century town

The little town of Carcoar has had both an interesting history and the good fortune to have been well preserved. In the early 1840s, this was the second-largest settlement west of the Blue Mountains; copper and gold discoveries later added to its prosperity. In 1863 it was the scene of Australia's first daylight bank hold-up, when bushrangers John Gilbert and John O'Meally, members of Ben Hall's gang, robbed the Commercial Bank (still standing and now a private residence). On a walking tour of the town you can visit the 1882 court house, with its cedar joinery and original fittings, and the convict-built Stoke Stable, now a small museum. Other heritage buildings house art and craft galleries and specialist shops.

► *51 km south-west of Bathurst via Mid Western Hwy.*

13 Cowra

Where wartime enemies became peacetime friends

During the Second World War, Cowra was the location of a prisoner-of-war camp and in 1944, in the chilly dark of an August night, the greatest mass escape of prisoners in modern military history occurred here when about 1000 Japanese prisoners stormed the camp's fences. More than 200 died from wounds or suicide and four Australian guards were killed. Information boards in the ruins of the camp tell the story. But from this tragedy came a lasting friendship, symbolised by the Australian and Japanese War Cemeteries and the beautiful Japanese Garden and Cultural Centre. Flowering cherry trees along Sakura Ave link the three sites, and each tree bears a plaque with the name of a local resident and a Japanese counterpart. A replica of the United Nations World Peace Bell, awarded to Cowra in 1992 for its commitment to international understanding, stands in Civic Square.

► *4 km north of Mid Western Hwy via Sakura Ave.*

14 Abercrombie Caves

Small but impressive cave system

These caves contain one of the largest natural limestone arches in the world – a 200-m-long tunnel, 60 m across at its widest point and with a roof height that in places soars to 30 m, which has been in existence for more than 2 million years. The cave system was used by bushrangers as a hideout in the 1830s; gold prospectors later built a dance floor in one section that has since been used for various events from boxing matches to weddings.

► *Abercrombie Karst Conservation Reserve, 72 km south-west of Bathurst via Old Goulburn Rd.*

Blue Mountains

The broad, river-carved plateau of the Blue Mountains was an early obstacle to European colonial expansion, and even once crossed it remained a wilderness, now protected by enormous national parks. Stupendous panoramas open out on all sides of the plateau and within are deep gorges, waterfalls and majestic rock formations.

1 Newnes

Atmospheric ruins of once thriving shale-mining town

Trees have reclaimed the skyline and much of the land. The houses are gone – mostly dismantled and transported elsewhere. Nevertheless, the substantial remains of this former oil-shale-mining town at the head of the beautiful Wolgan Valley convey a clear sense of what a bustling centre this once was. Founded in 1906 and abandoned in 1931, Newnes was home to 2000 people at its peak and had numerous shops, a school and a railway station; today only the old hotel is maintained, as an information kiosk. The Newnes Historic Ruins Walking Track winds through the remains of beehive-shaped coke ovens, chimneys and oil-storage tanks; kangaroos, wallabies and wombats are frequently spotted around the site. Halfway back down the Wolgan Valley, another track (8 km, 4 hours return) leads uphill to an old railway tunnel, now home to a large glow-worm colony.

▶ *47 km north-east of Lithgow via Castelreagh Hwy and Wolgan Rd.*

BRICK COKE OVENS ARE AMONG THE INTRIGUING RUINS AT NEWNES.

2 Zig Zag Railway

Astonishing feat of railway engineering

Reaching the western side of the Blue Mountains in 1866, railway engineers faced a monumental challenge: how to descend the almost sheer escarpment. Their ingenious solution, built over the next three years, involved the construction of zig-zagging railway lines, supported by tunnels and retaining walls, traversing back and forth across the cliff face. Replaced by another route in 1910, the line is now plied by tourist trains – steam locomotives and a diesel-powered vintage motor. Hop aboard to experience the stately steam-age pace and spectacular views over cliff, valley and viaduct.

▶ *Clarence Railway Station, 10 km east of Lithgow.*

3 Mount Wilson

Summer retreat of the wealthy, renowned for its gardens

The settlement is an oddity: tucked away amid wild bushland, far from the major centres of the Blue Mountains, with no shops and few services, yet brimming with grand homes surrounded by magnificent formal gardens. Wealthy Sydneysiders started coming here in the 1870s, building holiday homes where they could escape the summer heat. The volcanic soils – Mount Wilson sits atop a basalt outcrop – allowed them to grow an abundance of Old World plants and create elaborate formal gardens. Many are open to the public at weekends. You can also get a sense of the rich native vegetation that preceded the gardens at delightful picnic spots such as the Cathedral of Ferns, and descend to lookouts and gorges, notably that of the Wollangambe River, popular with canyoners.

▶ *25 km north-east of Great Western Hwy at Mount Victoria via Darling Causeway and Bells Line of Road.*

4 Mount Tomah Botanic Garden

Extensive collection of cold-climate plants in scenic location

Perched on terraces overlooking the Grose Valley, the gardens here harbour cold-climate plant species from all over the world, with roughly two-thirds coming from the Northern Hemisphere. Pathways lead through a rhododendron collection, Old-World formal garden, sphagnum bog, heathland and mist forest. Among the intriguing Southern-Hemisphere species are fine examples of the Wollemi pine, rediscovered in the Blue Mountains in 1994. Particularly attractive in autumn and spring, the gardens have a fine restaurant.

▶ *33 km east of Mount Victoria via Darling Causeway and Bells Line of Road.*

5 Hartley Historic Site

Early settlement bypassed by modernity

Once a busy staging post on the road west across the mountains, Hartley was left high and dry when the Great Western Railway was built further north in 1887. The residents drifted away, but the village remained intact and is now beautifully maintained by the NSW National Parks & Wildlife Service. The site encompasses 17 buildings of historic significance. The imposing Greek Revival–style court house, built in 1837, operated for 50 years. St Bernard's Church, completed in 1842, still holds services. Look out, too, for Old Trahlee Cottage (1840), the Shamrock Inn cottage (1841) and the post office (1846). Guided tours are available.

▶ *Great Western Hwy, 10 km north-west of Mount Victoria.*

Visitor information

Glenbrook 02 4738 5203
Katoomba 02 4780 5799
Lithgow 02 6350 3230
Oberon 02 6329 8210

6 Jenolan Caves

Labyrinthine system of tunnels, chambers and caverns

Talk about a grand entrance! After a hair-raising approach along a narrow road clinging to the steep sides of a spur of the Great Dividing Range, on arrival at Jenolan the bitumen disappears into the black, gaping maw of the 24-m-high Grand Arch. Not surprisingly, this archway caught the eye of the first-known European visitor, a convict bushranger, James McKeown, who used it and other caves nearby as hideouts. After he was captured in 1838, the caves drew a steady stream of visitors. Further exploration revealed a system of 300 or so subterranean chambers, 11 of which are open to visitors on guided tours that recount their origins and highlight their spectacular formations.

▶ *43 km south of Lithgow via Jenolan Caves Rd.*

7 Kanangra–Boyd National Park

Magical plateau above yawning chasm

The vantage points along the easy Lookout Walk (10 minutes from the car park) reveal breathtaking views of Kanangra Walls, the sheer sandstone cliffs that rim the Boyd Plateau, and, below, a giddying 500-m drop to Kanangra Creek. Beyond, row upon row of pyramidal bush-cloaked hills extend as far as the eye can see. Take the time to walk the Plateau Track (4 hours) across the heath-covered tops and yet more wonders will be revealed, including a cave once used for dances, vertigo-inducing views from the cliff edge, and startlingly diverse birdlife, including firetail finches and glossy black cockatoos. The road from the highway is unsealed but usually suitable for 2WD.

▶ *66 km south of Lithgow via Jenolan Caves Rd.*

8 Mount York Historic Site

Follow the tortuous descent of the original Cox's Road

Occasional traffic jams on the Great Western Highway may make the motorist's blood boil, but a visit to Mount York shows that we have little to lament compared to early travellers. Building the first road across the Blue Mountains in 1814 (see p. 152), William Cox reached this spot high above the plains at Hartley and carved out a steep, winding track down the north-eastern side of the narrow headland. Today you can walk down the old road, viewing convict-built walls and drainage culverts, taking in the sublime valley and bushland views, and marvelling that any carriage or bullock train ever made it down in one piece. A safer route via Lawsons Long Alley was built in 1823, and 10 years later the road was diverted via Victoria Pass, where the highway still runs.

▶ *5 km north-west of Mount Victoria.*

9 Govett's Leap

Peer into the depths of the grand Grose Valley

From the lookout atop 160-m cliffs, a deep, thickly forested valley flanked by towering escarpments snakes into the distance. Visible to the right and accessible via a clifftop track is beautiful Bridal Veil Falls, whose slender column of water sways in the breeze while tumbling 190 m to the valley floor. Prominent along the northern side of the valley is a columnar outcrop known as Pulpit Rock, which can be reached via a delightful walking track along the escarpment (3 hours return) or via Hat Hill Road and a shorter 400-m walk from the road. It is crowned by spectacular viewpoints reached by means of a series of stairs and ladders – not for the faint-hearted!

▶ *Blue Mountains National Park, 3 km east of Blackheath via Govetts Leap Rd.*

KANANGRA-BOYD
NATIONAL PARK

The way west

For much of its route across the Blue Mountains, the Great Western Highway follows the track taken by the plateau's first, convict-built road.

On his return in 1814 from plotting a road route over the Blue Mountains, surveyor George Evans asserted that a dozen men 'might clear a good road in three months for a cart to travel over the mountains'. Delighted by this assessment, Governor Lachlan Macquarie immediately appointed William Cox, a former soldier who had settled on a farm near Windsor, to oversee construction of the road, starting at Penrith and ending at Bathurst on the edge of the Western Plains.

Though they didn't quite meet Evans' target, the builders accomplished a remarkable feat. Thirty convicts took just six months to clear a carriageway through the thick bush, atop sandstone ridges rising up to 1000 m high. The 161-km road thereafter became the fledgling colony's lifeline, as settlers began to flow westward and the bounty of the pastoralists' labours was hauled back to the coast. As a reward, all the convicts who worked on the road were granted a full pardon.

10 Hydro Majestic Hotel

Ornate Art Deco establishment with suitably grand views

From the highway, the Hydro Majestic is eye-catching enough, with its domes, turrets and porticos; seen from the Megalong Valley below or from a lookout such as Hargraves Lookout west of Blackheath, it is revealed as truly dramatic, its string of cream buildings perched at the very edge of a precipitous slope dropping hundreds of metres to the valley below. The hotel was opened in 1904 by retailer Mark Foy, who had transformed three earlier buildings on the site to create a luxurious 'hydropathic establishment' offering spa therapies, and was soon attracting glamorous guests from all over the world. A network of walking tracks was constructed below the hotel and can still be accessed from adjacent side streets. The hotel's cafe and restaurant make the most of the spellbinding views.

▶ *Great Western Hwy, Medlow Bath.*

11 Echo Point

Iconic vista of vast wilderness landscape

The view from this wide lookout is the most famous in the Blue Mountains: the trio of rock pinnacles known as the Three Sisters dominates the foreground; straight ahead is the broad mesa of Mount Solitary; and beyond, on all sides, on a clear day, forested ridges, rounded peaks and cliff-rimmed tablelands stretch as far as the eye can see. Walking tracks follow nearby cliff lines to lookouts offering varying perspectives on this grand panorama, and descend via hundreds of hewn steps to and along the thickly forested floor of the Jamison Valley. An easier descent and, more importantly, ascent are available at nearby Scenic World, via the adrenalin-boosting Scenic Railway, a historic mining track that drops 250 m through a gorge (it's said to be the steepest incline railway in the world), or the more sedate Scenic Cableway, a Swiss-manufactured cable car; both connect with a rainforest boardwalk.

▶ *Blue Mountains National Park, 3 km south of Great Western Hwy at Katoomba.*

12 Everglades Gardens

Delightful landscaped terraces on the edge of the escarpment

Seeking to create a mountain retreat on a grand scale, businessman Henri Van De Velde in 1933 employed renowned Danish-born horticulturist and landscape designer Paul Sorenson to tame and transform 5 ha of steeply sloping ground overlooking the Jamison Valley. With the assistance of 60 labourers, Sorenson levelled terraces, laid pathways, built drystone walls and even excavated a grotto. Trees, shrubs and flowers were planted in intriguing formal arrangements and planned to produce broad splashes of colour at different times of year. Today, visitors can wander the picturesque pathways to arbours and lookouts, and enter Van De Velde's stylish Art Deco residence, which now incorporates tearooms and a shop.

▶ *2 km south of Great Western Hwy at Leura.*

13 Wentworth Falls

Follow in the footsteps of Charles Darwin, and share his delight

Emerging from the walking track that now bears his name at the top of this waterfall in 1836, Charles Darwin was thunder-struck by the sight that met his eyes: 'Suddenly & without any preparation, through the trees, which border the pathway, an immense gulf is seen … thickly covered with forest.' Much the same scene meets today's visitor, who can penetrate further into the Jamison Valley and aptly named Valley of the Waters via stairways and walking tracks. Outstanding among the many walks is the 4-hour National Pass, which at one point runs for 3 km along a broad ledge, halfway down the escarpment, en route to the falls. Atop the cliffs, described by Darwin as 'certainly [the] most stupendous cliffs I have ever seen', are lookouts, picnic areas and the stylish Conservation Hut cafe.

▶ *Blue Mountains National Park, 2 km south of Great Western Hwy at Wentworth Falls.*

14 Norman Lindsay Gallery

Showcase for prolific artist

Painter, cartoonist and writer Norman Lindsay was a controversial figure in his time, scandalising society with his voluptuous nudes and bohemian lifestyle, though to many today he is best known as the author of the raucous children's book *The Magic Pudding*. Purchased in 1912, the house was, in effect, a large canvas on which Lindsay could further display and extend his artistry. He added Classical-style colonnades, built a pool flanked by terraces, and adorned the garden with statues of nymphs and satyrs. All can still be viewed today, along with a large range of paintings, etchings, sketches and illustrations on display in the main house. Adjoining Lindsay's former etching studio is an excellent cafe.

▶ *3 km north of Great Western Hwy at Faulconbridge (follow signs).*

15 Red Hands Cave

Where the Blue Mountains' original inhabitants left their mark

It was during a search for a missing child in 1913 that Europeans first discovered this remarkable gallery, hidden deep in the bush in the lower Blue Mountains. On the cave wall is a colourful array of stencils of hands, created by Dharug people between 1600 and 500 years ago. You can drive to the site, but it's far better to walk in from Glenbrook Causeway car park along the 6-km (3-hours-return) Red Hands Cave Track, which skirts picturesque pools and creeks and traverses extensive eucalypt woodland. At roughly the halfway point is a short (400-m) detour via the Link Track to view axe-grinding grooves atop a rock, made by Dharug people when sharpening axes on the stone.

▶ *Blue Mountains National Park, 1 km south-east of Great Western Hwy at Glenbrook.*

Sydney Region

Australia's largest city sprawls across more than 1800 sq km, west to the Blue Mountains, north to the Hawkesbury River and south to Botany Bay, and encompasses a huge range of historical and cultural sites and natural wonders along its bush-clad bays, dramatically eroded sandstone cliffs, and sandy coves.

1 Windsor

Unrivalled collection of colonial buildings

Following floods along the Hawkesbury River, in 1810 Governor Lachlan Macquarie ordered the creation of five settlements on safe, high ground in the valley. The 'Macquarie towns' as they became known – Windsor, Richmond, Wilberforce, Pitt Town and Castlereagh – were the first towns founded outside of Sydney. Of these, Windsor was the largest. Planned around a village square, it became the administrative centre of the region, and today it probably retains more early colonial buildings than any other town in Australia. The jewels in its architectural crown are St Matthew's Anglican Church (1817–20) and the court house (1820), both designed by Francis Greenway, but there are at least 50 other heritage buildings, including the country's oldest pub, the Macquarie Arms (1811).

► *56 km north-west of Sydney via M2 and Old Windsor Rd.*

2 Barrenjoey Head

Lighthouse-capped outcrop with sweeping views

Ten thousand years ago, the delightful walk along Station Beach to Barrenjoey Head would not have been possible: the headland had then been cut off from the mainland by rising sea levels and was only reconnected when sand later accumulated to form a spit. From the base of the head-land today, the track winds uphill to lookouts affording magnificent views of tranquil Pittwater, the wide inlet to the west, and out over the ocean to the east. At the summit is Barrenjoey Lighthouse, designed by NSW Colonial Architect James Barnet, completed in 1881, and recently carefully restored, along with the nearby lighthouse-keepers' cottages.

► *Palm Beach, 42 km north of Sydney.*

LOOKING SOUTH FROM BARRENJOEY HEAD

3 Elizabeth Farm

Australia's oldest homestead and birthplace of its wool industry

Not only has this handsome 1793 building been restored to its original state, but also the interior is filled with reproductions of the furniture and artefacts that belonged to its first owners, the Macarthur family. Visitors are thus transported back in time and given an authentic sense of the lifestyle of early colonial days. John Macarthur arrived here in 1793 to take up a grant of 100 acres (40 ha) of prime land, and named the property after his wife. He steadily expanded his operations, developed an interest in woolgrowing, and brought the first merino sheep here from Spain.

▶ *70 Alice St, Rosehill, 22 km west of Sydney.*

4 Cockatoo Island

Spend a day – or a night – exploring convict and maritime heritage

The largest island in Sydney Harbour, Cockatoo Island is now World Heritage–listed as one of 11 significant Australian convict sites. It was a prison between 1839 and 1869, and the convict barracks, mess hall and guardhouse can still be viewed. In 1857, the convicts completed Australia's first dry dock, which became the basis of major dockyard operations after the jail closed. In the 20th century, the island was the site of a shipbuilding facility that produced dozens of warships and maintained hundreds of others. Slipways, workshops and cranes still line the docks. Public ferries service the island, guided tours are on offer, and there's even a camp site if you want to stay longer.

▶ *Sydney Harbour, 10 km west of city centre, north of Balmain.*

Visitor information

Clarendon (Hawkesbury Valley) 02 4578 0233
Parramatta 02 8839 3311
Sydney 02 9240 8788

TARONGA, A ZOO WITH A VIEW

5 Taronga Zoo

Enthralling menagerie in eminently desirable location

Leafy surrounds, immaculate gardens, sweeping harbour views, ferry service at the door: it's the kind of residence most Sydneysiders dream about and few can afford. The residents of Taronga Zoo may not fully appreciate their salubrious accommodation, but visitors will certainly relish it, along with its wonderful range of exhibits. Hop off the ferry and onto the zoo's 'Sky Safari' cable car for a thrilling overview, then wander the twisting pathways through bushland to beautifully designed displays. Ranger talks take place several times a day, and you can even arrange a 'Roar & Snore' – an overnight stay in safari tents.

▶ *Bradleys Head Rd, Mosman, Sydney.*

6 Sydney Harbour Bridge

Iconic, still-impressive engineering marvel

The climb to the apex of the giant metal arch, 134 m above the sea, certainly enhances your appreciation for the 1400 workers who toiled for eight years to piece together this magnificent structure, which on completion in 1932 was the world's longest single-span bridge (it's still the largest and widest). It also rewards your not insignificant effort – the climb involves steep ladders, catwalks and many, many steps – with astounding 360-degree views, encompassing the city's cluster of towers, rows of headlands, boats flitting across the harbour and, disconcertingly far below, the steady flow of traffic and trains across its 503-m span. But it's not essential to join a commercial tour to partake of the bridge's splendour and the achievement it embodies: a stroll across the footpath, an ascent of the Pylon Lookout (a mere 200 stairs), or even just silent contemplation from a nearby waterside park can suffice.

▶ *Bradfield Hwy, Sydney.*

7 The Big Dig

Where plague preserved the past

In 1900, bubonic plague struck Sydney. Fearing that the dilapidated houses in The Rocks would become breeding grounds for the disease, the state government purchased the century-old buildings on Cribbs and Carahers lanes and demolished the houses. The area was later paved over to provide parking, but no other buildings were constructed. In 1994, when the paving was removed, it revealed a treasure trove of the footings of some of the country's earliest buildings and more than a million artefacts from the earliest days of settlement. The stylish Sydney Harbour Youth Hostel now stands here, but has been built in such a way that 85 per cent of the archaeological site is visible at ground level. Explanations and artefacts are displayed in interpretive panels on adjacent lanes and streets, enhancing appreciation of this window onto the city's beginnings.

▶ *Cumberland St, The Rocks, Sydney.*

8 Sydney Opera House

A unique building in a magical setting

One of the marvels of Danish architect Jørn Utzon's extraordinary design, still vibrant and modern decades after the building's completion in 1973, is that you never quite feel as though you have the measure of it, even after repeated visits. Approach from a different angle or follow another route around the exterior and you discover an entirely new perspective, the huddle of peaked arches somehow reconfiguring themselves into a fresh arrangement of towering forms and shadows, their tiled surfaces taking on subtly different shades in the everchanging light. The building's splendid isolation on Bennelong Point and the shimmering backdrop of the harbour enhance these effects magically. Inside, guided tours are the best way to learn about the turbulent history of construction, view the interior's monumental concrete beams, glass walls and timber-lined halls, and peek backstage in the concert hall and theatres. Taking in a performance rounds off a visit perfectly.

▶ *Bennelong Point, Sydney.*

9 Fort Denison

Distinctive island fortress in the heart of Sydney Harbour

Concerns about foreign designs on British colonies prompted the construction of various defensive structures around Sydney in the mid-19th century. By far the most distinctive of the significant number still standing is this fortress on what was a tiny rocky island known to Aboriginal people as Mat-te-wan-ye and to Europeans as Pinchgut. Construction began in 1841 but was not completed until 1857, at which point the fort was named after the then governor of New South Wales, Sir William Denison. The imposing defences include a Martello tower, the only one in Australia and the last to be built in the British Empire. Ferries depart from Circular Quay and Darling Harbour, guided tours are available, and there is a stylish restaurant.

▶ *Sydney Harbour, 3 km north-west of city centre.*

TAKING IN THE VIEW FROM
SYDNEY HARBOUR BRIDGE

10 Royal Botanic Gardens

Exquisite harbourside refuge

Set beneath the city centre's skyscrapers on the shores of Farm Cove (site of the colony's first farm), the gardens display more than a million plants belonging to 11,000 species, spread over more than 30 ha. Pathways wind through themed plantings including a rose garden, fernery, palm grove and succulents garden, to picturesque picnic spots, cafes and harbourside vantage points, notably Mrs Macquarie's Chair, a stone bench carved in 1810 by convicts so that Governor Macquarie's wife, Elizabeth, could savour the splendid view. Wildlife resident in the park includes more than 100 species of birds and the Sydney region's only colony of pearl white butterflies.

► *Enter via Opera House forecourt, Macquarie St or Mrs Macquarie's Rd, Sydney.*

11 Hyde Park Barracks

One of Sydney's earliest and best-preserved buildings

This three-storey red brick structure, completed in 1819 and designed by the convict-architect Francis Greenway, is one of the most graceful in the city. It was built on the orders of Governor Lachlan Macquarie as accommodation for convicts working at various sites around Sydney, and after 1848 became lodgings for female immigrants and an asylum for destitute women, and later government offices. The museum housed in the refurbished building today uses interactive displays and re-enactments to recount the story of the barracks' diverse occupants and, by reflection, the history of the city.

► *Macquarie St, Sydney.*

SYDNEY AREA

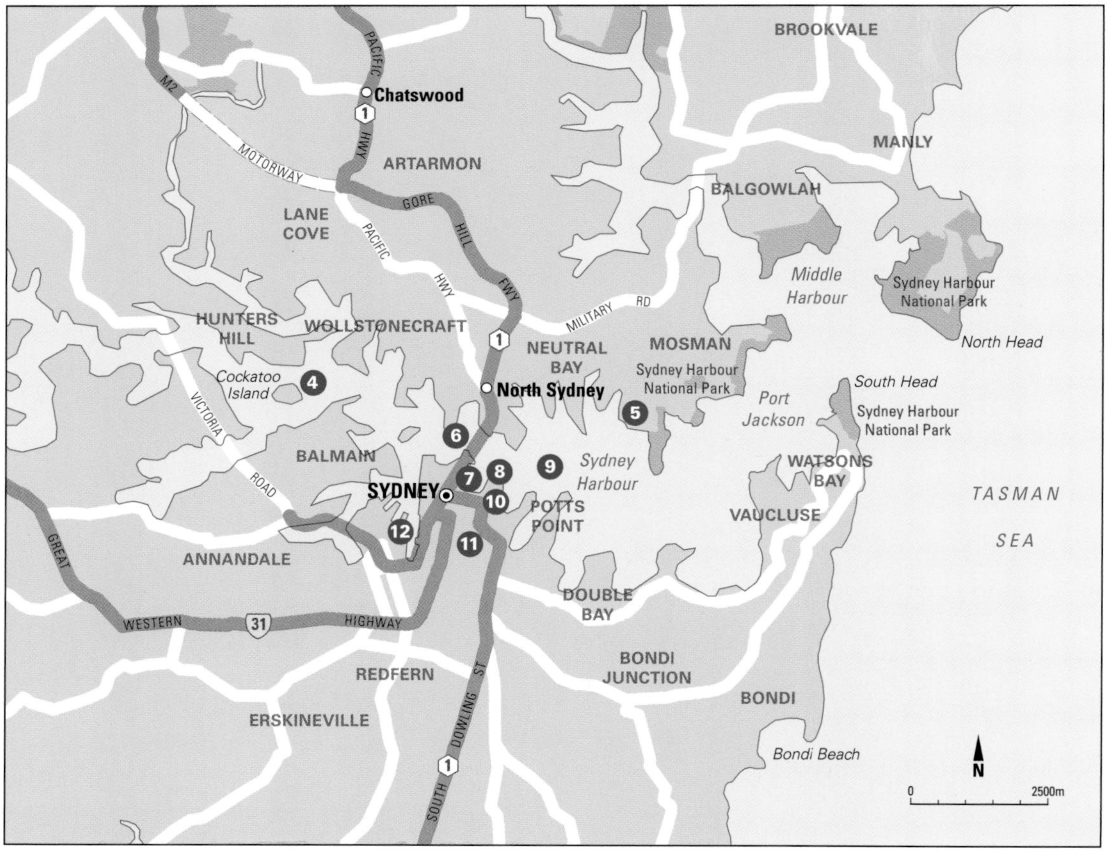

The people's harbour

Few cities encompass a harbour as splendid as Sydney's, and even fewer have managed to preserve such large tracts of foreshore for public enjoyment.

As early as 1879, islands in the harbour were being set aside for recreation, and several stretches of shoreline were gazetted as public reserves in the early 1900s. Through the 20th century, environmentally minded figures campaigned for a major harbour reserve and in 1975 Sydney Harbour National Park was created to preserve a diverse collection of islands, reserves and historic sites.

Waterside walks

One of the chief benefits of the park is that it protects extensive areas threaded by superb harbourside bushwalks. Just a short ferry ride away from Circular Quay, the track around Bradleys Head skirts bushland, rock platforms and secluded beaches, and provides wonderful views back to the city. At South Head, a trail leads to beautiful Camp Cove, where the First Fleet camped for a night before landing at what is now Circular Quay the next day, and along the cliffs to headland lookouts. More challenging and bracing is the 10-km walk from Spit Bridge to Manly Cove, which climbs to high coastal heath with majestic views and takes in rainforest pockets, a lighthouse and secluded coves.

Views of the past

The park also protects a range of historic artefacts and structures. There are fine Aboriginal rock engravings at Shark Point and Dobroyd Head, and colonial fortifications at Georges Head. Goat Island is the site of an 1830s powder magazine and water police station. At North Head, whose tall cliffs provide some of the finest views across the harbour entrance and back to the city, you can tour and even stay at the 1830s quarantine station, now a hotel.

12 Australian National Maritime Museum

Exploring the nation's links with the sea

The founding of Australia and its early growth were dependent on the endeavours of ocean-going explorers and traders. This splendid maritime museum, housing more than 40,000 artefacts, thus reveals much about the city's history, as well as a wealth of information on the worldwide development of ships and navigation. The museum has one of the world's largest fleets of historic vessels – 14 vessels, including a replica of Cook's *Endeavour*; a former navy submarine, HMAS *Otway*; and the retired destroyer HMAS *Vampire*.

▶ *Darling Harbour, Sydney.*

13 Captain Cook's Landing Place

Site of Cook's fateful first mainland visit

On 29 April 1770, James Cook's *Endeavour* landed at what is now Kurnell. For eight days, the crew explored the coast, making the first contact with Aboriginal people, while the expedition's botanists Joseph Banks and Daniel Solander gathered specimens – so many that Cook named the adjacent inlet Botany Bay. A monument marks the site of the landing, and displays in the Discovery Centre chronicle the 'Eight Days That Changed the World'. The Burrawang Walk (1 km) offers a fine introduction to native plants. You can also follow the Muru and Yena tracks (2.5 km) to the coastal cliffs, or drive out to Cape Solander, a prime whale-watching spot during the May-to-November migration.

▶ *Kamay Botany National Park, 37 km south of Sydney.*

Southern Highlands and Illawarra

This region has two distinct parts. Inland, on the highlands, are handsome and historic villages and towns with both gentle farmlands and mountainous wilderness within easy reach. In the east, a narrow strip lies between a striking coastline of headlands and beaches and the sandstone cliffs of a high escarpment.

1 Box Vale Tramway

Follow a former tramway to a superb gorge-edge lookout

Built in 1888, the tramway operated until 1896 and carried to Mittagong coal hauled in skips up a steep incline from a mine at the bottom of Nattai Gorge. Today the tramway makes a fine and fairly level elevated walkway (9 km return). The route includes narrow fern-filled cuttings and an 85-m-long tunnel (a torch is a big help in negotiating the dimly lit rutted floor). At the end are the old coal-loading area and new clifftop picnic tables, where you can enjoy superb views north to the Blue Mountains. Along the way are information panels and photographs of the tramway in use.

▶ *2 km north of Hume Hwy at Mittagong via Box Vale Rd.*

2 Berrima

Picture-perfect colonial village, complete with prison

Even on a wintry day, few visitors can resist a stroll around the compact collection of graceful old buildings – fine civic structures of local sandstone and neat Georgian cottages – that make up the village of Berrima. But they may feel a chill, even on a summer's day, as they stand in front of the bench in its imposing court house (1838), site of the colony's first trial by jury and now a museum, or gaze from its grand Doric façade across the road to the high walls of the country's oldest jail, notorious, among other reasons, for the execution here in 1885 of a member of Captain Moonlight's bushranging gang. For today's visitors, Berrima's saving grace was being twice bypassed, first by the Southern Railway in 1867 and more than a century later, in 1992, by the Hume Highway, leaving its unique heritage and attractive streetscapes remarkably intact.

▶ *8 km north-west of Moss Vale.*

3 Harper's Mansion

Georgian home with a heritage garden and a modern maze

This is not quite a mansion, but when built by James Harper in 1834, the two-storey structure was certainly the grandest house in the village. Now restored and filled with period furnishings, it is open on Sundays for inspection. Of equal interest is its refurbished cottage garden, which is filled with heritage roses and cool-climate shrubs, and the kitchen garden, planted with early forms of the fruits and vegetables it once contained, to mirror the original as closely as possible. Entirely new, though, is the lavender-edged maze that covers the area once occupied by the coach-house and stables.

▶ *Wilkinson St, Berrima.*

FITZROY FALLS AND LOOKOUT

4 International Cricket Hall of Fame

You'll be bowled over by this, in a thoroughly modern way

It sits alongside the Bradman Museum, in the home town of the great Don, and on the edge of the picturesque oval that bears his name: not a museum, but a series of themed galleries with interactive experiences that bring the game and its legends to life. You can play a match with friends using touch screens to try different batting strokes and bowling techniques; view on-demand footage of the best players of all time; and, using the centre's database of interviews, ask questions of modern cricket greats. Afterwards, visit the Bradman Museum with its extensive collection of cricketing memorabilia.

► *St Jude St, Bowral, 11 km east of Hume Hwy via Old Hume Hwy.*

5 Fitzroy Falls

Lacy waters plummet into deep, rainforest-filled ravine

It's slightly unnerving, stepping onto the steel mesh platform that juts into space beside the falls. Look down through the mesh, and way beneath your feet is a glistening tumble of water-worn boulders, while just to your left Yarrunga Creek begins its misty 82-m dive into the abyss. The lookout is reached from the visitor centre by an elevated walkway. From here walking tracks continue east and west around the rim of the horseshoe-shaped escarpment to further vantage points.

► *Morton National Park, 35 km south-east of Hume Hwy via Illawarra Hwy, Moss Vale and Kangaloon Rd.*

Visitor information

Kiama 02 4232 3322
Mittagong 02 4871 2888
Shellharbour 02 4221 6169
Wollongong 02 4227 5545

Follow the shoreline

The coast-hugging Grand Pacific Drive runs for 140 km from Stanwell Park to Nowra, sweeping south under the coastal escarpment, past pockets of rainforest and a string of former coal-mining villages.

Signs marked with a logo showing a road curving across the landscape point the way. At the northern end, Bald Hill, above Stanwell Park, hang-gliders soar through the air, harnessing the same onshore winds that led Edward Hargrave to fly box kites here in experiments that influenced early aircraft design. The view south along the scalloped coast is sensational and offers a preview of the drive's route and first glimpse of its undoubted highlight, the 665-m Sea Cliff Bridge, jutting dramatically out over pounding waves. Many take advantage of the parking bay at the bridge's southern end to stop and walk its length (allow 45 minutes return) – keep an eye out for whales in winter.

Rising on the west are the forested slopes and sandstone crests of the mighty Illawarra Escarpment. Beneath it run seams of high-grade coal, and throughout the 20th century collieries at Coalcliff, Scarborough, Wombarra and Coledale fed the steel-making industry of Wollongong. But times are changing and today modern mansions outnumber workers' cottages in these old villages, reflecting the region's diversification from heavy industry into education and technology.

Beaches, lakes and bays

South of Wollongong's sandy surfing beaches and pretty, park-edged boat harbour, the route passes the steel-works of Port Kembla to skirt the eastern edge of Lake Illawarra, then continues on through lush lands once logged for their dense forests and now a prime dairy district. Near Kiama century-old dry-stone walls divide some of the paddocks. The drive ends with the crossing of the Shoalhaven River, at Nowra.

SPECTACULAR SEA CLIFF BRIDGE

6 Kangaroo Valley

Fertile valley encircled by sandstone bluffs

The beauty of Kangaroo Valley is best appreciated from the roads that follow the steep flanks of its guardian peaks and offer views down over the patchwork of lush fields and forested hills. On the valley floor, the medieval-style Hampden Suspension Bridge, known for its crenellated stone towers, provides a dramatic entrance across the river to Kangaroo Valley township. It was completed in 1898 – just in time, as it happened: five days later a sudden flood washed away the old timber bridge it replaced. The river here is popular for swimming and canoeing, while the adjacent Pioneer Museum Park features an 1840s settlers hut, bush school, pioneer household and farm equipment and an interactive sound system describing life in the 1900s.

▶ *19 km north-west of Princes Hwy at Berry via Kangaroo Valley Rd.*

7 Cambewarra Mountain Lookout

Misty mountain high

Reached by a twisting drive, this lookout atop the Cambewarra Range commands sweeping views of the coastal plain, from Coolangatta Mountain in the north to Pigeon House Mountain (see p. 170) in the south. At an altitude of almost 680 m, it can be wreathed in mist even in summer, as warm air rises up the mountainside. You'll find picnic and barbecue facilities on the top, as well as a tearoom.

▶ *10 km north-west of Princes Hwy at Bomaderry via Moss Vale Rd.*

8 Bundanon

Where painted landscapes come to life

True to his belief that 'you can't own a landscape', artist Arthur Boyd, and his wife Yvonne, granted this property – the 1860s Bundanon Homestead and 1100 ha of pristine bushland overlooking the Shoalhaven River – to the Australian people. A visit here includes a guided tour of the homestead to view artworks in the impressive Bundanon Collection, which includes art and crafts by Arthur Boyd and five generations of the Boyd family dynasty, as well as works by Sidney Nolan, John Perceval, Joy Hester and Charles Blackman. Follow up with an inspection of the artist's studio and a walk through the riverside scenery that inspired much of his work. Open every Sunday.

▶ *22 km west of Princes Hwy at Nowra via Illaroo Rd.*

9 Royal National Park

Breathing space for a growing city

Bequeathed to the public in 1879 by far-sighted forefathers, this was the first national park in Australia and the second in the world. Despite its 'Royal' prefix, adopted after a visit by the Queen in 1954, this has always been a peoples' park, easily accessible by car and public transport, with a range of activities and tightly packed with a diversity of habitat and scenery. Its offerings range from Edwardian pleasure grounds at Audley, with hire boats and riverside picnic lawns, to the cliff-top grandeur and sparkling beaches of its eastern edge and the high sandstone plateau of heathland, woodland and open wetlands that stretch west.

It is crisscrossed by walking tracks, including Lady Carrington Drive (10 km, 3 hours one way, easy), which follows the Hacking River through rainforest – listen and look for lyrebirds.

▶ *3 km south of Princes Hwy at Loftus via Farnell Ave.*

10 Mount Keira Lookout

Panoramic coastal vantage point

On a clear day, the staggering vista from the summit of Mount Keira, some 457 m above sea level, stretches from Kurnell, 50 km to the north, to Jervis Bay 60 km to the south. Spread out below are the beaches and suburbs of Wollongong and glittering Lake Illawarra; offshore is the wave-ringed cluster of Five Islands. You can enjoy a picnic lunch here, or take advantage of a superbly sited cafe. The Mount Keira Ring Track (5.5 km, 4 hours, medium difficulty) encircles the summit, in part following the route of an early convict-built road; sweeping views open up at points along the way.

▶ *6 km west of Princes Hwy at West Wollongong via Mount Keira Rd.*

11 Nan Tien Temple

Magnificent modern Buddhist temple

The name translates as 'paradise of the south'. Strikingly dramatic and a world away from the surrounding suburbia and nearby industry, this grand, red-roofed Buddhist temple, complete with a towering pagoda, was built using traditional techniques and materials by Chinese craftsmen and opened in 1995. Enter the 22-ha complex by the impressive Mountain Gate to stroll in the landscaped gardens, inspect the temple interiors (the main shrine has five large Buddhas surrounded by 10,000 smaller ones) and visit the museum. Then relax in the tranquil teahouse with a coffee or exotic tea.

▶ *2 km east of Princes Hwy at Berkeley via Five Islands Rd, Glastonbury Ave and Berkeley Rd.*

12 Illawarra Fly Treetop Walk

Exhilarating bird's-eye views

Two walkways, 25 m above the forest floor, take visitors on a 500-m swaying stroll through the canopy of a temperate rainforest and right to the edge of the escarpment. In your perch in the treetops you may be joined by some of the locals – kookaburras, cockatoos and rosellas – and you'll certainly share their outlook over Lake Illawarra to the ocean. And there is more in store. The walkway culminates in a spiralling tower with a platform 45 m from ground level for truly top views.

▶ *Budderoo National Park, 30 km north-west of Princes Hwy at Kiama via Jamberoo Rd.*

13 Minnamurra Rainforest Centre

A rare remnant of once widespread forest

Protected in a canyon at the base of the Illawarra Escarpment is a surviving tract of the varied rainforest that once swathed these hills. Bird's-nest fern, elkhorns and orchids cling to the trunks and boughs of towering trees and can be seen from an elevated boardwalk that meanders beneath the canopy to a viewing platform (1.6 km, 1 hour). Birdlife is prolific, and you may even spot a normally shy lyrebird.

▶ *Budderoo National Park, 15 km north-west of Princes Hwy at Kiama via Jamberoo Rd.*

14 The Blowhole

Awesome quirk of nature

Kiama's star attraction is the Blowhole. Here the ocean waves have hollowed out a cavern under the rocky headland and, when seas are running strongly from the south-east, water driven into the opening is forced upwards and out through a hole in the rocks above. The spray can burst upwards to a height of 60 m; fenced viewing areas allow you to safely watch the spectacle. If the 'big' Blowhole isn't performing, you'll find a smaller version – the Little Blowhole – a few headlands to the south along the scenic Kiama Coast Walk. Displays here depend on the prevailing north-east seas, and so are more frequent, while the smaller opening means the plume, while of less volume than its larger relative, is tall and straight.

▶ *Blowhole Point, Kiama, 2 km east of Princes Hwy via Terralong St.*

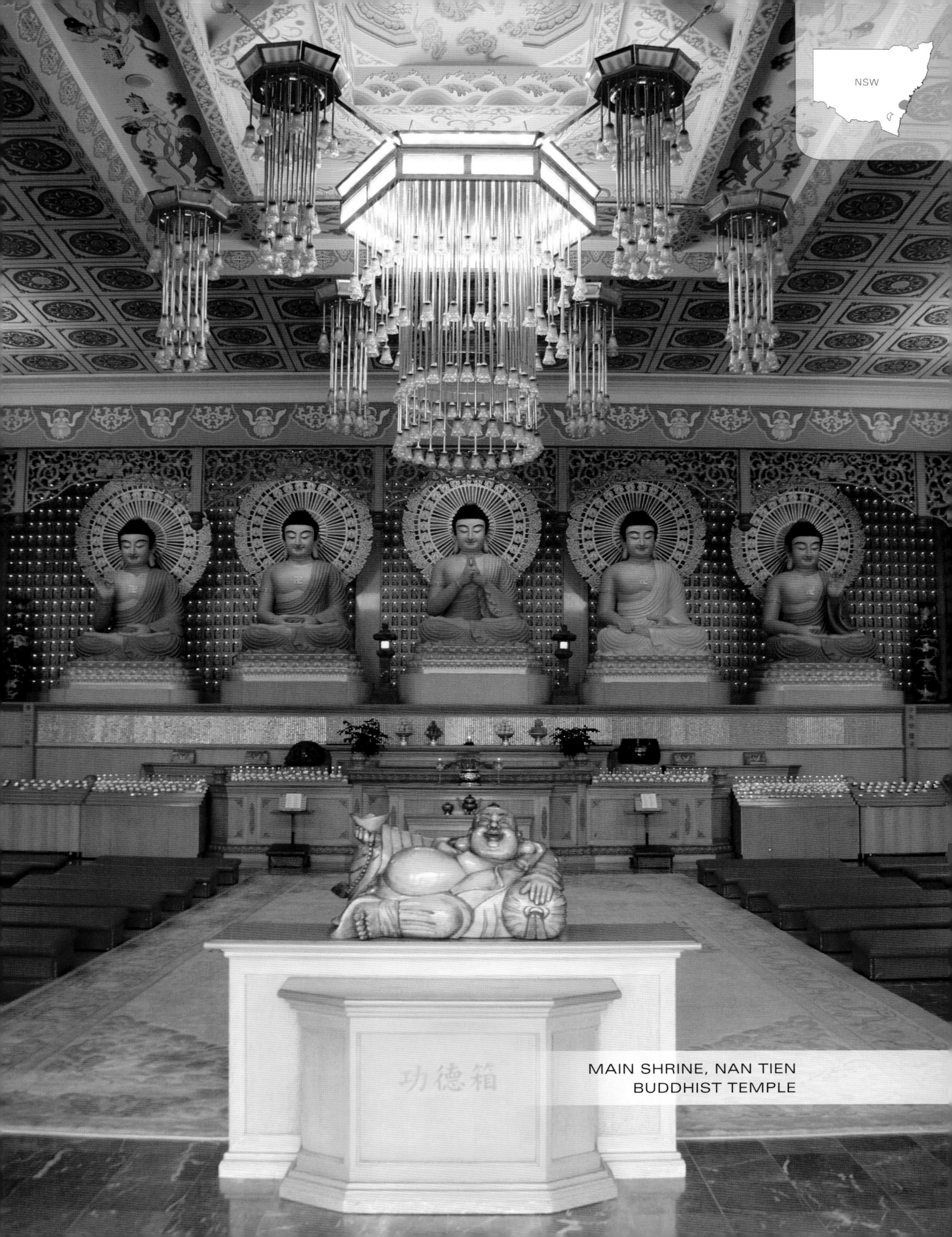

MAIN SHRINE, NAN TIEN
BUDDHIST TEMPLE

Southern Tablelands

The scenic rolling uplands on the western flank of the Great Dividing Range between Sydney and Canberra were the site of early and prosperous pastoral properties. Still tranquil and unspoiled, many of the farming settlements here are now home to other endeavours, including arts and crafts and winemaking.

1 Wombeyan Caves

Five show chambers of extraordinary formations

These remarkable caves were long known to the local Gandangara people and feature in Dreaming stories – they are said to have been created when one ancestor being was trying to extract another from a hiding place. John Macarthur and John Oxley visited the caves in the 1820s and they were opened to the public in 1865. Today, access to four of the largest caves is by guided tour, while visits to a fifth, Fig Tree Cave, can be self-guided. Kooringa is the smallest of the caves, but perhaps the most beautiful, with its richly adorned shawls and stalagmites. Wollondilly Cave is noted for its spectacular flowstones.

► *71 km north of Goulburn via Oberon–Goulburn Rd and Wombeyan Caves Rd.*

2 Taralga

Charming, tranquil heritage village

Founded in the 1820s, this quiet farming settlement is lined with early timber-slab and stone buildings of a distinctive style: substantial, with large windows, and mainly built of local stone dug up from the surrounding land as it was cleared for pasture. Pick up a map from one of the local shops and wander the quiet streets. Among the earliest structures is the former Commercial Hotel (1860), now a private residence; the still-operating Argyle Inn dates from 1856. No fewer than four churches were built here in the 1860s: the Presbyterian church (1861), St Ignatius Roman Catholic Church (1864), St Luke's Anglican Church (1866) and the Methodist church (1868). This last is now the site of the local historical society's museum (open weekends); in the adjoining grounds are an old dairy building and restored settler's slab hut.

► *49 km north of Goulburn on Oberon–Goulburn Rd.*

3 St Saviour's Cathedral

Unfinished, but still one of Australia's grandest Gothic churches

When construction began in 1874 on what would become this magnificent cathedral, a church called St Saviour's already existed on the site – its bricks now form the cathedral's floor. The bishop of Goulburn, Mesac Thomas, had commissioned noted architect Edmund Blacket to come up with a design based on the parish church at Heckington, Lincolnshire, England. The builders remained true to Blacket's ambitious, dramatic vision until it came to the belltower, which was put on hold time after time and not finished until 1988; the proposed spire was never built. Nevertheless, the cathedral is a major work, considered one of Blacket's finest. The interior is rich in carved stonework, including a magnificent pulpit and exquisitely carved roundels, as well as stupendous stained glass.

► *Church St, Goulburn.*

Visitor information

Bungendore 02 6238 1422
Goulburn 02 4823 4492
Queanbeyan 02 6299 7307
Yass 02 6266 2557

4 Goulburn Brewery

Sample the ales in Australia's oldest surviving brewery building

The brewery is part of a remarkable industrial complex, Bradley Grange, designed for brothers Thomas and William Bradley by the famous colonial architect Francis Greenway and built in 1835. Around the brewing hall stand a flour mill, maltings, a tobacco kiln and a cooperage. The brewery operated continuously, under various owners, until 1929, when it closed. Renovated in the 1980s, it now incorporates a hotel, theatre-restaurant and tearooms, and once again brews its own fine ales. Guided tours take place at weekends and there is a monthly crafts market on the fourth Saturday of every month.

▶ *Bungonia St, Goulburn.*

5 Bungonia Gorge

Sheer-walled chasm throws down the gauntlet to walkers, cavers and climbers

The centrepiece of Bungonia National Park, one of the state's oldest conservation areas, is this narrow limestone 'slot' canyon with near-vertical walls rising 300 m high. Fine views of the gorge can be enjoyed from The Lookdown and Adam's Lookout, both only a short stroll from the road and linked by the easy Green Track walk, which follows a 5.5-km circuit around the plateau, taking in lookouts with superb views. Fit, adventurous visitors can descend the Red Track (3.8 km, 5 hours) into the gorge and follow Bungonia Creek between the towering walls, but must be alert to falling rocks. The gorge walls are a popular, challenging climbing spot, and the park also encompasses some of Australia's deepest caves, but these are open only to expert cavers.

▶ *25 km south-east of Goulburn via Bungonia.*

Hilltop harvests

Vineyards scattered across the rolling hills north of Canberra have established an international reputation for cool-climate wines.

Although vines were first planted at Yass in the 1850s, wine production on the tablelands didn't really get underway until the 1970s, when a small number of winemakers achieved some remarkable results with cool-climate grapes, notably riesling, chardonnay and pinot noir. Today, 33 wineries operating in three main clusters – Hall, north-west of Canberra; Murrumbateman, south of Yass; and Lake George, Bungendore – constitute what's known as the Canberra Wine Region (even though most of it is in New South Wales).

The majority of the wineries offer cellar-door tastings and some have restaurants, and their predominantly upland sites enjoy wonderful views over the scenic surrounds. Along with the excellent wines, you can savour superb smoked foods from the onsite smokehouse at Poachers Pantry near Hall, and take in stunning panoramas of the Murrumbidgee Valley from Brindabella and Surveyor's Hill and of Lake George (see p. 169) from Milimani Estate. Some local wineries also offer accommodation.

6 Cooma Cottage

Restored residence of famed explorer

The pioneering 1824 expedition of Hamilton Hume and William Hovell forged an overland route from Sydney to Port Phillip. In doing so, it opened the Yass region to development as a woolgrowing area. Returning to the area in 1839 – with some satisfaction, one assumes – Hume elected to stay, and purchased a cottage built in 1835 by pastoralist Cornelius O'Brien, along with 40 ha of land. Over the next 20 years, Hume enlarged the building, adding a Palladian wing and a Greek Revival–style portico. Today the cottage (open Thursday to Sunday) is a fascinating museum of the explorer's life, with lovely gardens and picnic areas. Hume died at the house in 1873 and is buried in Yass Cemetery.

► *4 km south-east of Yass via Yass Valley Way.*

7 Gundaroo

Artistry on display in 1850s buildings

The main street of this quiet settlement on the Yass River is lined with shops selling a fine range of local arts and crafts. The village took shape in the 1850s and many of the buildings date from that period. The local common, or 'Great Paddock', is the site of a cemetery containing several pioneer graves. Bushrangers were active in the district and Gundaroo's merchants were held up on two occasions. To learn more of the history and get the most out of a tour of the streets, pick up a heritage guide at the Gundaroo Store, built in 1893 and now a crafts gallery.

► *28 km south of Hume Hwy via Sutton Rd.*

HANG-GLIDING OVER THE EMPTY EXPANSE OF LAKE GEORGE

8 Lake George

Now you see it ...

Europeans first discovered Lake George, known to Aboriginals as Wee-ree-wa (Werriwa), in 1820. Governor Lachlan Macquarie visited it that year and described it as a 'magnificent sheet of water'. But on at least six occasions since, and often for long spells, the lake has been empty of water, most recently between 2002 and 2010, during which time it was bone dry. The fluctuations are due to the fact that the lake has a small catchment and is very shallow, so that in times of drought the water evaporates easily and quickly; conversely, it can fill rapidly following heavy rains. Empty or full, it's a splendid sight, stretching 10 km east from the lookouts and picnic areas along the highway to the hills on the eastern shore – now the site of the Capital Wind Farm – and roughly 25 km from north to south.

▶ *Federal Hwy, 33 km north-east of Canberra.*

9 Bungendore

Historic village showcases local produce

This picturesque village was founded in 1837 and traces of the early days abound in the form of beautifully preserved mid-19th-century stone-and-timber buildings, notably the post office, Anglican church and Bungendore Inn. But another major drawcard is the array of galleries and antique shops displaying and selling art, crafts and collectables. Of particular note are the stylish Bungendore Wood Works Gallery, which exhibits work by the country's foremost carvers and furniture designers, and Bungendore Fine Arts, owned and operated by a group of local artists. Bungendore is also one of the hubs of the Canberra Wine Region (see p. 167) and local cool-climate wines are on sale in its cafes and bars.

▶ *40 km east of Canberra via Federal Hwy, Macs Reef Rd and Bungendore Rd.*

10 Braidwood

Smart farming centre with superb architectural heritage

The town takes its name from Dr Thomas Braidwood Wilson, a naval surgeon who accompanied a number of convict transport ships to Australia. Taking up land here in the 1830s, he built a court house at his own expense and petitioned for the town to be proclaimed. Farming maintained the first settlers and today dominates the local economy, but it was gold, discovered at Araluen in 1852, that ensured the town's future and funded the grand, predominantly Georgian streetscapes you see today. The entire town is classified by the National Trust; early gems include the original post office and general store, built in the 1840s; the grand homesteads Bedervale (1842) and Deloraine; and the old Royal Hotel (1845), which now houses the excellent Braidwood Museum.

▶ *87 km south-east of Canberra via Kings Hwy.*

South Coast

Pristine beaches, rocky headlands and superb fishing are perhaps most strongly associated with the South Coast, but this long narrow region also harbours historic river, steamer and whaling ports, as well as a hinterland of wild, forested ranges.

1 Booderee National Park

Wildlife haven hemmed by stunning white beaches

Step onto the blindingly white, squeaky-clean sands (literally – listen as you walk) at Green Patch, or the exquisite bush-backed cove at Murrays Beach, where the transparent turquoise waters of Jervis Bay lap the sheltered shore, and you'd have to agree there are few more beautiful beaches in the state than those in Booderee National Park. What's more, the park encompasses swathes of coastal heath and forests of swamp mahogany and blackbutt, and waters home to dolphins and myriad fish species. Walking tracks link the bayside beaches with headlands from where migrating humpback whales are often seen (May to October), as well as the wilder ocean beaches, where kangaroos and wallabies graze on beachside grasses. Booderee Botanic Gardens, at the centre of the park, highlights the use of south-eastern flora by Aboriginal peoples.

▶ *34 km south of Nowra via Princes Hwy and Jervis Bay Rd.*

Visitor information

Batemans Bay 02 4472 6900
Bega 02 6491 7645
Booderee National Park 02 4443 0977
Eden 02 6496 1953
Merimbula 02 6495 1129
Narooma 02 4476 2881
Nowra 02 4421 0778
Ulladulla 02 4455 1269

2 Pigeon House Mountain

Distinctive peak affords majestic views

Aboriginal people referred to it as Didthul, 'Big Mountain', but Europeans adopted the name chosen by James Cook as he sailed past in 1770, coined for the peak's resemblance to a dovecote. The region's most prominent landmark, it rises to 719 m in the south-eastern corner of Morton National Park. The climb to the top is challenging, requiring at least 4 hours for the return trip and involving the ascent of a series of metal ladders up the steep sides of the blunt-topped summit, but it repays with stupendous 360-degree views over plateaus, escarpments and forest, and deep gorges carved by the Clyde River and its tributaries. In clear weather, you can see as far north as Point Perpendicular (the northern headland at the entrance to Jervis Bay), and as far south as Mount Dromedary near Central Tilba (see p. 172).

▶ *27 km west of Princes Hwy at Milton.*

3 Pebbly Beach

Scenic shoreline home to tame wildlife

Take a stroll on the grassy foreshore early or late in the day, and you're unlikely to be alone. Not that this remote beach is often crowded with tourists; it's just that it abounds with eastern grey kangaroos, so habituated to the presence of humans that they are unlikely to even look up from their browsing. Though the beach was named for the stones heaped across its southern edge, it is mainly sandy and a top spot for a swim. There are cabins and a camping area, and Depot Beach, 4 km to the south, has a fine rainforest walk.

▶ *Murramarang National Park, 22 km north of Batemans Bay via Princes Hwy and Mount Agony Rd.*

INQUISITIVE EASTERN GREY KANGAROOS AT PEBBLY BEACH

4 Nelligen

Picturesque river port of yore

Walking along the waterfront of this sleepy town at a tranquil bend in the Clyde River, it's hard to picture it a bustling port, alive with the sounds of bullock teams and horses, and wharfies hauling supplies onshore and loading timber, wool, gold and oysters. Yet a major port this once was, the principal outlet for produce from the goldfields and forests of the tablelands, with a regular steamer service to Sydney that ran from 1861 right up to 1952. Stroll the historic streets, lined with timber cottages, or join a guided river cruise, and you'll start to get a sense of the way things once were.

▶ *8 km north-west of Batemans Bay via Princes Hwy and Kings Hwy.*

5 Mogo Zoo

World-class collection of native and exotic wildlife

Built up from scratch over 20 years by Sally and Bill Padey, this impressive zoo rivals many of its metropolitan counterparts for the breadth of its collection and its achievements in breeding and conservation. More than 200 animals are on display, including 41 rare and exotic species; among the most unusual are a group of white lions, distinguished by their very pale colouring. Interactive experiences allow you to feed a tiger, stroke a 7-m boa constrictor, play with mischievous meerkats and snuggle up to a Nepalese red panda. Recent breeding successes include the birth of a baby silvery gibbon, born to one of only nine captive breeding pairs in the world.

▶ *Tomakin Rd, Mogo, 12 km south of Batemans Bay.*

6 Montague Island

Home to the state's largest little penguin and fur seal colonies

Aboriginal peoples were well aware that this small granite island harboured abundant wildlife, and hunted here regularly, as middens and other archaeological sites show. Now fully protected within Batemans Marine Park, the island is home to around 8000 pairs of little penguins and huge nesting colonies of crested terns and sooty, short-tailed and wedge-tailed shearwaters. Up to 1000 Australian and New Zealand fur seals bask on the rocky shores at any one time, and dolphins, whales and green turtles are often spotted offshore. Guided tours – the only way to visit the island – explore Montague's natural and human history, visiting the bird and seal colonies and the 1881 lighthouse. Contact the Narooma tourist office for details.

► *6 km east of Narooma.*

7 Central Tilba

Quaint village little changed in a century

Nestled at the foot of Mount Dromedary, this charming settlement of attractive weatherboard houses developed during a short-lived gold rush; the inhabitants quickly turned to dairy farming when the gold ran out. Many of the businesses that occupy the buildings today – woodturning, weaving, saddlemaking – hark back to those early times. There are also several galleries and cafes, as well as the renowned ABC Cheese Factory, which offers tastings and sales. Nearby Tilba Tilba is smaller but equally pretty; its attractions include the lovely Foxglove Spire Open Gardens, a 2-ha cottage garden with rose-covered arbours, woodlands, a pond and a cafe.

► *Princes Hwy, 13 km south-west of Narooma.*

8 Tathra Wharf

The state's only remaining coastal steamer wharf

The large, handsomely restored wharf is the most striking feature of this attractive coastal settlement and in fact it stood here long before the rest of the town. It was constructed in 1862 to ship goods and passengers between Sydney and thriving pastoral properties around Bega, and until 1876 its warehouse was the only building in the district – steamship passengers arriving from Sydney, a journey of 24 hours, were whisked off to the nearest lodgings, at Bega. Today the huge wharf still evokes the steamer era, provides magnificent coastal views and is one of the South Coast's finest fishing spots.

► *17 km south-east of Bega via Tathra Rd.*

THE GRAND TIMBER WHARF AT TATHRA

9 Goodenia Rainforest

Forest reserve provides an inspiring sample of a vast wilderness

To experience an environment in stark contrast to the surf and sand of the coastline, head inland to this rainforest reserve in the hills above Pambula. It is part of South East Forest National Park, which protects enormous tracts of temperate rainforest and old-growth eucalypts in the far south-eastern corner of the state. From the Goodenia Picnic Area, an easy (1.2 km, 45 minutes) walking track leads through a gully of dense ferns beneath a lofty canopy of lilly pilly and sassafras trees. Listen for the whipcrack-like call of the eastern whipbird and lyrebirds scratching in the understorey – you might even be lucky enough to hear them imitating other birds. Rarer inhabitants include koalas, tiger quolls and sooty owls.

► *17 km north-west of Princes Hwy at South Pambula.*

10 The Pinnacles

Striking sandcastle-like formation

In a narrow gully just off the beach, water and wind have fashioned the cliffs into a multihued, multitiered extravaganza. Layers of deep red gravelly clay cap lower layers of paler clay and white sand, forming bands of bright colour. Water running down the lower layers has cut deep clefts and columns – pinnacles – of brittle rock. The approach to the formation is along a pleasant, easy walk (1 km) through forest, woodland and heath, passing vantage points with fine coastal views. After admiring the cliffs, take the time to descend the shore to enjoy the golden sands of Long Beach.

► *Ben Boyd National Park, 10 km north of Eden via Princes Hwy and Haycock Rd.*

11 Eden

Fascinating former whaling town in magnificent location

Beneath a backdrop of forested hills, Eden perches on a promontory jutting out into beautiful Twofold Bay. This vantage point – check out the jaw-dropping views from Eden Rotary Park Lookout – made it an ideal location for a whaling station, founded in 1818 and only closed in the 1930s. The wonderful Eden Killer Whale Museum has displays on the colourful history of whaling here, including the skeleton of Old Tom, a killer whale that assisted whalers by herding humpbacks into the harbour. These days, of course, the whales are protected and boats sail out to view the giant marine mammals as they pass by on their southward migration to Antarctica (September to November); a wide range of cruises is available, along with diving and deep-sea fishing charters.
▶ *Princes Hwy.*

12 Boydtown

Relics of a grandiose scheme

He was nothing if not ambitious. Benjamin Boyd, former London stockbroker and banker, not only set about building an entire whaling settlement here, but was determined that it would become a city to rival Sydney. From 1842 to 1849, he had 500 men working for him, putting up buildings, looking after flocks of sheep, operating whaleboats and running a steamship service. Miscalculations and a recession put paid to the scheme, and by 1870 the inhabitants had all shifted to Eden. Boyd, meanwhile, had long since moved on to the California goldfields before disappearing mysteriously in the Solomon Islands in 1851. The elegant Seahorse Inn, now a boutique hotel, and an adjacent ruined church are intriguing remnants of the entrepreneur's dream.
▶ *Princes Hwy, 7 km south of Eden.*

BOYD'S TOWER AT RED POINT

Days of harpoon and whaleboat

The lucrative but perilous business of whaling shaped the fortunes and landscape of Twofold Bay.

The first whaling station off Eden was established by Thomas Raine in 1828, and by 1847 there were two shore stations: the government-run station at Eden and Benjamin Boyd's at East Boyd. The original targets of the whalers were female southern right whales, which came into Twofold Bay to calve; great profits could be made from their thick blubber and the flexible baleen from their mouths, often called 'whalebone'.

By the 1840s, the southern right whales had been hunted almost to extinction, and the whalers turned their harpoons on a new quarry, sperm whales. The oil-rich organ in a sperm whale's head yielded enormous quantities of valuable oil used for fuel and making candles – Benjamin Boyd made £42,000 from sperm whales in a single year, a colossal sum for his day.

The industry was wound down in the 1920s, but Eden maintains its links with whales through seasonal whale-watching trips. Fascinating relics of the whaling industry can be seen in the museum at Eden and at Boydtown (see entry) and at the former Davidson Whaling Station Historic Site on Kiah Inlet.

13 Boyd's Tower

Former lookout atop majestic headland

There's no mistaking the originator of this handsome sandstone structure: carved into the stonework around the crenellated turret in bold capital letters is the name 'BOYD'. Benjamin Boyd built this tower at Red Point, south-east of Twofold Bay, as a lighthouse, in 1847, but the local authorities prevented him lighting it. It was subsequently taken over by other whalers, the Davidson family, who used it as a whale lookout to try to steal a march on their competitors: as soon as a whale was spotted, an observer would fire a gun to alert a crew in nearby Kiah Inlet. The panorama of Twofold Bay and the coastline from nearby viewpoints is superb, and far below waves crash onto the crumpled, red-hued metamorphic rocks that give the point its name.

▶ *Ben Boyd National Park, 15 km north-east of Princes Hwy via Edrom Rd.*

14 Green Cape

Experience the lonely life of the lighthouse keeper

With the adjacent inlet having a name like Disaster Bay, it was almost inevitable that a lighthouse would be built here. Completed in 1883, it was at the time the largest mass-concrete structure in New South Wales and it is still the state's tallest and most southerly lighthouse. Unfortunately, it wasn't enough to prevent subsequent catastrophes, notably the wreck of the steamer *Ly-ee-moon* in 1886, which sank with the loss of 76 crew and passengers, some of whom are buried in the graveyard nearby. Looking out over an infinity of sapphire-blue ocean, the 29-m-high octagonal tower and adjacent lighthouse-keepers' cottages are beautifully maintained. Two of the cottages can be rented as holiday accommodation.

▶ *Ben Boyd National Park, 41 km south-east of Eden via Princes Hwy and Green Cape Rd.*

Snowy Mountains

The mighty granite mountains here are the highest in the land. Pierced in places by tunnels that carry power-generating rivers west, their forested flanks and high plains are a refuge for endangered animals and are the home of Dreaming stories and, in more recent times, stirring tales of cattlemen and horsemen.

1 Lake Burrinjuck

Young lake fills time-worn valley

Encircled by slopes of unspoiled bushland, this sprawling lake under the southern escarpment of Mount Barren Jack looks to have always been part of the landscape. In fact its waters have lain here only since the completion of the Burrinjuck Dam wall in 1927. Although its purpose was and still is to supply irrigation to the farmers of the western plains, the lake soon became a playground for the residents of the new national capital, Canberra. Today, with waters stocked with trout and Murray cod, it is a popular fishing spot and also offers swimming, water-skiing and bushwalks.

▶ *Burrinjuck Waters State Park, 20 km south of Hume Hwy west of Yass via Burrinjuck Rd.*

2 Adelong

Scattered relics of former boomtown

This was one of the state's major goldfields. Over nearly a century, from 1857 until 1942, its rich deposits of alluvial and reef gold yielded more than 21,000 kg of the precious ore. Ruins at Adelong Falls Reserve, just north of the town, are reminders of the heady days of the 1860s and 1870s when up to 20,000 miners toiled here and 14 crushing batteries clanked and groaned around the clock. Signposted walking tracks start from the picnic area and take in the battery complex with its historic mining equipment. And, as many a fossicker here has discovered, there's still gold to be panned from the creek.

▶ *18 km west of Tumut via Snowy Mountains Hwy.*

3 Blowering Dam Wall

A dam wall with an astounding view

You can drive across the top of this dam wall. At 112-m high, it's as tall as a 35-storey building, so it's not surprising that the views are impressive. Winding away below the wall to the north is the wooded valley of the Tumut River; filling the reservoir to the south is the vast expanse of its captured waters. Completed in 1968, the dam stores water collected from the Snowy Mountains Scheme in winter for summer irrigation use. When full, it holds more than three times the volume of Sydney Harbour.

▶ *13 km south of Tumut via Blowering Dam Access Rd.*

4 Pioneer Women's Hut

Exhibits and stories testify to the ingenuity of rural women (and men)

In this unusual museum (open only on Wednesdays and weekends), once you've slipped on a pair of white gloves, you can handle many of the artefacts on display, which were gathered from pioneer homes. Feel the weight of a flat iron, examine the stitching on a nightdress, or the wirework repair that keeps a de-handled china cup in service. Life in the early days was tough and little was wasted or thrown away – clothes were patched and patched again and recycled as rag rugs; hessian bags made aprons and wooden crates were turned into toy cupboards. There are also doilies galore and a collection of touching postcards sent by young and homesick First World War soldiers to their mothers.

▶ *Tumbarumba, 50 km south-east of Hume Hwy via Tumbarumba Rd.*

Double dividend

The Snowy Mountains Hydro-Electric Scheme diverted the headwaters of snow-fed rivers to irrigate agricultural lands to the west, while at the same time harnessing the force of their waters to generate electricity.

To achieve its objectives, the scheme employed, between 1949 and 1974, a workforce of more than 100,000 from 30 nations to build 16 major dams, drill 145 km of huge tunnels through mountains to carry the water, and construct seven major power stations. To house the workers, 7 towns and 100 camps were established, many with schools for the workers' children. Today, as it travels down the escarpment, the harnessed water passes through a series of power stations driving the turbines in each, before flowing on to holding reservoirs ready for release into the Murray and Murrumbidgee rivers for farmers. On its way, it generates the energy that helps light up centres as far way as Brisbane and Adelaide.

5 Yarrangobilly Caves

Imposing chambers crammed with water-worn creations

For more than a million years, water seeping and dripping through a belt of limestone here carved out numerous tubes, sinkholes and caves, and decorated some of them with striking and varied formations. Of the dozens of caves identified, only three are open year-round to the public: South Glory Cave can be explored on a self-guided tour, but entry to Jersey (featuring a 4-m-high column dubbed Cleopatra's Needle) and Jillabenan (with delicate displays of straw stalactites, shawls and cave corals) is by guided tour only. Finish your visit with a soothing swim in the natural thermal bathing pool, which is a constant 27°C.

► *75 km south of Tumut via Snowy Mountains Hwy.*

6 Coolamine Homestead

Historic dwelling-place of pioneering cattlemen and their families

The winding unsealed road follows a traditional route used for centuries by the Aboriginal people of the area, and later by the cattlemen who grazed stock in summer on the high plains here. The homestead complex consists of four buildings, all restored, and excellent examples of three different styles of building. The oldest, a slab hut, dates back to 1839; the later structures, two homesteads and a log cabin cheesehouse, were built in the 1880s. The complex was home year-round to the cattlemen and their families. A fascinating feature is newspapers plastered over timber walls to keep out the wind; some date back to the 1890s.

► *40 km north of Kiandra via Snowy Mountains Hwy and Long Plain Rd.*

Visitor information

Cooma 02 6450 1742
Jindabyne 02 6450 5600
Tumbarumba 02 6948 3333
Tumut 02 6947 7025

7 Kiandra

Gold-rush remains amid stark landscape

Despite appearances to the contrary, this was once the site of a major goldmining town with a population in 1860 of more than 5000, and 25 stores and 14 hotels. Little remains today but mullock heaps, scarred hillsides, abandoned mining equipment and just four buildings. Nevertheless, a self-guided heritage walk signposts the sites of many of the original buildings and conveys a vivid impression of pioneer life. A highlight is the newly restored court house, an impressive building optimistically constructed in 1890, many years after the gold rush, in the belief that the mining would continue. It later saw service as a hotel and ski chalet – Kiandra became the birthplace of organised skiing in Australia in 1861, when Norwegian miners introduced the sport using fence palings for skis.

▶ *89 km south of Tumut via Snowy Mountains Hwy.*

8 Adaminaby

A town that moved

How must they have felt, the residents of the original Adaminaby township, as they watched their homes levered from foundations and then hauled, one by one, from the valley to a new site 9.5 km to the north-east, in 1958? Churches, too, including the 1886 Uniting Church, were dismantled stone by stone and re-erected. In all, more than 100 buildings were relocated. What wasn't moved – fencing, sheds and abandoned farm equipment – now lies under the waters of Lake Eucumbene, formed by the damming of the Eucumbene River for the Snowy Mountains Scheme. Today Adaminaby is also known for its huge fibreglass rainbow trout, reminding visitors that the lake that laps almost at the town's new doorstep is a handy spot for trout fishing.

▶ *53 km north-west of Cooma via Snowy Mountains Hwy.*

ALPINE PANORAMA FROM MOUNT KOSCIUSZKO

9 Mount Kosciuszko

Make a flying start on the way to the top

It's a walk in the park like no other. The chairlift seat slides under you and you're off, cranking up the steep flanks of the Crackenback Range. Most of the Summit Walk from the top of the chairlift (13 km return; allow 4 hours) is a raised mesh pathway that snakes across herbfields and over streams. In midsummer these uplands are bright with flowers; in spring and autumn tiny alpine shrubs frame embedded boulders, resembling miniature Japanese gardens. The walk passes glacial Lake Cootapatamba, the highest lake in Australia, then climbs through granite formations. At the top (2228 m above sea level), you may find a queue for the coveted spot on the cairn, where, briefly, you can be the highest person in the country. And there's excellent mobile coverage if you want to call a friend.

► *Thredbo, 34 km west of Jindabyne via Alpine Way.*

10 Nimmitabel

Charming settlement with a windmill that won't frighten the horses

Known to the locals as 'Nimity-belle', this small township grew to serve traffic heading north to the Kiandra goldfields and by the 1870s was a busy centre with two hotels, a post office, bank, police station (which now has a museum in one of its decommissioned cells), court house, general store and an imposing stone windmill which became a subject of some controversy. The mill was built by German settler and storekeeper John Geldmacher, who initially fitted wooden sails; however, he was forced to remove them as local laws did not permit their use so close to a road where they might startle horses. The tower-like structure still stands.

► *28 km south of Cooma via Snowy Mountains Hwy.*

Riverina and Murray

Stretching from the foot of the south-west slopes to the outback, this is a region of semiarid flatlands, nevertheless intensely farmed thanks to major irrigation schemes. Its diverse centres harbour intriguing cultural attractions, while in more remote areas historic sheep stations occupy vast plains beneath immense skies.

1 Willandra Station

Legendary pastoral property

It's a long way off the bitumen, but your reward for the dusty drive is a fascinating insight into the pastoral history of the region. Willandra Homestead, surrounded by gardens and overlooking peaceful Willandra Creek, has been restored to its former glory and recalls the time when Willandra was famed for its high-quality wool clip. There's a pontoon off the homestead lawn for swimming, and you will also find picnic areas, camping grounds and walking tracks. The access road may be impassable in wet weather.

> *Willandra National Park, 66 km north-west of Hillston via Hillston–Mossgiel Rd.*

2 Shear Outback

The legends and reality of shearing culture

This is a region immortalised in outback songs of the Murrumbidgee shearers who 'shore at big Willandra' and 'on One Tree Plain', so there could hardly be a more appropriate setting for a centre celebrating shearing's culture and colourful characters. Hear yarns from the past, learn the language of the sheds and meet the shearers, shed hands, cooks, classers, cockies, sheep and dogs who work in the industry today. Then watch shearing demonstrations in the historic Murray Downs shed, which was relocated here from the Swan Hill region of Victoria.

> *Cnr Sturt Hwy and Cobb Hwy, Hay.*

SHEAR OUTBACK CENTRE, HAY

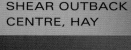

3 Hermit's Cave

One man's self-made Utopia

In the early 1930s, Italian-born Valerio Riccetti sheltered from rain in a cave here, and, finding it to his liking, moved in. Over the following ten years, and working at night so that he would not be seen, the former mason used his skills to create rooms, a chapel, a water cistern and terraced cliffside gardens. During the Second World War, Riccetti was interned in a prisoner-of-war camp, and at the end of the war he returned to Italy, but his extraordinary gardens were later restored by members of a local service club.

▶ *Scenic Dr, Griffith.*

4 Ron Clarke Steel Sculptures

Striking oxy-torch roadside artworks

Drivers on the Sturt Highway around Waddi who encounter Clydesdales plodding beside the road, or perhaps a stagecoach drawn by four horses, should not be alarmed. They are life-like silhouettes created by local artist Ron Clarke, who is renowned for his sculptures cut with an oxy torch from sheets of steel. Clarke's work ranges from motorbikes and oversized koalas to figures of Ned Kelly, and examples are on display around his workshop at Waddi.

▶ *Sturt Hwy, Waddi.*

Visitor information

Albury 1300 252 879
Griffith 02 6962 4145
Gundagai 02 6944 0250
Hay 02 6993 4045
Holbrook 02 6036 2422
Jerilderie 03 5886 1666
Leeton 02 6953 6481
Wagga Wagga 02 6926 9621

5 Leeton

Capital design for an irrigation town

It's no coincidence that Leeton's circular street pattern is reminiscent of the national capital – both are by the same designer, Walter Burley Griffin. Griffin was engaged to prepare plans for the expansion of Leeton, then the administrative centre of the fledgling Murrumbidgee Irrigation Area, in 1914. A city with sweeping plazas and imposing buildings was envisioned. Although much of the grand design stayed on the drawing board, features such as the decorated water towers crowning the hill and intended as portals to the town give an idea of what might have been. Leeton is also known for the fine Art Deco architecture of its commercial centre.

▶ *58 km south-east of Griffith via Griffith Rd.*

6 Junee Roundhouse Museum

Giant repair shop for locomotives

In railway terms, a roundhouse is a large circular building where locomotives are serviced. Because early engines normally travelled forwards only, the defining feature of the structure is a mighty turntable in the centre to deliver rolling stock to a repair bay and return it to the rails facing in the right direction. The Junee Roundhouse, with its massive 33-m turntable surrounded by 42 repair bays, opened in 1947 and was the last in the country to be built for steam trains. Today, half of the doughnut-shaped building is home to a workshop that maintains and repairs rolling stock, while the rest is occupied by a museum displaying steam and diesel locomotives – some restored, some in the process of restoration – as well as other heritage items. Guided tours are available.

▶ *Harold St, Junee.*

7 Monte Cristo Homestead

Join a ghost tour of this haunted house

Empty rooms that sometimes blaze with light, invisible force-fields, ghostly voices, phantom footsteps and unexplained feelings of grief – it all adds up to what is said to be Australia's most haunted house. Wealthy local businessman Christopher William Crawley spared no expense in the construction of Monte Cristo, a grand, two-storey mansion set high on a hill to reflect his status and completed in 1885. But all was not happy in the house. A child died mysteriously on its stairs, and Crawley himself met an untimely end by blood-poisoning from a carbuncle that became infected as a result of the constant rubbing of his starched collar. For the rest of her 23 years, Crawley's widow rarely left the building. Join a ghost tour here, and you may feel her presence.

▶ *Homestead Ln, Junee.*

8 The Marble Masterpiece

Master workmanship in miniature

Each of the 20,948 pieces of marble that make up this fanciful 1.2-m-high Baroque-style palace/cathedral was cut, turned and polished by hand. Its creator, Frank Rusconi, was a monumental stone-mason who believed passionately in Australian marble as a building material and collected examples from around the state to use in his business. Crafted in his spare time as a tribute to the stonemason's art, the structure took 28 years to complete and showcases 20 different types of marble. Rusconi also sculptured the model for Gundagai's iconic Dog on the Tuckerbox statue north of town; his other work includes tombstones, funerary monuments and Gundagai's two war memorials.

▶ *Sheridan St, Gundagai, 1 km east of Hume Hwy.*

9 Prince Alfred Bridge

Wooden viaduct spanning the Murrumbidgee flood plain

In 1852, a disastrous flood virtually wiped out the first settlement here and drowned one-third of its residents. The town moved up the slopes and continued on with its main purpose, accommodating travellers on the main Sydney–Melbourne route and ferrying them across the river. When a bridge was eventually built, in 1867, its designers acknowledged the risk of high floods. The crossing measures 921 m from end to end, with most of its length made up of wooden approaches – the longest such structures in the land – that strut high over the river flats. The bridge was an immediate hit with locals, who now had not only an easy way to cross the river but also an agreeable place to take a Sunday stroll. Today, although traffic is now carried by the 1977 steel-and-concrete Sheahan Bridge to the west, the heritage-listed Prince Alfred still stands proud, an important record of former methods of bridge design and construction.

▶ *Gundagai, 1.5 km east of Hume Hwy via Sheridan St.*

10 National Art Glass Gallery

Cutting-edge artworks

Wagga Wagga may seem an unlikely place for the nation's largest collection of modern glass sculptures. But step inside this purpose-built and light-filled gallery, itself shaped like a shard of glass, and that's just what you'll find. The 500-piece collection celebrates glass as an artistic medium and features blown, engraved, etched, kiln-fired, cast and sand-blasted glass art. Wagga Wagga Art Gallery began collecting glassworks in 1979 in response to a request from the Australia Council that regional galleries specialise in particular fields of art; its success was acknowledged with the 'National' title in 1992.

▶ *Morrow St, Wagga Wagga.*

Water to wine

A grand vision and willing workers turned semiarid plains into one of the world's most intensive fruit-, wine- and rice-producing regions, the Murrumbidgee Irrigation Area.

In these dry but fertile lands, a modest supply of water is the difference between abundance and failure. In the early 1900s, experiments conducted by pastoralist Samuel McCaughey in diverting Murrumbidgee River waters through channels to his 'Yanco' property showed the effectiveness of dryland irrigation. In 1906, to put McCaughey's methods into practice, the state government resumed nearly 270,000 ha of ideally suited flat land and set about building an elaborate network of weirs, canals and holding ponds. Farmers, many of them Italian, came on the promise of cheap land, healthy subsidies and a regular supply of water. In 1912 this key component began flowing south down the Murrumbidgee after release from the Burrinjuck Dam storage, a journey that took a week. By 1914, 622 farms on 9700 ha were irrigated, and today the region is a patchwork of agriculture covering 660,000 ha. Nearly all of Australia's rice and 20 per cent of its wine are produced here, and the region grows 90 per cent of the state's citrus crop.

IRRIGATED RICE PADDIES OUTSIDE GRIFFITH

CONCRETE COLONNADES
ATOP HUME DAM WALL

11 Lockhart

Century-old streetscapes tell their story

The history of this Riverina wheat town can be read on the walls and pavements of its National Trust–classified main street. Plaques on the restored century-old shop façades list historic details. At ground level, the pavement is a community artwork portraying historic events, individual endeavours and local features, and made up of contributions from the Wiradjuri people, descendants of the first European settlers and more recent arrivals. Continuous old-style overhanging verandas bring shade and add character.

▶ *61 km south-west of Wagga Wagga via Sturt Hwy and Collingullie–Jerilderie Rd.*

12 HMAS *Otway*

Unusual monument reflects an inland town's links to the sea

This 90-m-long submarine standing high and dry beside the highway (in fact it is only the sub's outer casing) is a startling sight, but just as intriguing is the tale of how it came to be here. During the First World War, the town's name was changed from Germanton to Holbrook, to honour Commander Norman Holbrook, the first Naval recipient of the Victoria Cross. Holbrook made regular visits to 'his' town, which in turn developed close ties with the Royal Australian Navy Submarine Squadron. In 1995, when the *Otway* was decommissioned, he determined to buy it as a memorial to submariners; this was achieved with financial assistance from Holbrook's widow. Today the *Otway* fronts a museum with displays of photographs and memorabilia and mock-up areas of the submarine interior, including a control room with working periscope, engine room, galley and living quarters.

▶ *Holbrook, Hume Hwy.*

13 Albury Railway Station

Monument to colonial differences

In the days before Federation, there was no uniformity to the railway system and the trains of Victoria and New South Wales ran on tracks of different gauges. From 1883, when Sydney–Melbourne rail services began, until 1962, when Victoria adopted the standard gauge, passengers travelling through Albury had to change trains at the border. This required a covered platform of sufficient size to accommodate the entire length of both trains – one on either side. The result is a 450-m-long platform, one of the longest in the country, sheltered by solid awnings on cast-iron fluted columns. The extravagance of the grand Italianate red-and-white brick station building, symmetrically arranged beneath a 22-m clock tower, may owe something to the rivalry between the two colonies.

▶ *Railway Pl, Albury.*

14 Lake Hume

A vast and scenic body of water

Locals like to claim that the volume of water held behind the Hume Dam – 3 million megalitres when full – is six times that of Sydney Harbour. And Lake Hume *is* big. Its shoreline of 350 km is so big in fact, that it has its own volunteer coastguard. The lake is roughly crescent-shaped, with two long arms arcing north and south across the border. It was created by the damming of the Murray River, and its purpose is to capture spring rain for release in summer, thus maintaining a regular water supply for farmers and settlements as far downstream as South Australia. At the time of its completion, in 1936, this was one of the largest dams in the world. Although it has since slipped in the rankings, it is still impressive, and a walk across the 1.5-km dam wall gives some idea of the immensity of the project.

▶ *13 km from Hume Hwy via Thurgoona Dr, Bowna Dr and Riverina Hwy.*

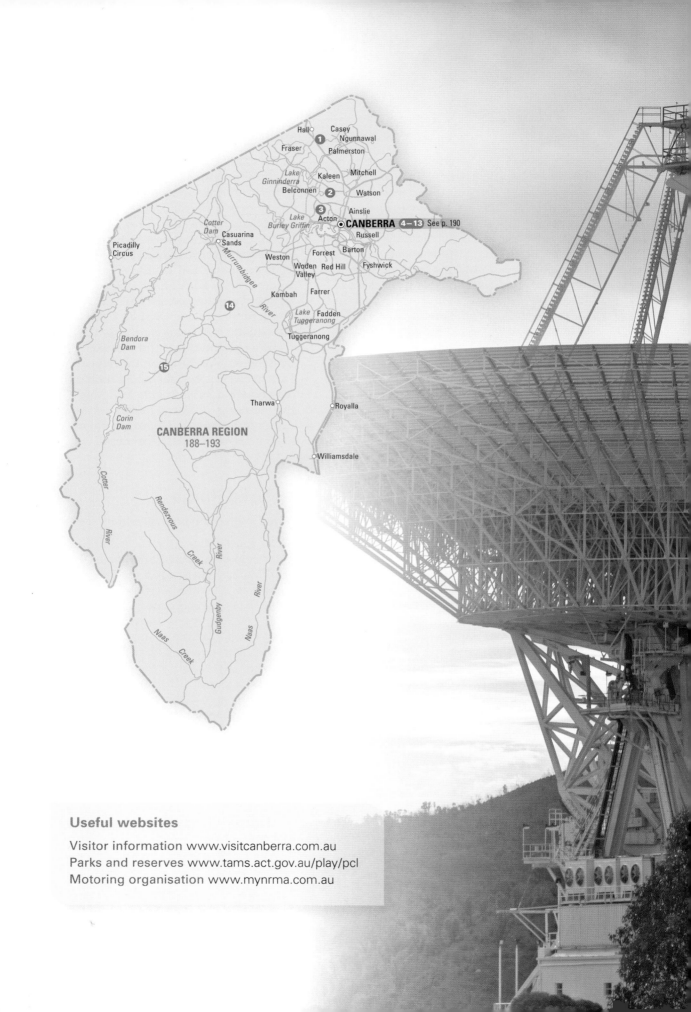

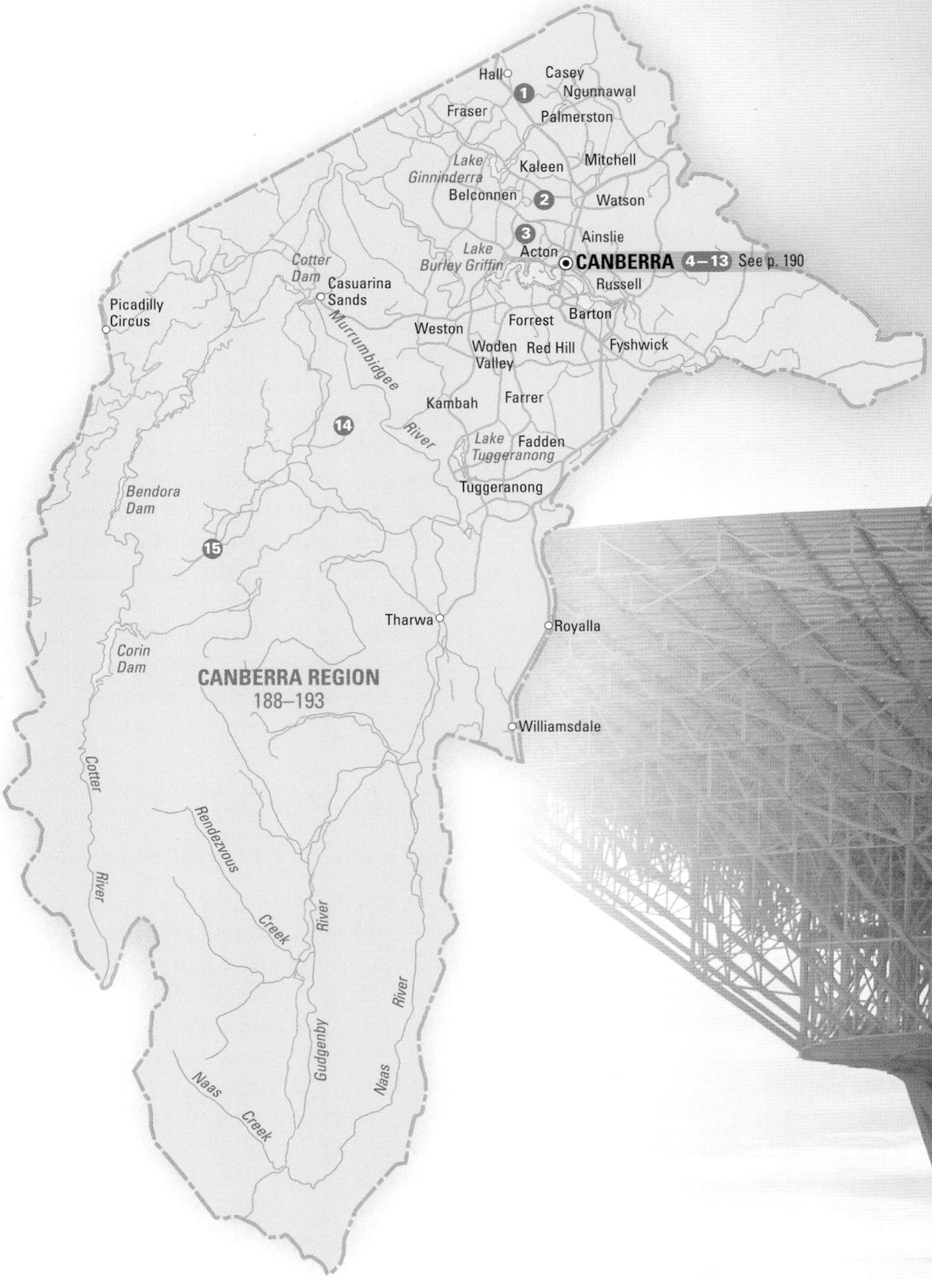

Useful websites

Visitor information www.visitcanberra.com.au
Parks and reserves www.tams.act.gov.au/play/pcl
Motoring organisation www.mynrma.com.au

Australian Capital Territory

The federal capital's superb array of monuments, museums and galleries is so absorbing that it's easy to forget that the surrounding Territory also encompasses scenic grazing lands and pastoral properties, and, in the south, extensive and unspoiled bush-clad ranges home to abundant wildlife.

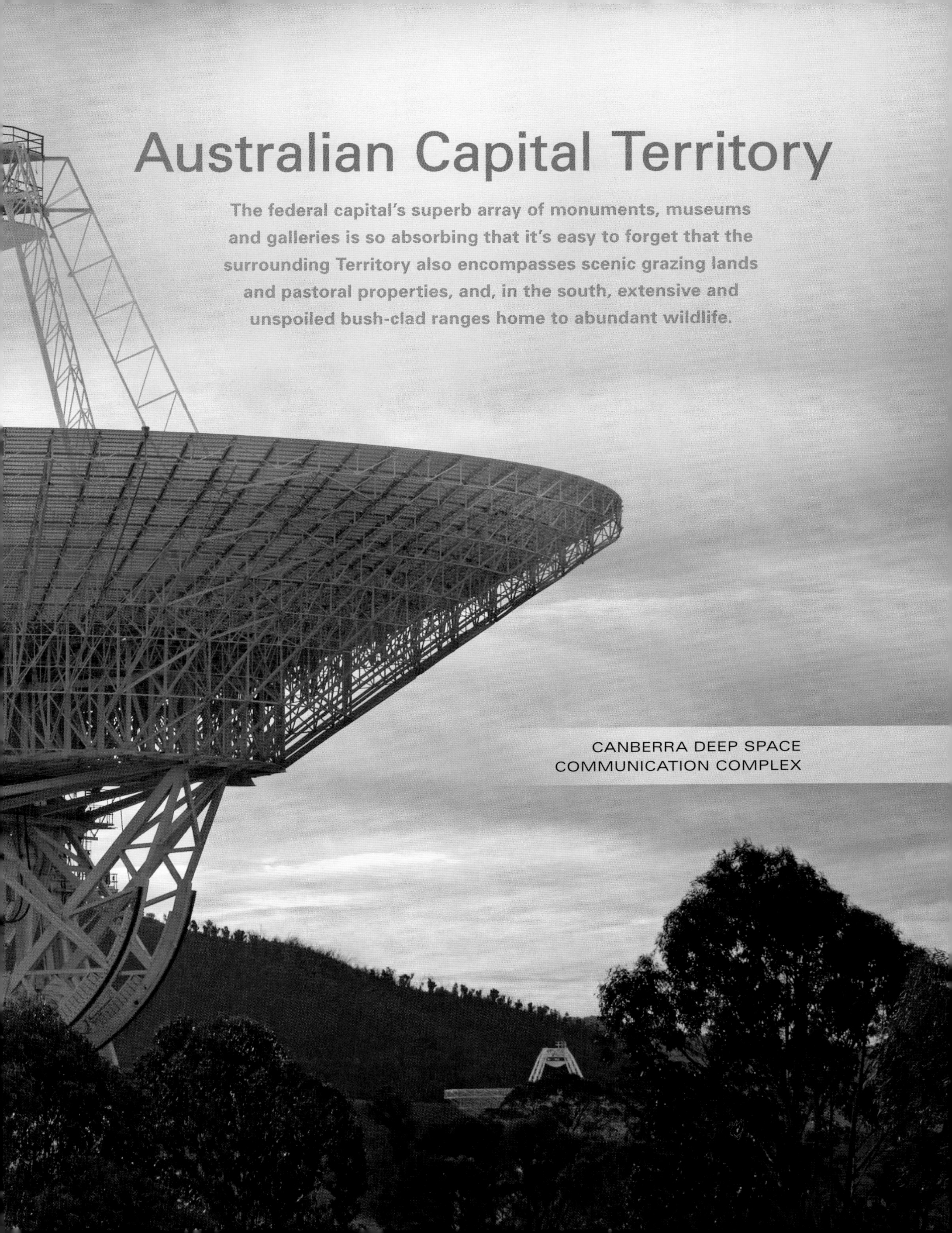

CANBERRA DEEP SPACE COMMUNICATION COMPLEX

Canberra Region

Home to the Australian Federal Parliament and an extensive range of national institutions, Canberra is a sophisticated cultural centre with an unusual, intriguing layout. But it also displays a wilder side, notably in the forested reserves that dot its suburbs and climb the surrounding hills.

1 Cockington Green

See the world – in miniature

The bird's-eye view of the Ukrainian church of St Andrij is magnificent, and the Roman ruins of Palmyra, Syria, can be studied without trekking through desert – this is certainly one of the easiest ways to take in the architectural wonders of 30 countries. The buildings here are intricately rendered scale models. Those in the 'International Garden' were sponsored by Canberra embassies, happy to highlight their nation's attractions. But the first objective of Cockington Green was to re-create the architectural heritage of the British Isles and hence the 'Original Display' consists of models of a thatched village (Cockington, England, after which the gardens are named), country pub, Victorian canal, Scottish castle and even Stonehenge. These are flanked by miniature figures (playing cricket, fishing, supping beer), and real but matching-scale trees and shrubs bordered by lovely floral displays. You can wander the pathways or hop on a miniature steam train, and there is a quaint – full-size – cafe.

▶ *Barton Hwy, 15 km north of Canberra.*

2 Australian Institute of Sport

Watch top athletes train, and find out how you measure up

Who hasn't dreamed of sporting glory? Well, here's your chance to find out what the reality might entail (or have entailed!). Daily tours (90 minutes each) of this national training centre are conducted by elite athletes and you're likely to see other leading competitors working out in the gym or doing their laps in the pool. Displays recount the stories of Australia's sporting legends, and at the Sportex interactive exhibit you can try rock-climbing, wheelchair basketball and virtual downhill skiing, and test your speed, strength and ball skills.

▶ *Lavender St, Bruce, Canberra.*

3 Black Mountain Tower

Majestic city panoramas, day and night

Perched atop Black Mountain, one of Canberra's highest points, the 195-m tower was built to house vital communications facilities. Its observation decks (outdoor and indoor) provide perhaps the most magnificent 360-degree panorama of any viewpoint in the territory. To the south, the vista takes in landmarks such as Parliament House, Woden Valley and the Brindabella Ranges beyond; to the east are the Australian War Memorial and National Library; and to the north the Federal and Barton highways snake through suburbs and rolling farmland. The tower is open late, and one of the best times to visit is as the sun is setting and the city lights gradually appear and brighten. To spin things out, you can enjoy a leisurely meal in the revolving restaurant, Alto Tower.

▶ *Black Mountain Nature Reserve, Canberra.*

Visitor information

Canberra 1300 554 114

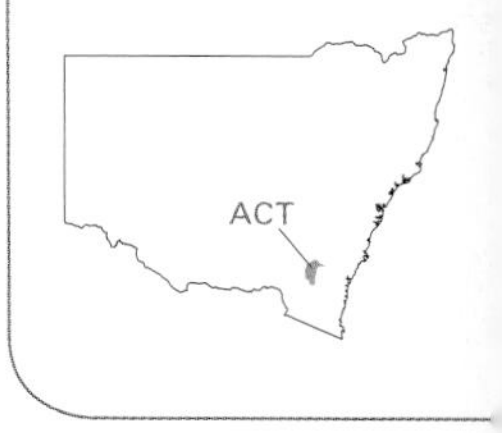

4 National Film and Sound Archive

Australia's past, recorded, shot and screened

From the first muffled sounds and jittery moving images ever recorded in Australia, in the 1890s, through the early days of 'wireless', the emergence of 1960s pop culture, and the flourishing of modern-day Australian cinema, this audiovisual collection encompasses more than 1.6 million recordings and associated documents. Wander through the absorbing interactive displays and you can view excerpts from movies, including what is arguably the first-ever feature film, *The Story of the Kelly Gang*; listen to radio shows, pop hits and jingles; and peruse scripts, stills and posters. The Arc cinema screens classics, lost gems and ground-breaking international releases, and free guided tours are on offer at weekends.
▶ *McCoy Cct, Acton, Canberra.*

5 National Museum of Australia

Quirky chronicle of the nation housed in striking structure

This museum takes a fresh look at the nation's past and cultural heritage – no gloomy rooms of staid, dusty artefacts here; instead the marvellously open, colourful and bright interior presents a series of intriguing thematic exhibitions featuring engaging narratives and unusual exhibits ranging from James Cook's magnifier and the embalmed heart of racehorse Phar Lap to Greg Chappell's cricket cap. Among the exhibitions, Australian Journey traces the routes followed to and from Australia by a range of famous and not-so-famous people; First Australians highlights the diversity of Aboriginal and Torres Strait Islander culture; and Eternity conjures the emotional heart of the nation through the personal and affecting stories of 50 ordinary Australians.
Lawson Cres, Acton Peninsula, Canberra.

COVERED WALKWAY, NATIONAL MUSEUM OF AUSTRALIA

CANBERRA CITY CENTRE

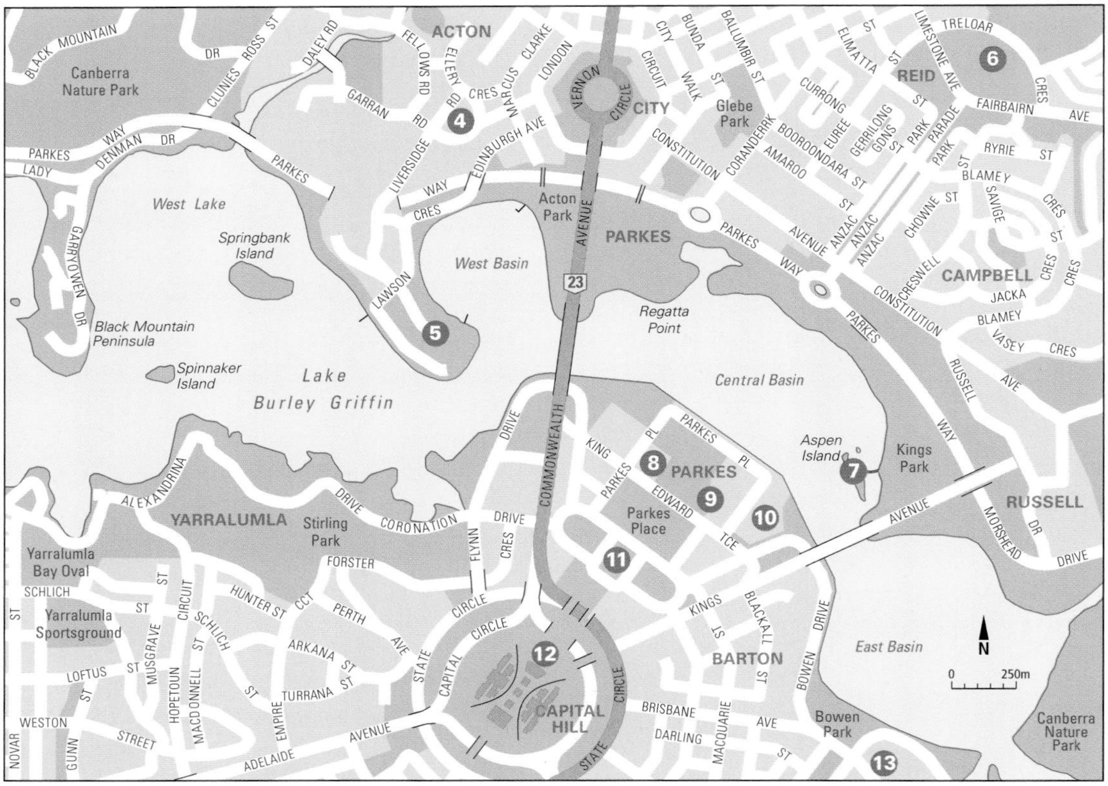

6 Australian War Memorial

Commemoration of the country at war

An immensely moving tribute to the nation's war dead, this is at once shrine, monument and archive. The Roll of Honour at the entrance lists the names of the fallen on bronze panels; beyond, in the Hall of Memory, is the Tomb of the Unknown Soldier, a First World War serviceman killed on the Western Front. Thousands of war-related books, diaries, maps and other documents are held in collections here. More prominently, the museum chronicles Australia's participation in major conflicts in vivid fashion, through displays of photographs, arms and uniforms, impressive dioramas of key battles, and, in the cavernous and strikingly lit Anzac Hall, affecting sound-and-light shows and magnificently restored military vehicles and aircraft, including a massive Lancaster bomber.

▶ *Anzac Pde, Canberra.*

7 National Carillon

Towering musical instrument

It's an enchanting experience to stand on the shore of Lake Burley Griffin as the magical sounds of tolling bells ring out across the water. The heaviest of all musical instruments, a carillon consists of a collection of at least 23 large bells that can be played by pressing a connected keyboard with feet and hands. A gift from the British Government to the Australian people on the occasion of Canberra's 50th anniversary, this one has 55 bronze bells (each weighing up to 6 tonnes) and is housed in an imposing angular tower rising 50 m high. The carillon is played most Sundays and for special events, and there are occasional open days.

▶ *Aspen Island, Lake Burley Griffin, Canberra.*

8 Questacon

Fun ways to get to grips with science

Experience an earthquake inside a full-scale model house. Learn about the physics of motion on a rollercoaster simulator. Develop a new appreciation for gravity (and soft landings) on the 6-m Free Fall. Play a light harp. The 200-plus interactive exhibits here will keep kids and curious adults amused for hours while enhancing their understanding of the workings of our planet. Regular talks and workshops provide more in-depth experiences.
► *King Edward Tce, Parkes, Canberra.*

9 National Portrait Gallery

Faces that tell the nation's story

One part of the enjoyment here is putting not-so-well-known faces to famous Australian names: early explorers (Edward Eyre, Hamilton Hume), statesmen (Arthur Philip, Henry Barkly) and artists (John Glover, Arthur Streeton). Another is noting the infinitely diverse ways face and figure can be rendered, from the gloriously lively society oils of Tom Roberts to the playful ceramic cast of pediatrician Dr John Yu adorned with tiny children, and the DayGlo spray-can colours of Howard Arkley's bold depiction of singer Nick Cave. A beautifully designed space and a stylish cafe add to the absorbing and rewarding experience.
► *King Edward Tce, Parkes, Canberra.*

10 National Gallery of Australia

Masterpieces of all artistic media, from Australia and beyond

Appropriately, the focus here is on Australian art, and the exhibits constitute an unrivalled survey of the nation's artistic endeavours. Highlights include a forest of 200 hollow log coffins from Arnhem Land, a gallery of 1970s Papunya desert painting, a superb range of works by Australian Impressionists, and Sidney Nolan's *Ned Kelly* series. But the scope of the gallery is broader still, with works on display from all over the world and spanning the full range of styles and forms, including sculpture, photography, and installations such as James Turrell's *Within Without*, an extraordinary outdoor structure that harnesses sunlight to create remarkable and awe-inspiring optical effects.
► *Parkes Pl, Parkes, Canberra.*

LANCASTER BOMBER, ANZAC HALL, AUSTRALIAN WAR MEMORIAL

VIEW FROM PARLIAMENT HOUSE FOYER TOWARDS OLD PARLIAMENT HOUSE

11 Old Parliament House

Pivotal events still echo in these halls

They're long gone, the ministers and prime ministers, the secretaries and civil servants, and the journalists who doggedly recorded every speech and scandal. But you can still sense their presence, almost hear their purposeful footsteps in the corridors and feel the tension of pivotal, nation-changing decisions. This was the venue of the Federal Parliament from 1927 to 1988, and much of its original decor and furnishings remain intact. You can view the desk used by every prime minister who served here, visit the Cabinet Room to learn about momentous enactments such as the 1939 declaration of war, stand on the steps where Gough Whitlam addressed the crowd following the dismissal of his government in 1975. The Museum of Australian Democracy, which today occupies the building, provides fascinating background and a compelling complementary account of the evolution and experience of democracy in Australia.

► *King George Tce, Parkes, Canberra.*

12 Parliament House

Tour the nation's political control centre

Dramatically embedded in the flag-capped grass dome of Capital Hill, Parliament House, which opened in 1988, forms the apex of the so-called Parliamentary Triangle. The building's design centres on two massive, curved walls separated by a great mall; the forecourt features a stunning mosaic designed by Aboriginal artist Michael Nelson Jagamara. Inside, the walls are lined with fine Australian timbers and adorned with magnificent works by Australian artists and master craftspeople, including superb marquetry and a giant tapestry based on a painting by Arthur Boyd. Visitors can observe the proceedings of the House of Representatives and the Senate when they are in session; tickets for Question Time can be booked in advance. Guided tours take place daily.

► *Capital Hill, Canberra.*

13 Canberra Glassworks

Absorbing displays of an ancient craft

Observing a group of people heft a huge but hugely delicate glass vase in and out of a blazing furnace, rotate it steadily as the glassmaker fashions the glass with a flame, then repeat the process over and over, you develop a keen appreciation of the skill, care and sheer hard work involved in crafting the beautiful glassware on display in the adjacent galleries. Leading artists come here to use the extensive facilities, which are housed in the former Kingston Powerhouse, built in 1915 – the city's oldest public building. Visitors can watch them at work from the mezzanine, study exhibits on glassmaking techniques and the history of the Powerhouse, and even sign up for glassmaking workshops.

▶ *Wentworth Ave, Kingston, Canberra.*

14 Canberra Deep Space Communication Complex

Where they seek to unlock the secrets of the universe

Dominated by its four massive antennas, the complex is part of NASA's Deep Space Network, a group of three deep-space communications facilities (the other two are in California and near Madrid, Spain) that monitor outer space and support spacecraft exploring the solar system. At the visitor centre here, you can find out more about the complex's role and what it's like to voyage through space, and view the antennas, rocks brought back from the Moon, models of spacecraft, and the latest images and recordings from space.

▶ *Paddys River Rd, Tharwa, 40 km south-west of Canberra.*

15 Tidbinbilla Nature Reserve

Easily accessible wilderness and wildlife

Set in a delightful valley framed by granite ridges and peaks, the reserve encompasses forest, grasslands, wetlands and, higher up, true subalpine wilderness. Well-marked walking tracks make it easy to explore these environments and there are regular guided tours. The Sanctuary, a wetland enclosed by predator-proof fences, protects abundant, highly visible fauna – you'll almost certainly see kangaroos and brush-tailed rock wallabies, lizards scuttling across the outcrops and, if you are sharp-eyed, platypuses in the pools. Koalas and lyrebirds are frequently seen along the Peppermint Trail and Koala Path.

▶ *Paddys River Rd, Tharwa, 35 km south-west of Canberra.*

A unifying feature

Though appearing to be part of the natural landscape, Lake Burley Griffin was as carefully planned as Canberra's streets and buildings.

For the first 50 years of Canberra's existence, there was no lake and the settlement was, in effect, two villages divided by the flood plain of the Molonglo River. It was only in 1963 when the Scrivener Dam was completed and the river's waters were backed up to create an artificial lake that the vision of the city's designer was fully realised. As Walter Burley Griffin had foreseen, the many-armed waterway tied the disparate suburbs together and provided a central, marvellously scenic focus. It also yielded a superb recreational resource: the banks of Lake Burley Griffin are mostly given over to parks threaded by walking tracks and cycleways. From many a lakeside vantage point, you can enjoy splendid views of city landmarks and the surrounding hills, on calm days all mirrored in the placid waters.

MELBOURNE REGION
226–231
YARRA VALLEY AND DANDENONG RANGES
232–235
MORNINGTON PENINSULA AND PHILLIP ISLAND
236–239
5–11 See p. 229
MELBOURNE
Sunbury
Melton
Bacchus Marsh
Sunshine
Werribee
Geelong
Ocean Grove
Queenscliff
Torquay
Port Phillip
Frankston
Mornington
Rosebud
Mornington Peninsula
Phillip Island
French Island
Wonthaggi
Inverloch
Leongatha
Lang Lang
Cranbourne
Pakenham
Drouin
Warragul
Dandenong
Ringwood
Lilydale
Yarra Glen
Healesville
Marysville
Warburton
Olinda
Emerald
CALDER
HUME FWY
MAROONDAH HWY
WESTERN
FWY
PRINCES
SOUTH
GIPPSLAND
HWY
MURRAY
196–199
DAYLESFORD AND MACEDON RANGES
208–213
GOLDFIELDS
204–207
GRAMPIANS
200–203
HIGH COUNTRY
214–219
GIPPSLAND
240–245
GREAT OCEAN ROAD
220–225
MELBOURNE REGION
SEE INSET ABOVE
MORNINGTON PENINSULA AND PHILLIP ISLAND
SEE INSET ABOVE
YARRA VALLEY AND DANDENONG RANGES
SEE INSET ABOVE
Murray River
STURT HWY
Mildura
Red Cliffs
Cullulleraine
Robinvale
Narrung
Sunset Country
Hattah
Ouyen
MALLEE
Nyah
Vinifera
Lake Tyrrell
Swan Hill
Sea Lake
Big Desert
Lake Albacutya
Hopetoun
Kerang
Koondrook
Cohuna
Birchip
Rainbow
Lake Hindmarsh
Jeparit
Wycheproof
Charlton
Warracknabeal
Nhill
Dimboola
Little Desert
Wedderburn
St Arnaud
Logan
Inglewood
Bendigo
Natimuk
Horsham
WIMMERA
Edenhope
Stawell
Halls Gap
The Grampians
Ararat
Avoca
Maldon
Maryborough
Castlemaine
Heathcote
Balmoral
Rocklands Reservoir
Glenelg River
Casterton
Cavendish
Hamilton
Dunkeld
Beaufort
Ballarat
Daylesford
Kyneton
Kilmore
Broadford
Skipton
Enfield
Ballan
Bacchus Marsh
Sunbury
Craigieburn
Melton
Sunshine
MELBOURNE
Werribee
Penshurst
Lismore
Cressy
Lake Corangamite
Heywood
Mortlake
Tyrendarra
Camperdown
Portland
Cape Bridgewater
Port Fairy
Warrnambool
Port Campbell
Colac
Otway Ranges
Lorne
Glenaire
Apollo Bay
Cape Otway
Geelong
Queenscliff
Torquay
Port Phillip
Dromana
Mornington Peninsula
Frankston
Phillip I.
Wonthaggi
Echuca
Numurkah
Cobram
Yarrawonga
Rutherglen
Wodonga
Lake Hume
Tallangatta
Shepparton
Wangaratta
Beechworth
Stanhope
Rushworth
Murchison
Nagambie
Benalla
Myrtleford
Bright
Mount Beauty
Mitta Mitta
Seymour
Mansfield
Mt Buller
Lake Eildon
Eildon
Alexandra
Jamieson
Omeo
Dargo
Marysville
Yarra Glen
Healesville
Lilydale
Warburton
Baw Baw Alpine Village
Walhalla
Noojee
Dandenong
Pakenham
Lang Lang
Warragul
Moe
Traralgon
Morwell
Maffra
Sale
Bairnsdale
Lakes Entrance
Mirboo North
Boolarra
Leongatha
Yarram
Woodside
Foster
Yanakie
Corner Inlet
Cape Liptrap
Wilsons Promontory
Ninety Mile Beach
Golden Beach
GREAT DIVIDING RANGE
CALDER HWY
SUNRAYSIA
MIDLAND
HUME
WESTERN HWY
HAMILTON HWY
PRINCES HWY
GREAT OCEAN ROAD
SOUTH GIPPSLAND HWY
GREAT ALPINE
OMEO HWY

Victoria

Crammed between the Murray River in the north and Victoria's long, rugged seashore is a remarkable range of intriguing attractions, from pink lakes and thermal springs to towering escarpments, and from paddle-steamer ports and opulent gold-rush architecture to the grand streetscapes, galleries and gardens of the capital.

TWELVE APOSTLES,
GREAT OCEAN ROAD

Useful websites

Visitor information www.visitvictoria.com
Parks and reserves www.parkweb.vic.gov.au
Motoring organisation www.racv.com.au

Murray

The Murray River meanders west through avenues of red gums, past sandy beaches, farming lands and the 150-year-old wharves of former river ports. Trees from which Aboriginal people cut bark for canoes still stand on its banks. In more recent times, the river was a highway to market for western pastoralists.

1 Rio Vista

Handsome museum of local history

Little has changed in the appearance of this Queen Anne–style mansion built in 1899 by irrigation pioneer William Chaffey. Overlooking the Murray, Rio Vista ('River View') is a grand construction of red brick and ornate timberwork. Inside you'll find jarrah and cedar floors, Italian tiles in the hallway and, in the basement, a ballroom with a sprung floor for dancing. The drawing room has been returned to its original decor and colour schemes – even the wallpaper is as it once was, re-created from scraps found under layers of later adornments. Upstairs, five bedrooms contain a variety of Victorian-era furniture and fittings. And an elegant fountain still plays in the formal garden.

▶ *Cureton Ave, Mildura.*

2 Pink Lakes

A splash of colour in an arid land

For most of the year, these salt lakes glisten silver. But in spring the arrival of warmer weather sparks a population explosion of *Dunaliella salina*, algae that stain the salty waters with a red pigment. By the end of summer, the water has evaporated – leaving shimmering beds of pink-tinged salt. It was the commercial harvesting of this seasonal bounty that in 1916 attracted settlement here. A town was established and men using horsedrawn scrapers toiled in the salt mines; the bagged product was hauled to railheads by camel teams. Operations ceased in 1979 when the area became a national park. Spring is also the best time to see the park's wild flowers.

▶ *Murray–Sunset National Park, 72 km west of Ouyen via Mallee Hwy and Pink Lakes Rd.*

Echoes of the riverboat age

Reaching far inland, the Murray, Darling and Murrumbidgee rivers provided convenient transportation routes in the early days of European settlement.

The first paddle-steamers on the Murray River were the *Lady Augusta*, skippered by Francis Cadell, and William Randell's *Mary Ann*; in 1853 the pair raced each other upstream from Goolwa to Swan Hill to show that the river was navigable. Soon everything from roofing iron to pianos was being carried inland by water, while hides, tallow, chaff and wool bales were loaded from outback wharves for the return run. Fluctuating water levels meant that navigation was always tricky. In times of low water, the tops of the banks might be 10 m above the deck, at other times they disappeared beneath floodwaters. The hub of river transport on the Murray was the Echuca–Swan Hill stretch, where 17 steamers churned up and down in the 1860s. But by the turn of the century, the boats had lost out to the railways, and today a number of restored vessels ply a different trade: tourism.

RIVER RED GUMS FRINGING THE MURRAY RIVER IN BARMAH NATIONAL PARK

3 Pioneer Settlement

Relive the romance of a riverboat port

The arrival of the first paddle-steamers in 1853 set the port of Swan Hill on its way as a thriving 19th-century commercial centre. Today, at the Pioneer Settlement, a working re-creation of a Mallee township and river port, you can walk the streets and experience the lifestyle of that bustling era. Here, more than 50 original and replica heritage buildings, including an 1850s slab cottage and an 1880s school, form authentic streetscapes; on their outskirts are a number of relocated pioneer homesteads. Visitors can dress in period costume, take a carriage ride, tour a working blacksmith's workshop, bakery and general store, and board a paddle-steamer for a short trip up the Murray.

▶ *Monash Dr, Swan Hill.*

Visitor information

Corryong 02 6076 2277
Echuca–Moama 03 5480 7555
Mildura 03 5018 8380
Shepparton 03 5831 4400
Swan Hill 03 5032 3033
Wodonga 02 6051 3751
Yarrawonga 03 5744 1989

4 Barmah National Park

Vast red gum forest that relies on rejuvenating floods

The massive red gums – up to 45 m in height and 500 years old – that line the Murray and its waterways depend for survival on the river's regular inundation of the surrounding land. Their roots can endure months of submersion; their reward is that the river's waters wash their seeds away to germinate. The largest remaining stand of these iconic trees is protected in Barmah National Park, which extends for more than 100 km along the twisting Murray frontage and across the associated flood plain. In times of flood, visitors can boat between the mighty trunks; when the waters recede, the forest floor is a lush green meadow dotted with wild flowers and home to kangaroos, emus and koalas. The park is also an internationally recognised freshwater wetland providing vital habitat for over 200 bird species – brolgas, night herons, spoonbills and sea eagles can all be seen here.

▶ *34 km north-east of Echuca via Cobb Hwy and Barmah Rd.*

5 Echuca Wharf

Grand historic wharf and restored riverfront precinct

The scale of this wharf, towering on great trunks of red gum at the river's edge, is best appreciated from the water, so take advantage of the paddle-steamer cruises that regularly depart from here to get a captain's-eye view. In the 1860s, Echuca was the largest inland port in the country; it lies on the part of the Murray closest to Melbourne and therefore offered the fastest rail link for wool headed to the southern capital. Today it remains a working port and home to a painstakingly maintained fleet of paddle-steamers that operate much as they did 150 years ago, but now carry sightseers, not wool. Watch shipwrights at work, visit the cargo shed museum and duck into the illegal underground bar of the Star Hotel, with its escape tunnel that delivered drinkers to the back lane should the law arrive.

▶ *Echuca, 2 km north of Murray Valley Hwy via High St.*

6 Cactus Country

Amazing assemblage of cacti and succulents

The contrast between the surrounding irrigated farmlands and the clusters of spiky balls and towering multi-armed cacti could hardly be greater. Once a peach orchard, this 5-ha property is now planted with more than 4000 species of cacti and succulents from North America, South America and Africa – more than 10,000 desert plants in all – all grouped by country of origin along colour-coded trails. Take a self-guided tour to learn about their adaptations to harsh desert environments. Plants are available for sale.

▶ *Strathmerton, 19 km west of Cobram.*

PADDLE-STEAMERS AT HISTORIC ECHUCA WHARF

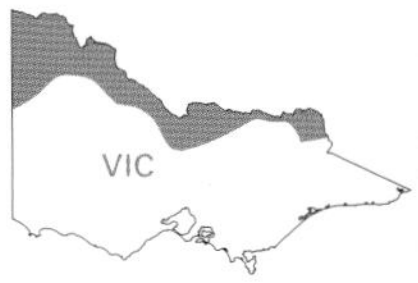

7 Shepparton Art Gallery

Outstanding collection of ceramics

Representing all of the major developments in Australian ceramics history, this permanent exhibition of more than 3000 pieces ranges from examples of some of the earliest ceramics produced in Australia – by convict potters – to modern artworks. Highlights include an 1830s ginger-beer bottle made at Jonathan Leak's pottery at Brickfield Hill in Sydney, and *The Lovers' Platter*, made in the 1950s by Arthur Boyd.
▶ *Welsford St, Shepparton.*

8 Byramine Homestead

Custom-designed safe house for colonial widow and children

Elizabeth Hume, sister-in-law of explorer Hamilton Hume, was not going to be caught unawares. The central octagonal room that is a key feature of her homestead allows a clear view through its doors and windows to all parts of the property; safety features include low door handles that could easily be reached by the children, shutters for all the windows and walls 50 cm thick (made of handmade bricks). Elizabeth had reason to be wary: when she took up land here in 1842, she was a widow with young children, her husband having died at the hands of bushrangers. It is believed that the plans for the house were originally prepared by an English architect for use in India. Open Sunday, Monday, Wednesday and Thursday.
▶ *Murray Valley Hwy, Yarrawonga.*

9 Man from Snowy River Museum

Chronicles of high-country life

The grand high plains that surround the Upper Murray township of Corryong were settled in the late 1830s by a band of hardy pioneers who brought their cattle to the lush alpine pastures for the spring and summer months. This high country was also home to Jack Riley, who is believed to have been the inspiration for the horseman in Banjo Paterson's epic ballad *The Man from Snowy River*. Riley is buried in the town, and his story is told in this museum. Also on display here are household items, quilts and a collection of antique skis.
▶ *Corryong, 116 km east of Wodonga via Murray Valley Hwy.*

Grampians

The steep escarpments and forested slopes of the starkly beautiful Grampians rise abruptly from a flat expanse of farmland. In the forested wilderness beneath the bare peaks, you'll find colourful wild flowers, prolific wildlife, and ancient rock art that speaks of a long and rich human heritage.

1 Little Desert National Park

Neither little, nor a desert

Early settlers who shunned the nutrient-poor soils of this region – misleadingly called a desert – unwittingly preserved an extraordinary pocket of mallee habitats from axes and scrub-rollers. Today this 132,000-ha park is a natural wild-flower garden in spring, with more than 670 species ranging from woodlands and heaths to a colourfully named selection of orchids, including greenhoods, pink fingers and red beaks. It is also a refuge for endangered birds, particularly the shy mallee fowl (see p. 203) and mammals such as the silky desert mouse. By day, stumpy-tailed lizards and bearded dragons bask in the sun; at night, bats flit overhead.

► *10 km south of Nhill via Nhill–Harrow Rd.*

Visitor information

Ararat 03 5355 0281
Dunkeld 03 5577 2558
Halls Gap 03 5361 4444
Horsham 03 5382 1832
Stawell 03 5358 2314

2 Mount Arapiles

Where cliffs challenge climbers

The flat lands of western Victoria are about the last place you'd expect to find a world-class rock-climbing site. But in the elevated world of serious mountaineers, the steep-sided outcrop of Mount Arapiles is regarded as one of the country's best climbs. More than 2000 routes have been developed on its fissured cliffs and crags, and are graded in difficulty with thought-provoking names such as 'Agamemnon', 'Spasm in the Chasm' and 'Anxiety Neurosis'. For non-climbers, there are other ways to get to the summit – you can take a walking trail or cycle or drive to a car park where a short steep track leads to a lookout with stupendous views across a sea of wheatfields to the Grampians.

► *Mount Arapiles–Tooan National Park, 30 km west of Horsham via Wimmera Hwy and Mount Arapiles Summit Rd.*

3 The Balconies

Rocky ledges frame jaw-dropping views

On the crest of Mount Bagara nature has sculpted the Grampians sandstone into a striking series of weathered platforms that jut out over Victoria Valley. Known as The Balconies, these fanciful formations include a much-photographed pair that resemble mighty open jaws. To the south are sweeping views of the Victoria Range and valley and, to the north, Lake Wartook and the Mount Difficult Range. The 2-km easy return walk to The Balconies starts from Reed Lookout car park.

► *Grampians National Park, 30 km south-west of Stawell via Halls Gap.*

JAWS FORMATION
AT THE BALCONIES

THE DRIVES, SEPPELT GREAT WESTERN WINERY

4 Boroka Lookout

Look down on Wonderland

This lookout in the Mount Difficult Range offers an eagle's-eye view south over the sharp ridge of the Wonderland Range, one of several ranges that run north–south in the Grampians and were formed by the upward tilt of a thick bed of sandstone some 400 million years ago – molten granite later filled cracks in the sandstone. Just east of its craggy edge and cradled in the Fyans Valley lies the township of Halls Gap. Lake Bellfield gleams further to the south and the panorama continues across the plains to the town of Stawell.

▶ *Grampians National Park, 30 km south-west of Stawell via Halls Gap.*

5 Brambuk the National Park and Cultural Centre

Essential stop for an Indigenous perspective on the Grampians

Brambuk incorporates the National Park information and Brambuk Aboriginal Cultural centres. It is owned and operated by Aboriginal people and is the longest-running Aboriginal cultural centre in Australia. Here you can learn of the long cultural heritage of Gariwerd (the Grampians) through displays of artefacts (clothing, tools and weapons), presentations in the Gariwerd Dreaming Theatre, and activities such as didgeridoo playing, traditional dance, basket-weaving, boomerang-throwing and finding bush tucker. Aboriginal guides lead tours to ancient rock-art sites and teach you how to recognise Gariwerd's six seasons through changes in plants and animal behaviour.

▶ *Halls Gap, 27 km south-west of Western Hwy via Grampians Rd.*

6 Stawell Gift Hall of Fame

Museum dedicated to a famous dash

The Stawell Gift is the country's oldest and richest short-distance footrace. Apart from four years during the Second World War, the event has been run every Easter since 1878. It began as a 130-yard fun run for goldminers, but now attracts professional athletes from around the world who race 120 m across the grass of Stawell's Central Park oval. The story is told through artefacts, memorabilia and archives dating back to the first race. Portraits of past winners watch over a fascinating collection that includes starting blocks, running shoes, medals and cups.

▶ *Main St, Stawell, 1.5 km north of Western Hwy.*

7 Bunjil Shelter

Outstanding Indigenous art site

In traditional belief, Bunjil is a principal creation figure. It was Bunjil who heated the sun, which then warmed the earth, causing it to open so the first humans could emerge from its interior. Bunjil then brought rain to make grass and roots grow for their nourishment, and is also credited with shaping the landscape. The painting on the wall of this rock overhang in the Black Range shows Bunjil with two helper dingoes. The 200-m track to the site looks west across the plains to the Grampians.

▶ *Black Range Scenic Reserve, 8 km south of Stawell.*

8 Seppelt Great Western Winery

Underground vaults stacked with sparkling wines

You may think it strange to find a gaping shaft entrance in the centre of this winery's elegant tasting room. Peer down, and you'll see dusty bottles and hand-dug passageways disappearing into the darkness. Known as 'The Drives', this labyrinth of tunnels was gouged through soft rock by out-of-work goldminers in the 1870s as cellars for the Best brothers, founders of the winery. As the demand for wine grew, the drives were extended. Today, the 3 km of tunnels still serve their original purpose – sparkling wines are bottle-aged here at an even, year-round temperature of 14–15°C. You can see them for yourself on an underground tour.

▶ *Great Western, Western Hwy.*

9 Gum San Chinese Heritage Centre

Rich seam of history and culture

In the 1850s, thousands of Chinese gold-seekers made their way to Australia. One such group, trudging overland from the South Australian port of Robe to the Victorian diggings, made a fortuitous stop in the foothills here and, by chance, while topping up water supplies at a spring, discovered the Canton Lead, a 5-km-long alluvial goldfield. They stayed, of course, and thus Ararat became the only Australian town to be founded by Chinese. Set in a Chinese garden, adorned with dragons and designed according to Feng Shui principles, the Gum San Chinese Heritage Centre brings this story to life, and explores the history of immigrant workers on the goldfields and the influence of Chinese culture in Australia.

▶ *Lambert St, Ararat, Western Hwy.*

Nature and nurture

Reserves in western Victoria protect some of the last remaining habitat of a solitary, hard-working bird, the mallee fowl.

In parks such as Little Desert National Park (see p. 200), visitors can see evidence of the remarkable breeding activities of the mallee fowl. The bird builds a large incubator mound, roughly 3–4 m across, in which it buries its eggs along with leaves and bark. It then covers the mound with sand so that the vegetable material decomposes and increases the temperature to incubate the eggs.

While the female bird gathers food, the male maintains the mound, using his beak as a thermometer to check its warmth and adding material as required to keep the incubator at just the right temperature. Curiously, after all this effort, the birds' interest ceases once the offspring hatch. After struggling to the surface through perhaps a metre of debris, the chicks must wander off alone to fend for themselves.

Goldfields

In the 1850s, the rolling hills of central Victoria were transformed by the discovery of gold. The material and cultural benefits live on in the imposing architecture of its vibrant centres, the unspoiled streetscapes of its 19th-century villages, a rich Chinese heritage and the history-making site of the Eureka Rebellion.

1 Melville Caves

Look down from a robber's retreat

With gold came bushrangers. One such was Frank McCallum, also known as Captain Melville, who, after relieving gold transports of their load, withdrew to a hideout in these 'caves' – a labyrinth of cavities and crevices in a jumble of granite boulders atop Mount Kooyoora. These shelters and overhangs gave protection from the weather, and shallow depressions in the rocks captured rainwater. They had been used for millennia by Aboriginal people, and many stone artefacts have been found in their sandy floors. The hideout also offered clear views over the plains to the south, where gold-bearing coaches passed in the 1850s. Today's visitors can enjoy these views from Melville Caves Lookout, reached by a 1-km-loop track from a picnic area.

▶ *Kooyoora State Park, 14 km west of Calder Hwy at Inglewood via Kingower Rd.*

2 Pall Mall

Imposing streetscape funded by goldmining wealth

It's called 'boom style' – the highly ornate architecture of the 1880s that reflected the sudden and extraordinary wealth generated in south-eastern Australia by goldmining – and there is probably no purer example than the grandiose public buildings of Bendigo's Pall Mall. Here, no expense was spared and buildings often combined many architectural styles. The highlight is the 1887 French Second Empire–style Bendigo Post Office and Law Courts complex, with its elaborate façades and decorative roof forms. Other grand sights include the 1897 Shamrock Hotel, rebuilt three times with each incarnation more lavish than the last, and the 1881 Alexandra Fountain, made from 20 tonnes of granite. A self-guided walk is marked by information panels, or you can hop on the vintage 'Talking Tram', which runs an 8-km route from the city's majestic heart to the Central Deborah Mine, a 411-m-deep mine now restored and open to the public.

▶ *Pall Mall, Bendigo.*

3 Golden Dragon Museum

Where record-holding dragons rest

Sun Loong, the world's longest imperial (five-clawed) dragon, and Loong, the world's oldest (and now retired) dragon are both on permanent display here. Made near Canton (Guangzhou), China, of bamboo, silk, papier-mâché and mirrors, Loong first walked the streets of Bendigo in 1892; in 1970 he was replaced by Sun Loong, 100 m long, covered with beads and mirrors and so heavy he needs 52 carriers to help him make his spectacular annual outing at the Bendigo Easter Fair. Six other dragons complete the family.

▶ *Bridge St, Bendigo.*

Visitor information

Ballarat 03 5320 5741
Bendigo 03 5434 6060
Castlemaine 03 5471 1795
Maldon 03 5475 2569
Maryborough 1800 356 511

ORNATE FAÇADES ADORN THE BUILDINGS OF PALL MALL, BENDIGO.

4 Maryborough Railway Station

'A railway station with a town attached ...'

American author Mark Twain's remark is not so much a put-down of Maryborough – it's a handsome, well-planned town – but an acknowledgment of the magnificence of its 25-room, red-brick railway station. Built in 1890, it has 1010 m of covered platform, its foyer is laid with elaborate tessellated tiles, the ticket-box windows are surrounded by intricate carving, and there are marble dressing tables in the women's toilets. You can still take tea in the oak-panelled waiting room, where antiques are on display and on cool days a fire glows in the grate. In 2010, passenger trains, absent from Maryborough for more than a decade, began running again.

► *Victoria St, Maryborough.*

5 Maldon

Victoria's best-preserved gold town

You would not call the buildings of Maldon's commercial centre grand. Instead they are of an appealing human scale and present a streetscape that is for the most part unchanged since the turn of the 20th century, with many buildings outwardly still as they were in the 1860s. Gold from rich reefs was mined here from the 1850s. The town grew in a hasty, unorganised manner, with meandering streets and mixtures of styles and materials, from wattle-and-daub and mud brick to bluestone and wrought iron. It was the charm of these irregularities that led the National Trust, in 1966, to declare Maldon a 'notable town'. Pick up a self-guided heritage walk map from the visitor centre and spend an hour or two investigating what today's merchants have on offer.

► *18 km north-west of Castlemaine via Castlemaine–Maldon Rd.*

6 Castlemaine Diggings National Heritage Park

Evocative remains of gold era

From 1851 to 1854, the Castlemaine area was the richest shallow alluvial goldfield in the world. By 1852, more than 40,000 migrant fortune-seekers were crammed onto the fields here, uprooting forests of towering ironbark and overturning flats and gullies in the search for gold. A large swathe of the former diggings lies within this park, where an extensive network of roads and walking tracks accesses sites and relics that hold tales of the mining past. These range from the stone axle supports of the massive (24 m in diameter) Garfield Water Wheel, which supplied power to a quartz-crushing stamping battery, to the cemetery at Pennyweight Flat, where the graves of children and adults (including Chinese) lie in rows among eucalypts.

▶ *2 km east of Castlemaine via Pyrenees Hwy.*

7 Buda Historic Home and Garden

Stronghold of a family of talented women

The five Leviny women, unmarried daughters of silversmith Ernest Leviny, lived long and cultured lives in this 1860s hilltop house. Each was creative in some form of art or craft, and examples of their work, displaying the influence of the Arts and Crafts Movement of the early 20th century, can be seen throughout the house. The range includes embroidery, metalcraft, photography and woodwork; also on display are works by artists whose works the sisters collected, including Margaret Preston. After the death of their father in 1905, the women modified and redecorated Buda to their taste; the last sister, Hilda, lived here until 1981 and the house and its formal gardens are much as she left them.

▶ *Hunter St, Castlemaine.*

SOUND AND LIGHT SHOW AT SOVEREIGN HILL, BALLARAT

Site of the diggers' stand

More than just a stand against an unfair tax, the Eureka Rebellion was also about the right of ordinary people to have a say in how they were governed.

Seeking to secure a share of the wealth being dug from the Ballarat goldfields, in August 1854 the Victorian government introduced a licence fee, to be paid a month in advance, for the right to mine. This was beyond the resources of most miners, and at a mass meeting in late November they demanded not only the abolition of the fee – some burned their licences in a gesture of defiance – but also the right to vote and stand for parliament (at this time only male property-owners could vote). This was refused, and in the mounting tension the government brought in troopers while the miners, under the leadership of Peter Lalor, barricaded themselves into a hastily built stockade. Some 28 miners and six troopers died in the battle that ensued. In the aftermath, public opinion was firmly on the side of the rebels. They won the right to vote, and in 1855 Lalor was elected to parliament.

8 Sovereign Hill

Living museum re-creates Ballarat's gold-rush days in thrilling style

Built directly over the site of one of Ballarat's richest mines, this open-air museum fairly throbs to the beat of the boom times. Spend a day here and you'll find yourself caught up in both the frenzy of gold fever and the political upheaval of the Eureka Stockade. Pan for real gold (and keep what you find), take a tramway deep into the mine, ride in a Cobb and Co coach, then, as night falls, stand shoulder to shoulder with the Eureka rebels in the 'Blood on the Southern Cross' sound and light show. The faithful representation of the past continues with working machinery, ingots poured every day and period-costumed guides.

► *Bradshaw St, Ballarat.*

9 Eureka Stockade Gardens

Where diggers fought for a fair go

For many, this is hallowed ground, a place to imagine, reflect on and honour all who died here in the battle between miners and troopers in the early hours of 3 December 1854 (see above). Mining continued after the uprising, burying or obliterating visible relics of the Eureka Stockade, until 1869, when these gardens were established by the people of Ballarat to mark its site. The monument erected in 1884 stands on a spot chosen by general agreement as being the location of the stockade. In 2004, as part of the 150th anniversary of the rebellion, the artwork 'Eureka Circle', depicting aspects of the Eureka story in 20 steel panels, was added to the gardens.

► *Eureka St, Ballarat.*

10 Art Gallery of Ballarat

Born of gold-rush wealth and Victorian-era civic pride

The battle-tattered Eureka flag lies in a darkened room here, a major attraction but by no means this gallery's only drawcard. Ballarat's magnificent collection is regional Australia's oldest and largest and features several iconic 19th- and 20th-century works, including Tom Roberts's *Wood Splitters* (once stolen from here and held to ransom), as well as paintings by Eugene von Guérard, Russell Drysdale and Norman Lindsay.

► *Lydiard St, Ballarat.*

Daylesford and Macedon Ranges

This region's dramatic and mysterious rock formations and its concentration of mineral springs – the country's largest – are both the result of past volcanic turmoil. The more recent upheaval of the gold rushes has engendered a magnificent legacy of picturesque villages and diverse cultural influences.

1 Anderson's Mill

Boom-times mill by a babbling brook

Prospects were promising in 1861 when the Scottish Anderson brothers built this imposing, four-storey bluestone mill to tap into the local farming and population boom generated by the gold rushes. But the mill's prosperity was short-lived; Smeaton was bypassed by the railway and even wheat-growing moved on, shifting north and west to the plains of the Wimmera. The Andersons turned to oats, and the mill ground on through the wars and the Depression until 1959. Much of the machinery was then sold, but the mighty iron waterwheel remains in place. The building is only open on the first Sunday of each month, but the excellent information boards and the sheer charm of its grounds (with picnic tables) make a visit worthwhile on any day – you can even see the waterwheel through strategically placed peepholes.

▶ *Smeaton, 13 km north-east of Creswick via Creswick–Newstead Rd.*

2 Hepburn Springs

Take the waters amid striking architecture

Beneath a layer of volcanic rocks, an underground reservoir here absorbs salts and minerals before bubbling to the surface in at least 75 locations. The springs provided miners in the 1850s with clean drinking water and also attracted the particular interest of the large number of Swiss Italians on the fields, who were familiar with European spas and in time used this resource to develop a fashionable health resort. By the late 1880s, Melbourne's wealthy were travelling to Hepburn for the reputed restorative powers of its waters and a bathhouse has been in operation here since 1895 (the current building dates from a century later). Bring a bottle and join the locals to fill up from the hand pumps located nearby.

▶ *4 km north of Daylesford via Hepburn Rd.*

3 Daylesford

From 'Satan's stronghold' to centre of stylish indulgence

In the 1850s, isolated Daylesford was a lawless mining town and, according to the local Methodist preacher, 'one of the most wicked and abandoned places'. Not so today. Gourmet eateries and outlets rub shoulders with galleries and crafts shops along its historic main street and luxurious spas and boutique hotels are sprinkled around the hillsides. Tranquil Lake Daylesford lies over Wombat Flat, site of the original rowdy diggings and later a Chinese market garden; it was created in 1929 with the building of a dam. Every Sunday, heritage trains make a 35-minute round trip from Daylesford through scenic forest and farmlands.

▶ *Midland Hwy.*

4 Trentham Falls

A geology lesson in slow motion

This waterfall originally formed about 2 km downstream. Several million years ago, lava flowed into an old valley here and solidified into basalt. As the young stream that is now the Coliban River tumbled over its edge, the force of falling water and debris exposed and cut back into the softer sedimentary rock beneath, undermining the overlying basalt and causing it to collapse. This ongoing erosion has seen the waterfall retreat slowly upstream to its present position, where it plunges 32 m in an unimpeded fall – making it the longest single-drop waterfall in Victoria. Information boards on the short walk from the pleasant picnic ground explain the geological process. Around the falls are stately native forests of manna gum, messmate and stringy-bark.

► *23 km east of Daylesford via Daylesford–Trentham Rd.*

5 Keystone Viaduct

Marvel of mid-1800s engineering

An impressive bluestone viaduct with five elegant arches, each 18 m wide, carries the Melbourne–Bendigo railway line high above the waters of the Coliban River. About 100 masons worked on the viaduct's construction. The first stone was laid in 1859, the keystone in the central arch was placed in 1860 and the viaduct opened in 1862, at which time it was the longest bridge in Australia. A scenic 4.5-km walk meanders through Malmsbury's Botanic Gardens and past the viaduct.

► *Malmsbury, 2 km north-west of Calder Fwy.*

Visitor information

Bacchus Marsh 03 5367 7488
Daylesford 03 5321 6123
Kilmore 03 5781 1319
Kyneton 03 5422 6110
Woodend 03 5427 2033

TRANQUIL DAYLESFORD

Coach class

The Cobb and Co coach company, established in 1853 by American Freeman Cobb, reaped rich rewards on routes north from Melbourne.

Cobb and Co's first coaches (see also p. 100) were imported from the United States. They were light and robust vehicles, suspended on leather straps attached at either end to iron jacks and were reliable on rough bush roads – an advantage on the Melbourne to Bendigo route, which was dusty and bumpy at the best of times and a mud bath in wet weather. Cobb and Co used experienced US coach drivers and changed horses frequently, enabling them to keep to their timetable. A later company innovation was to breed horses especially suited to the task of pulling a fully laden coach at a gallop. Pride of the fleet in the 1850s was the *Leviathan*, a mighty coach that ran between Castlemaine and Kyneton (see Piper Street), pulled by 22 horses, each wearing a blue rosette over its ears. It carried up to 75 passengers and the driver had as many as four postilions to help him with the reins.

6 Piper Street

Colonial streetscape highlights heritage and fine food

Piper Street's handsome buildings of local bluestone date from the gold-rush days, when Kyneton was a staging post and supply town for the diggings. The Royal Hotel, now a hatted eatery, opened in 1852 as the Diggers Arms Hotel to provide refreshments on the way to the goldfields. Other historic buildings now serve as restaurants and cafes – showcasing the region's food and wine – art and crafts shops, antique shops and galleries. The former Bank of New South Wales, erected in 1856, houses the Kyneton Museum, which has changing exhibits in the original banking chamber, period-furnished rooms in the manager's quarters upstairs and, at the rear, the kitchen, laundry, stables and buggy house and the relocated 1838 Theaden Cottage.

▶ *Kyneton, 5 km south-west of Calder Fwy via Kyneton Main Rd.*

7 Kilmore

Celtic heritage and historic buildings

Founded in the early 1840s, Kilmore is one of Victoria's oldest inland towns and was the first coach stop on the route from Melbourne to Sydney via north-eastern Victoria. Fine stone buildings grace its streets, including the 1862 post office, the 1863 court house and 1850s St Patricks Church, the state's oldest Catholic parish church outside Melbourne. Many of the first settlers were from Ireland, Scotland and Cornwall and the town celebrates this heritage each June with a Celtic Festival.

▶ *56 km east of Kyneton via Lancefield.*

8 Hanging Rock

Volcanic formation with a mystical pull

This was the setting for Joan Lindsay's novel *Picnic at Hanging Rock*, about the mysterious disappearance of a group of girls during a school outing to the rock in 1900, as well as Peter Weir's film adaptation. These works have endowed the place with a brooding air of mystery, and today few set off on the scenic track to the top without at least a tremor of trepidation. Rising 105 m from a farmed plain, the rock is the weathered remains of dense lava that squeezed through the earth's crust 6 million years ago and formed a mound. Rent with cracks and fissures, it is steeped in Aboriginal history and was once the lair of notorious bushranger Mad Dog Morgan. From the peak, the panorama extends from Mount Macedon in the south to the Cobaw Ranges in the north; less strenuous tracks encircle the rock, providing opportunities for spotting wildlife including koalas, wallabies and rosellas. You'll also pass a number of attractive picnic areas.

▶ *Hanging Rock Recreation Reserve, 6 km east of Calder Fwy via Lancefield–Woodend Rd and South Rock Rd.*

JUMBLED BOULDERS CROWN HANGING ROCK.

9 Mount Macedon Memorial Cross

Highly visible tribute to fallen soldiers

The 21-m-high cross on the summit of Mount Macedon can be seen from 50 km away. The original tiled cross was built in the 1930s at the instigation of local businessman William Cameron to honour those who died in the First World War. Time took a toll on the structure: in 1975 it was hit by lightning and it was further damaged in the 1983 Ash Wednesday bushfires; in 1995 it was replaced by the present steel cross. It and the surrounding gardens now commemorate all those who served in wars and conflicts. The view from the summit takes in the entire southern plain towards Port Phillip Bay.

► *Macedon Regional Park, 12 km north-east of Calder Fwy via Mount Macedon Rd.*

10 Dromkeen National Centre for Picture Book Art

Beautiful artworks and manuscripts from children's books

This assemblage of original illustrations, artworks and manuscripts shows young and old the complex process of producing picture books. Numbering approximately 8000 pieces, the collection was established in 1974 and is spread over three galleries in an 1849 homestead owned by Scholastic Australia, publishers of books for children. In the grounds, picture-book heroes come alive in bronze garden sculptures – among others, you'll come across the Gumnut Babies, Shy the Platypus and the Bunyip from Berkeley's Creek, as well as elegant strutting peacocks.

► *Kilmore Rd, Riddells Creek, 8 km east of Calder Fwy via Gisborne–Kilmore Rd.*

MOUNT MACEDON MEMORIAL CROSS

11 Werribee Gorge State Park

Where the cliff walls tell a story

The walls of the steep-sided 200-m-deep gorge carved by the Werribee River provide a layer-cake cross-section of 500 million years of geological history. The lowest levels are gently curving bands of ancient seabed sediments containing tiny marine fossils laid down between 400 and 500 million years ago. Above is a deep layer of pebbles and powdered rock, now hardened into sandstone, left by a glacier that several times, between 250 and 290 million years ago, ground its way inland from the south-west then retreated. You can see examples of both on the River Walk (3 km return). More recent is the basalt capping, the result of volcanic activity a mere 3 to 4 million years ago. It is best viewed above the gorge at Picnic Point on the Circuit Track (10 km). Care is required on the narrow gravel road to the picnic and parking area.

▶ *6 km south of Western Fwy via Pentland Hills Rd and Myers Rd.*

12 Avenue of Honour

Living monument to First World War locals

'Each tree stands as a silent sentry representing a gallant soldier': so read a report of the 1918 planting of the Avenue of Honour in a local newspaper. More than 240 of the 281 Canadian elms planted that August by relatives and friends of those serving abroad remain in place and, with the addition of later trees, today form a dramatic 3-km-long avenue of mature, 30-m-high elms arching over the road. Each tree bears a plaque naming the soldier for whom it was planted.

▶ *Bacchus Marsh.*

13 Brisbane Ranges National Park

Rocky refuge rimmed by eroded turrets

There is perhaps no richer wild-flower habitat in the state than the rugged plateau protected by Brisbane Ranges National Park. Here the sandy soils ignored by farmers support more than 600 plant species, representing nearly a quarter of Victoria's native flora, including many species that have long since vanished from other regions and some, such as the locally common golden grevillea, that are unique to the area. In spring the display is gloriously colourful. The park is also home to abundant wildlife including the highest density of koalas in the state. A network of walking tracks provides access to lookouts.

▶ *30 km south of Bacchus Marsh via Geelong Rd.*

14 Steiglitz Historic Park

Fluctuating fortunes of a gold-rush town

Gold was mined here from the mid-1850s to the early 1900s. Steiglitz's population rose and fell with the success of the mines, peaking in the 1860s at more than 1500 residents, who were served by four hotels, several churches, a newspaper, a variety of shops and an undertaker. But as gold production petered out the population dwindled, and the town's buildings were sold for removal to other settlements. Today the empty streets and surrounding area are protected in the 469-ha Steiglitz Historic Park. Atmospheric reminders of its boom days include the 1875 court house – one of the few buildings to escape demolition and relocation and now housing a display of photographs and relics from the gold years – a cemetery and extensive mining remains.

▶ *55 km south-east of Ballarat via Midland Hwy and C142.*

High Country

Gold-rush relics and the legend of Ned Kelly loom large in this region's historic towns. Large tracts of majestic alpine wilderness invite exploration through the summer months, while abundant winter snows draw skiers from near and far.

1 Tahbilk Winery

Sample top-flight wines amid protected wetland wilderness

Established in 1860, Tahbilk is one of the state's oldest and best-known wineries and is renowned for its red, white, sparkling and fortified wines, which can be sampled in its handsome vaulted brick cellar. But it's not just the quality of the wine, or the attractive buildings, capped by the distinctive weatherboard tower, that make this such an appealing destination. It's also the remarkable surrounding property: 1200 ha of rich river flats including 11 km of Goulburn River frontage, much of it protected by the Tahbilk Wetlands Reserve. More than 4 km of paths and boardwalks allow you to examine this environment and its bountiful wildlife at close quarters. On weekends and public holidays, guided cruises explore the waterways further.

► *10 km south-west of Goulburn Valley Hwy at Nagambie.*

2 Cathedral Range

Wonderful walks along and atop a razorback ridge

Testimony to titanic tectonic forces, the Cathedral Range is a 7-km-long outcrop of sedimentary rock that aeons ago was uplifted and overturned, leaving uppermost what elsewhere are the lower, older layers of rock. Fascinating from a geological point of view, the range is also a distinctive regional landmark and a top-notch bushwalking and climbing destination. Numerous walking tracks climb and traverse its flanks, ranging from the easy 1-hour Friends Nature Trail through manna forest and the medium 1.5-hour ascent of Neds Peak to the demanding 2-hour trek between The Farmyard and 910-m Sugarloaf Peak.

► *Cathedral Range State Park, 21 km south of Alexandra via Maroondah Hwy.*

3 Snobs Creek Fish Hatchery

Learn about the intriguing aquatic life of the High Country

The hatchery breeds brown and rainbow trout for stocking Victoria's High Country waterways – more than 1 million trout are released from here into rivers and streams each year. Displays and exhibits explain the breeding process and you are even encouraged to thrust a hand into a tankful of trout and give them a tickle. Other aquatic animals are also on view, including long-finned eels and long-necked turtles, as well as a rare growling grass frog. Upstream from the hatchery is scenic Snobs Creek Falls, whose waters cascade appealingly over tiers of granite boulders.

► *21 km south-east of Alexandra via B340.*

Visitor information

Alexandra 03 5772 1100
Beechworth 03 5728 8065
Bright 03 5750 1233
Dinner Plain 1300 734 365
Mansfield 03 5775 7000
Mount Beauty 03 5755 0596
Wangaratta 03 5721 5711

4 Lake Eildon

Victoria's largest inland waterway

Formed in the 1950s by damming the Goulburn River, Lake Eildon irrigates much of northern Victoria. Snaking through several valleys, it has more than 500 km of deeply indented shoreline and is hemmed by steep-sided mountains rising to over 1000 m and protected by the eponymous national park. Scenic landscapes abound along its fringes and the waterway is a paradise for boaters, anglers and rowers. The most accessible part of the park and lake is at Jerusalem Creek, while Mount Pinniger, just outside Eildon, has the best views, encompassing the lake and dam wall, as well as the mountains to the north and east.

▶ *Eildon, 27 km south-east of Alexandra via B340.*

DELATITE ARM, LAKE EILDON

5 Benalla

Enjoy sublimely colourful works of nature and art

Arrive here in early summer and you'll be able to savour the stunning sight and heady scents of more than 2000 varieties of roses in full bloom. Victoria's 'City of Roses' prides itself on its floral displays and they are indeed extraordinary: roses line the highways and spill over garden fences, building to a crescendo of colour in the beautiful rose garden within the Benalla Botanic Gardens, established in 1886. Another reason to visit is the splendid Benalla Art Gallery, housed in a striking modernist building on the lakeshore. It encompasses the remarkable Ledger Collection, assembled by local stock and station agent LH Ledger, which includes superb examples of Australian works from the colonial era, the Heidelberg School and the early 20th century, and the impressive Gallery Collection of modern and contemporary art.

▶ *4 km north of Hume Fwy via Midland Hwy.*

6 Glenrowan

Retrace the route of Kelly's last stand

There's no mistaking the main business of this somewhat unprepossessing settlement: at the entrance to town a giant statue of Ned Kelly, clad in his now-iconic home-made armour, looms above a line of museums, shops and cafes dedicated to the perpetuation of the bushranger's myth. Pick up a copy of the Glenrowan Siege Site Walk guide from the tourist centre and follow its route around town and you become absorbed in a fascinating, dramatic and well-told story: Kelly's final, fateful battle. On 27 June 1880, at Jones's Glenrowan Inn, now ruins, Kelly and his gang held more than 60 townsfolk hostage while awaiting the arrival of a police train they hoped to derail. Tipped off, the police surrounded the inn and, despite making an almost otherworldly appearance amid the morning mists in his armour, Kelly was captured and sent to Melbourne for trial.

▶ *1 km north of Hume Fwy.*

7 Chiltern

Atmospheric streetscapes favoured by film-makers

Chiltern's tranquil charm belies its boisterous gold-rush past, when buildings rose on fortunes made on the surrounding diggings and the streets were packed with people. Among the many remnants of those heady days are the Grapevine (formerly Star) Hotel, whose courtyard contains Australia's largest grapevine, planted in 1867; the adjacent Star Theatre (1866), preserved to this day in period style; Dows Pharmacy (1859), which houses displays of early pharmaceutical items; and the Federal Standard (1861), the office of the town's first newspaper, which displays early printing equipment. Handsome Lakeview House was the childhood home of author Henry Handel Richardson (Ethel Florence Richardson). Described in her novel *The Fortunes of Richard Mahony*, it has been restored in period style and displays Richardson memorabilia. So well preserved is the town centre that it has been used as a set for many movies.

▶ *Hume Fwy.*

8 Yeddonba Aboriginal Site

Sacred site harbouring ancient art

The centrepiece of this important art site is a rare painting of a thylacine, also known as the Tasmanian tiger, alongside a goanna and a snake. This makes the painting at least 2000 years old, for that's when the thylacine became extinct on the Australian mainland. A self-guided tour winds through the bracken to the granite rock shelter where a viewing platform allows close-up inspection of the art. Interpretive boards explain the detail in the images and how the surrounding land – mainly box–ironbark forest – was used by Aboriginal people.

▶ *Chiltern–Mount Pilot National Park, 15 km south of Chiltern.*

9 Eldorado Gold Dredge

Grand, rusting monument to days of gold

Now home to just a few hundred people, Eldorado was a bustling town of 4000 in the 1870s and continued to prosper as a gold-producing centre until the mid-20th century. Many intriguing buildings from the early days can be viewed, and the Eldorado Museum recounts the full story, but the most imposing relic is the Eldorado Gold Dredge. Built in 1936, when it was the largest dredge in the Southern Hemisphere, it operated until 1954, hauling more than 70,000 ounces of gold (2000 kg) and 1380 tons of tin from the gravel beds of Reedy Creek. A walking track circles the pond where the dredge sits, and signs explain its operation and history.

▶ *Eldorado Historic Reserve, 23 km east of Wangaratta via Wangaratta–Eldorado Rd.*

10 Yackandandah

Pretty National Trust–listed village amid forested hills

With its veranda-lined shopfronts, Yackandandah is reminiscent of a North American frontier town – perhaps not surprising, as many of the region's early settlers were miners from Sacramento and the Klondike goldfields who had abandoned their US diggings for what they hoped would be richer pickings here. The main street remains broad and beautifully preserved, and historic buildings also line the side streets, many shaded by grand old oak trees. Notable among the many National Trust–listed buildings are the 1864 Court House, the 1850s Colonial Bank and Dean's Grocery and Hardware Store, dating from 1870.

▶ *25 km south of Wodonga via Beechworth–Wodonga Rd.*

11 Beechworth

Immaculately preserved goldmining town

In 1870, aged 16, Ned Kelly appeared in Beechworth's court on trial for a minor misdemeanour; ten years later, after his capture at Glenrowan (see entry), he was arraigned for trial in the same court before being taken to Melbourne and hanged. Stepping out of the 1858 building, now a museum, into Beechworth's thoroughfare, Ford Street, it's not difficult to imagine the town as it was then, so little has it altered. Take time to admire the 1859 prison, the handsome Italianate post office (1870), the former Bank of Victoria (1867) and the 1858 Town Hall – just some of the 32 National Trust–listed buildings. Beechworth Cemetery contains the graves of thousands of Chinese miners, some marked by ceremonial towers. The Burke Museum, named after explorer Robert O'Hara Burke, superintendent of police here in the 1850s, chronicles the region's history.

▶ *40 km south of Wodonga via Beechworth–Wodonga Rd.*

12 Mount Buffalo National Park

Magical granite tableland

Driving up the steep, winding road from the park entrance, you soon become aware of giant outcrops and immense rocks half-hidden by the dense forest of the slopes – a taste of things to come. Atop the steep-sided plateau, measuring 11 by 7 km, amid subalpine vegetation, spectacular granite formations are everywhere: piles of stones like giant cairns; colossal, precariously balanced boulders; and towering rock spires. At The Gorge, sheer granite walls plummet more than 300 m, and lookouts reveal dizzying views over 240-m Crystal Brook Falls to the valley below. The 360-degree view over the Australian Alps from the park's highest point, The Horn (1723 m high), a towering pyramid of rock ascended via a 1.5-km (45 minutes return) walk, is awe-inspiring.

▶ *15 km north-west of Bright via Great Alpine Rd.*

Huts of the high plains

For 150 years, stockmen used the high plains as summer pasture for cattle, leaving a legacy of pathways and rustic tin and timber huts.

Cattlemen first discovered the Bogong High Plains (see entry) in the 1850s, and by the 1880s drovers across the region were undertaking the spring drive up the mountains every year. As many as 40,000 cattle at a time, as well as thousands of sheep and horses, were grazed on the high plains, and the practice continued until 2003.

The cattlemen blazed trails and built shelters across the High Country, several of which can still be visited. The oldest, Wallace Hut, dating from 1889, is also one of the most accessible, lying just 750 m off the Bogong High Plains Road (allow 45 minutes for the return walk). An 8-km (3.5 hours return) walk leads to the Tawonga Huts, nestled on a snow plain beneath a rocky outcrop, and a 10-km (4 hours return) track winds past snow gums to the picturesque 1903 Fitzgerald Hut, which was rebuilt after a fire in 1991.

SUNSET LIGHT COLOURS SNOW NEAR MOUNT HOTHAM.

13 Mount Hotham

Enjoy the views from on high – snow or no snow

The alpine village of Mount Hotham, situated just below the summit of the same name, is Victoria's highest settlement. Established by goldminers in the late 1850s, it was one of the state's first ski villages and is today one of the country's leading resorts, with 320 ha of skiable terrain. Most of this terrain lies below the resort, meaning that you don't have to ski to enjoy the tremendous views from the village and roadside viewpoints (on the crest of the Great Alpine Road) down both the northern and southern flanks of the Australian Alps – there's a real sense here of being 'on top of the world'. Moreover, the panoramas are equally impressive, and often clearer, in summer, when the snowfree slopes are ideal for hiking, mountain-biking and horseriding.

▶ *51 km south of Bright via Great Alpine Rd.*

14 Bogong High Plains

Mountain fastness home to rare wildlife

Heavy snows place this plateau off limits to all but the hardiest cross-country skiers in winter, but come spring, when the plains briefly blaze with the colours of wild flowers, an enchanting world opens up to walkers. Rimmed by forests of colourful snow gums, the plains are a vast expanse of high grasslands, heathlands, herbfields and bogs. Walking tracks wind across these open spaces to ridges, sheltered gullies and tumbling streams, revealing wonderful panoramas. This is the realm of some fascinating creatures, including the rare alpine pygmy possum, the only alpine marsupial in the world, and the summer gathering place of the famous Bogong moth. As well as several day walks, the 650-km Australian Alps Walking Track traverses the plains, and a 60-km (five-day) section can be walked from Mount Hotham to Mount Bogong.

▶ *Alpine National Park, 65 km south-east of Bright via C536, C531 and Bogong High Plains Rd.*

Great Ocean Road

An extensive limestone plain stretches west from Port Phillip Bay to beyond the South Australian border. Along its ocean rim, dubbed the Shipwreck Coast, wind and wave have fashioned a string of spectacular natural features, and coastal settlements recall the days of whaling and frequent shipwrecks. Inland rise the fern-filled forests of the Otway Ranges.

1 Lower Glenelg National Park

Majestic works wrought by water

In its lower reaches the Glenelg River cuts a spectacular 15-km-long, 50-m-high gorge through ancient limestone. Over the years, water percolating through has peppered its cliffs with caves. The most majestic of these is Princess Margaret Rose Cave, claimed to be the most decorated cave per square metre in the country. Here the constant drip of waters enriched with dissolved minerals has deposited delicately tinted stalactites, stalagmites, straws, columns, shawls and cave coral. The best way to experience the gorge and also take the guided tour of the cave is by cruise boat upstream from Nelson.

▶ *Nelson, 53 km north-west of Portland via Portland–Nelson Rd.*

Visitor information

Apollo Bay 03 5237 6529
Geelong 03 5283 1735
Lorne 03 5289 1152
Nelson 08 8738 4051
Port Campbell 03 5598 6089
Port Fairy 03 5568 2682
Portland 03 5523 2671
Queenscliff 03 5258 4843
Torquay 03 5261 4219
Warrnambool 03 5564 7837
Werribee 03 9742 0906

2 Cape Bridgewater

Sea spray, stony stumps and basking seals

The parking area at the top of the volcanic hump of Cape Bridgewater reveals grand views along the rugged coastline and, in windy conditions, spouts of spray from a blowhole. From here it is a short walk to the 'petrified forest', an intriguing cluster of 1-m-high limestone tubes that look like tree trunks turned to stone. If you have time, press on to an observation platform (a further 3.5 km) which juts out over a colony of some 1000 fur seals that live below in a watery cave; groups can usually be seen basking on the kelp-covered rocks. You can also take a boat ride to the colony for a sea-level view.

▶ *28 km south-west of Portland via Portland–Cape Bridgewater Rd.*

3 Portland Maritime Discovery Centre

Whalebones back from the grave

The 14-m-long whale skeleton that greets visitors to the centre comes from a sperm whale that died and was buried on a nearby beach in 1988. A decade later its remains were exhumed and the piles of bones sorted and then sent to the South Australian Museum for 'degreasing' before the entire skeleton was reassembled and wired together. Also on display is the lifeboat used to rescue 19 people from the *Admella* shipwreck in 1859.

▶ *Lee Breakwater Rd, Portland.*

PRINCESS MARGARET ROSE CAVE,
LOWER GLENELG NATIONAL PARK

4 Port Fairy

Historic seafaring township

Settlement at Port Fairy followed its use as a base by whalers and sealers in the early 1800s. In the mid-1840s, as whaling declined, the port was developed as a planned town and families from England, Ireland and Scotland were encouraged to settle here. Port Fairy's rich variety of 19th-century buildings includes the 1841 Merrijig Inn, once a watering place for whalers; a row of 1860s cottages; 1840s Motts Cottage; and the Caledonian Hotel, continuously licensed from 1844. Griffiths Island, reached by footbridge, is a muttonbird sanctuary. When the birds are in residence (September to April) a dusk visit to the observation deck may be rewarded by the sight of thousands returning at the same time from feeding. To avoid damage to nests, please keep to the marked track that encircles the island.

► *28 km west of Warrnambool via Princes Hwy.*

5 Tower Hill

Drive into a volcanic crater

Tower Hill was formed in a violent eruption 30,000 years ago. Just off the highway are views from its rim of three volcanic cone islands surrounded by a moat-like lake. A one-way 3-km circuit drive descends to the crater floor to loop past Tower Hill (the tallest of the three cones) and the Worn Gundidj Visitor Centre, which houses cultural displays and has an adjacent shady picnic area, and along the lakeshore before climbing back up the rim. Several short walks start at the picnic area; frequently seen wildlife includes koalas and fearless emus. A short drive north is the vantage point used by Eugene von Guérard for his 1855 painting of Tower Hill; a century later the painting was used as a guide when the crater was being replanted with native vegetation earlier cleared for grazing.

► *17 km west of Warrnambool via Princes Hwy.*

6 Flagstaff Hill Maritime Museum

Bustling port comes to life

Tragic tales of the Shipwreck Coast and an opportunity to time-travel to Warrnambool in the 1870s share the limelight here. Re-created dockside street-scapes offer an interactive journey through Victoria's early maritime history. A spine-chilling highlight is *Shipwrecked!*, an evening-only sound-and-laser show that relives the sinking of the *Loch Ard* (see Loch Ard Gorge). Also on display is the most famous relic from the wreck, a life-sized porcelain peacock; salvaged virtually unscathed (there is a small chip on its beak), it was made by Minton Potteries and bound for Melbourne's 1880 Great International Exhibition. On nearby Cannon Hill, a traditional Portuguese marble marker, or *padrão*, commemorates possible links with early Portuguese navigators, as posed by the mystery of the 'Mahogany Ship' believed to have run aground along the coast here in the 1500s.

► *Merri St, Warrnambool.*

7 London Bridge

Has fallen down

Until January 1990, this striking formation was a headland with two arches. The collapse of the landward arch (temporarily stranding two startled sightseers who were later winched off by helicopter) left it as an island with an arch. In time the second arch will also give way, leaving two stacks. A short walk through coastal heath reaches platforms with views over swirling seas to the increasingly endangered landmark.

► *Port Campbell National Park, Great Ocean Rd, 7 km west of Port Campbell.*

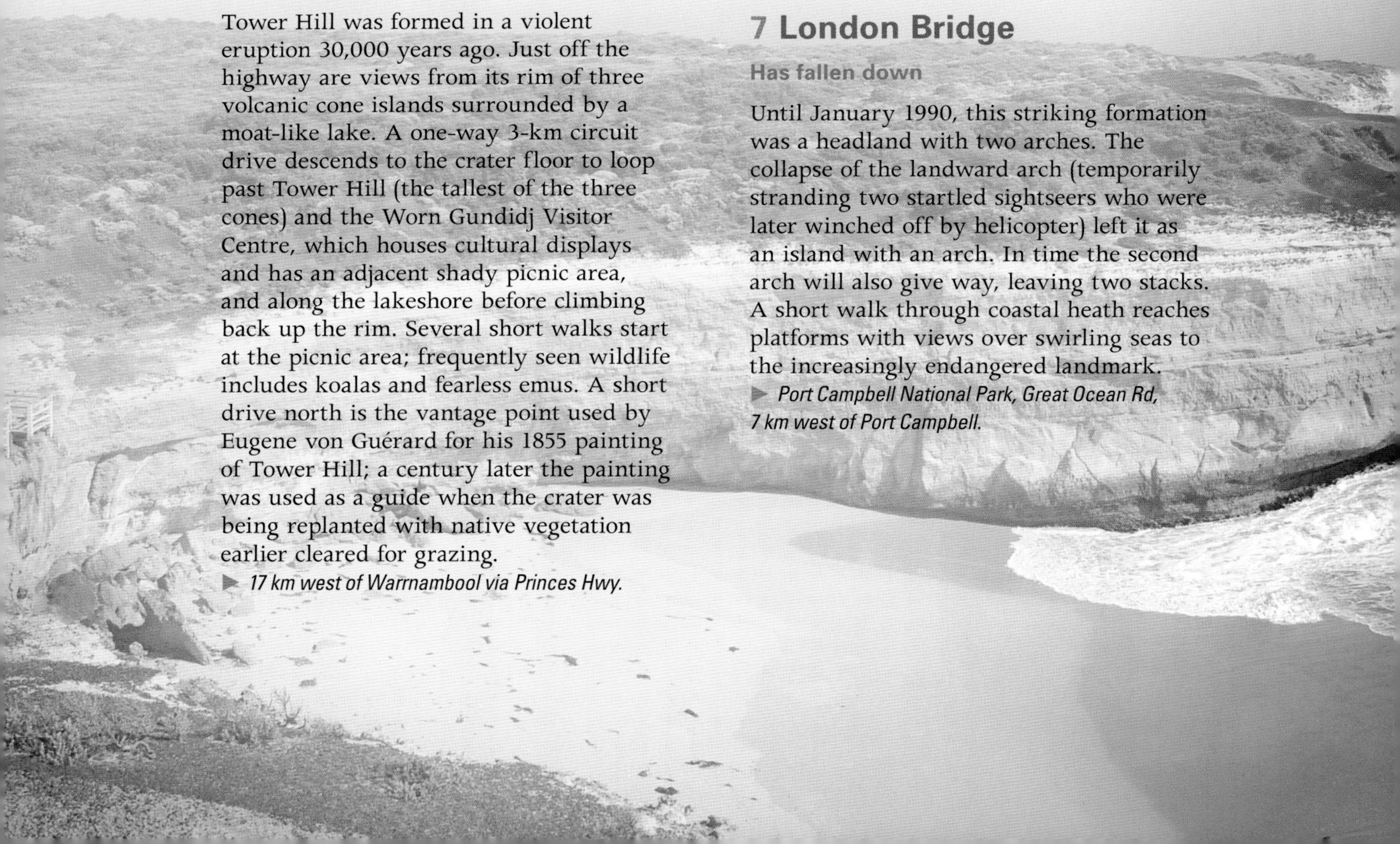

8 Loch Ard Gorge

Site of harrowing shipwreck and remarkable survival

Something of the tragedy played out in its waters seems to linger in the narrow enclosure of Loch Ard Gorge. In 1878 the *Loch Ard*, nearing Melbourne after a three-month voyage from London, struck cliffs just outside the gorge and sank in 20 minutes. Just two of its 54 passengers survived: Eva Carmichael and Tom Pearce. Today, steps lead down to the beach where they struggled ashore. Four of the five bodies recovered lie in the tiny cemetery above the western end of the beach. From the cemetery, a path reaches a lookout with views across to Muttonbird Island; the wreck lies in 25 m of water off its south-eastern tip.

▶ *Port Campbell National Park, Great Ocean Rd, 8 km east of Port Campbell.*

9 Twelve Apostles

Falling one by one

You won't be able to count 12. Until 2005 there were nine, then the sudden collapse of one of the group reduced the line-up to eight. The missing Apostles may have disappeared since the group was named, or perhaps never actually existed. In a continually repeated cycle, the relentless assault of the Southern Ocean will eventually claim each one of these rocky towers, but the same forces will also carve new disciples from the cliffs. Although awe-inspiring at any time of day, the Apostles are particularly magnificent in the glow of the late-afternoon sun.

▶ *Port Campbell National Park, Great Ocean Rd, 12 km east of Port Campbell.*

LONDON BRIDGE'S OUTER ARCH IS NOW AN ISLAND.

BLACK LIGHTHOUSE AT FORT QUEENSCLIFF

10 Cape Otway Lightstation

Beacon of hope on the Shipwreck Coast

Beyond the dramatic promontory of Cape Otway lies Bass Strait, one of the most treacherous stretches of water in the world. This 18-m-high clifftop lighthouse marks the mainland side of its narrow western entrance and was built in 1841 in response to the alarming number of shipwrecks that had already occurred here. Its London-made lantern was fuelled first by whale oil, then by kerosene, diesel and finally electricity, and its light provided reassuring guidance for vessels entering the 'final strait' after the long ocean voyage until 1994, when it was replaced by a solar-powered light. Today, guided tours visit the heritage buildings and the lighthouse, revealing sweeping views of the foaming waters and cliff-lined shores. Outside the historic precinct, an easy walking track leads to a cemetery containing the graves of drowned sailors and lighthouse-keepers' children.

► *14 km south of Great Ocean Rd via Otway Lighthouse Rd.*

11 Maits Rest

A rainforest pit stop

Maitland Bryan was the district's first forestry officer. Based at Apollo Bay, he often rested himself and his horses in this rainforest glen as he travelled the track now followed by the Great Ocean Road. Walking into the cool, dim gully is like descending into a different world. Huge fronds glisten with dewdrops, as the raised boardwalk winds through clusters of tree ferns and around the moss-covered roots of ancient trees; one, a triple-trunked myrtle beech estimated to be 300 years old, is registered as a historic tree with the National Trust.

► *Great Otway National Park, south side of Great Ocean Rd, 17 km west of Apollo Bay.*

A breathtaking memorial

Winding for more than 240 km, the Great Ocean Road is one of the world's great scenic drives – and one of its largest war memorials.

It was an inspired idea: a road commemorating Victorian soldiers killed in the First World War that would also give employment to returned servicemen, attract tourists and end the isolation of the region's coastal settlements. Construction began in 1919 and advanced slowly as there was no machinery available – all work was done with picks, shovels and explosives. The road finally opened in 1932 when, it is said, motorists held their breath for two reasons: the narrowness of the rough track cut into the cliffside, as well as the grandeur of the scenery.

The Memorial Arch at Eastern View (the original starting point) and plaques along the roadside wall at Mount Defiance (a particularly difficult section for the builders) pay tribute to lost servicemen. Extensive improvements to the route have been made over the decades and today the Great Ocean Road stands as a monument not only to fallen soldiers, but also to the men who built it.

12 Barwon Park Homestead

Where rabbits ran wild

Built in 1869 for Thomas and Elizabeth Austin, this imposing 42-room bluestone mansion, still largely in original condition, reflects the prosperity of the region's pastoral heritage. It features elegantly proportioned rooms, a grand central staircase and an iron lace veranda. As a member of the Acclimatisation Society, Thomas Austin imported many species from England and is remembered especially for breeding rabbits – their offspring, it is thought, are the ones that spread across the continent.

▶ *Inverleigh Rd, Winchelsea, 37 km west of Geelong via Princes Hwy.*

13 Baywalk Bollards

Maritime city's colourful chroniclers

Geelong's Baywalk (4 km), which runs the length of the city's revamped waterfront, is enlivened with more than 100 large bollards carved from pier timbers and brightly painted to represent figures from the city's past and present. You'll meet Matthew Flinders in his naval uniform, Eureka Rebellion leader Peter Lalor (given sanctuary here in 1851 after being wounded in the miner's uprising), newspaper editor and refrigeration pioneer James Harrison, a footballer in the jersey of Geelong's first team, players from Geelong's 1860s Volunteer Rifle Band, a fisherman and a sailor highlighting links to the sea, and saucy beach belles wearing bathing fashions from the 1890s to 1930s.

▶ *Geelong waterfront.*

14 Black Lighthouse

Providing guidance through the Rip

Queenscliff's 'black lighthouse' is built of unpainted Melbourne bluestone. It lines up with the nearby 'white lighthouse' (built of the same stone, but painted) to give vessels entering Port Phillip Bay a safe bearing through the centre of the dangerous Rip that churns across its narrow entrance. The Black Lighthouse dates from 1862 and lies within the walls of Fort Queenscliff, a later structure that was built between 1874 and 1884 to repel a feared Russian invasion.

▶ *Queenscliff, 30 km south-east of Geelong via Bellarine Hwy.*

Melbourne Region

Melbourne spreads eastwards from horseshoe-shaped Port Phillip Bay across the coastal plain bisected by the Yarra River towards the Dandenong Ranges. The city's gracious centre is well-endowed with cultural and historic institutions and pretty parklands. Beaches and seaside suburbs fringe the bay's southern shores.

1 Organ Pipes National Park

Basalt columns, long and short

The Organ Pipes are part of a 1-million-year-old lava deposit that, as it cooled to form basalt, cracked into columns. The columns stand in correct organ-pipe order, with the tallest in the centre tapering to the shortest at either end. Nearby, the Tessellated Pavement, consisting of what appear to be hexagonally jointed basalt tiles, is actually the tops of columns that have been worn down to ground level.
▶ *Organ Pipes National Park, 20 km north-west of Melbourne via Calder Fwy and Organ Pipes Rd.*

2 Heide Museum of Modern Art

Historic hub of modern art scene

Between the 1930s and 1950s, wealthy champions of modern art Sunday and John Reed made their home, Heide, the focus of the Australian avant-garde art scene. Sidney Nolan painted 26 of his original 27 Ned Kelly paintings here; others closely associated with Heide include Albert Tucker and Charles Blackman. Today the heritage-listed farmhouse shares its extensive gardens with two galleries where changing exhibitions display contemporary Australian and international works.
▶ *Templestowe Rd, Bulleen, 16 km north-east of Melbourne via Eastern Fwy and Bulleen Rd.*

Visitor information

Melbourne 03 9658 9658
Werribee 03 9742 0906

3 Melbourne Zoo

Walk through a range of wildlife habitats

In the nation's oldest zoo (it dates from 1861), a number of walkways passing through re-created habitats safely bring visitors and animals almost face-to-face. In the Orang-utan Sanctuary, an elevated boardwalk climbs into the treetop world of the orang-utan. A pathway winds through the bird aviary, a bridge crosses over the lion's park and viewing points reach right into the rainforest home of a gorilla family. Other displays include a butterfly house and the Trail of the Elephants, which takes visitors into an Asian village setting that is home to the zoo's five elephants.
▶ *Elliott Ave, Parkville.*

4 Abbotsford Convent

Arts hub in medieval-style buildings

This complex of 11 buildings is remarkable for both the grandeur of its architecture and its extraordinary preservation of a rural landscape just 4 km from the city centre. It was built in the 1860s by the Sisters of the Order of the Good Shepherd to provide shelter and spiritual support for vulnerable females, and in the 1990s was acquired by the state government for an arts, education and cultural precinct. Now, the buildings have taken on a new life as artists' studios, creative spaces for writers and designers, galleries, workshops, a bakery, cafes, restaurants and bars.
▶ *St Heliers St, Abbotsford.*

CELL BLOCK IN OLD MELBOURNE GAOL

5 Queen Victoria Market

Lively and historic marketplace

So tempting is the produce here that the market has become a lip-smacking tourist attraction in its own right. Trading since 1878, the elegant 'Queen Vic' retains many of its original halls and open-sided buildings where more than 1000 merchants noisily sell a multicultural array of dairy, meat, fish, fruit and vegetables and deli goods, as well as clothing, antiques and bric-a-brac. The market is closed on Monday and Wednesday.

▶ *Elizabeth St, Melbourne.*

6 Old Melbourne Gaol

Crime and justice, 19th-century style

Travel back to the 'good old days' – when seven prisoners shared a cramped cell and hangings were commonplace. Old Melbourne Gaol is a salutary reminder of what penal conditions were really like, even in 1929, when this grim place finally closed. It was the scene of 135 hangings including, in 1880, the bushranger Ned Kelly, whose death mask is on display. You can tour the cells, inspect the gallows and, if you dare, join a hangman's candle-lit tour (four nights a week).

▶ *Russell St, Melbourne.*

Homes away from home

Three longstanding cultural precincts – Chinatown, Lonsdale Street and Lygon Street – celebrate Melbourne's vibrant ethnic diversity.

Chinatown, centred around Little Bourke Street in the heart of the city, dates from the 1850s gold-rush days when a small Chinese community here supplied food, lodging and equipment to recently arrived countrymen on the way to the diggings. Today, marked by five traditional arches, the area is home to Chinese restaurants and Asian shops and in February is the focus of Chinese New Year Celebrations.

Melbourne is home to one of the largest Greek-speaking populations in the world outside Athens and, since the early 1900s, Lonsdale Street, a block north of Chinatown, has been its meeting place. It encompasses cafes, restaurants, clubs and cultural events, including the exuberant Antipodes Greek Festival held each March.

On the northern edge of the CBD is Carlton, where many Italians settled after the Second World War, and its lively Lygon Street. Often referred to as 'Little Italy', it is noted for its pavement restaurants and cafes, food stores, boutiques and, each October, the Lygon Street Festa, a four-day food-and-fun street party. A more recently created cultural enclave is the cluster of Vietnamese shops and food outlets to the east, in Richmond.

7 Cook's Cottage

Family home of the great navigator, far from its original location

This simple 1755 stone cottage once stood in Great Ayton, Yorkshire, and was the home of James Cook's parents. In 1933, the building was dismantled and shipped to Melbourne where it was reassembled under leafy European trees in Fitzroy Gardens. Today, surrounded by a traditional English cottage garden and filled with appropriate period furniture, it houses an exhibition devoted to the navigator's life and achievements.

▶ *Fitzroy Gardens, Wellington Pde, Melbourne.*

8 Melbourne Cricket Ground

Where big men fly and wickets fall

For many, the MCG is the heart and soul of Australian sport. Established in 1854 (and in the decades since, extensively upgraded into a mighty stadium), it is a hallowed venue for Test cricket, the location of the Australian Rules Football Grand Final and was the main stadium for both the 1956 Olympic and the 2006 Commonwealth games. Go to a match or, on non-event days, take a behind-the-scenes tour that includes the Long Room and (when available) the dressing rooms and arena. The MCG is also the location of the National Sports Museum, which houses exhibits ranging from a collection of baggy green caps worn by Australian Test cricketers and the 'Blackham ball' used in the first cricket defeat of England by Australia in 1882 to interactive holograms of sporting champions.

▶ *Brunton Ave and Jolimont Tce, Melbourne.*

9 Great Hall, NGV International

Mighty ceiling of stained glass

A major feature of this building housing the gallery's impressive international collection is decidedly Australian – the Leonard French stained-glass ceiling that fills the Great Hall with a dappled glow of coloured light. Measuring 51 m long by 14 m wide, it is made up of 224 triangular pieces of glass in 50 colours and took five years (1965–70) to construct. French described it as 'using glasswork to paint with light'. It is one of the largest glass ceilings in the world.

▶ *NGV International, St Kilda Rd, Melbourne.*

10 Polly Woodside Maritime Museum

Tall ship tells compelling tales of the city's seafaring heritage

The iron-hulled, Belfast-built *Polly Woodside* first set sail in 1885 and made many voyages carrying freight around Cape Horn and across Australasian waters before coming to rest, in the 1940s, in Port Phillip Bay. Today, meticulously restored by the National Trust, which acquired the ship in 1968 for the payment of just one cent, the permanently moored vessel is the centrepiece of a museum featuring displays about life at sea, the crew, navigation, maritime language and Melbourne's docks. But you'll need your sea legs to go through its rotating entry area, which mimics the motion of a ship at sea.

▶ *Clarendon St, South Wharf, Melbourne.*

MELBOURNE CITY CENTRE

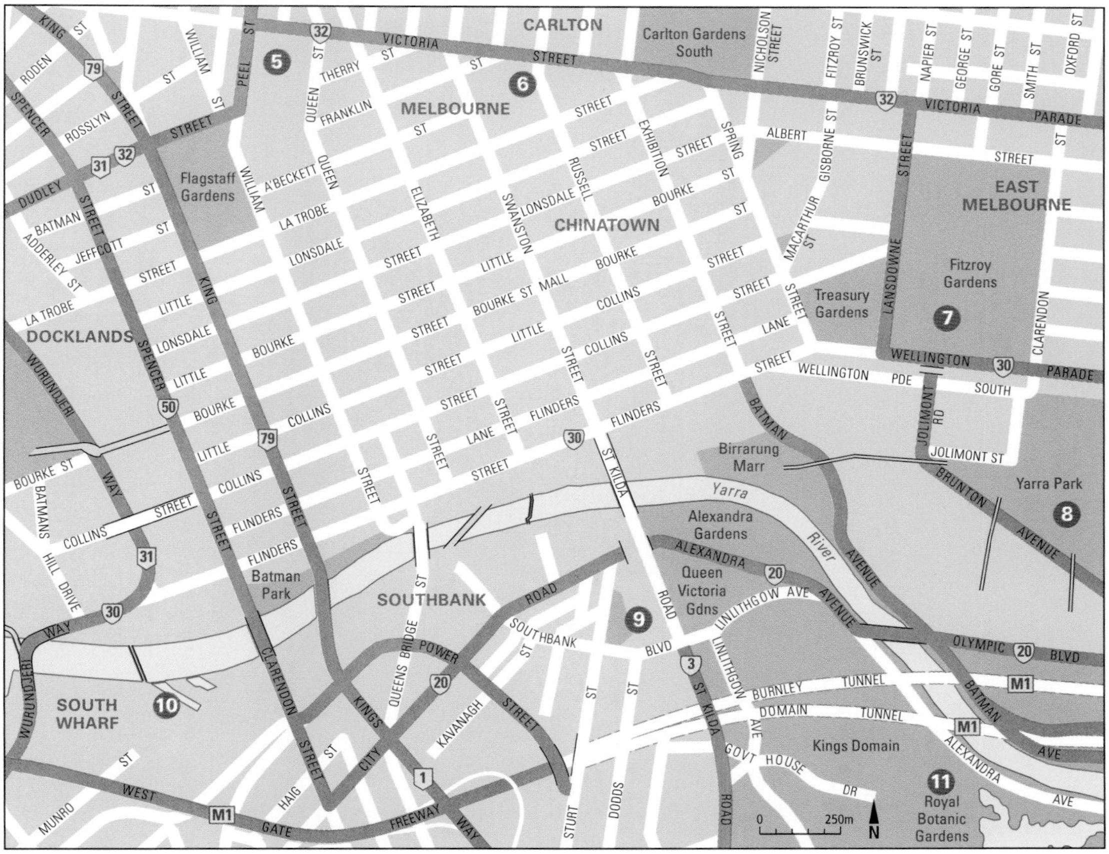

11 Royal Botanic Gardens Melbourne

Skilfully landscaped showcase

Aficionados regard these gardens as among Australia's finest. Characterised by scenic panoramas across lakes and sweeping lawns, they display more than 50,000 plants in diverse collections ranging from 300 varieties of delicate camellia and 40 species of oak (some more than 130 years old) to a grey garden – an ornamental collection of silver-, grey- and blue-leaved plants – that thrives in a site exposed to extremes of heat and wind. Other features include the Children's Garden, with a host of weird and wonderful plants and a range of activities that encourage play, exploration and appreciation of the natural world; Guilfoyle's Volcano, a reservoir built in the 1870s in the form of a volcanic crater, which provided irrigation to the gardens; and the tropical hothouse, best visited in winter when it offers a refuge from the cold as well as orchids in flower.

▶ *Birdwood Ave, South Yarra.*

12 Como House

Luxurious lifestyles of the colonial elite

To cross the threshold here is to enter a sumptuous world of wealth, privilege and romance. Built in 1847, Como House was named for the location of a marriage proposal (Italy's Lake Como) and over the decades it has seen many a glamorous gathering of Melbourne's social set. For 95 years it was home to the Armytage family, who in 1959 gave it to the National Trust. Furnished as they left it, the house provides a glimpse into the lives and prosperous times of a dynasty in colonial Victoria. The magnificent gardens have been returned to their original glory.

▶ *Cnr Williams Rd and Lechlade Ave, South Yarra.*

FORMAL GARDENS ENFOLD WERRIBEE PARK MANSION.

13 St Kilda

Funky seaside suburb with iconic landmarks

St Kilda boomed from the 1880s till the early 1900s as a favoured beach resort for Melbourne's elite and its many Victorian and Edwardian mansions date from that era. Then decline set in until the late 20th century, when a period of rejuvenation saw it once again become a fashionable address, known for its multicultural community and its cafes, especially the outstanding cake shops in Ackland Street. At weekends, large crowds browse the craft market on The Esplanade and enjoy rides at the Luna Park funfair – its laughing face façade and roller-coaster have both been classified by the National Trust. Dating from 1853, St Kilda Pier provides views of the Melbourne skyline and Port Phillip Bay, and is popular for strolling, cycling and fishing. Nearby you might spot members of a breeding colony of little penguins that has taken up residence on the St Kilda Breakwater, constructed for the 1956 Olympic Games as a safe harbour for yachts.

▶ *8 km south of Melbourne via St Kilda Rd.*

14 Rippon Lea

Grand estate embodies Melbourne's boom times

Frederick Sargood, the creator of Rippon Lea, made his fortune on the goldfields not as a miner but as a merchant, becoming one of the richest men in the land, a leader of Melbourne society and a notable political figure. Rippon Lea was built in the ornate Italianate style much favoured in the boom years and is an expression of his success. Today the grand estate remains largely intact and open to the public. Spend an hour or two meandering through the mansion then explore the garden with its sweeping lawns, lookout tower, magnificent trees, tranquil lake and waterfall, fernery and orchard (harbouring more than 100 varieties of heritage apples and pears).

▶ *Hotham St, Elsternwick.*

15 Werribee Park Mansion

A rich man's world

Surrounded by 10 ha of manicured formal gardens, this 60-room Italianate mansion is said to be the largest and most elaborate private residence in the state. It was built by the pastoralist Chirnside family between 1873 and 1877, and for much of the 20th century it was a Catholic seminary. Now government-owned, it is open to the public. You can explore the mansion, visit the original farm buildings and find a spot to enjoy a picnic on the banks of Werribee River.

▶ *Werribee Park, Werribee South; 3 km south of Princes Hwy at Werribee via Duncans Rd and K Rd.*

16 You Yangs Regional Park

Timeless landmark

The name comes from Aboriginal words meaning 'big mountain in the middle of a plain' and, though reaching only 352 m high, the granite peaks of the You Yangs are without doubt the dominant feature of the landscape here. In 1802 explorer Matthew Flinders and three of his crew climbed to the summit now known as Flinders Peak. On a clear day, the reward for following in their footsteps (3.2 km return from the parking area) is a panorama stretching from Mount Macedon to Corio Bay. Also seen from the track is the 2006 stone sculpture of a wedge-tailed eagle, representing the creation figure Bunjil. For those less keen on walking or with limited time, the Great Circle Drive (12 km, gravel) provides an overview of the park's diversity of habitats, which are home to more than 200 species of birds and a variety of mammals including kangaroos, koalas and ringtail possums.

▶ *55 km south-west of Melbourne via Princes Hwy and Forest Rd.*

Yarra Valley and Dandenong Ranges

Rising on the south-eastern edge of Melbourne, the forested slopes, waterfalls, grand public gardens and charming mountain villages of the Dandenong Ranges have for more than a century been a place of recreation and retreat for city-dwellers. The Yarra Valley, to the west, has excellent wineries and fascinating wildlife.

1 Steavenson Falls

Light fantastic

With a drop of 84 m, Steavenson Falls is one of the highest cascades in the state, and while its three tiers put on an attractive display at any time, at night, when illuminated by floodlights, they are particularly enchanting. The power for this is provided by hydro-electricity generated by the falls' own thundering water. New viewing platforms were built after the 2009 bushfires, which devastated this area. Several walks explore the nearby Steavenson Falls Reserve.

▶ *4 km south-east of Marysville via Falls Rd.*

2 Gulf Station

The most complete group of timber slab farm buildings in Victoria

A rich array of aged timber buildings, including a school house, piggery, stables, smithy, dairy, shearing shed and slaughterhouse, runs in a ribbon along a gentle rise. This is Gulf Station, a self-sufficient pastoral property farmed for a century from 1851 onwards by the Bell family, who began their enterprise by supplying meat and other produce to the goldfields. Restored by the National Trust, the complex is open to the public as a working pioneer farm, whose original farm buildings, together with farm tools, household utensils, farm animals and a cottage garden, provide a vivid picture of 19th-century farm life.

▶ *Melba Hwy, Yarra Glen.*

3 Yering Station

Pioneering Victorian winery

In 1838, the Ryrie brothers planted 600 grapevine cuttings, the first in Victoria, on their cattle property Yering Station; they made their first wine in 1845. In the 1850s, the property was sold to Paul de Castella (marathon runner Robert is a descendant), who was impressed by wines made by the Ryries and so extended the vineyards and engaged the services of a winemaker; at the 1889 Paris Exhibition a Yering cabernet won a Grand Prix, an honour usually reserved for French wines. De Castella was also responsible for the avenue of 300 elms that still line the driveway – it was planted to welcome his bride. By the early 1900s, the devastation of phylloxera and a shift in tastes from table to fortified wines saw Yering Station return to dairy farming. All this changed again in the 1980s, when the vineyards were replanted and a massive winemaking and hospitality complex was built. The original 1859 winery now incorporates the cellar door and art gallery.

▶ *Melba Hwy, Yarra Glen.*

Visitor information

Dandenong Ranges 03 9758 7522
Marysville 03 5963 4567
Yarra Valley (Healesville) 03 5962 2600

4 TarraWarra Museum of Art

Grand vision of art and architecture

This not-for-profit museum displays works of Australian art from the 1950s to the present day, chosen from the private collection assembled over half a century by its founders, Eva and Marc Besen. Opened in 2003, it is housed in a striking, contemporary building with curved external walls of mainly rammed earth set into a hillside within a vineyard. Three large spaces display themed exhibitions that change with the seasons.

► *Healesville–Yarra Glen Rd, Healesville.*

5 Healesville Sanctuary

Head here to gain a better understanding of Australian wildlife

The Healesville Sanctuary has been attracting wildlife lovers since the 1920s, when Dr Colin McKenzie, a noted anatomist and philanthropist, was granted 30 ha of bushland here to establish an institute to study native animals. In the 1940s it became the first place to breed a platypus in captivity. Now managed by Zoos Victoria and home to more than 200 species of Australian animals, its involvement in breeding programs for endangered species continues. Sanctuary highlights include the World of the Platypus, where visitors meet these shy creatures in their creekside home, and the Platypusary, a behind-the-scenes peek into their world via glassed tunnels and nesting chambers; the Birds of Prey presentation of swooping raptors; and an inspection of the Wildlife Health Centre.

► *Badger Creek Rd, Healesville.*

WINE BAR RESTAURANT BUILDING, YERING STATION

6 Rainforest Gallery

Spend time with nature's old masters

On the southern slopes of Mount Donna Buang is an exhibition in two parts. First, a 40-m-long, 17-m-high aerial walkway takes visitors through a forest of 60-m-tall mountain ash, some up to 300 years old, to an observation deck. Then, also leading from the car park, is a staircase which descends to a lower walkway through myrtle beech forest with trees that are up to 400 years old.

▶ *Yarra Ranges National Park, 7 km north of Warburton via Acheron Way and Mount Donna Buang Rd.*

7 William Ricketts Sanctuary

Sculptor's inspiring legacy

This is no ordinary garden. It was created in the 1930s by sculptor William Ricketts as an expression of his personal philosophy, inspired by the culture of Aboriginal people, that we should all act as custodians of the natural environment. More than 90 ceramic sculptures of humans and animals are scattered along the paths – half-hidden in ferny glades or rising from moss-padded rocks as if growing there. Ricketts lived at the Sanctuary until into his nineties, and made sculptures until his death in 1993.

▶ *Mount Dandenong Tourist Rd, Mount Dandenong.*

8 National Rhododendron Gardens

Banks of brilliant colour

The hilltop setting framed by the ramrod-straight trunks of mountain ash against a backdrop of the Australian Alps could hardly be more spectacular, and in late winter and spring the garden fairly dazzles as 15,000 rhododendrons, 12,000 azaleas, 3000 camellias and 250,000 daffodils bloom brightly. Wide paths wind through 43 ha of massed shrubbery, cherry tree groves, exotic trees and shady lawns dotted with gazebos and picnic areas.

▶ *The Georgian Rd, Olinda.*

PUFFING BILLY CROSSING THE 1899 TRESTLE BRIDGE

An urban retreat

On the edge of suburbia, sun-dappled roads and walking tracks wind through soaring forests and valleys lush with tree ferns.

Located just 40 km east of Melbourne, Dandenong Ranges National Park is an ideal day-trip destination. It is an amalgam of five areas: the longstanding and much-used Ferntree Gully Forest (see entry), first reserved in 1882; Sherbrooke Forest, which until 1950 supplied the capital's timber needs and is now prized for its towering mountain ash (the tallest flowering plant in the world); the less accessible Doongalla Forest, sloping steeply at the foot of Mount Dandenong and also once logged; Olinda State Forest; and Mount Evelyn Forest. Together, these reserves constitute a 3500-ha forest haven that protects a superb lyrebird population as well as rosellas, cockatoos, kookaburras and honeyeaters, as well as more than 30 species of native mammals, notably night-feeding gliding possums. Numerous picnic areas and bushwalking trails enhance the experience.

9 Ferntree Gully

Well-loved tracks and picnic grounds

Once the summer hunting grounds of the Wurundjeri people, by the 1870s these green glades had become a favoured destination for Melbournites. The gully's network of walking tracks (some following paths forged by the Wurundjeri) ranges from the Ramblers Track Loop, an easy 1.5-km stroll through fern gullies, and the more demanding 3-km Living Bush Nature Walk to the 4-km Lyrebird Loop, a steep climb through shady rainforest where resident superb lyrebirds may be heard scratching in the undergrowth, and the similarly challenging Kokoda Track Memorial Walk, which honours those who fought in the 1942 Kokoda campaign in New Guinea. The 100-m red-brick path walk from the car park to the 1909 kiosk building was made by local residents after the 1997 bushfires; each brick carries a carved message of hope and renewal.

▶ *Dandenong Ranges National Park, Burwood Hwy, Upper Ferntree Gully.*

10 Puffing Billy Railway

Steam through stunning mountain and forest scenery

A chugging locomotive on the Puffing Billy line is one of the signature sights – and sounds – of the Dandenongs. The railway is a great survivor, the only one of four set up in the early 1900s to develop rural areas that is still running regularly. Although closed in 1953 after a landslide, public affection for the mountain track kept the line alive; a bypass was built and service resumed in 1962. Today, maintained by a band of volunteers, the railway is a major tourist attraction, with a fleet of restored 'Puffing Billy' locomotives and vintage carriages carrying sightseers from its headquarters at Belgrave through forests, fern gullies and farmlands along 24.5 km of the original narrow-gauge track.

▶ *Burwood Hwy, Belgrave.*

Mornington Peninsula and Phillip Island

This region has long been an accessible holiday haven for Melbournites, and strung around the southern edge of Port Phillip are some of the state's earliest beach resorts. To the east, beyond picturesque rolling hills, lie wilder shores and the large but tranquil islands of Western Port.

1 Point Nepean National Park

Scenic headland dotted with historic sites

Commanding the southern headland of the narrow entrance to Port Phillip, Point Nepean occupies a strategically significant location. From 1852, it was the site of a quarantine station used to monitor ships for disease. Infected passengers were escorted to hospitals and bathhouses while their clothes and goods were fumigated in disinfecting chambers; today's visitors can move more freely through the site, inspecting the restored buildings and chambers on guided and self-guided tours. Numerous fortifications were built around the headland from 1880 on. Particularly impressive is Fort Nepean, from where the first shots of each world war were fired in Australia, the first time at a German freighter, the second at an unidentified ship that turned out to be Tasmanian. You can walk or cycle between sites (bikes can be hired) or hop on the 'transporter' (carriages towed by a tractor).

▶ *21 km west of Rosebud.*

Visitor information

Dromana 1800 804 009
Frankston 03 9768 1433
Phillip Island 1300 366 422

2 Sorrento

Site of the state's first European settlement, later a colourful resort

The first birth, death and marriage in Victoria all took place at Sorrento, after a settlement was founded here in 1803. Most of the early settlers departed a year later, but a few fishermen stayed on. Sorrento's transformation into a fashionable holiday town was mainly down to entrepreneur George Coppin. In the 1870s he built smart hotels, shops, rotundas, lookouts and walking tracks, and laid on a paddle-steamer service and steam tramway to bring in middle-class Melbournites. Many of Coppin's creations still stand, most notably the 1875 Hotel Continental.

▶ *37 km west of Mornington via Point Nepean Rd.*

3 Peninsula Hot Springs

Soothing waters amid glorious gardens

Bubbling up from 637 m underground, natural hot spring water is directed into an array of beautifully designed pools flanked by sundecks, terraces, rockeries and lush vegetation. The main bathing areas are the Bath House, which includes a family bathing area, and the more secluded and exclusive Spa Dreaming Centre. Pool and treatment options include Turkish baths, mud baths, cold plunge pools, massages and saunas. After a restorative dip you can opt for a massage or don a bathrobe and have a coffee or a meal at the cafe or kiosk.

▶ *Springs La, Fingal, 31 km south-west of Mornington.*

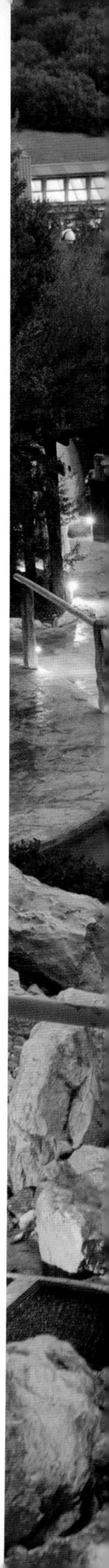

4 Cape Schanck Lighthouse

Early coastal light with intact original mechanism

There are more than 20 lighthouses along the rugged, storm-battered Victorian coast, but the 21-m limestone tower at Cape Schanck stands out in more ways than one. For one thing, the coastal views from the cape are truly magnificent; for another, this is one of the best preserved of Australia's early lighthouses – built in 1859, it's the state's second oldest – and one of very few to retain its original clockwork mechanism, on display in the tower. Guided tours take place daily and accommodation is available in the keeper's cottage. There is also a small museum.

▶ *35 km south of Mornington.*

5 McCrae Homestead

Pioneer home housing fine museum and intriguing artworks

The first permanent white settler on the Mornington Peninsula, Andrew McCrae, established a cattle run between Rosebud and Dromana in 1843 and a year later completed this rustic homestead (open Wednesday and weekends). It has been restored to its original state, right down to the furniture, paintings and household items, and provides a powerful evocation of pioneer life. Andrew's wife, Georgina, was a skilled portrait artist and many of her works are on display in the adjoining McCrae Gallery. Also on the site, the Burrell Twycross Gallery exhibits artefacts and artworks belonging to the Burrell family, who lived at the homestead from 1851 to 1925, as well as photographs taken by descendant John William Twycross.

▶ *Beverley Rd, McCrae, 17 km south-west of Mornington via B110 and Mornington Peninsula Fwy.*

Comings and goings

Phillip Island had a busy history long before it became one of Victoria's major sporting venues and tourist attractions.

Middens along the shores testify to long Aboriginal occupation of this 10,000-ha landmass. The first European to visit was George Bass, in 1798, and soon whalers and sealers were calling in for the yearly killing season. In 1826, Captain Wright set up a military post and two 6-pounder guns to repulse any French attempt at establishing a foothold in Port Phillip Bay, but a shortage of water forced him out. In 1842, the McHaffie brothers became the first permanent settlers and rural development then accelerated. Four towns with British names were established: at Cowes, Newhaven, Rhyll and Ventnor. A mainstay of the early economy was chicory growing, but the industry declined with the advent of instant coffee. Alongside tourism, fishing is a major activity, with fleets based at Newhaven and San Remo.

6 Arthurs Seat

Diverse attractions cap bushclad landmark

With its spurs and valleys radiating down from its 314-m summit, Arthurs Seat is perhaps the Mornington Peninsula's most distinctive landmark. It was named in 1802 after a rocky outcrop in Edinburgh, Scotland, by Lieutenant John Murray. Pathways and mountain-biking trails around the peak traverse she-oak and messmate woodlands, and lead to scenic spots such as Kings Falls. A short walk from the peak is Seawinds, a formal garden adorned with sculptures by William Ricketts (see p. 234); also nearby is the Enchanted Maze Garden, featuring topiary and indoor mazes, slides and gardens.

21 km south of Mornington.

7 Royal Botanic Gardens Cranbourne

Bushland enclave in the midst of suburbia

This annexe of the Royal Botanic Gardens in Melbourne encompasses 363 ha of heathlands, wetlands and woodlands. Walk up to the Trig Point to enjoy a fine overview. Adjacent to the visitor centre is the Australian Garden, a landscaped area of themed plantings emphasising the beauty of native Australian habitats: the Red Sand Garden focuses on the striking colours of arid environments, while the Eucalypt Walk highlights the diversity of Australian tree species.

Cnr Ballarto Rd and Botanic Dr, Cranbourne, 16 km south of Dandenong via South Gippsland Hwy.

8 French Island

A short hop by ferry, but a world away

The ferry trip from Stony Point on Mornington Peninsula to Tankerton on French Island takes just 10 minutes, but given the wild, almost deserted feel of the island, you'd think you had travelled much further. Though sizeable (11,000 ha), and just 65 km from Melbourne, French Island, named Île des Français by French mariner Nicolas Baudin in 1802, has been little developed. Two-thirds of it is national park, and from 1916 to 1975 an open prison operated here and access was restricted. So even today there are few buildings, no sealed roads, just 70 or so residents, and an abundance of wildlife, including 230 bird species and the world's largest disease-free koala colony. Moreover, the former prison is now an innovative organic farm, McLeod Ecofarm, offering an unusual farmstay experience.

► *Stony Point is 26 km south-east of Mornington.*

9 Penguin Parade

Heart-warming wildlife show

They're an endearing, often comical sight: emerging every evening from the sea as the sun sinks below the horizon, groups of little, or fairy, penguins surf onto the shore, set themselves upright then waddle speedily up the beach, heads swivelling, alert to predators, bound for their burrows in the dunes. It's a scene that thrills large gatherings of human spectators year-round at this purpose-built facility. You can observe from a seat on the terraces overlooking the beach, or pay extra to get up close in the company of a ranger. The birds seem unperturbed by the human observers and have even been known to nest under local houses.

► *Summerland Beach, Phillip Island.*

10 Grand Prix Circuit Visitor Centre

Live out your revhead fantasies

The venue for the Australian Motorcycle Grand Prix, as well as V8 Supercar races, the internationally renowned Phillip Island Grand Prix Circuit occupies a dramatic setting atop coastal cliffs. You can admire vintage and modern vehicles and learn about the history of the circuit in the visitor centre. Outside, you can go-kart around a scale replica circuit, join a guided circuit tour that provides access to the control tower, pits, media centre and winner's podium, or strap yourself in for a 'Hot Lap' ride around the track with an experienced racing driver. Then you might need to recover in the Champions Cafe.

► *Back Bay Rd, Phillip Island.*

LITTLE PENGUINS WADDLE ASHORE ON PHILLIP ISLAND.

Gippsland

Occupying much of eastern Victoria, this region is bordered to the south by a long, wild coastline indented by inlets and enclosing large lakes. To the north, the alpine foothills encompass gorges and caves, and picturesque upland towns.

1 George Bass Coastal Walk

Invigorating coastal hikes and scenery

Named after navigator George Bass, who mapped 600 km of this coastline in 1797, this walking track runs for 7 km along the clifftops west of Kilcunda, weaving through grasslands and pockets of original vegetation including coast banksia, beard-heath boobiallas, and coast tea-tree. Panoramic views unfold at every turn and short detours descend to secluded coves and beaches. Gulls soar above the surf and nankeen kestrels and black-shouldered kites seek prey on the pastures just inland. Come in winter and you'll have a good chance of spotting southern right whales migrating along the coast.

► *15 km north-west of Wonthaggi via Bass Hwy.*

2 Wilsons Promontory

Wild peninsula rimmed by stunning shores

A rugged 40-km-long granite peninsula, the 'Prom' is linked to the mainland via a narrow isthmus. This limited access and its longstanding status as a national park have preserved its marvellous landscapes, rich vegetation and abundant wildlife. Wind-pruned heathland, pockets of tea-tree, banksia and hakea, and valleys lush with tree ferns climb to granite slopes topping out at 754 m. Along the 130-km shoreline, fur seals haul themselves onto rock ledges and broad sweeps of pristine, deserted sands are sheltered by rocky headlands. The myriad walking tracks range from easy strolls, such as the lovely 300-m walk to magnificent Whisky Bay, to the challenging 3.4-km climb to the summit of Mount Oberon and multiday hikes around the entire peninsula.

► *30 km south of South Gippsland Hwy at Foster.*

3 Agnes Falls

Victoria's highest single-span falls

From the quaint 1860s village of Toora, a winding drive climbs to Agnes Falls Scenic Reserve, yielding magnificent views back towards Wilsons Promontory. The 200-m walk from the car park to the falls is a delight, threading through forests of blue gum, blackwood and silver wattle, which once spread across the surrounding Strzelecki Ranges. And the scene that opens up at the end of the track is more enchanting still: the Agnes River plummets almost 60 m into a scenic, fern-lined gorge that echoes with the calls of birds.

► *Agnes Falls Scenic Reserve, 11 km north of South Gippsland Hwy at Toora.*

4 Walhalla

Former goldmining town with narrow-gauge railway

Tucked into picturesque hills, Walhalla was founded following the discovery of one of Australia's richest pockets of gold in 1862, which was mined for the next 50 years. By the 1880s, the town had 40 shops, several hotels and 4000 residents. Just a handful of people live here now, but the town retains many historic buildings, including the 1865 bakery, 1886 post office, 1896 rotunda and 1890s Windsor House, the town's only brick structure. You can still pan for gold in Stringers Creek and fish for trout. Not to be missed is a ride on the Walhalla Goldfields Railway, whose vintage trains weave through forested Springers Creek Gorge over a series of timber trestle bridges.

► *45 km north of Princes Hwy at Traralgon.*

5 Tarra-Bulga National Park

The Strzelecki Ranges as they once were

If you want to know what the Strzelecki Ranges once looked like, this is the place to come. The 2015-ha reserve preserves virtually all that remains of the original cool-temperate rainforest, and it is truly spectacular: rows of 60-m-high mountain ash trees loom over stands of myrtle beech, sassafras and blackwood and treeferns. Follow the Fern Gully Nature Walk (720 m, 15 minutes return), with its interpretive signs, to learn about the mountain ash forest, or walk to historic Corrigan Suspension Bridge (1.2 km, 25 minutes one way), which stands level with the rainforest canopy, far above a fern-filled gully. Further south, the 1.4-km (35 minutes) Rainforest Walk winds through a gully to lovely Cyathea Falls.

► *25 km north of Yarram via Tarra Valley Rd.*

6 Port Albert

Heritage architecture graces one of the state's oldest ports

It took him five attempts, but in 1841 explorer Angus McMillan finally succeeded in forging a route from the high inland pastures to the coast. Soon he had established a port here and a successful business shipping cattle to Tasmania. And when gold was discovered in Gippsland, Port Albert became a bustling entry point and outlet for livestock, butter, hides and timber, as well as gold. Though much more sedate now, the town retains prominent reminders of that affluent era, notably the 1864 post office, the Port Albert Hotel – Victoria's longest continually licensed inn – and the 1860s bank building that now houses the intriguing Gippsland Regional Maritime Museum, a treasure trove of seafaring memorabilia.

► *13 km south of Yarram via South Gippsland Hwy.*

Visitor information

Bairnsdale 03 5152 3444
Inverloch 03 5671 2233
Korumburra 03 5655 2233
Lakes Entrance 03 5155 1966
Metung 03 5156 2969
Traralgon 03 5174 3199
Wonthaggi 03 5671 2444

RAINFOREST IN TARRA-BULGA NATIONAL PARK

Inland waters

The narrow sand ribbon of Ninety Mile Beach encloses the largest enclosed waterway system in Australia, the Gippsland Lakes.

A million years ago, what is now the Gippsland Lakes was a huge bay. As the sea surged in and out, over thousands of years, it deposited vast amounts of sand. These deposits accumulated in places to form a 600-sq-km network of lakes, marshes, lagoons and channels and, finally, the long narrow ribbon of sand called Ninety Mile Beach, which separates the system from the sea. The three main lakes – Victoria, King and Wellington – are linked and fed by rivers that descend from the High Country, and for 70 years these waterways served as a busy transport network. Today, they are a recreational playground and a haven for the region's abundant wildlife. The major access points are Paynesville, a fishing port; stylish Metung, site of a smart marina; and Lakes Entrance, a lively holiday resort. All three offer boat hire, cruises and ferry services to isolated islands and spits.

LAKES ENTRANCE AND NINETY MILE BEACH

7 Ninety Mile Beach

All the space you could ever want, and more

In the otherwise densely populated south-eastern corner of Australia, this is one of the most secluded and least spoiled places – even today the only access to the most remote parts of the beach is by boat – and for its unbending, unwavering form, something of a topographical marvel. From Seaspray past Lakes Entrance to Croajingolong National Park, the beach runs almost poker-straight for 90 miles (145 km), its unblemished golden sands uninterrupted by headlands or even rocky outcrops. You can walk for kilometres along the sands (and not see a soul), cast a line offshore, or take a dip in the pristine but often turbulent waters – the beaches at Woodside Beach and Seaspray are patrolled in summer.

▶ *Access from South Gippsland Hwy via Woodside Beach, Seaspray, Golden Beach, Loch Sport or Lakes Entrance.*

8 Eagle Point

Bird's-eye view of an extraordinary geological formation

Silt jetties are long, parallel spits of sand and silt deposited on either side of a river as it enters the sea or a lake; undoubtedly the most famous such formations are those of the Mississippi River, which fan out around that river's huge delta. It's far less well known that the second-largest silt jetties in the world are here, at the mouth of the Mitchell River, where it enters Lake King. More than 8 km long, they can be most clearly seen from Eagle Point, but you can also drive out along the road atop the main jetty, following the river, to Port Dawson, from where you'll enjoy marvellous views over the lake.

▶ *14 south of Bairnsdale via Bairnsdale–Paynesville Rd.*

9 St Mary's Catholic Church

Breathtaking religious art

Grand though its bell tower is, the exterior of Bairnsdale's cathedral, built of red brick between 1913 and 1937, is rather austere. Inside, however, it's a different story. Here the altar and ceiling are a riot of colour, adorned as they are with bright, intricate and impressive murals depicting biblical scenes, visions of heaven, hell and purgatory, and trompe-l'oeil architectural elements. These extraordinary and exuberant designs are the work of an unemployed Italian painter, Frank Floreani, who was offered the chance to work here by the church authorities during the Depression – an opportunity he clearly seized with both hands.

▶ *Princes Hwy, Bairnsdale.*

10 Omeo

Famously lawless gold town that gained new life as a pastoral centre

Perched amid rolling hills at an altitude of 643 m, where the alpine air is crisp and untainted, Omeo still has the look of a frontier town and a collection of fine historic buildings. But fortunately, its pace of life is more sedate and its inhabitants more welcoming than in the mid-1800s, when this was one of the roughest, toughest goldfields in the land. Signs of those times are in evidence in the Omeo Justice Precinct, the state's most intact example of a judicial complex, which encompasses a log lockup (1858), court house (1859–61), police residence (1882–83) and a second court house (1893), designed in grand Federation Romanesque style. West of town are the Oriental Claims, the remains of a large hydraulic gold-sluicing operation run by Chinese miners.

▶ *123 km north-east of Bairnsdale via Great Alpine Rd.*

11 Buchan Caves

Tip of a vast underground realm

Though only two chambers in this system of around 350 limestone caves are open to the public for guided tours, they are not only fabulously beautiful in themselves but also convey a clear sense of the rich subterranean world beyond. Fairy Cave harbours delicate stalactites and stalagmites, while Royal Cave features larger chambers and calcite-rimmed pools. Above ground, the Buchan Caves Reserve encompasses a visitor centre, beautiful deciduous forest (whose autumn colours are a marvellous sight), and native bushland crisscrossed by walking tracks and inhabited by koalas, kangaroos and 100 species of birds.

► *Caves Rd, Buchan.*

12 Little River Gorge

Dramatic drive into state's deepest gorge

For 20 million years or so, the Snowy River has been carving a winding channel through the foothills of the Australian Alps, in places cutting deep into the bedrock and forming deep canyons. The deepest of these canyons – and the deepest in Victoria – is Little River Gorge. Reaching the gorge involves a dramatic drive along a dipping, twisting cliff-side road, followed by a walk along a rough 400-m path to a clifftop lookout where, all at once, a breathtaking panorama opens out over the awe-inspiring chasm. The hair-raising road continues eastward to McKillop Bridge on the Snowy River, where the 2-km Snowy River Nature Trail and the 15.5-km Silver Mine Walking Track explore the riverbank, adjacent cypress-pine forest and mining sites.

► *65 km north of Buchan via C608.*

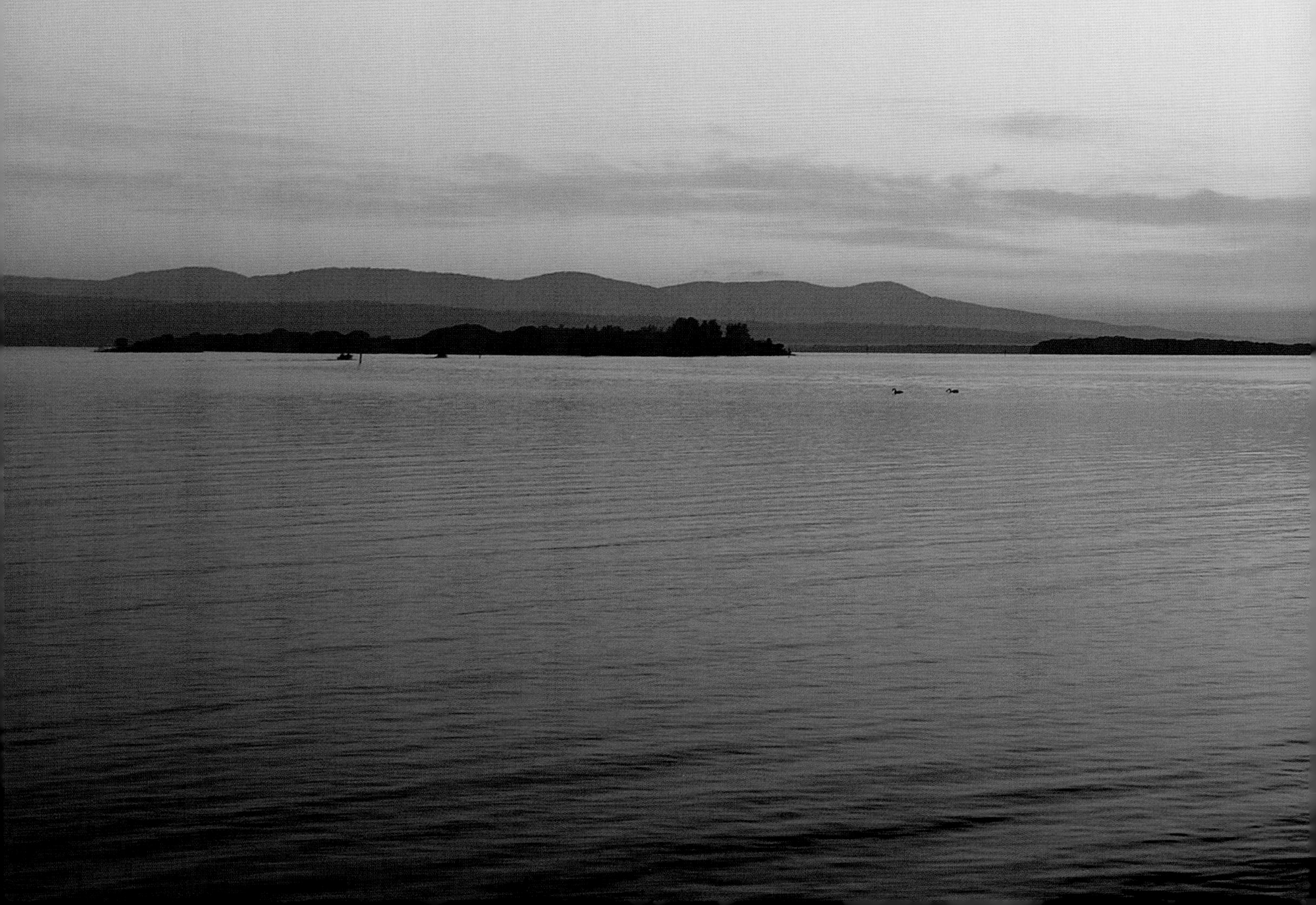

13 Point Hicks

Spectacularly sited lighthouse towers over breathtaking coastal landscape

'I have named it Point Hicks because Lieutenant [Zachariah] Hicks was the first to discover this land.' So wrote James Cook in his log for 19 April 1770, after first sighting the Australian mainland here. The headland remains much as it would have looked then, save for the 37-m-high lighthouse, built of concrete in 1888, and its two wooden keepers' cottages. You can rent one of the cottages or enjoy an exhilarating wild camping experience at nearby Thurra River. There, walking tracks explore 30-m-high sand dunes, lead to windswept beaches with views of the wreck of the SS *Saros*, and ascend to a viewpoint on 371-m Mount Everard, revealing wonderful vistas across heathland and forest to the ocean.

▶ *Croajingolong National Park, 47 km south of Princes Hwy at Cann River.*

14 Mallacoota Inlet

Deep harbour enveloped by wilderness

Wild but sheltered, remote but well serviced by a sizeable holiday town, Mallacoota Inlet is a beautifully scenic spot at the south-eastern tip of Australia. Around its deeply indented shoreline rise forested hills; just across its narrow harbour entrance are beautiful beaches. Join a cruise, hire a boat to explore the wide waterway at your own pace, or stretch your legs on the 7-km Mallacoota Walking Track, which leads through forest, over heathland and along the shore. At the head of the inlet, Gipsy Point has yet more tranquil waterways, fine fishing and a tame mob of grey kangaroos.

▶ *22 km south of Princes Hwy at Genoa via Genoa–Mallacoota Rd.*

SUNSET COLOURS AT MALLACOOTA INLET

Cape Wickham
Egg Lagoon
King Island
1
Currie
Grassy
Stokes Point
Outer Sister I
Inner Sister I
Palana
FURNEAUX GROUP
Cape Frankland
Flinders Island
Marshall Bay
Emita
Prime Seal I
Whitemark
Lady Barron
Badger I
Cape Barren Island
Clarke Island
Banks Strait
Hunter I
Three Hummock I
Cape Grim
Robbins I
BASS STRAIT
Waterhouse Point
Cape Portland
Ringarooma Bay
West Sandy Point
Noland Bay
Stony Head
Anderson Bay
3
Stanley
Montagu
Smithton
Forest
BASS
Rocky Cape
HWY
Wynyard
Somerset
Burnie
Sulphur Creek
Penguin
Ulverstone
LAUNCESTON AND NORTH
248–253
Marrawah
2
Arthur River
Arthur
Roger River
River
Ridgley
4
5
Hampshire
Devonport
6
George Town
Beauty Point
8
7
Beaconsfield
Lebrina
Pipers Brook
9
Bridport
Waterhouse
Tomahawk
Gladstone
Poole
1
Eddystone Point
Ansons Bay
Bay of Fires
4
Scottsdale
2
Weldborough
Ringarooma
St Helens Point
3
Pyengana
St Helens
Temma
Latrobe
BASS
Exeter
Targa
Barrington
Railton
Wilmot
Sheffield
Legana
Sandy Cape
Moina
HWY
12
Launceston
Upper Blessington
Mathinna
Scamander
Savage River
Liena
10
Deloraine
Westbury
11
Hadspen
Perth
Evandale
Mole Creek
Longford
13
5
St Marys
1
Corinna
Lake Mackintosh
Cradle Valley
2
Lake Pieman
Tullah
LAKE
Nile
Cressy
MIDLAND
South
Esk
R
Fingal
Chain of Lagoons
HWY
MIDLANDS AND EAST COAST
254–259
Rosebery
Breona
Granville Harbour
3
Zeehan
WESTERN WILDERNESS
266–271
Poatina
Avoca
Great Lake
Conara
Campbell Town
10
Bicheno
4
Trial Harbour
Arthurs Lake
TASMAN
Lake Leake
Lake St Clair
9
Miena
Lake Sorell
6
Ross
Friendly Beaches
Queenstown
5
LYELL
Derwent Bridge
Steppes
Coles Bay
Strahan
6
Lake Burbury
10
Lake Echo
Interlaken
Tunbridge
Swansea
Wineglass Bay
11
12
Great Oyster Bay
Freycinet Peninsula
Macquarie Harbour
8
HIGHWAY
7–8
Oatlands
HWY
Schouten I
Lake King William
Tarraleah
Little Swanport
7
Franklin River
Wayatinah
HIGHWAY
9
Bothwell
Gordon
Ouse
Tunnack
Woodsdale
Triabunna
Kempton
Colebrook
Orford
Point Hibbs
Hamilton
Buckland
13
Maria Island
Lake Gordon
River
11
12
Brighton
Campania
Strathgordon
Maydena
1
3
Richmond
Marion Bay
13
New Norfolk
2
4
Glenorchy
HOBART
5–8
See p. 263
9
10
11
Forestier Peninsula
Low Rocky Point
Lake Pedder
Huonville
HWY
Kingston
13
14
Eaglehawk Neck
Franklin
Snug
Tasman Peninsula
Nubeena
Southwest National Park
12
Geeveston
HUON
Woodbridge
15
Port Arthur
Cape Pillar
Nth Bruny I
Port Davey
Dover
South Bruny I
HOBART AND SOUTH-EAST
260–265
Southport
Tasman Head
South West Cape
Catamaran
South Cape
South East Cape
Maatsuyker Group

Tasmania

The next amazing place is never far away in this compact island state. And what Tasmania may lack in size, it more than makes up for with the monumental scale of its coastal, forest and mountain landscapes, the richness of its colonial towns, historic sites and cultural attractions, and the range and uniqueness of its animal and plant life.

Useful websites

Visitor information www.discovertasmania.com.au
Parks and reserves www.parks.tas.gov.au
Motoring organisation www.ract.com.au

DEEP CREEK BEACH, MOUNT WILLIAM NATIONAL PARK

Launceston and North

This coastline sculpted by the boisterous waves of Bass Strait and punctuated by dramatic headlands is home to much-loved colonies of little penguins. In the relatively low-lying lands to the south are sunken forests, limestone caverns, imposing colonial estates and fields of scented lavender.

1 King Island

Relive turbulent times on the Shipwrecks and Safe Havens Trail

The windswept summit of a drowned mountain, King Island stands like a sentinel at the western entrance to stormy Bass Strait. These are treacherous waters indeed, with more than 60 ships having come to grief here, including, in 1845, the immigrant ship *Cataraqui*, driven in a howling gale onto jagged rocks with the loss of 399 lives. The Shipwrecks and Safe Havens Trail visits 12 sites – eight overlook the locations of major shipwrecks, the remainder are lighthouses and safe harbours – to give an insight into the lives of the shipwrecked, the rescuers, and the lighthouse-keepers whose beams warned shipping away from dangerous shores.

▶ *Flights to Currie from Devonport, Melbourne and Moorabbin; no ferry services.*

2 Dismal Swamp

Slide or stroll into a sunken forest

Dismal Swamp is a 40-m-deep sinkhole, a natural depression formed over thousands of years by the slow dissolution of the dolomite bedrock by water from the region's high rainfall. But the unique forest of tall blackwood, myrtle and eucalypt that flourishes on the ferny sinkhole floor here is anything but dismal. Visitors can first gaze into its green depths from a rim-edge walkway suspended over the treetops, then choose their method of descent: either a gentle 10-minute stroll down a sloping pathway or, for the adventurous, an exhilarating 110-m spiralling slide through the tree canopy to reach the bottom in less than 15 seconds. There, boardwalks meander in dappled light through dense wet forest; information signs and large-scale artworks inspired by this unusual environment add to the experience.

▶ *Togari, 32 km south-west of Smithton via Bass Hwy.*

THE TABLE-TOPPED FORM OF THE NUT, STANLEY

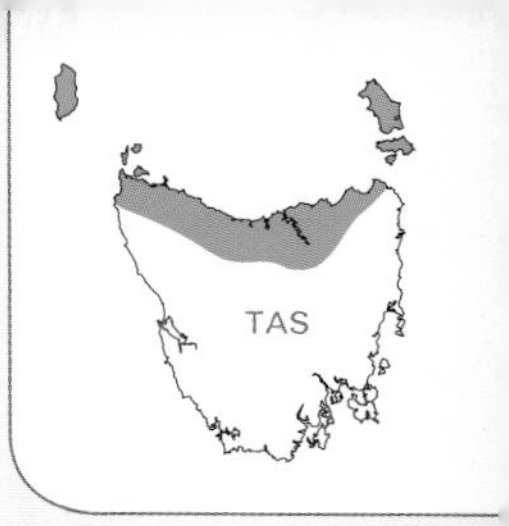

An ambitious private venture

The history of Tasmania's north-west coast is inextricably linked to a pastoral company set up in London in 1824 by a syndicate of businessmen.

The Van Diemen's Land Company (VDLC) was set up to develop land in Tasmania and thereby ensure a cheap and steady supply of wool for the English mills. In 1826, the company took up land grants totalling 140,000 ha in north-western Tasmania – at Cape Grim, on nearby islands and near present-day Burnie.

The company founded a town, Stanley, incorporating its headquarters at Highfield, a handsome bluestone property that can be visited today. Cultivation commenced and sheep – Cotswolds, Saxon Merinos and Leicesters – were imported. Problems with management and the sheep adapting to local conditions made the early years difficult. The shareholders lost heavily, and in 1853, the VDLC was restructured.

Long-term gain

Nevertheless, despite the fact that the primary purpose of the venture failed, the whole colony profited from the VDLC's activities and explorations, which helped open up the unknown hinterland to settlement. From 1848 to 1858, the company tried to recoup its losses by selling land. Luckily, it retained its holdings at Mount Bischoff near Waratah, and thereby benefited greatly from the 1871 discovery of tin in that district; later, VDLC timber supplied the paper mill at Burnie. Today, the much diminished Van Diemen's Land Company still raises cattle and sheep at its property 'Woolnorth', on Cape Grim, a unique link with the early colonial past.

Visitor information

Burnie 03 6430 5831
Deloraine 03 6362 5280
Devonport 03 6424 4466
Exeter 1800 637 989
Launceston 03 6336 3133
Stanley 03 6458 1330

3 The Nut

Prominent relic of geological upheaval

The Nut is a plug of solidified lava, remnant of Tasmania's last volcanic period, some 10 to 20 million years ago. Rising abruptly from the sea to a height of 150 m, it is one of several that dot the northern coastline. Matthew Flinders, who came across its rocky bulk in 1798, described it as 'a cliffy round lump resembling a Christmas cake'. Its summit can be reached on foot or by the ease of a chairlift, and yields views over Bass Strait and the town of Stanley.

Browns Rd, Stanley.

4 Makers Workshop

Handsomely housed crafts hub

They like to make things in Burnie. For more than 70 years, until the mills closed in 2009, it was paper. Now, at the Makers Workshop, skilled paper-makers are keen to show traditional methods, and then help visitors produce their own textured paper from local fibres that range from lavender to roo poo. The workshop is based in a striking waterfront building that also houses the Burnie visitor centre. And also working in studios here, depending on the day, will be one or several of more than 20 makers in other crafts – painters, milliners, wood-turners, ceramicists and even papier-mâché sculptors.

▶ *Bass Hwy, Burnie.*

5 Penguin

For all things penguin, including the birds themselves

Little penguins have a big presence here. The town takes its name from the colonies along the coastline, and the 3-m-tall Big Penguin on its main street pays homage to the region's best-known residents. For a close-up view of the real thing, join a twilight guided tour to Penguin Point, nearby to the east, to watch the birds surf ashore after a day's fishing then waddle up the beach to their rookeries to feed waiting chicks. The tours run from September to March.

▶ *19 km south-east of Burnie via Bass Hwy and Preservation Dr.*

6 Mersey Bluff

Repository of Tasmanian rock art

Mersey Bluff headland dominates the western shore of the Mersey River, with impressive views of the coast and the cross-Tasman ferry terminal of Devonport. Moreover, it is a traditional Aboriginal sacred site and one of the few places in Tasmania where Aboriginal rock engravings are still well preserved. At the Tiagarra Aboriginal Culture Centre and Museum (*tiagarra* means 'keeping place') walking tracks access 10 engraving sites, and exhibitions and displays of art and artefacts pay tribute to the history and present-day cultures of Tasmanian Aboriginal people.

▶ *Bluff Rd, Devonport.*

7 Beaconsfield Mine and Heritage Centre

Record of tragedy, resilience and dramatic rescue

It's hard to imagine even one person inside the 1.5-m-square metal cage that is the centrepiece of the mine-rescue display here, but in 2006 two miners – Brant Webb and Todd Russell – spent two cramped weeks in a cage such as this, trapped almost 1 km underground following a rockfall that killed fellow worker Larry Knight. The museum has been in operation since 1980 and is centred on the Grubb Shaft, which closed in 1914; it adjoins the Hart Shaft, scene of the disaster. Now extended, it honours the rescued miners, who helped plan the exhibits, and their rescuers. The display includes the torn overalls the men were wearing, accounts of how they survived and the difficulties faced by the rescuers. Gold has been mined here, on and off, since the 1880s, and the museum also houses working models, photographic collections, mining artefacts and industrial machinery that chronicle the town's golden past.

▶ *West St, Beaconsfield.*

8 Beauty Point

Enter the worlds of two bizarre creatures

In this pretty town at the mouth of the Tamar River – actually named for a prize bull and not its pleasant surroundings – you can find out all you need to know about two intriguing creatures. Seahorse World was established in 1999 to study the life cycle of the pot-bellied seahorse, native to these waters, and today is a working seahorse farm, breeding and displaying thousands of these odd fish; all, including males with young in an incubating pouch, can be seen on a guided tour. Visitors to Platypus House, a centre for breeding and research, can watch these shy animals feeding and playing and then wander through the echidna garden where their spiky cousin (both the platypus and echidna are monotremes – egg-laying mammals) can be encountered roaming free in a bushland setting. Seahorse World and Platypus House share a riverside wharf.

► *Inspection Head Wharf, Flinders St, Beauty Point.*

9 Bridestowe Estate Lavender Farm

Fragrant fields of French lavender

Bushes on this working lavender farm were grown from seed imported from the European Alps in the 1920s and planted in curved rows to suit the land contours and maximise soil and water conservation. Because the plants have not been cross-pollinated, the strain is remarkably pure. The highly prized oil is exported for perfume manufacture. The prime time to visit is summer, from December to mid-January, when blooms turn the hills into an undulating sea of purple; this is followed by a month of harvesting, when visitors can watch the cut lavender being distilled and enjoy the scent of lavender oil in the air. The farm has a cafe and a picnic area shaded by century-old oak trees, and a range of lavender products is available for purchase.

► *Gillespies Rd, Nabowla, 21 km west of Scottsdale via B81.*

FRAGRANT FIELDS AT BRIDESTOWE ESTATE LAVENDER FARM

10 Marakoopa Cave

Glittering underground galleries

The myriad of tiny lights twinkling in the unlit recesses of the sprawling Marakoopa cave system looks for all the world like the starry night sky in miniature. In fact these pinpoints of light are grubs, the larvae of a mosquito-like fly, and better known as glow-worms. The glow is produced by a chemical reaction in their bodies designed to lure prey, and this massed show of their enticing ways is the largest publicly accessible glow-worm display in Australia. The 45-minute Underground Rivers and Glow Worms guided tour to Marakoopa's lower chamber suits all fitness levels and also reveals sparkling crystals and pools studded with stalactites. Sharp-eyed visitors may spy Tasmanian cave spiders, which have a leg span of up to 12 cm. Wear warm clothing before descending – the year-round temperature is a chilly 9°C.

▶ *Mole Creek Karst National Park, 31 km west of Deloraine via B12.*

11 Entally Estate

Colonial spread in park-like grounds

This gracious house was built in 1819 by Thomas Reibey II, son of Mary Reibey, former convict turned successful businesswoman. Its heyday was in the era of Thomas's son, Thomas III, who became the local member of parliament and, in 1876 and just for one year, premier of Tasmania. In the 1850s, Thomas III extended the house and added the stone chapel; Entally was then the scene of grand parties and even offered hospitality to visiting royals. Today, the house is open to the public; lavish furnishings include cedar furniture, an 18th-century mahogany mirror and paintings by John Glover. The gardens were established more than 150 years ago and feature oaks, radiata pines, sequoias, elms and poplars, and a conservatory and a cricket ground, both of which are thought to be the oldest of their kind in Australia.

▶ *Meander Valley Hwy, Hadspen, 18 km south-west of Launceston via Bass Hwy.*

12 Cataract Gorge

Spectacular scenery on the edge of town

Just 15 minutes walk from the heart of Launceston is dramatic Cataract Gorge. Here towering granite walls channel the waters of the South Esk River as they rush north and on to their meeting with the Tamar. Early settler William Collins, the first European known to have visited the site, was clearly impressed, declaring 'the beauty of the scene is probably not surpassed in the world'. Today the area is a scenic reserve where walking tracks reach lookouts and wind through wilderness to ornamental gardens with peacocks and picnic areas. Those with a head for heights can view it all from the chairlift that glides across the ravine, then return via the suspension bridge.

▶ *Off Basin Rd, Launceston.*

13 Woolmers

Old World home where roses bloom

The neat, sweet-smelling hawthorn hedges and stately mansions of the Longford area bear witness to the desire of its early British settlers to re-create the landscapes of their homeland in the Tasmanian bush. And nowhere more so than at Woolmers, established in 1819 by Thomas Archer and home to his descendants until 1994. As well as the imposing homestead, the historic buildings include the former chapel, workers' cottages, blacksmith's shop, stables and bakehouse – a virtual village where up to 100 people lived and worked at one time. A colourful addition is the National Rose Garden, of formal 19th-century design and planted with hundreds of heritage and new roses. There are guided tours of the main house and self-guided tours of the outbuildings and rose garden.

▶ *Woolmers La, Longford.*

SWIFT-FLOWING WATERS
AT CATARACT GORGE

Midlands and East Coast

Tasmania's spectacularly scenic east coast is famed for white sands, clear waters, forests and abundant wildlife. To the west, threaded along the cross-island Midland Highway, are Georgian towns, graceful bridges and colonial estates of finely crafted sandstone – lasting monuments to the skills of convict masons.

1 Mount William National Park

Orange rocks and marsupial lawns

Tucked into the remote north-eastern corner of the state, this little-known park is not, as its name might suggest, a place of rugged mountain scenery, but instead consists of sweeping beaches, grassy flats and low, wooded ridges. Huge granite boulders lie scattered along the shore and, encrusted with patches of flame-coloured lichen, create an arresting colour scheme against the snow-white sands and blue-green sea. The lichen also aids the weathering of the granite, which due to its high quartz content produces the coast's pure sand as it breaks down. In the north of the park, nocturnal grazing by kangaroos, wallabies and wombats keeps grassy swathes behind the dunes almost as trim as a suburban lawn – a dawn or dusk excursion around Forester Kangaroo Scenic Drive will reveal mobs of kangaroos busy at this task.

▶ *17 km north-east of Gladstone via C843 and C845.*

Visitor information

Oatlands 03 6254 1212
Ross 03 6381 5466
St Helens 03 6376 1744
Scottsdale 03 6352 6520
Triabunna 03 6257 4772

2 Legerwood Memorial Trees

Carved trunks honour fallen heroes

In 1918, an avenue of trees was planted in this rural hamlet to honour local men who died in the First World War. By 2001, the trees had grown to a dangerous height and some had become unstable. Rather than remove them completely, the town found a novel solution to retain its memorial – the tops were lopped off and the solid trunks carved into likenesses of each of the fallen men; other tree sculptures depict scenes from the era of the First World War.

▶ *23 km east of Scottsdale via Tasman Hwy and Carisbrook La.*

3 St Columba Falls

Lush forests edge cascading waters

Here the headwaters of the George River plunge 90 m from the Mount Victoria foothills down a boulder-strewn cliff into the valley of the South George River. This is one of the highest waterfalls in Tasmania, and, although it can be seen from the car park, to fully appreciate the power of the cascade it's worth taking the time to follow the moderately steep, but well-formed, walking track (40 minutes return) that winds through a forest of tree ferns, sassafras and myrtle down to a viewing platform at its base. There are benches where walkers can rest in the shade of the rainforest, and a picnic area near the road.

▶ *10 km south-west of Tasman Hwy via Pyengana and St Columba Falls Rd.*

JACOBS LADDER, THE DRAMATIC ASCENT TO BEN LOMOND NATIONAL PARK

4 Bay of Fires

Leave footprints in dazzling sands

The startlingly beautiful Bay of Fires sweeps south from Eddystone Point to the township of Binalong Bay. It is the site of a famed 4-day, 27-km walk and, at the finishing line, an acclaimed eco-lodge. You can join a guided tour or sample part or all of the walk under your own steam. Either way, you will find a glorious selection of picnic, camping and swimming spots, many beside coastal lagoons or facing the turquoise sea and fringed by boulder-studded beaches. If you just want to look, drive north from Binalong Bay to The Gardens – named in the 1840s by Lady Jane Franklin, the wife of Governor John Franklin, for its masses of spring wild flowers – for a view north of white sands and sparkling waters. The bay itself was named in 1773 by Captain Tobias Furneaux for the number of Aboriginal campfires seen along the coast.

▶ *21 km north of St Helens via C850.*

5 Ben Lomond

Climb Jacobs Ladder to a majestic plateau

The founder of Launceston, Scotsman Colonel Paterson, named Ben Lomond after a mountain in his homeland, but this elevated plateau – 14 km long, 6 km wide and 1572 m above sea level at its highest point – is considerably taller than its Scottish counterpart. The plateau is flanked by cliffs of columnar dolerite and many prominent features have colourful names – Misery Bluff, Plains of Heaven and Little Hell. Vehicle access to the tops is via a series of six very steep hairpin bends known as Jacobs Ladder. In winter, snowfields here attract downhill skiers; in summer two cross-country ski routes double as walking tracks. The scenery is magnificent year-round.

▶ *Ben Lomond National Park, 50 km south-east of Launceston via C401.*

6 Ross Bridge

Convict-sculpted with skill and wit

In 1812, a military post was established here, beside a ford over the Macquarie River, for the protection of travellers. As the township grew, the need for a bridge became apparent, and the Ross Bridge, built from the same golden stone as the town's other buildings, took shape from 1831 to 1836. Apart from its simple elegance, the most striking thing about the three-spanned bridge is the 186 intricately carved faces, animals and swirling Celtic symbols that decorate the edge of each rib of the three arches. Most are the handiwork of convict mason and ex-highwayman Daniel Herbert. His skill earned him a pardon, despite the fact that his carvings include some very unflattering likenesses of well-known figures of the day. The carvings are best viewed from the adjacent riverside park.

► *Ross, Midland Hwy.*

7 Oatlands Topiaries

Historic highway hedges

In the 1960s, roadworker Jack Cashion began spending his lunch hours clipping hedges along the Midland Highway north of Oatlands into the shapes of animals. Long a distinctive feature of this stretch of road, these whimsical topiaries have been joined in recent years by a series of similar works designed by sculptor Stephen Walker and placed in and around Oatlands. These include an emu at the corner of High and Gay streets, a shepherd at the junction of High and Church streets, and a drover at the southern entrance to the town, as well as a giraffe, swans and a golfer.

► *Oatlands, Midland Hwy.*

ROSS BRIDGE'S QUIRKY CARVINGS WERE MADE BY CONVICT STONEMASONS.

8 Callington Mill

Old mill sails on

Built in 1837, the five-level Callington Mill is the third-oldest windmill in Australia and the only one in Tasmania. Steam power was added in the 1850s, and the mill, towering centrepiece of a mini-estate of workers' cottages, granary and bakery, ground on until 1892. In 1909, a storm ripped off its sails, and, while the mill stood firm, it was not until a century later, in 2010, that they were replaced in a major renovation. Now in full sail, the mill is once again operational and producing locally grown flour, just as it did in the colonial period. It can be seen from the highway, and tours of its interior allow visitors to inspect its workings.

▶ *Oatlands, Midland Hwy.*

9 Bothwell

Site of Australia's oldest golf course

Bothwell's Scottish and golfing connections originate from a group of families who settled here on the banks of the Clyde River in the late 1820s. With the help of convict labour, the village of Bothwell took shape in the 1830s, and by 1839 Alexander Reid had laid out Australia's first golf course on his farm at Ratho – then, as now, grazing sheep keep the fairways trim. The course, with its unusual square putting greens, is open to the public and visitors can hire clubs from the Australasian Golf Museum in Market Place, where an extensive collection of golfing memorabilia is on display. Bothwell itself has more than 50 buildings of architectural and historical interest, many of which can be viewed on a self-guided walk – ask for a brochure from the Golf Museum.

▶ *Lake Hwy.*

Highway through history

The Midland Highway still follows much of the original road carved out in the 1820s by convict labour.

The Midland Highway had its beginnings in 1807, when the surveyor Charles Grimes pioneered a track, fit only for travel on foot or horseback, between Hobart and Launceston. This was the route followed in 1811 by Governor Macquarie, who, accompanied by his wife, took nearly six days to travel its length, leaving a legacy of place names and an order to his surveyor James Meehan to 'mark out a road for travellers'. When Macquarie returned in 1821, much of the route was trafficable by carriage.

Rich rewards

Convict gangs, under the supervision of engineer soldiers, toiled on, and by 1826 the road was complete. Prisoners were also used to build a string of settlements to serve the needs of travellers and farmers. Their labours can be appreciated in the historic buildings that are a feature of many of the highway's towns, including Campbell Town and Oatlands (see Oatlands Topiaries and Callington Mill). In 1834 a coach service commenced, with change stations every 16 km, a journey that took passengers 12 hours. Soon after, a mail coach replaced the walking mailman (his beat took a week each way); it was an easy target for bushrangers, so armed guards rode with it. By the 1870s, visiting English writer Anthony Trollope declared the road to be 'as good as any road in England' and, no doubt due largely to the hawthorn hedgerows and deciduous trees planted by the English, Scottish and Irish settlers, 'in appearance exactly like an English road'.

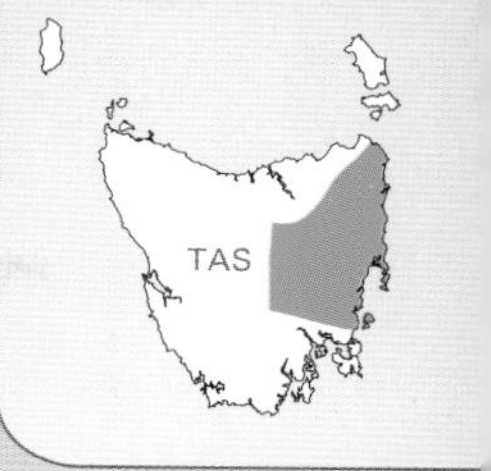

10 East Coast Natureworld

Fighting for the devils

Set among 160 ha of natural parkland and lagoons, East Coast Natureworld is a wildlife park with a difference – it also functions as a rescue and rehabilitation centre for wildlife injured on the roads (fully recovered animals are returned to the wild), and as a disease-free refuge and breeding centre for Tasmanian devils, at present under threat from facial-tumour disease. Here you can watch these fierce little creatures being fed, and also meet a range of other animals, from exotic birds to koalas, quolls and long-necked turtles.

▶ *7 km north of Bicheno via Tasman Hwy.*

11 Wineglass Bay

Postcard perfect

A moderately difficult uphill track from the car park to the Wineglass Bay Lookout (1 to 2.5 hours return) reaches a boulder-flanked platform perched in a saddle between the pink granite peaks of the Hazards. Below, an arc of white sand traces a half-moon sweep between clear, turquoise waters and wooded slopes. This is Wineglass Bay, the gleaming jewel in the crown of Freycinet National Park. Beyond is the glowering granite bulk of Mount Graham and Mount Freycinet (620 m). For those with a day to spare, this is the start of one of the most scenic walks in Tasmania. Hike down the rocky slope, then stroll to the southern end of the beach to look back at the magnificent Hazards. Return to the car park across the low marshy isthmus to tranquil Hazards Beach and around the base of Mount Mayson, about 11 km in all. The fastest way back, though, is to prearrange a pick-up by aqua taxi.

▶ *Freycinet National Park, 45 km south of Bicheno via Coles Bay Rd.*

12 Spiky Bridge

Smoothing the journey

This unusual dry-stone bridge, now just off the highway, is named for its distinctive jagged parapets of large and small upright rocks. It was built in the 1840s by convicts from the Rocky Hills probation station, down the hill to the south. More of a causeway than a bridge, it spans a sharp dip across a small but steep gully. You can walk across the bridge, then clamber down into the hollow to inspect the stonework of the buttresses and arched culvert.

▶ *Tasman Hwy, 8 km south of Swansea.*

13 Maria Island

From penitentiary to Australian ark

Serene Maria Island, 15 km off the coast, was once a grim place of incarceration. A penal station was established here in 1825 and many of the buildings, erected using bricks made on the island and sandstone excavated from its sea cliffs, still stand. Today the watery isolation that kept convicts captive makes the island an ideal refuge for native animal and plant species under threat elsewhere. Wildlife is abundant. Some species, such as the pademelon and the endangered forty-spotted pardalote, occur naturally on the island; others, including Forester kangaroos, Bennett's wallabies, Tasmanian native hens and Cape Barren geese, have been introduced since the 1960s. Parts of the surrounding waters are a marine reserve, and seals, dolphins and whales can be seen offshore. The island is a car-free zone (but bikes are welcome and available for hire) and has no electricity or shops.

▶ *Ferry from Triabunna, Tasman Hwy.*

AERIAL VIEW OF WINEGLASS BAY AND THE HAZARDS

Hobart and South-East

Hobart, the nation's second-oldest state capital, lies between the bulk of Mount Wellington and the Derwent River and offers heritage buildings and impressive cultural collections. Upriver lie colonial townships of great charm and to the south-east are the rugged landscapes and sombre ruins of the Tasman Peninsula.

1 Salmon Ponds

Despite the name, it's all about trout

British settlers hankering after familiar plants and animals introduced many species from home but, until the 1860s, failed with fish. This all changed when a shipment of live eggs of salmon and trout arrived here in 1864, having survived the 91-day voyage from England in an ice chest against incredible odds, on a journey that involved first a clipper, then a steamship, a river steamer and, finally, packhorses. Salmon are migratory fish and those released chose to complete their life cycle elsewhere, but descendants of the trout went on to stock Tasmanian, mainland and New Zealand waterways. Visit the Trout Fishery Museum and the historic hatchery to learn about trout breeding, then lunch in the restaurant or picnic under the trees.

▶ *Salmon Ponds Rd, Plenty, 10 km north-west of New Norfolk via Glenora Rd.*

2 New Norfolk

Historic town of industrious settlers

This is one of Australia's oldest towns, founded in 1808 by settlers transferred here from Norfolk Island. At the time, food was in short supply, so their arrival was met with dismay; however, they brought skills that helped the colony survive and soon set about farming in the fertile Derwent Valley. The town was named for their forsaken island and its orderly street plan is a legacy of Governor Macquarie, who visited in 1811. Historic buildings include the two-storey Bush Inn, built in 1815 and the Old Colony Inn, built in 1835 as a cottage, later used as a barracks and now a restaurant and museum. Here also is St Matthew's Church, dating from 1823, Tasmania's oldest Anglican church. By the 1860s the valley was an important hop-growing area and it is still dotted with oast houses (used for drying the plant).

▶ *Lyell Hwy.*

3 Richmond

Mixture of heritage gems and grim past

This delightful and well-preserved Georgian village was a military post and convict station from the 1830s until the 1870s. Today its mellow stone buildings house galleries, outlets for gourmet foods and local produce, craft shops, eateries and accommodation. Its main road crosses the oldest bridge still in use in Australia, built by chain-gangs between 1823 and 1825 and best appreciated from the grassy banks of the Coal River, below, where obliging ducks often gather for food scraps and photo opportunities. The 1825 convict-built Richmond Gaol sheltered local work gangs and prisoners in transit between Hobart and Port Arthur; the original solitary confinement cells, chain-gang holding rooms, flogging yard, cookhouse and women's section are all open for public inspection. In the 1870s a new route east bypassed Richmond, leaving the village as a handsome relic of a harsh era.

► *13 km north of Tasman Hwy at Cambridge.*

4 MONA

Not your typical museum

Owner David Walsh describes MONA – the Museum of Old and New Art – as a 'subversive adult Disneyland'. The largest privately owned collection of antiquities and modern art in Australia, it is housed in a striking, purpose-built gallery. The more than 400 pieces range from Egyptian funerary art to confronting contemporary works (there is a content warning and map showing visitors how to avoid images that might offend), and are arranged to show them as works of art rather than chronologically, so you might find an ancient mummy beside a high-tech multimedia work. Unlike Disneyland, admission is free.

► *Main Rd, Berriedale, 10 km north of Hobart; ferry from Brooke St, Hobart.*

Visitor information

Hobart 03 6238 4222
Huonville 03 6264 1838
Port Arthur 03 6251 2371

MONA'S BOLD AND COLOURFUL DESIGN REFLECTS ITS COLLECTION.

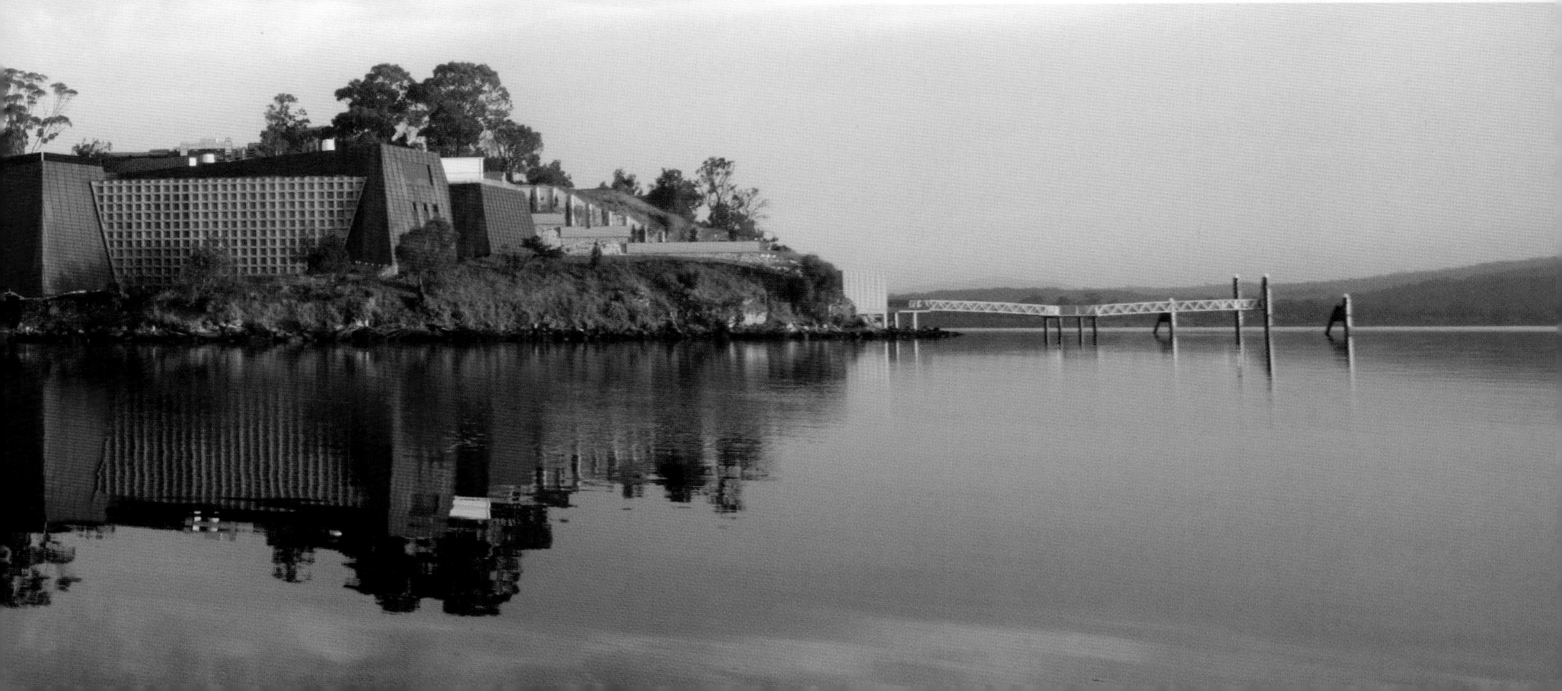

Faltering start

The first site on the Derwent River to be settled was Risdon Cove, scene of the first conflict between Tasmanian Aboriginals and the British.

In 1802, a French scientific expedition led by Nicolas Baudin visited Tasmania, suggesting to Britain that its rival might soon try to claim the island. In response, Lieutenant John Bowen was sent to the Derwent in the following year, with a party of soldiers and convicts, to assert British rights. The expedition established an encampment at Risdon Cove, on the east bank of the river, but it lasted barely a year. In 1804, Lieutenant-Colonel David Collins decided that Sullivans Cove, with its better soil and more reliable fresh water, offered better prospects and shifted the government settlement there.

Little has changed at Risdon Cove since then. Archaeological excavations have uncovered traces of the buildings erected by the settlers, making it the only site of a major European settlement in its original state. The symbolism is different for Tasmanian Aboriginals, however. In 1804, a number of members of a hunting party were killed here in a clash with armed soldiers, the first in a shameful sequence that came close to removing all traces of the island's original inhabitants. In acknowledgment of traditional ownership, the land was returned to the Aboriginal community in 1999.

5 Theatre Royal

'The best little theatre in the world', in the opinion of Sir Laurence Olivier

This is the oldest theatre in the nation. It was built in 1837 at the instigation of a group of leading citizens to the design of Peter Degraves, founder of the Cascade Brewery, and has walls of convict-carved stone. Since then it has been remodelled, refurbished and restored, several times threatened with demolition – most notably in the 1940s, when Sir Laurence leaped to its defence – and in 1984 was seriously damaged by fire; it reopened two years later after major reconstruction. Today it still presents a full program of drama. Tours of the building are conducted on Monday, Wednesday and Friday mornings.
▶ *Campbell St, Hobart.*

6 Tasmanian Museum and Art Gallery

Diverse in content, broad in scope

Treasured heritage buildings on the Hobart waterfront, including the 1808 Commissariat Store, house the wide-ranging collections of this combined museum, art gallery and herbarium. Permanent exhibitions include 'Ningenneh tunapry', meaning 'to give knowledge and understanding', which celebrates and explores Tasmanian Aboriginal culture, and Islands to Ice, which takes visitors on a journey from Hobart across the wild Southern Oceans to the icy Antarctic, as well as early colonial art, 250 items of Chinese art and antiquities, a collection of Roman coins, and photographs and preserved remains of the extinct thylacine.
▶ *Macquarie St, Hobart.*

7 Salamanca Place

Where market day in historic surroundings echoes the bustle of bygone days

The splendid, two- and three-storeyed sandstone warehouse terraces of harbour-front Salamanca Place are the only such group of buildings still standing in Australia. Built between 1835 and 1850, they were the hub of Hobart's trade and commerce. Many have made the transition to the 21st century as shops, restaurants and galleries. Every Saturday the area is closed to traffic and transformed into a lively, open-air market where hundreds of stalls offer fresh produce, local arts and crafts, clothes, flowers and books.

▶ *Salamanca Pl, Hobart.*

HOBART CITY CENTRE

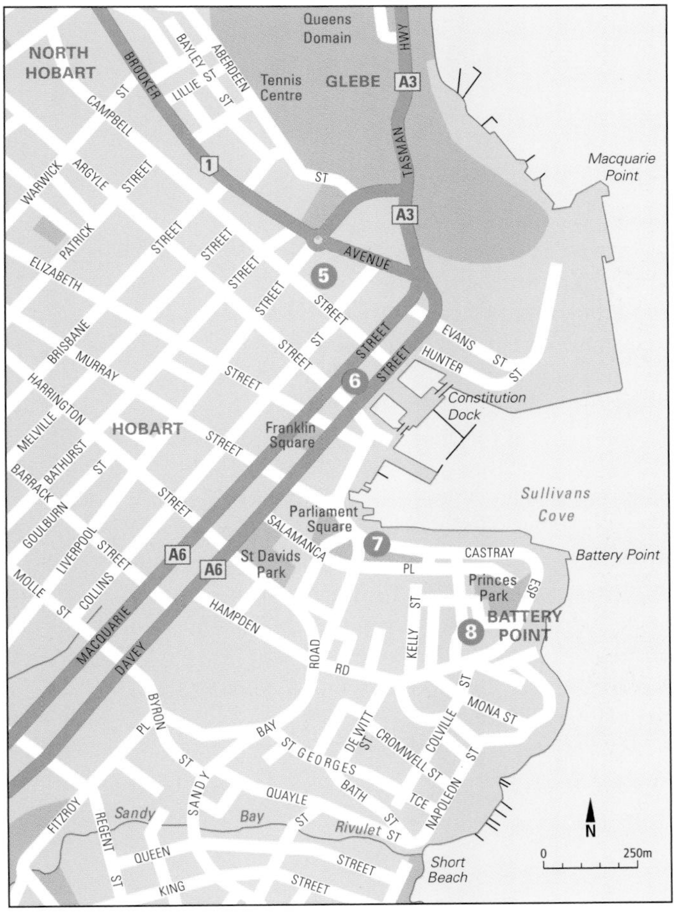

8 Battery Point

Walk the narrow streets of a maritime village

This is perhaps the most complete colonial village remaining in Australia, once the haunt of sailors, merchants, whalers, shipwrights and fisherfolk and outwardly little changed from the 1840s. At its heart is Arthur Circus, consisting of 15 single-storey brick cottages, many with tiny dormer windows, originally built around a village green. The area takes its name from the Mulgrave battery of guns built in 1818 to protect the port.

▶ *Battery Point, Hobart.*

9 Mount Wellington

Crown of Hobart's mountain backdrop

Mount Wellington is so close to Hobart it is possible – for the fit and experienced – to walk from the city centre to the summit and back in a day. The great majority of visitors, however, make the round trip by car. On a bright clear day, the view is breathtaking. All of Hobart is spread out below, from its historic heart to the suburban fringes. In the middle distance the long sweep of the Derwent winds seaward through its neat river valley to the D'Entrecasteaux Channel, World Heritage Area wilderness rims the north-western horizon, while the Tasman Peninsula can be seen to the south-east. Winds, often icy, can whip in, setting the mountain-top television towers singing. At 1271 m, this is one of the highest peaks in Tasmania, and is sometimes under cloud; in winter it is capped with snow.

▶ *Pinnacle Rd, 21 km west of Hobart via B64 and C616.*

10 Cascade Brewery

Castle-like headquarters of the nation's oldest brewery

Its imposing architecture and leafy setting suggest a grand château rather than a brewery. The oldest parts of the complex date from 1824 and are the original flour and saw mills of the brewery's founder, Englishman Peter Degraves; the extensions that gave the building its current majestic shape were added a century later. Although much was destroyed in the disastrous 1967 Black Tuesday fires, the metre-thick walls stood firm and the brewery was rebuilt almost immediately. The twice-daily tours inside the building examine the brewing process (they involve climbing many flights of stairs, and bookings are essential). The lawns, playground and rhododendron beds of nearby Cascade Gardens are the upstream end of a park that follows Hobart Rivulet to the city.

▶ *4 km west of Hobart via Cascade Rd.*

11 Shot Tower

Monument to perseverance

This 48-m-high, tapering cylinder of stone was built in 1870, almost single-handedly, by Scottish architect, engineer and carpenter Joseph Moir. Its purpose was to make lead shot, but for Moir, as a plaque above the door reveals, 'the secrets of shot-making had [still] to be discovered'. With practice, he eventually perfected the process: molten metal was poured from a vast cauldron set up at the top of the tower through a great iron colander, forming drops of lead that became spherical as they fell to a water tank in the base; there the shot was checked, graded and polished ready for use. Sadly for Moir, while his method was successful, the costs of labour and importing lead made the enterprise a commercial failure. Today, the top of the tower can be accessed via a 259-step staircase and offers spectacular views up, down and across the Derwent River; there is a museum at the base of the tower.

▶ *Channel Hwy, Taroona, 11 km south of Hobart.*

12 Tahune AirWalk

Wander in the leafy tops of forest giants

To the early European explorers, the heavily timbered Tahune rainforest looked so inhospitable that they condemned it as unsuitable for settlement. Today 102 ha of the forest are protected in the Tahune Forest Reserve, the setting for Forestry Tasmania's Tahune AirWalk, a 40-m-high steel pathway that takes walkers on a 50-minute loop through the forest canopy of celery-top pine, sassafras, myrtle, blackwood and stringy-bark to a viewing platform over the confluence of the Huon and Picton rivers. Ground-level walks include the Swinging Bridge Circuit (3 km return), which follows the rivers and crosses both on modern swinging bridges.

▶ *Tahune Forest Reserve, 28 km north-west of Geeveston.*

13 Coal Mines Historic Site

Hellhole where convicts of the 'worst class' toiled

This was Tasmania's first coalmine and served a dual purpose. It reduced the colony's dependence on costly New South Wales coal and, by using convicts as a cheap source of labour, functioned as a place of further punishment for troublesome prisoners from Port Arthur. Working conditions in the mines were atrocious, and for those who continued to offend, four damp and dark solitary cells were constructed deep in the subterranean labyrinth. The mine shipped its first coal in 1834 and was operational for more than 40 years, but from 1848 on it was leased to private concerns. Today the collapsed mine shafts can still be seen, as well as the remains of the above-ground cells and the officers' barracks.

▶ *36 km west of Eaglehawk Neck via Arthur Hwy and B37.*

PROMINENT AMONG PORT ARTHUR'S BUILDINGS IS THE 1842 GUARD TOWER.

14 Tessellated Pavement

Handiwork of nature

They may look like the enormous hand-crafted tiles of a giant stonemason, but the neat, almost squared-off patterning of this shoreline rock platform is actually the result of natural forces. Between 160 and 60 million years ago, stresses in the Earth's crust fractured a great slab of flat-lying siltstone into sets of lines. Erosion by seawater has since worn smooth the surface of the rock and scoured these cracks into deep, evenly spaced grooves.

▶ *7 km north-east of Eaglehawk Neck via Arthur Hwy.*

15 Port Arthur

Sobering reminder of a brutal system

Despite the beauty of the surrounding landscape, Port Arthur's grim history invests the site with a brooding atmosphere. From 1830 to 1877, this former penal settlement housed some 25,000 male convicts, sent here for committing crimes after transportation and subjected to 'the most unceasing labour' and 'harassing vigilance'. Among the punishments, perhaps none was worse than incarceration in the Model Prison, where inmates were held in solitude, silence and often total darkness for weeks at a time. More than 30 other buildings are scattered around the site and include the Penitentiary, built as a granary in 1842 and turned into prison accommodation 15 years later, an elegant church and an interpretation centre. Guided tours and cruises are available.

▶ *Port Arthur Historic Site, Arthur Hwy.*

Western Wilderness

Western Tasmania encompasses enormous tracts of wilderness, ranging from the granite peaks of Cradle Mountain to the 'wild rivers' of the central west and the untamed realm of Southwest National Park. Isolated outposts of settlement include former penal colonies, river ports and mining towns.

MAJESTIC LANDSCAPES SURROUND CRADLE MOUNTAIN.

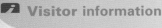

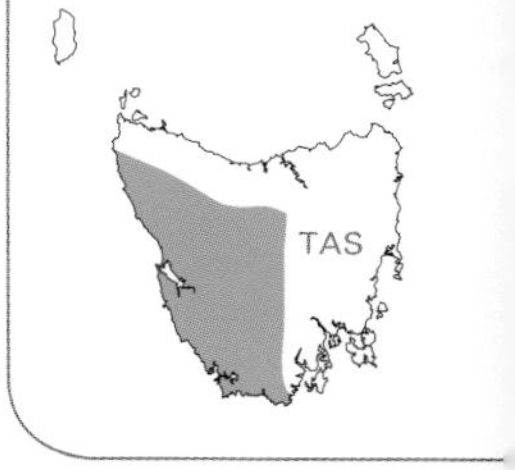

1 Pieman River

Cruise a remote waterway through Australia's largest temperate rainforest

Bounded to the north by the Arthur River, to the south by the Pieman River and to the east by the Murchison Highway, the Tarkine is the largest myrtle-beech rainforest in Australia, covering some 450,000 ha, and is traversed by few roads. Cruises and tours from the former gold-rush settlement of Corinna, now reinvented as an ecotourism resort, provide rewarding experiences of this ancient wilderness. Hop aboard the *Arcadia II*, a 1939 cruiser built of Huon pine, to drift downriver on glassy, tannin-stained waters reflecting seemingly impenetrable stands of native pines and tree ferns, while watching for sea eagles and azure kingfishers. At the river mouth, you can explore a little-visited stretch of coastline edged by white-sand beaches, massive dunes and rock formations.

► *Corinna, 50 km north-west of Zeehan via Heemskirk Rd and Corinna Rd.*

Visitor information

Strahan 03 6472 6800

2 Cradle Mountain

Invigorating walks through glacier-fashioned scenery

The view across Dove Lake to the ragged dolerite ridge of Cradle Mountain is one Australia's most iconic and most photographed, and on a clear day in the limpid, invigorating mountain air, with the waters mirroring the majestic landscape, it is truly one of the country's great sights. The easy, 2-hour Dove Lake Loop Track offers varying perspectives on the peak as it leads along the lakeshore and through cool temperate forest on the lower slopes. Wallabies are abundant and you may spot platypuses in the waterways. One approach to climbing Cradle Mountain involves walking the first section of the famous Overland Track past Crater Lake, a glacial tarn enclosed by towering cliffs, then negotiating a jumble of weathered, lichen-decorated boulders and dolerite scree. The summit views reveal the scoured, often snow-dusted surrounds in all their glory; to get there and enjoy them, you'll need a full day, good fitness, all-weather gear and (fingers crossed) good weather.

► *Cradle Mountain–Lake St Clair National Park, 5 km south of Cradle Valley.*

3 Montezuma Falls

Hike to towering falls via abandoned mining camps and rail tracks

The 5.5-km, 3-hour-return walk to the falls begins at Williamsford, an old zinc-mining settlement, then follows the route of the North East Dundas Tramway, which served the region's mining sites between 1898 and 1925, through rainforest of myrtle, leatherwood, sassafras and tree ferns. It then arrives at a suspension bridge across the base of the imposing falls, which, with a drop of 104 m, are among the tallest in Tasmania. The name of the falls derives from the Montezuma Mining Company, which once held leases here.

► *Williamsford is 8 km south of Rosebery via Williamsford Rd.*

VIEW FROM THE LYELL HIGHWAY OVER LAKE BURBURY TO FRENCHMANS CAP

4 West Coast Pioneers Memorial Museum

Impressive collection, ranging from rare crystals to giant locomotives

Housed in the handsome 1894 School of Mines building, the museum has a fine collection relating to the history of western Tasmania and the 1880s boom times in Zeehan, when a huge silver–lead deposit was discovered and the population surged to 10,000. Also on show are an outstanding array of gems and minerals, and steam locomotives and rolling stock. A bonus is that your entry fee also includes access to the recently revamped 1898 Gaiety Theatre, where audiences once came to hear singers of the highest calibre, including Dame Nellie Melba and Enrico Caruso, and watch the magic tricks of Harry Houdini and the provocative dances of Lola Montez.

► *Main St, Zeehan.*

5 Queenstown

Hauntingly bare hillsides reflect environmental toll of mining

It's a memorable but sobering scene that greets the driver approaching Queenstown: hillsides stripped bare of vegetation (for fuel) and stained strange shades of yellow, pink and ochre by pollution from copper smelters encircle the town. Despite the closure of the smelters in 1969, there has been little regrowth. You can learn more about the history (and impact) of mining here at the Eric Thomas Gallery Museum inside the former Imperial Hotel, built in 1898, which has a fine collection of photographs, minerals and artefacts, and by taking a tour of the still-operational Mount Lyell Mine, which travels 6 km into the mountainside. For another perspective on the town's past, visit the Paragon Theatre, a beautifully restored Art Deco cinema, where you can watch a series of films covering the evolution and human history of the Western Wilderness.

► *Lyell Hwy.*

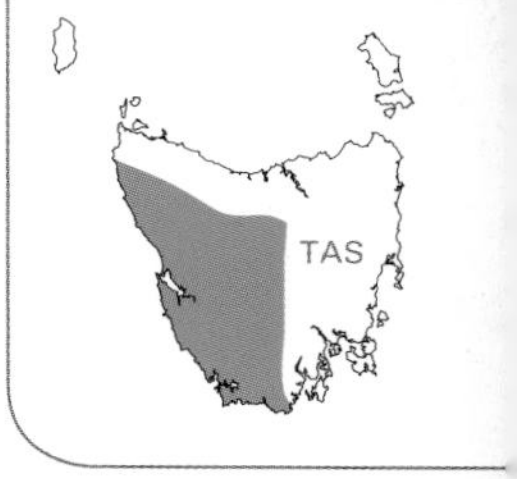

6 Strahan

Atmospheric heritage waterfront

Strolling along the waterfront admiring timber stores and piers, the customs house and Union Steamship buildings, you can almost hear the rumble of logs rolling onto decks, and the cries and banter of wharfies. In the late 1800s, Strahan was Tasmania's third-largest port, serving the timber and mining industries. Though the port closed in 1970 and the population dwindled, the waterfront has found a new lease of life serving the tourist industry. Cruises depart from here to explore Macquarie Harbour – one of the world's largest natural harbours – and head up the lower reaches of the beautiful Gordon River through dense rainforest. The West Coast Wilderness Railway runs for 35 km from Strahan to Queenstown along rivers, through gorges and past old mining camps.

▶ *41 km south-west of Queenstown.*

7 Sarah Island

The most feared of all colonial prisons

Surveying the poignant ruins of the prison on Sarah Island, it's hard to imagine a more dismal, lonely and soul-destroying fate for an inmate of the early-19th-century British penal system: transported to the other side of the world, sent to a trackless wilderness roamed by who knew what, then placed on a tiny stud of rock in the middle of Macquarie Harbour's dark, frigid waters to toil (logging the Huon forests and building ships) and suffer. Reserved for the most recalcitrant of prisoners, the brutal regime here was vividly described in Marcus Clarke's novel *For the Term of His Natural Life*. Many inmates died. Incredibly, some escaped into the bush, sometimes only to turn on and cannibalise their companions. The penitentiary operated only from 1822 till around 1833, but it cast a large shadow and is still an affecting place.

▶ *Macquarie Harbour; cruises depart from Strahan.*

8 Frenchmans Cap

Snow-white even in summer

Rising to 1443 m, Frenchmans Cap is the most prominent topographic feature in the vast Franklin–Gordon Wild Rivers National Park. It often retains a cap of snow well into summer, and even when the snow melts remains white due to the quartzite rock that makes up the 300-m-high half-dome peak. The easiest way to view the peak is from Donaghys Hill Wilderness Lookout, a 40-minute-return walk from the Lyell Highway, which reveals a splendid panorama with the mountain at its centre. Alternatively, you can take a scenic flight over the mountain from Strahan, or, if you are an experienced, fit and well-equipped bushwalker, tackle the 46-km-return hike to the summit; it requires three to five days but rewards with magnificent scenery, and stupendous views from the top.

▶ *Franklin–Gordon Wild Rivers National Park, Lyell Hwy, 35 km west of Derwent Bridge.*

9 Lake St Clair

Explore Australia's deepest lake

The grandeur of this lake's setting amazed early visitors, notably Tasmanian governor Sir John Franklin, who in 1842 declared it the most beautiful lake he had ever seen – and after many years exploring the Arctic, he was a man who knew a thing or two about dramatic landscapes. Set in a basin gouged by glaciers, the 167-m-deep lake is rimmed by forested slopes and towering peaks. From the visitor centre at Cynthia Bay, follow the shoreline and savour the views across to Mounts Olympus, Rufus and Hugel; along the way you'll almost certainly see pademelons and red-necked (Bennett's) wallabies. Then take the 1-hour-return Watersmeet Track through a variety of vegetation zones abounding in waratahs, banksias, hakeas and orchids. For a more extensive but leisurely lake tour, hop on the ferry that runs 13 km north to Narcissus Bay, site of a restaurant and terminus of the Overland Track.

▶ *Cradle Mountain–Lake St Clair National Park, 5 km north of Lyell Hwy at Derwent Bridge.*

10 The Wall in the Wilderness

Remarkable in-progress artwork

In a studio just off the highway near Derwent Bridge, an extraordinary work of art is slowly taking shape. Since 2005, artist Greg Duncan has been carving a series of wooden bas-reliefs depicting the history of the Tasmanian central highlands. Each panel is 1 m wide and 3 m high, and eventually there will be 100 of them; Duncan estimates the task will take ten years. Scenes carved so far show people who have shaped the region, including Indigenous inhabitants, miners and hydro workers, as well as iconic animals such as the Tasmanian tiger and wedge-tailed eagle. Drop in to admire the artistry and you might even see the artist at work.

► *Lyell Hwy, 2 km south-east of Derwent Bridge.*

11 Gordon Dam

Astonishing feat of engineering

The Gordon River Power Development scheme encompasses Lakes Gordon and Pedder, which together form Australia's biggest reservoir, and supplies around 13 per cent of Tasmania's energy. The centrepiece of the scheme is this colossal dam, whose construction controversially flooded the pristine bays and valleys bordering the original lakes. Made of concrete and standing 140 m tall, it flanks a power station built to house five massive generators. There is a visitor centre and you can walk along the top of the dam and peer into the yawning chasm below. If you are game and fit, you can even abseil down its face in the company of trained guides.

► *15 km north-west of Strathgordon via Gordon River Rd.*

12 Mount Field National Park

Majestic highland plain punctuated by peaks and lakes

The road to Mount Field climbs steeply through a fascinating cross-section of Tasmanian habitats: from eucalypt forest to fern groves up through rainforest, thick with sassafras, leatherwood, beech, celery-top pine and wattle, to the park's alpine plateau, with its icy tarns, stands of swamp gums and snow gums, and abundant waterfalls. The most impressive of these are glorious Russell Falls, reached via an easy 10-minute circuit walk, where curtains of water drop from a multitiered cliff and, 100 m upstream, pretty Horseshoe Falls. Linked tracks take in lovely Lady Barron Falls and a stand of swamp gums on the Tall Trees Walk. Another visitor area at Lake Dobson offers longer high-country hikes as well as skiing.

► *40 km north-west of New Norfolk via Lyell Hwy and B61.*

13 Styx Big Tree Reserve

Walk among forest giants

The 'Big Tree' itself, a swamp gum (also known as mountain ash), is one of Australia's tallest known living trees, standing 97 m tall. It's in lofty company here in the Styx Valley, in a forest that contains some of the tallest and mightiest hardwood trees on Earth. Many rise more than 30 storeys high and are more than 300 years old. Among the highlights are the trees known as Gandalf's Staff and Bell Bottom, whose base measures 5.8 m in diameter. Raised boardwalks permit close examination of these prime specimens.

► *17 km south of Maydena.*

HORSESHOE FALLS, MOUNT FIELD NATIONAL PARK

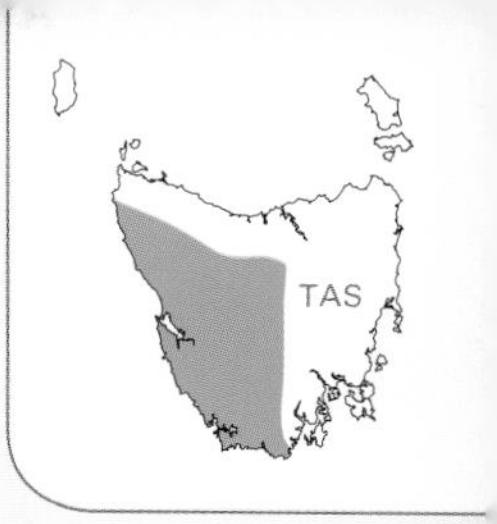

Last frontier

South of Lake Pedder extends the island's most intractable wilderness, much of it off-limits to all but the hardiest bushwalkers.

Covering more than 600,000 ha, Southwest National Park is at once a forbidding and inspiring realm of wind-scoured scrub, jagged dolerite peaks, dense rainforest and storm-battered coastline. It forms a substantial part of the 1.4-million-ha Tasmanian Wilderness World Heritage Area, which also takes in Cradle Mountain–Lake St Clair, Franklin–Gordon Wild Rivers and adjacent reserves.

Ways into the wild

You can sample the park's grandeur without enduring any serious hardship by driving the sealed road to Gordon Dam (see entry) or the unsealed road to Scotts Peak Dam, where a spectacular natural amphitheatre of colossal, steep peaks – Mounts Anne, Eliza and the densely clustered summits of the Western Arthurs – arcs around the southern end of Lake Pedder. Located near the start of the Scotts Peak Road, the Creepy Crawly Nature Trail is an easy 20-minute stroll through cool temperate rainforest.

Coastal pathways

The southern sector of the park is reached via Cockle Creek, 148 km south-west of Hobart, where an easy walk (allow 2 to 3 hours) follows rugged coastline to Fishers Point Light, and the South Cape Bay Track crosses buttongrass plains to the isolated bay. To the west, the internationally renowned South Coast Track is a challenging 85-km hike along a rough and often muddy route to Melaleuca, at the end of a long, narrow inlet on majestic Bathurst Harbour. From there, you can retrace your steps, catch a flight back to Hobart, or, if you are a glutton for punishment, continue north to Scotts Peak along the 70-km Port Davey Track (allow another five days).

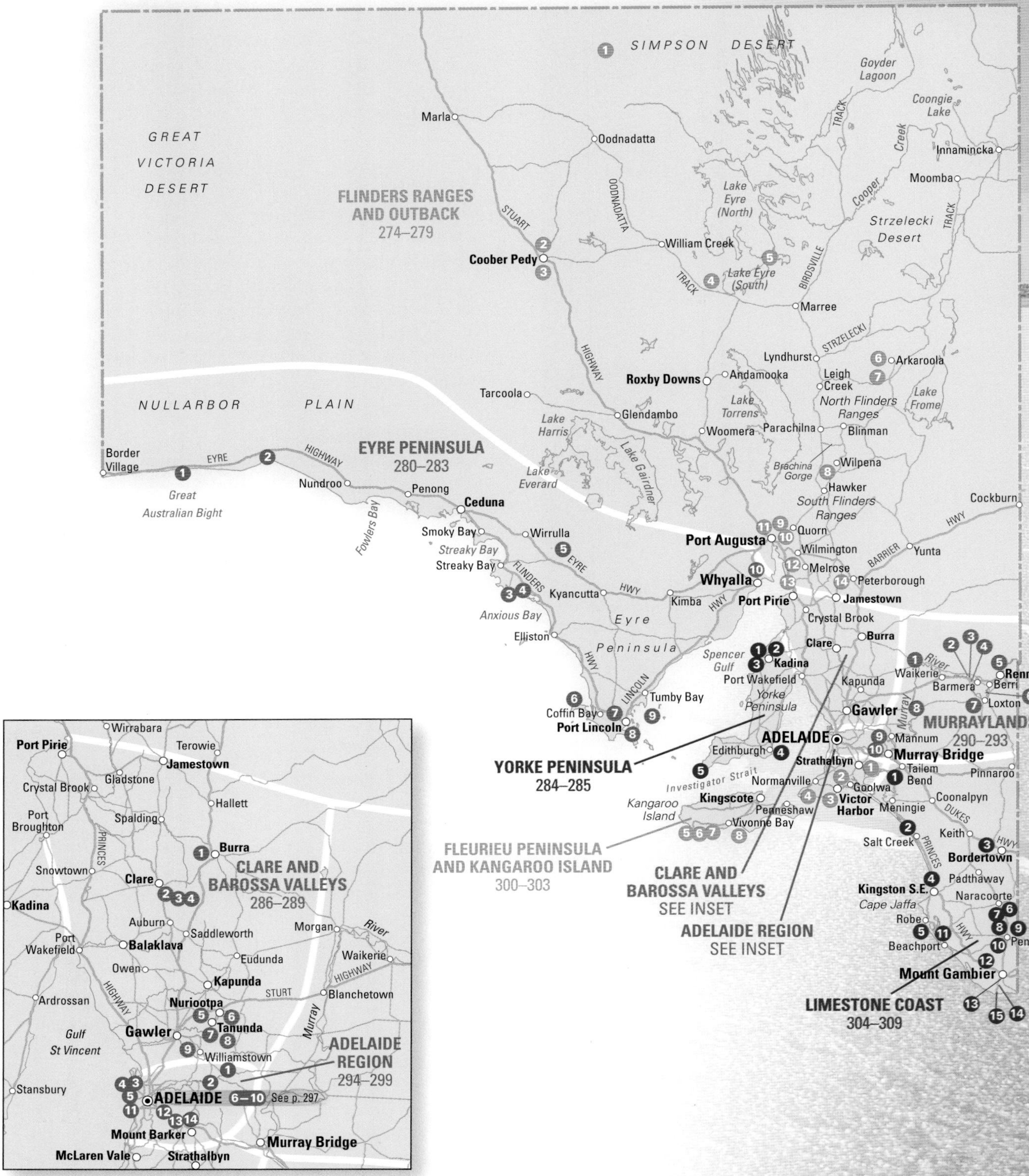
SIMPSON DESERT
GREAT VICTORIA DESERT
Goyder Lagoon
Coongie Lake
Marla
Oodnadatta
Innamincka
Moomba
FLINDERS RANGES AND OUTBACK
274–279
STUART
OODNADATTA
TRACK
Lake Eyre (North)
Cooper Creek
Strzelecki Desert
William Creek
Coober Pedy
Lake Eyre (South)
BIRDSVILLE
Marree
HIGHWAY
STRZELECKI
Lyndhurst
Arkaroola
Roxby Downs
Andamooka
Leigh Creek
NULLARBOR PLAIN
Tarcoola
Lake Torrens
North Flinders Ranges
Lake Frome
Lake Harris
Glendambo
Woomera
Parachilna
Blinman
Border Village
EYRE
HIGHWAY
EYRE PENINSULA
280–283
Lake Gairdner
Brachina Gorge
Wilpena
Nundroo
Lake Everard
Hawker
Great Australian Bight
Penong
South Flinders Ranges
Cockburn
Ceduna
HWY
Fowlers Bay
Smoky Bay
Wirrulla
Quorn
Port Augusta
Streaky Bay
Wilmington
BARRIER
Yunta
Streaky Bay
FLINDERS
Melrose
Whyalla
Peterborough
Kyancutta
Kimba
Port Pirie
Jamestown
Anxious Bay
Eyre Peninsula
Crystal Brook
Elliston
Clare
Burra
Spencer Gulf
Kadina
River
Renmark
LINCOLN
Port Wakefield
Waikerie
Barmera
Berri
Kapunda
Loxton
Tumby Bay
Yorke Peninsula
Coffin Bay
Gawler
Murray
MURRAYLANDS
290–293
Port Lincoln
ADELAIDE
Mannum
Edithburgh
Murray Bridge
YORKE PENINSULA
284–285
Strathalbyn
Tailem Bend
Investigator Strait
Normanville
Goolwa
Pinnaroo
Kingscote
Victor Harbor
Coonalpyn
Kangaroo Island
Penneshaw
Meningie
DUKES
Vivonne Bay
Keith
HWY
Salt Creek
FLEURIEU PENINSULA AND KANGAROO ISLAND
300–303
PRINCES
Bordertown
CLARE AND BAROSSA VALLEYS
SEE INSET
Padthaway
Kingston S.E.
Naracoorte
Cape Jaffa
ADELAIDE REGION
SEE INSET
Robe
Beachport
Penola
Mount Gambier
LIMESTONE COAST
304–309
Wirrabara
Port Pirie
Terowie
Jamestown
Crystal Brook
Gladstone
Hallett
Port Broughton
Spalding
PRINCES
Burra
Snowtown
Clare
CLARE AND BAROSSA VALLEYS
286–289
Kadina
Auburn
Morgan
River
Port Wakefield
Balaklava
Saddleworth
Eudunda
Waikerie
Owen
HIGHWAY
HIGHWAY
Kapunda
STURT
Blanchetown
Ardrossan
Nuriootpa
Murray
Tanunda
Gulf St Vincent
Gawler
ADELAIDE REGION
294–299
Williamstown
Stansbury
ADELAIDE
6–10
See p. 297
Mount Barker
Murray Bridge
McLaren Vale
Strathalbyn

South Australia

Clustered in the state's south-eastern corner are world-famous wineries, picturesque ports and villages, magnificent cave systems and pristine shorelines, as well as Adelaide's gracious architecture and parks and picturesque backdrop of hills. Further afield and spread more widely are spectacular desert ranges, salt lakes and magical coastal reserves.

Useful websites

Visitor information www.southaustralia.com
Parks and reserves www.environment.sa.gov.au/parks
Motoring organisation www.raa.com.au

LAKE EYRE, LAKE EYRE NATIONAL PARK

Flinders Ranges and Outback

Running in a straight line for 200 km north-east from the fringes of South Australian settlement on Spencer Gulf, the ancient Flinders Ranges encompass stunning rock formations, fascinating pioneer history and abundant arid-country wildlife. Beyond and to the west lies a vast untamed desert realm.

1 Dalhousie Springs

An oasis in the desert

The far north of the state is a forbidding realm of gibber plains and sand dunes. Creekbeds are normally dry, lake waters quickly evaporate. But in places artesian waters bubble to the surface, and the cluster of 120 or so mound springs at Dalhousie – the largest in Australia – has long been a lifeline for Irrwanyere people, European travellers and wildlife. Fringed by trees and mounds of crystallised minerals, the springs contain unique aquatic species, including the Dalhousie goby. The water in the Main Spring is usually a bathlike 36°C, and therefore ideal for a leisurely dip. From the 1870s to the early 1900s, sheep and cattle were grazed here and the ruins of a homestead and farm buildings can be visited, too. Access to the springs requires a 4WD, camping gear and a Desert Parks Pass.

▶ *Witjira National Park, 350 km north-west of Stuart Hwy at Marla via Oodnadatta Track.*

2 The Breakaways

Spectacular desert ranges favoured as a cinematic backdrop

This extraordinary landscape of multihued and dramatically eroded sandstone mesas and buttes – also known as breakaways – might just look familiar. For not only does it conjure up the dramatic settings of American Westerns, but it has also been used as a location by a range of Australian film-makers, enhancing scenes in movies ranging from *Mad Max III* to *The Adventures of Priscilla, Queen of the Desert*. Directional and interpretive signs guide drivers through the formations, and there are wonderful views from the Main Lookout. You'll need a day pass, available in Coober Pedy.

▶ *39 km north of Coober Pedy via Stuart Hwy.*

DALHOUSIE SPRINGS

COOBER PEDY'S SERBIAN ORTHODOX CHURCH LIES DEEP IN THE SANDSTONE.

3 Coober Pedy

There's more to this town than meets the eye – and most of it's underground

When the mercury regularly hits 50°C in summer and there's not a skerrick of shade in sight, you have to take drastic action to stay cool. The opal miners who flocked to this remote community from the 1920s on quickly decided, no doubt after enjoying the darkness of their mining tunnels by day, to take up more permanent residence underground, and began excavating subterranean dwellings. The practice has been maintained and today you can tour subsurface homes, cafes, shops, galleries – and mines, of course. You can even take part in services at various subterranean places of worship including the Anglican Catacomb Church and Roman Catholic Church of Saints Peter and Paul. Above ground, mining has created a bizarre but dramatic landscape of holes and craters.

► *Stuart Hwy.*

Visitor information

Coober Pedy 1800 637 076
Leigh Creek 08 8675 2315
Peterborough 08 8651 2708
Port Augusta 1800 633 060
Port Pirie 1800 000 424
Quorn 08 8648 6419
Wilpena Pound 08 8668 4250

4 Coward Springs

Wash off the dust in a natural spa

After a hot drive along the Oodnadatta Track, one of Australia's most historic and scenic 4WD routes, there's nothing more appealing than a soothing soak. At Coward Springs, a former Old Ghan railway settlement, you can pitch your tent and unwind in the 29°C waters of an artesian spa, alongside a wetland flanked by rushes, reeds and palms. Formed after a bore was sunk here in the 1880s, the wetland supports 99 plant species and 126 kinds of birds. The old Station Masters House and Engine Drivers Cabin have been restored, and the latter houses a museum.

► *236 km east of Coober Pedy via Oodnadatta Track.*

Rocks of ages

The ancient, contorted rockscapes of the Flinders reveal a tumultuous geological evolution.

The origins of the Flinders Ranges, Australia's second-longest mountain range, date back at least 500 million years, when thick layers of sediments were deposited on the floor of an ancient sea and slowly turned into sedimentary rock. Thrust upward by enormous tectonic forces, these rocks rose to form mountains as high as the Himalayas, before being whittled down, uplifted again, and finally gouged by water and scoured by wind into the ragged forms of today's ranges.

To the trained eye, traces of this history are evident almost everywhere: in buckled sedimentary layers, quartzite outcrops, eroded domes and gravel-filled basins. The Brachina Gorge Geological Trail, a 20-km drive lined with interpretive panels, constitutes an illustrated, annotated chronicle of this geological evolution. In the gorge walls, rock layers are clearly visible – sandstone, siltstone, shale and more – some tipped at precipitous angles. Another fascinating perspective on the Flinders' past can be enjoyed at the Wadlata Outback Centre in Port Augusta, where displays track the formation of the ranges as well as their human history.

5 Lake Eyre

An astonishing sight – empty, full or anywhere in-between

It's Australia's largest lake, at 9500 sq km (the size of the Netherlands!), but it seldom contains any water. Indeed, from 1840 to 1949, it was long thought to be permanently dry, but since then it has been established that water from its enormous catchment usually inundates at least part of the lake every eight years or so on average – it filled to a depth of 6 m in 1974, and flooded for three years in a row from 2009 to 2011. Dry, it is still an awe-inspiring sight, its sparkling white salt crust stretching to the far horizon. Following floods, hordes of birds – terns, stilts, pelicans, cormorants – arrive to feed and breed, and aquatic creatures, including bony bream and shield shrimp, magically appear in the waters. You can drive out to Halligan Bay in a 4WD and camp, but you'll enjoy more spectacular views and gain a better sense of the lake's vast scale from the air – scenic flights depart from William Creek and Marree.

▶ *227 km east of Coober Pedy via William Creek Rd.*

6 Arkaroola Wilderness Sanctuary

Awe-inspiring maze of ridges and ravines

At Sillers Lookout, the road suddenly heads skyward at an alarming angle before coming to an abrupt halt, seemingly in midair. Climbing out of the 4WD, you find yourself perched atop a small, rocky summit and surrounded by breathtaking views. Visible across a huge tract of desert to the east is the immense salt-encrusted expanse of Lake Frome; behind you are row upon row of jagged red-granite ridges. The lookout is one of the highlights of a guided tour of Arkaroola Wilderness Sanctuary, a privately owned reserve that protects 60,000 ha of the Flinders Ranges' most dramatic scenery. Gorges and waterholes, hot springs and abandoned mines can also be explored here, and the resort has its own observatory.

▶ *120 km east of Leigh Creek.*

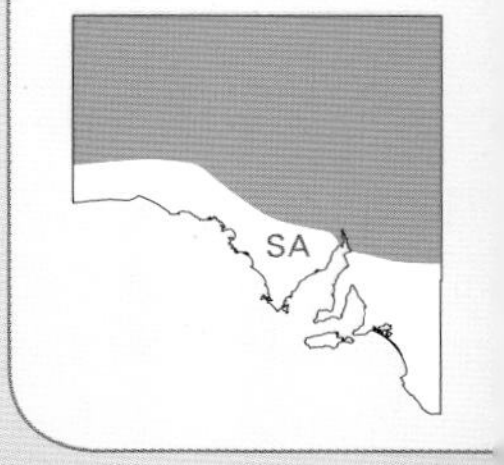

7 Weetootla Gorge

Unexpectedly lush, spring-fed valley in arid wilderness

Concealed amid the harsh red rockscape of the northern Flinders Ranges is this magical oasis. Flanked by huge river red gums and paperbarks and threaded by a burbling stream, it is often alive with birds – corellas, herons, finches, wrens – and shy yellow-footed rock wallabies can be spotted on rock ledges. The Balcanoona Creek Hike (6 km one way, 2.5 hours) leads up the gorge through the sheer, weathered cliffs known as Hells Gate to Grindells Hut, a former pastoral station building that is now a holiday cottage. Also nearby are the remains of the former Monarch copper mine.

▶ *Vulkathunha–Gammon Ranges National Park, 100 km east of Leigh Creek.*

8 Wilpena Pound

Colossal craterlike formation

The centrepiece of the Flinders Ranges is this immense, elevated natural amphitheatre covering an area of 5 km by 11 km and rimmed by sheer cliffs of reddish sandstone and quartzite. Its apparent symmetry is the result of massive earth movements, which folded and lifted sedimentary rocks. The softer rocks then weathered away, leaving a precipitous rim of more resistant material. Driving routes and walking tracks lead to formations and viewpoints on the rim; a 9-hour-return hike ascends the summit of St Mary Peak, the Pound's highest point. Walks around Wilpena Pound Resort, an ideal base, explore intriguing historic sites, including Hills Homestead and Old Wilpena Station.

▶ *Flinders Ranges National Park, 160 km north-east of Port Augusta via Hawker–Stirling North Rd.*

RAMPART-LIKE WALLS ENCIRCLE WILPENA POUND.

SOUND AND LIGHT SHOW AT THE STEAMTOWN HERITAGE RAIL CENTRE

9 The Dutchmans Stern

Ship-shape bluff looms above the plains

Rising dramatically from the flatlands to a height of more than 800 m, this peak was named by Matthew Flinders for its resemblance to the stern of a typical 18th-century Dutch ship. Several walking tracks lead through the park, including part of the long-distance Heysen Trail and an 8.2-km (4-hour) climb to the summit, from where the stupendous views encompass the Spencer Gulf, the Willochra Plain and Wilpena Pound, 100 km away. Flowering plants, notably wattles, are abundant, more than 50 species of birds have been recorded and endangered yellow-footed rock wallabies are often seen foraging on the slopes.

▶ *The Dutchmans Stern Conservation Park, 50 km north-east of Port Augusta via Hawker–Stirling North Rd.*

10 Pichi Richi Railway

Travel back to the age of steam

A route from Port Augusta to the Willochra Plain and the heart of the Flinders Ranges was forged through narrow, 400-m-high Pichi Richi Pass in the early 1850s by drovers seeking new runs for their sheep. In 1879, a railway was opened along the same route, to link Port Augusta with farms and mines, and as part of the narrow-gauge 'Old Ghan' railway that would eventually reach Darwin. One of the oldest intact railway systems in the world, the Pichi Richi Railway maintains a section of the original track, as well as locomotives and carriages. Its regular tours include the Pichi Richi Explorer, to and from Woolshed Flat (2.5 hours return), and the Afghan Express, a re-creation of the Old Ghan train, to Port Augusta (6 hours return).

▶ *Quorn, 41 km north-east of Port Augusta.*

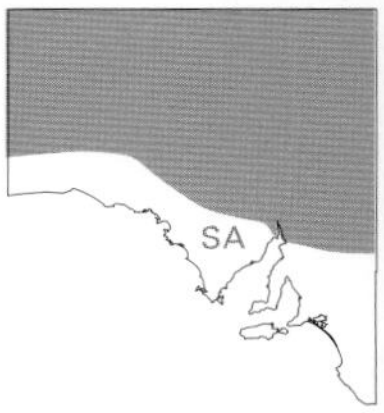

11 Australian Arid Lands Botanic Garden

Comprehensive collection of outback flora

There's no better place to learn about the extraordinary plant life of Australia's desert regions than at this beautifully designed garden. Covering 200 ha and commanding magnificent views of the Flinders Ranges, it encompasses a host of themed plantings crisscrossed by more than 12 km of walking tracks. Highlights include stunning displays of more than 155 varieties of eremophilas, colourful flowering shrubs that bloom in profusion in the desert, notably in the Flinders Ranges. Interpretive panels reveal the remarkable adaptations that many plant species have developed to cope with arid lands, and there are daily guided tours.

▶ *Stuart Hwy, 5 km north of Port Augusta.*

12 Alligator Gorge

Towering cliffs shade enchanting (croc-free) creek

You won't spot any alligators here (the origin of the name is uncertain), but you may well see other reptiles – lizards, goannas, skinks – as well as colourful birds, red kangaroos, rock wallabies and emus. All these creatures and more are drawn to this shady nook where Alligator Creek runs between sheer red quartzite cliffs before spilling into a wide, shallow basin. The Ali Lookout, reached by way of an easy 400-m-return walk, provides dramatic views into the gorge, while the 2-km Gorge Circuit Hike explores its full length. River red gums and cypress pines grow in open areas and in spring beautiful wild flowers, including purple native hibiscus and scented sun orchid, burst into bloom.

▶ *Mount Remarkable National Park, 57 km south-east of Port Augusta via Princes Hwy, B56 and Wilmington.*

13 Port Germein Wharf

Once the longest wooden jetty in the Southern Hemisphere

Port Germein had its heyday when the grain clippers plied Spencer Gulf, delivering stores and loading wheat and wool for the Australian and British mills. Initially, its shallow, muddy, mangrove-lined shore was unapproachable for vessels of almost any kind, but loading and unloading was soon facilitated by the construction of this jetty. Completed in 1883, when it was the longest wooden jetty in the country, it had to extend for more than 1.5 km to reach water deep enough for ships. Although the last tall-masted grain ships departed in the late 1930s, the wharf has been lovingly maintained since then. The adjacent waterfront, too, has changed little since the late 1800s.

▶ *21 km north of Port Pirie via Princes Hwy.*

14 Steamtown Heritage Rail Centre

Where three gauges met

Founded as Petersburg in 1880 – a name that was Anglicised during the First World War – Peterborough became the meeting point of three railways, from Adelaide, Port Augusta and Broken Hill. That made it a vital transport hub, obviously, but also presented local workers with a thorny problem: each of these railways ran on different gauges, or widths, of track – broad, standard and narrow. The only way to deal with this was to swap locomotives and exchange wheel assemblies on the carriages. A legacy of this laborious process is the handsomely preserved, heritage-listed, 23-bay workshop at Steamtown, with its massive three-gauge turntable – the only one of its kind left in the world. Other exhibits include an opulent 1923 first-class lounge car, carriages from the Old Ghan, and steam locomotives. After dark every night, the centre presents a sound-and-light show recounting the history of the town and the railways.

▶ *Telford Ave, Peterborough.*

Eyre Peninsula

Bounded to the west by the Nullarbor Plain, this region encompasses some of the continent's most dramatic shorelines, edged by idyllic beaches, massive dunes and towering cliffs. Isolated but busy ports reflect a fascinating maritime heritage.

1 Bunda Cliffs

Unrivalled panoramas of the Great Australian Bight

Sheer cliffs rising up to 100 m from the sea arc around the shore of the Great Australian Bight for 200 km, forming a towering wall with few inlets or beaches. It's one of the continent's great sights and there's no better place to view it than from this long chain of lookouts along the edge of the Nullarbor Plain. In either direction, the cliffs – dramatically banded in shades of grey, ochre and cream – stretch as far as the eye can see, along a series of wide, gently scalloped bays. From May to October, keep an eye out for migrating southern right whales in the ocean below. Take care at the cliff edges, though, as there are no barriers.

► *Eyre Hwy, 100 km west of Nullarbor Roadhouse.*

2 Head of Bight

Prime spot for watching whale migration

There's an audible gasp from the small group of onlookers as, 65 m below, in the transparent turquoise ocean, a huge adult whale propels itself above the water then flops backward languidly; later, a collective sigh as a calf approaches its mother to feed. Between May and October each year, this is one of the best places in Australia to observe breeding southern right whales at close quarters. Up to 100 of these creatures – adults can be up to 18 m in length – halt here during their long migration to rest and give birth. You can learn more about whale ecology at the interpretive centre, before following the boardwalk to the main viewing platform and a series of smaller lookouts.

► *12 km south of Eyre Hwy via Head of Bight Rd.*

Treeless plain

A formidable barrier between the major population centres of the south-west and south-east, the Nullarbor Plain is 200,000 sq km of arid, forbidding terrain.

To Aboriginal people, this realm was *bunda bunda* or 'high cliffs'; it was early European explorers who gave it its present name, from the Latin *null arbor*, meaning 'no trees'. Twenty million years ago, this flat, dry and empty region lay under a shallow sea, and the deposits on its floor formed a thick layer of limestone. This slab – the largest single slab of limestone in the world – was then uplifted to form the plain.

Although the surface is now waterless, subterranean rivers flow through underground chambers and passages. After countless centuries of water percolating, some of the chambers are as large as cathedrals. Some caves have yielded 40,000-year-old animal fossils.

A huge expanse of the plain is protected by Nullarbor Regional Reserve and Nullarbor National Park. Visitor facilities are limited, but gravel roads turn off the Eyre Hwy in places, permitting some exploration. You can visit Murrawijinie Caves, north of Nullarbor Roadhouse, and peer into Koonalda Cave further west, which harbours evidence of Aboriginal occupation from 20,000 years ago. More extensive exploration is off-limits to all but expert cavers.

Visitor information

Ceduna 08 8625 3343
Elliston 08 8687 9200
Port Lincoln 08 8683 3544
Whyalla 08 8645 7900

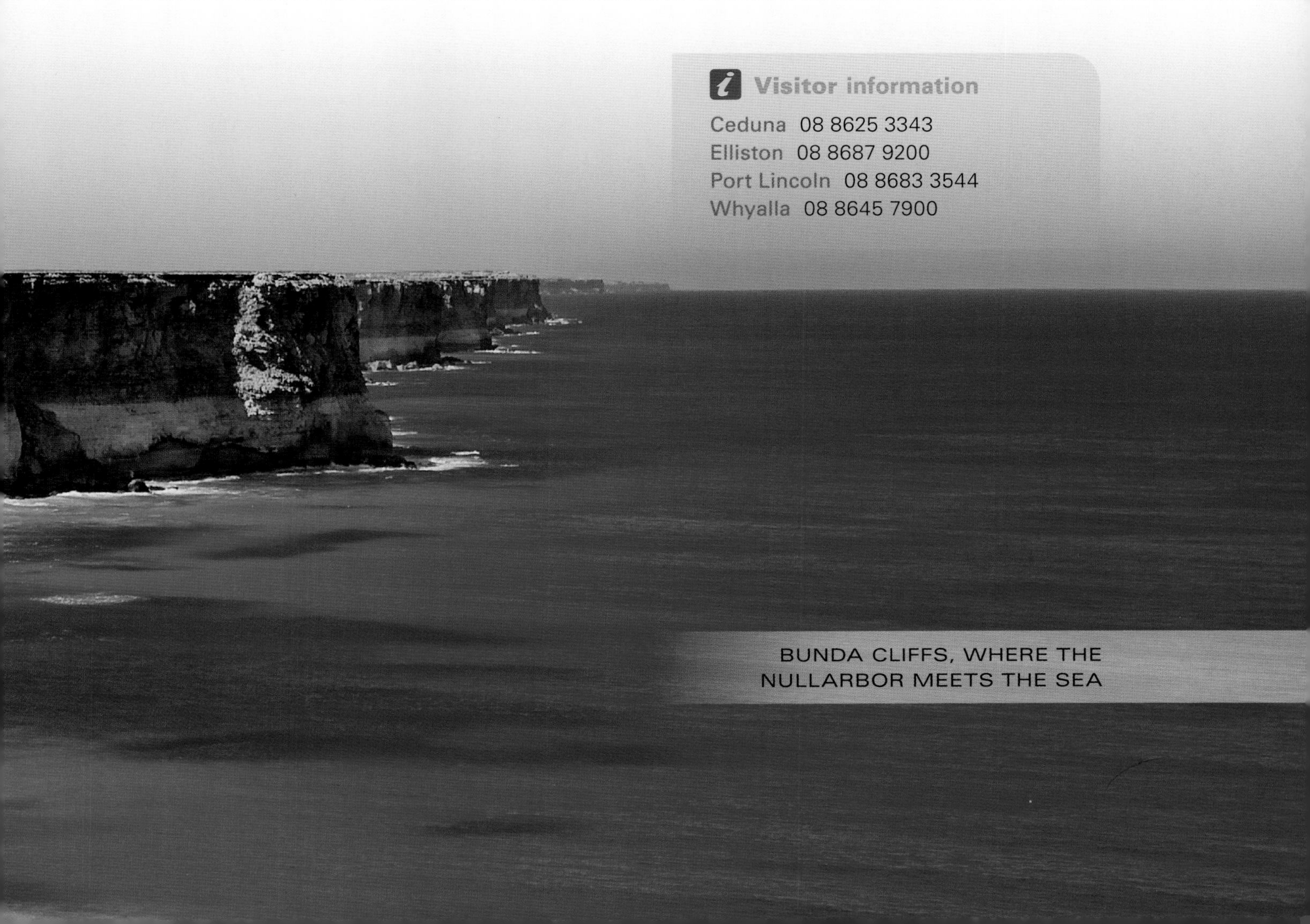

BUNDA CLIFFS, WHERE THE NULLARBOR MEETS THE SEA

3 Point Labatt Conservation Park

Home to Australia's largest mainland colony of breeding sea lions

Their colour helps conceal them on the brown and rosy-hued rocks and sand below the viewing platform atop the 60-m-high limestone cliffs. But look carefully (binoculars are recommended) and you'll spot sea lions all along the shore: hauling themselves out of the water, corralling pups on the sand, basking on boulders and ledges. After spells of two weeks or so feeding at sea, adult sea lions return here to their colony to rest, while their young play and swim around them. Cormorants, red-necked stints and crested terns mingle with the big mammals. Look to the rocks at the far point and you might spot a group of fur seals, distinguishable from the sea lions by their darker colour, pointed snouts and smaller stature. Look either way and you'll enjoy majestic views of this beautiful, remote peninsula.

▶ *50 km south of Streaky Bay via Calca–Sceale Bay Rd.*

4 Murphy's Haystacks

Deceptive granite formations

In the right light and seen from the right angle, the comparison is highly apt: these smooth-sculpted granite masses do indeed have the hue and shape of old-fashioned haystacks. They even stand in the middle of a wheat paddock. Named by early European settlers, the 'haystacks' are in fact outcrops of pink granite. Originally, they would have been part of a single large formation, of the kind known as an inselberg, which formed around 1500 million years ago. Erosion and weathering exposed and cracked the inselberg then buffed the smaller forms into these rounded shapes.

▶ *40 km south of Streaky Bay via Flinders Hwy and Calca Rd.*

5 Pildappa Rock

Granite outcrop edged by dramatic wave

The granite outcrops known as inselbergs can be found all over this region, and this is one of the most impressive. It is distinguished in particular by its 'wave formation' – a steep, concave wall running 100 m along its edge – which rivals Western Australia's much more famous Wave Rock (see p. 34) for grandeur. The wave is thought to have formed as water run-off combined with soil to erode the stone originally below ground level; the soil was then worn away, exposing the excavated stone. A one-way walk or drive trail circles the rock, taking in the wave and other formations such as boulders, sheared granite sheets and namma holes – natural hollows used as a water source by Aboriginal people. Two tracks lead to the summit, yielding wonderful views.

▶ *15 km north of Eyre Hwy via Mackenzie Rd.*

6 Coffin Bay National Park

Diverse perspectives on a remote coastal realm

From Templetonia Lookout, the view extends to the ocean across salt marshes, she-oak woodlands and huge rolling sand dunes, formed, according to Aboriginal belief, when two ancestral warriors, Marnpi and Tatta, piled up sand to halt a huge fire. The scene is unpeopled and wild. Further south along the park road at Point Avoid, a viewpoint atop a limestone headland, encircled by black tea-trees stunted to shrub height by salt-laden winds, reveals another magnificent view over islands, black-rock reefs and waves crashing ashore. To the north at sheltered Yangie Bay, shrub-cloaked land encloses stunning, shallow turquoise waters perfect for swimming and kayaking, and walking tracks traverse woodlands and climb to vantage points. A 4WD is recommended for exploring the even wilder western sector of the park.

▶ *15 km south-west of Flinders Hwy via Coffin Bay.*

7 Axel Stenross Maritime Museum

Boaties' treasure trove in a Finnish bloke's shed

It's not an imposing exterior: a cluster of corrugated-iron buildings, walls built of old tea chests, a slipway, a few boats under repair. But go inside and you find not only a collection of seafaring artefacts and shipbuilding tools, but also an abundance of information on the maritime history of Port Lincoln: photographs, ship's logs, charts and even high-tech touchscreens listing the vessels that have berthed in the port, right back to its early whaling days, when it was briefly considered for the site of the state capital. The collection was assembled by Finnish-born Stenross, who sailed the world and settled here in 1927, then founded the still-operating shipbuilding business for 60 years.

▶ *Lincoln Hwy, Port Lincoln.*

8 Lincoln National Park

Monuments, ruins, breathtaking scenery

Many places on the Eyre Peninsula were first mapped and named in 1802, and a cairn at the entrance to this magnificent park commemorates the navigator's visit. Climbing to Stamford Hill (1.1 km, 45 minutes return) – site of another monument to Flinders erected in the 1840s by another explorer, then governor of Tasmania, Sir John Franklin – is one of the best introductions to the astonishing scenery. From the summit, you can survey swathes of coastal mallee rolling south to rocky headlands and giant sand dunes, and look north over sheltered bays to Port Lincoln and Boston Bay. Descend and follow the road to Spalding Bay to enjoy one of the park's most attractive and safest swimming beaches, before continuing to Cape Donington, site of a short-lived 1870s settlement. Ruins and abandoned machinery testify to attempts to farm the land and harvest guano (dried seabird excrement) as fertiliser.

▶ *18 km south of Port Lincoln.*

9 Sir Joseph Banks Islands

Head offshore to a wildlife haven

In the 19th century, some of these islands were offshore sheep stations; today, they are predator-free breeding grounds for birds and marine life under threat elsewhere. Most notably, this is the site of the state's largest colony of Cape Barren geese, which graze on the swards and heaths and nest amid rock and tussock. The Australian sea lion also finds a refuge here, on English Island: huge bulls can be observed guarding their harems as pups snuggle up to their mothers. Dolphins are also frequently spotted here in large numbers. Guided tours offer the best access and chances of sightings.

▶ *By boat from Port Lincoln.*

10 Whyalla Maritime Museum

High and dry, the largest landlocked ship in the state

The prize exhibit at this fascinating museum stands outside: HMAS *Whyalla*, which in 1941 was the first ship to be built in the city's shipyards. About 57 m in length and weighing almost 600 tonnes, it was commissioned in 1942 and used by the navy as an antisubmarine and mine-sweeping vessel. It was involved in repelling the 1942 Japanese mini-submarine attack on Sydney, and saw service in New Guinea and Hong Kong. You can not only stroll its decks and peer into its cabins, but also walk under its hull. Inside the museum are exhibits on the Second World War, the history of Whyalla's shipyards and Spencer Gulf wildlife, as well as one of the country's largest scale-model railways.

▶ *Lincoln Hwy, Whyalla.*

Yorke Peninsula

This finger of land was the focus of a mid-1800s mining boom that drew thousands of settlers, especially from Cornwall, England, and the distinctive Cornish heritage of its towns remains a major attraction. While most of the hinterland is given over to barley growing, the lovely seascapes of its shoreline remain largely untouched.

1 Wallaroo Heritage and Nautical Museum

Enjoy the seafaring stories of this former windjammer port

Founded in 1861, when Captain Walter Hughes built a copper-smelting works, Wallaroo became the shipping outlet for copper from Moonta and Kadina and the entry point for the mainly Cornish and Welsh immigrants heading for the mines. Later, majestic windjammer ships sailed out of the port laden with grain; the last one departed in 1939. The whitewashed building at the centre of this complex was the town's first post office, built in 1865. The displays recount the history of the port and mining operations through photographs, charts, ship's logs, models and mementos – and an 8.5-m-long giant squid found in the stomach of a whale! Outside is the 1877 Tipara Reef Lighthouse.

► *Jetty Rd and Emu St, Wallaroo, 9 km north-west of Kadina.*

2 The Farm Shed Museum and Tourist Centre

Learn about life on the drylands, indoors and out

The somewhat bleak, arid interior of the northern Yorke Peninsula was not promising land for farmers, yet many persevered, eventually turning it into a productive cereal-producing region. Key to their success was the invention (in Ardrossan in 1876) of the famous stump-jump plough, which allowed farmers to plough cleared land still full of mallee roots (the stumps). An example and a full explanation are on display here alongside strippers and harvesters, tractors and trucks. You can also explore Matta House, built for a mine manager in 1863 and still furnished in Victorian style, and sit at a desk in a re-creation of a 1950s schoolroom.

► *14 km south-west of Kadina.*

3 Moonta

Hub of Little Cornwall

It was the discovery of copper-bearing rocks near a wombat hole, made by shepherd Paddy Ryan in 1861, that led to the rapid growth of this town. The rocks contained some of the purest copper ever found and soon the (mainly Cornish) miners flooded in. Modern Moonta is dotted with reminders of those days and retains a strong Cornish flavour – Cornish pasties are available in bakeries, there are locals who can speak Cornwall's Celtic language, and traditions are celebrated avidly at the annual Kernewek Lowender ('Cornish happiness') festival in May. Among the mining relics are the imposing Hughes Pump House and its huge chimney, built of limestone in the mid-1860s; the pump here operated 24 hours a day, removing water from the nearby Hughes Mine. The 1870 Miner's Cottage is typical of the dwellings built by the Cornish miners and contains period furnishings and gardens. Moonta Mines Museum fills out the historical background, and you can travel through the mining areas on the handsomely restored narrow-gauge Moonta Mines Tourist Railway.

► *69 km west of Port Wakefield.*

HUGHES PUMP HOUSE AND CHIMNEY, MOONTA

4 Troubridge Island

Away with the birds

A fragile sand island, Troubridge is an important bird sanctuary and has large breeding populations of little penguins, crested terns and black-faced cormorants. To protect the birds and their habitat, access is limited and a permit is required (contact Innes National Park Visitor Centre). Book into the heritage accommodation in the former lighthouse-keeper's cottage, built, like the adjacent red-and-white lighthouse, around 1850, and you can have the whole place to yourself.

► *Access via charter boat from Edithburgh.*

5 Innes National Park

Stunning seaboard scenery at lands' end

Preserved by the national park, the tip of Yorke Peninsula is a magnificent realm of jutting headlands, rocky clifftops, wave-cut platforms, deserted beaches and fascinating historic remains. The park road follows the coast and short tracks branch off it to the main sights. Explore the remains of the gypsum-mining port at Stenhouse Bay then follow the Stenhouse Bay Lookout Walk (2 km, 1 hour return) to enjoy superb views over Investigator Strait. The Inneston Historic Walk (2 km, 1 hour return) winds through the ruins of the main gypsum-mining camp. A short hike to West Head (1 km, 30 minutes) leads to the stainless-steel lighthouse and sweeping views of Pondalowie Bay (site of a renowned surf break) and Wedge and Althorpe islands; majestic vistas also unfold along the Royston Head Walk (4 km, 2 hours return) in the north.

► *2 km south-west of Marion Bay.*

Visitor information

Kadina 08 8821 2333
Minlaton 08 8853 2983

Clare and Barossa Valleys

Internationally renowned for their wines, these picturesque valleys are patchworks of vineyards and paddocks, sprinkled with pretty towns and villages complete with stone cottages and church spires. Fabulous local produce – food as well as wines – can be sampled at almost every turn.

1 Burra

One of the oldest and best-preserved mining towns in Australia

A copper find here in 1845 gave rise to one of the world's largest mines, the so-called Burra Monster Mine. It operated only until 1877 but yielded ore worth more than £5 million, most of it extracted by Cornish miners. Since then, time has stood still for much of Burra – the entire town has been designated a state heritage area. The Burra Mines Historic Site encompasses a cluster of period dwellings; the Powder Magazine, built in 1847 to store gunpowder for blasting; Peacock's Chimney, an updraught for engine-house boilers, dating from 1857; and the Morphett's Enginehouse Museum. Also part of the heritage area are miners' cottages, the Burra Smelting Works, and National Trust–listed Redruth Gaol, which featured in the film *Breaker Morant*.

► *Barrier Hwy.*

2 Sevenhill Cellars

The Clare's oldest vineyard

Thriving commercial Australian winery it may be, but Sevenhill retains an Old World, monastic air that proclaims its origins and ownership – it was established in 1851 by Jesuits from Austria and is still run by the order. Park-like grounds surround the complex of buildings, prominent among which are the lovely St Aloysius Church, built in 1875, and the 1854 College Building – at one time a Catholic college and still the Jesuits' main residence – as well as the stone winery building with its extensive vaulted cellars. The Jesuits planted the first vineyard with the intention of making sacramental wine, and in the 1940s began producing table wines too, which have since gained an enviable reputation and many awards. Take a tour then try them out.

► *8 km south of Clare via B82.*

3 Mintaro

Picturebook hamlet of slate cottages

Established as a resting place for drovers in the 1840s, Mintaro became a more permanent settlement following the discovery of extensive slate deposits nearby. Mid-1800s slate cottages still line the narrow streets, where flowers spill over dry-stone walls and eucalypts and centuries-old Moreton Bay fig trees cast their shadows. A delightful time can be had here strolling the lanes, admiring the old stone churches, browsing antique shops and enjoying refreshments in the quaint pub, the Magpie & Stump, which dates from 1850.

► *18 km south-east of Clare via B82 and Sevenhill–Mintaro Rd.*

Visitor information

Burra 08 8892 2154
Clare 1800 242 131
Gawler 08 8522 9263
Tanunda 08 8563 0600

4 Martindale Hall

Magnificent Georgian mansion, one of the stars of a famous film

In Peter Weir's movie *Picnic at Hanging Rock*, Martindale Hall turned in a convincing performance as an elite girls' boarding school in 1900. Its original function was somewhat different, but the building nevertheless harks back to the affluent lifestyles of the colony's wealthiest late-19th-century settlers. Pastoralist Edward Bowman brought craftsmen all the way from England to add ornate touches to his already grand sandstone home – elaborate carvings, a domed glass roof, parquetry floors – which was completed in 1879. Hunt meets were held here, the grounds were stocked with quail to provide shooting quarry, and a visiting English cricket team played on the property's own pitch. Preserved much as it was, Martindale Hall is open to day visitors as a museum and offers luxury accommodation.

▶ *20 km south-east of Clare via B82 and Sevenhill–Mintaro Rd and Mintaro–Manoora Rd.*

5 Seppeltsfield

Imposing winery, almost a village in itself

The approach via Marananga, along a road lined with hundreds of huge date palms, announces that you are heading somewhere special. Probably Australia's grandest winery, Seppeltsfield is a huge complex of buildings, established by Silesian merchant Joseph Ernst Seppelt in the 1850s and steadily expanded by his descendants. Manicured lawns and formal gardens surround castle-like winery buildings, a grand 1890s homestead, 1850s stables, a dining hall and a distillery. Another architectural highlight is the family mausoleum, built in the 1820s in the style of a Greek temple. A range of guided tours and tastings is available, and the complex also has a restaurant, cafe and art gallery.

▶ *3 km south of Sturt Hwy via Seppeltsfield Rd.*

BAROSSA VALLEY VINEYARDS
DRENCHED IN AFTERNOON SUN

CHÂTEAU TANUNDA'S GRAND BRICK-AND-BLUESTONE WINERY BUILDING

6 Angaston

Handsome colonial town renowned for fine fare

Angaston's lovely wide streets are lined with Moreton Bay fig trees and fine old buildings, including the 1843 Old Union Chapel, one of the state's oldest churches, an 1870s blacksmith's shop and the Angaston Hotel. The town was first settled by German immigrants in 1841 but named after George Fife Angas, the London-based chairman of the South Australian Company. Today Angaston has a reputation for a fabulous range of gourmet produce and the main thoroughfare, Murray Street, is a food-lover's delight, with fine restaurants, a bakery, the excellent Barossa Cheese Company, and Schulz Brothers, specialising in German-style smallgoods. Angaston is also the venue for the superb Barossa Farmers' Market, held every Saturday morning.

► *7 km south of Nuriootpa.*

7 Château Tanunda

Majestic, magnificently restored building houses pioneering winery

The vines established here in 1843 by Auguste Fiedler were among the first to be planted in the Barossa. The land was taken up in 1849 by JE Seppelt who, after experimenting with tobacco, cultivated and harvested the vines to produce his first vintages. Since 1998, the winery has been owned by the Geber family. Built in 1890, the winery building is Australia's largest chateau-style construction and at the time of its completion was the largest building in the state. Behind it is a huge sunken garden, and the winery also has a cricket ground and a croquet lawn. Inside you'll find tasting rooms and the Barossa Small Winemakers Centre, which promotes the wares of smaller growers in the valley.

► *Basedow Rd, Tanunda.*

Worthy of celebration

The Barossa Valley is one of Australia's oldest, most productive and best-known wine regions.

This 'Valley of the Vine' is about 30 km long and up to 14 km wide. South Australian author Colin Thiele memorably described it as 'a halved bottle with its bottom upturned near Truro and its neck corked by Lyndoch'. It was originally named *Barrosa*, 'hill of roses' in Spanish, by Colonel William Light, after a battle-field in Spain; the modern name is the result of misspellings on maps.

The local wine industry owes a great deal to German migrants from the Prussian region of Silesia (now in Poland). Fleeing persecution, they gratefully accepted the offer of George Fife Angas and the South Australian Company to provide passage to Australia in return for help establishing a colony. Familiar with viticulture, the Silesians planted grapes for their own use and found the valley ideally suited to their cultivation. Many subsequently became involved in establishing wineries.

Riesling was initially the grape of choice but modern producers have found the hot climate better suited to the production of full-bodied red wines such as shiraz, cabernet sauvignon and grenache. Today the valley hosts around 170 wine companies and you can sample their produce at around 75 cellar doors. The Tanunda visitor centre can assist with itineraries and recommend tours.

8 Bethany

The Barossa's oldest Lutheran settlement

In 1842, 28 Lutheran families began making a home for themselves in this corner of the Barossa – initially named New Silesia after their homeland – on land leased from the South Australian Company. They built a traditional Silesian village in what is known in German as *hufendorf* style: a line of cottages along a main street, each one with a long narrow strip of land behind it that extended to a common pasture. Today, Bethany – as it was renamed after the ancient town near Jerusalem (a word meaning 'fertile place') – remains one of the few surviving examples of the *hufendorf* style and preserves intriguing early buildings including cottages dating from the 1840s and 1850s, the 1883 Herberge Christi Church and the Pioneer Cemetery, the valley's oldest.

▶ *5 km south-east of Tanunda.*

9 Whispering Wall

Where your every word is amplified

The 140-m-long wall that holds back the Barossa Reservoir is an impressive feat of engineering in itself. But what makes it especially interesting are its remarkable acoustic properties, which have earned it the name of the 'Whispering Wall'. Stand at one end of the gently curved structure and have a friend stand at the other end, then get them to speak; you will hear their words loud and clear, no matter how quietly they whisper. The dam is surrounded by picturesque forest and has pleasant picnic spots.

▶ *13 km south-east of Gawler via Barossa Valley Way (B19).*

Murraylands

Contrasting red-ochre rockscapes and verdant wetlands line the Murray River, as it runs west from the Victorian border then south-west to spill into Lake Alexandrina. Atmospheric former ports are strung along its banks, and in the east bountiful orchards and vineyards are watered by ambitious irrigation schemes.

1 Morgan

Once the state's busiest inland port

Situated at a bend in the Murray where the river cuts through a landscape of towering cliffs and turns sharply south, Morgan was surveyed in 1878 and quickly connected to Adelaide by train. Very soon, it became the state's busiest river port. That status was short-lived, however: within a decade the railway had won out as chief conveyor of colonial trade. Quiet now, Morgan retains fine early buildings and a fascinating port area. Start at the Morgan Railway Museum, then follow the Morgan Heritage Walk through the 1878 wharf precinct, with its 12-m-high piers, and the old railway station and customs house.

► *44 km north-west of Waikerie.*

Visitor information

Barmera 08 8588 2289
Loxton 08 8584 8071
Mannum 1300 626 686
Murray Bridge 1800 442 784
Renmark 08 8586 6704
Waikerie 08 8541 2332

2 Overland Corner Hotel

Watering hole for drovers, cattle – and today's travellers

During the early 19th century, the grassy river flats at this 'corner' on the original overland stock route from New South Wales to the infant town of Adelaide were a popular resting place for drovers and their livestock. Built in 1860 to cater for these and other travellers, including businessmen, gold-diggers and station hands, the Overland Corner Hotel was constructed using local fossilised limestone and became the first stone dwelling in the Riverland. With walls up to half a metre thick, it is not surprising that it has withstood the rigours of time. The 1870s saw it take on the additional role of post office, which kept the business going after the growth of river and rail transport in the late 1800s led to a drop in demand for lodgings. Today, the establishment has found a new lease of life, offering food and beverages to locals and visitors; it also houses displays of historic artefacts.

► *Holmes Rd, Kingston-on-Murray, 1 km north of Sturt Hwy.*

BANROCK STATION WETLANDS

3 Banrock Station Wine and Wetland Centre

Fine blend of winery and nature reserve

In a district home to many a productive vineyard, Banrock stands out as a visitor experience by virtue of being more than a winery. You can, of course, sample its range of classic and special-release wines, and you can do it, with or without a gourmet meal, in the stylish surrounds of its rammed-earth, passive-solar visitor centre, perched on a ridge and looking out over the woodlands, flood plains and river. But you can also go for a walk through its remarkable wetlands reserve, which has been created to restore 250 ha of lagoons to their natural state and where interpretive trails meander for 8 km to viewpoints, bird hides and waterways brimming with wildlife. The importance of this place is not just local: the Ramsar Convention for the protection of wetlands has recognised it as a reserve of international significance.

▶ *Holmes Rd, Kingston-on-Murray, 1 km north of Sturt Hwy.*

4 Cobdogla Irrigation Museum

Home of the world's only working Humphrey Pump

A what pump? Its name may not ring many bells now, but the Humphrey Pump, known more colloquially as 'Big Thumper', was a godsend to these arid plains and the reason for Cobdogla's existence when it was installed here in 1919. Invented in England by Herbert Alfred Humphrey, the gas-powered pump employed a revolutionary design to lift water from the Murray and disperse it to surrounding farmland. Two such pumps supplied Cobdogla with water for the next 40 years, until superseded by electric models. As well as viewing the pump, you can peruse steam engines, tractors and other machinery, and learn about the vital role of irrigation in the Murraylands.

▶ *Trussell Tce, Cobdogla, 6 km west of Barmera.*

5 Olivewood

Rustic home of pioneering irrigators

Having been encouraged by the Victorian and South Australian governments to set up an irrigation scheme on the Murray (an area then described as a 'Sahara of hissing hot winds and red driving sand'), the Canadian Chaffey brothers, George and William, did much to establish the towns of Mildura (see Rio Vista, p. 196) and Renmark in the mid-1880s. They settled in Renmark and, perhaps experiencing a touch of homesickness, commissioned this huge Canadian-style log cabin as their home. Completed in 1887, it made concessions to the Australian climate with the addition of wide verandas. The richly furnished interior displays period photographs, artefacts and irrigation machinery. Outside are a stunning avenue of palms and beautiful groves of olives and orchards.

▶ *Cnr Renmark Ave (Sturt Hwy) and Twenty-first St, Renmark.*

6 Murray River National Park

Wetland wilderness vital to birdlife

Protecting almost 13,000 ha of internationally important wetlands, the park is divided into three sectors, with most of the visitor facilities concentrated in the largest, the Katarapko sector, nestled within a wide loop of the River Murray. The Murray Pine Drive provides the perfect introduction to the park's environments: woodlands, flood plains, mallee and swamps, home to kangaroos, echidnas, goannas and a host of birds. The 2-km (40-minute) Kai Kai Nature Trail allows a more leisurely perusal, and the Ngak Indau Wetland Trail (4.8 km, 1.5 hours) follows the river to a bird hide. On the Cragg's Hut Walk (2 km, 40 minutes), you can view the ruins of said hut, home in the mid-1800s to the pioneering Craigie family.

▶ *4 km south-west of Berri via Old Sturt Hwy.*

7 Loxton Historical Village

Handsome re-creation of a pioneer village

The town of Loxton was established in 1907, as a service centre for settlers, many of them German, who were then clearing the thick mallee scrub for grazing and cultivation. This extensive and convincing re-creation harks back to those times and provides a captivating experience of life in a frontier town. There are more than 35 historic buildings, including a farm complex, printworks, bakery, bank, garage and railway station, all operating as they would have a century ago. Vehicle and costume parades and demonstrations of sheep-shearing and printing bring the past vividly to life, and there is an interesting Irrigation Museum.

▶ *Allan Hoskings Dr, Loxton, 21 km south of Berri.*

8 Swan Reach

Imposing cliffs flank famous river crossing

On its long journey through the arid lands of northern South Australia, the Murray has, in places, cut deep into the limestone plains, creating a majestic riparian landscape of golden walls looming above stands of grand river red gums. One of the best places to view this scenery is at Swan Reach, where the so-called Big Bend has the river's highest and oldest cliffs – the walls here have yielded fossils dating back 20 million years. Traditionally the realm of the Ngaiawang people, the area was settled by Europeans in the 1840s. A ferry began to operate at Swan Reach in 1898 and still functions today. The Swan Reach Museum has a fine collection of photographs, including images of the river in flood.

▶ *28 km south of Sturt Hwy at Blanchetown.*

THE CLIFF-HEMMED MURRAY RIVER AT SWAN REACH

9 Mannum Dock Museum of River History

Captivating museum conjures up the paddle-steamer days

Every now and again, part of this museum sails off down the river. The PS *Marion* is one of the last operational, steam-driven paddle-steamers in the world, and it regularly carries passengers on short, dinner and overnight cruises; on other days, it remains wharfside as an integral part of the museum. Built in 1897, the vessel retains its original steam plant and has been lovingly restored; its three decks encompass a grand dining saloon, lounges and cabins. The rest of the museum uses fossils, artefacts and photographs to chronicle the history of the Murray from its geological origins through Aboriginal occupation, European settlement and the growth and demise of river trade.

▶ *Randell St, Mannum.*

10 Monarto Zoological Park

Set off on a global safari

This is probably the only place in South Australia where you might look out across the plains and behold a bison, or approach a waterhole and come face to face with a giraffe. Open-range enclosures and concealed fences make for as realistic an experience of the American prairies or the East African savannah as you can expect on this side of the world, and allow the animals a relatively close-to-natural lifestyle. Hop on the Zu-loop Shuttle to view the main exhibits – including lions, camels, cheetahs, chimps, miniature Przewalski's horses and scimitar-horned oryx – then hit the 10 km of walking trails to get close to zebras and elands, emus and kangaroos.

▶ *Old Princes Hwy, 4 km north of South Eastern Fwy.*

Adelaide Region

Backed by a beguiling hinterland of rolling hills, wooded valleys and picturesque villages, South Australia's elegant capital is an orderly city of wide avenues, parklands and church spires, with magnificent museums and galleries, colourful seaside suburbs and a historic port area.

1 Herbig Family Tree

An unusual place to start afresh

The German settlers who arrived in South Australia in the mid-1800s were nothing if not resourceful. Reaching the Adelaide Hills in 1855, Johann Herbig found he had enough money to buy a block of land but insufficient to build a house. Coming upon this 24-m-high red gum on his property he found the answer to his problem: the tree's hollow base was so wide – 7 m – that it could easily accommodate him and his modest possessions. After Herbig married in 1858, his wife, Caroline, moved in, and the couple's first and second children were born in the tree. At that point, Herbig saw the limitations of his abode and built a hut nearby – a prescient move, since he and Caroline eventually had 16 children.

► *Angaston Rd, Springton, 73 km north-east of Adelaide.*

2 National Motor Museum

A history of Australia on wheels

The country's largest collection of vintage, veteran and classic motor vehicles not only displays more than 300 historic vehicles – ranging from the 1899 steam-powered Shearer, the oldest Australian car still running, to enormous modern road trains – but also chronicles the impact of road transport on more than a century of Australian history. Regular events include the biennial Bay to Birdwood Run, in which more than 1000 vintage and early classic cars drive from West Beach Road, Adelaide, to the museum.

► *Shannon St, Birdwood, 50 km north-east of Adelaide.*

3 South Australian Maritime Museum

Experience sea life, without leaving port

Even the most steadfast of landlubbers will gain a real sense here of life on the ocean waves. Imaginative, interactive exhibits take you aboard a range of vessels of various kinds and eras. Settle into re-created cabins to find out what it was like to sail to Australia from Europe in the 1840s, 1910s and 1950s. Embark on *Active II*, a replica ketch, to learn about sea trade and travel in the late 1800s. Steel yourself for 'Action Stations!', a close look at naval life. Other highlights include a remarkable collection of ships' figureheads and a small heritage fleet anchored outside.

► *Lipson St, Port Adelaide.*

4 Fort Glanville

South Australia's first defensive structure

A symbol of how isolated and vulnerable the early colonists felt, the fort was built in the 1870s in response to a perceived threat of Russian invasion. Constructions began in 1878, but it was two years before the guns were in place and test fired. Within 10 years, the complex had been all but abandoned after the threat evaporated. Today the fort is one of the country's best examples of a 19th-century coastal fortification. Open days (third Sunday of the month, September to May) involve re-enactments of military drills.

► *Military Rd, Semaphore Park, 18 km north-west of Adelaide.*

THE BICENTENNIAL CONSERVATORY IN ADELAIDE BOTANIC GARDEN

5 Charles Sturt Museum

The search for an inland sea started here

It's intriguing to think of him sitting here, pondering the great unknown lands to the north, planning his daunting journey, perhaps daring to envision the immense body of water into which the eastern rivers he had explored must, it seemed, empty themselves. Sturt took up this then 200-ha property in 1839 and had the cottage built soon after. In August 1844, he departed from Adelaide, amid much fanfare, with a 15-man team and a boat, on a journey that he hoped would once and for all reveal the secrets of the Australian interior. After journeying thousands of kilometres and being stranded by drought and stricken by scurvy, he was forced homeward. Though now encircled by modern suburbia, the house (open the first and third Sunday of each month) has been faithfully restored to look as it did in Sturt's time and is an affecting evocation of the golden age of exploration.

▶ *Jetty St, Grange, 13 km west of Adelaide.*

Visitor information

Adelaide 1300 655 276
Glenelg 1300 422 008
Hahndorf 08 8388 1185
Mount Lofty 08 8370 1054
Port Adelaide 1800 629 888

6 Adelaide Botanic Garden

Wander through far-flung floral realms

A place of great serenity, the garden was laid out in the 1850s and encompasses formal lawns, themed plantings, artificial lakes and groves of trees, as well as three spectacular glasshouses. Inside the Bicentennial Conservatory – the largest single-span glasshouse in the Southern Hemisphere – is an unexpected sight so far from the tropics: a rainforest. A walkway takes visitors above the palms, ferns and vines, allowing close inspection of the lush canopy. Nearby, the Palm House is an ornate Victorian glasshouse imported from Germany in 1875, which now nurtures plants from Madagascar. The Amazon Waterlily Pavilion is a showcase for the astonishing *Victoria amazonica* lily, native to the Amazon; its flowers can reach 30 cm in diameter and its lily pads 1.65 m across.

▶ *North Tce, Adelaide.*

DIVERSE AND COLOURFUL INDIGENOUS ART IS ON DISPLAY AT TANDANYA.

7 Adelaide Oval

Picturesque sportsground, scene of legendary exploits

Tours of this handsome and historic sports venue allow you to take a close look at its stands, dressing rooms and famous Edwardian scoreboard, as well as the hallowed turf that has hosted some of the most stirring events in Australian sports history, including the tempestuous 1933 Bodyline Test matches and many of Don Bradman's most astonishing performances. Though he was brought up in New South Wales, Bradman settled in Adelaide, establishing a strong and lasting association with the ground, honoured today in the Bradman Collection Museum, which displays the Don's own memorabilia, including bats, clothing and scrapbooks.
▶ *War Memorial Dr, Adelaide.*

8 Migration Museum

Poignant record of epic journeys to a new homeland

Initially, they were mainly British, of course. But in the 1850s came Germans fleeing religious persecution in their native Prussia, in the 20th century increasing numbers of Italians, and, after the Second World War, boatloads of refugees from war-torn Europe. Today, migrants come to South Australia from all corners of the globe. Employing artefacts, documents, photographs and artworks, the museum documents the history of migration and the experiences of migrants, while celebrating the diverse heritages of Australians. One exhibit, 'Behind the Wall', surveys the history of the buildings that house the museum, once Adelaide's Destitute Asylum.
▶ *Kintore Ave, Adelaide.*

9 South Australian Museum

Indigenous collection shines amid remarkable assemblage of artefacts

This world-class museum of natural and human history, established in 1881, displays more than 3000 items over six floors of imaginative and engaging exhibits. Permanent fixtures include galleries of minerals and meteorites, fossils and megafauna, as well as an Ancient Egyptian room and a hall devoted to the exploits and achievements of Antarctic explorer Douglas Mawson. But the main drawcard is undoubtedly the Australian Aboriginal Cultures Gallery, a showcase for the world's biggest collection of Indigenous artefacts.

▶ *North Tce, Adelaide.*

10 Tandanya

Vibrant cultural centre highlights Indigenous creativity

A day spent at Tandanya, the National Aboriginal and Cultural Institute, rewards with keen and lasting insights into Indigenous modes of artistic expression. Start by perusing the art on display in the gallery space: exhibitions are everchanging but always thought-provoking, and often feature Aboriginal artists on the point of mainstream breakthrough. Catch the daily noon cultural performance, usually involving traditional dance or music, then check out the short films and documentaries showing in the theatre. A superb range of paintings and crafts is for sale in the shop, whose sales support artistic communities around the country.

▶ *Grenfell St, Adelaide.*

ADELAIDE CITY CENTRE

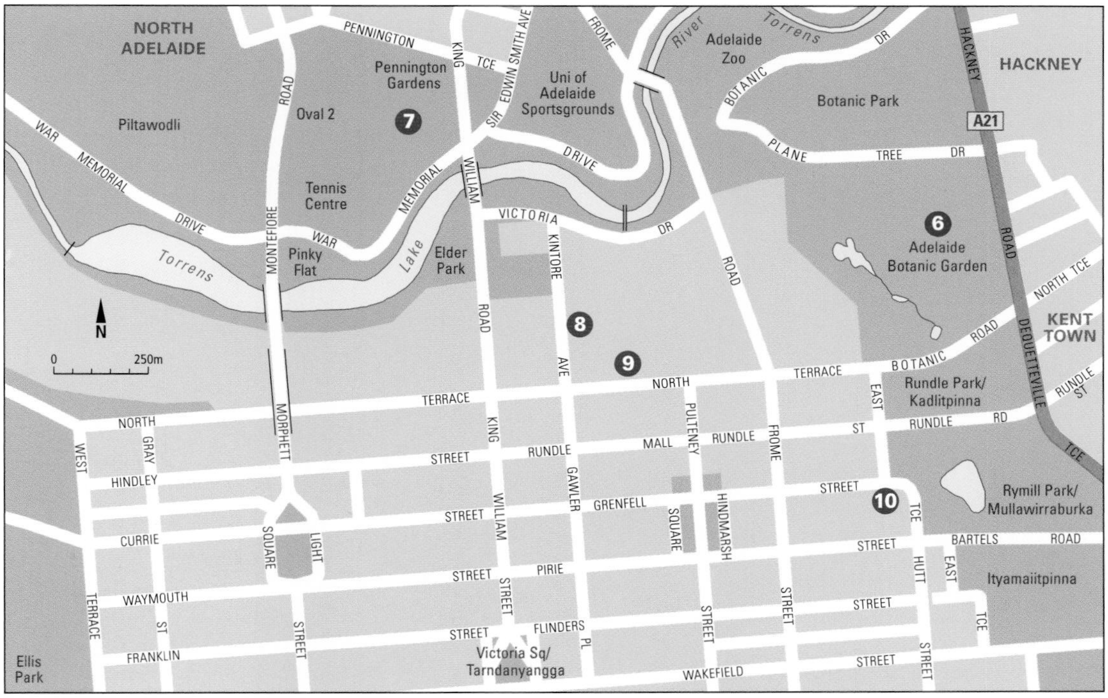

Enchanted hills

The Adelaide Hills are a car-tourer's delight, with inspiring views and intriguing sights unfolding at every turn.

Dubbed the 'enchanted hills' by Adelaide founder William Light, the hills are part of the ancient Mount Lofty Ranges, which extend for 320 km or so from the tip of the Fleurieu Peninsula to the Barossa Valley and divide the narrow coastal plain from the flatlands of the interior. The region was settled early, soon after the founding of Adelaide, by English, Scots and Germans, who quickly cleared forest and established pastoral properties and vineyards.

From Adelaide, roads climb through leafy hillside suburbs and quickly emerge in open country, winding on through gorges, past quaint villages and over rolling tablelands. From Lobethal, one of the first German settlements and site of Australia's oldest Lutheran church, a delightfully scenic route runs south along the valley of the Onkaparinga River through Woodside, with its heritage farm buildings and Hahndorf (see entry) to historic Clarendon, founded in 1840. The crowning glory – of the region and any day out – is Mount Lofty, at 727 m, the highest point in the ranges and site of a restaurant and a lookout with sensational views of Adelaide and the Gulf St Vincent.

VIEW OF ADELAIDE FROM THE HILLS AT SUNSET

11 HMS *Buffalo*

Replica of the ship that brought Adelaide's first colonists

In July 1836, ships belonging to the South Australian Company reached Kangaroo Island and established the future colony's first settlement at what is now Kingscote. A few months later, Captain John Hindmarsh and a group of 176 colonists set sail for the mainland aboard HMS *Buffalo*, arriving at what is now Glenelg in December and proclaiming the new colony. This replica of the ship stands on the spot where the colonists landed. In Macfarlane Street, north of the main beach area, is the oddly bent Old Gum Tree, where Hindmarsh is said to have read the proclamation establishing the government of the new colony. The replica houses a restaurant and a small museum; the original ship was wrecked off Mercury Bay, New Zealand, in 1840.

▶ *Anzac Hwy, Glenelg, 11 km south-west of Adelaide.*

12 Cleland Wildlife Park

Meet and greet a host of natives

Located just below Mount Lofty, this 35-ha reserve is home to more than 600 native animals from 130 species. Trails lead through bushland where many of the animals roam free. They are, however, so accustomed to the presence of humans that they are easily approached. Even closer acquaintances can be made at daily feeding sessions with lorikeets, dingoes, Tasmanian devils and snakes. The surrounding Cleland Conservation Park protects another 1000 ha of lovely bushland and gorges, and is the scene of a spectacular July-to-November wild-flower display.

▶ *Mount Lofty Summit Rd, 15 km south-east of Adelaide.*

13 Bridgewater

Charming village centred on historic mill

As the name suggests, this settlement was founded as a fording point, on Cox's Creek, in the early 1840s. It subsequently took shape around Bridgewater Mill, an impressive stone structure erected beside the creek by miller John Dunn in 1860. Originally powered by its 13-m-high water wheel, the mill was restored in the 1970s and now provides an atmospheric setting for Petaluma Winery's cellar door and outstanding restaurant. Two walking tours guide visitors to other heritage buildings, including the miller's cottage (1860), general store (1877) and old police station.

▶ *21 km south-east of Adelaide via South Eastern Fwy.*

14 Hahndorf

Australia's oldest German settlement

In December 1838, the ship *Zebra* landed at Port Adelaide carrying 200 Lutherans who had fled religious persecution in Prussia. The Danish captain of the *Zebra*, Dirk Hahn, went out of his way to help his passengers, eventually securing for them a lease on a parcel of land in the Adelaide Hills. In gratitude, the Lutherans named their settlement Hahndorf, 'Hahn's village'. Today's arrivals can best savour Hahndorf's distinctive atmosphere by wandering the attractive streets, lined with 1840s stone and half-timbered buildings, and visiting its German cafes, bakeries and smallgoods outlets. Architectural highlights include the Old Mill, dating from 1853 and now a restaurant; St Michael's Church, completed in 1859; and Hahndorf Academy, a schoolhouse built in 1857, which houses a museum of German migration and a small gallery.

▶ *26 km south-east of Adelaide via South Eastern Fwy.*

Fleurieu Peninsula and Kangaroo Island

A short drive south from Adelaide, white beaches, sandy coves, forest groves and seaside villages nestle below the steep, grassy hills of the scenic Fleurieu Peninsula. Across narrow Backstairs Passage, Kangaroo Island is a wildlife haven where an extraordinary range of animals can be observed at close quarters.

1 Bleasdale

Winemaking as it used to be done

As a prestigious winemaking operation, Bleasdale has to move with the times, and it employs the latest technology to create its renowned range of table and fortified wines. But every so often, its winemakers like to indulge themselves and squeeze out a special reserve using the National Trust–listed winery's remarkable range of antique equipment, most notably its colossal 1862 wine press. Built by founder Frank Potts and modelled on wine presses he had seen in Portugal, it is 15 m long, 7 m high and employs a 10-m, 3.5-tonne red gum tree as a lever. Take a look at the press then climb down into the domed cellar built in 1892, with its giant oak barrels, before lining up at the red-gum tasting bench to sample the excellent range of red, white, sparkling and fortified wines.

▶ *Wellington Rd, Langhorne Creek, 14 km south-east of Strathalbyn.*

BLEASDALE WINERY'S ANTIQUE WINE PRESS

2 Cockle Train

Enjoy a seaside outing on Australia's oldest iron-track railway

Explorer Charles Sturt suggested a settlement be built on the site of what is now Goolwa as early as 1830, and after the town's founding in 1840 there was talk of it being linked by canal to Encounter Bay to create South Australia's major seaport. Though nothing came of that idea, Goolwa evolved into a busy hub of river trade and in 1854 Australia's first public, iron-tracked railway – albeit horsedrawn – began hauling produce to Port Elliot for shipment to London. Today, steam- and diesel-powered locomotives pull tourists in vintage carriages along the same line between Goolwa and Victor Harbor (half an hour; Wednesday, Sunday and school holidays). It's a delightful trip, running practically along the beach south of Port Elliott and revealing superb sea views at every curve of the track. The name derives from the fact that in the early days Goolwa locals would take this train to the coast to gather cockles on the beaches.

▶ *Departs from Goolwa and Victor Harbor.*

3 Granite Island

Where a horse will take you to visit the penguins

An important cultural site for the local Ramindjeri people, this granite outcrop was a whaling station in the early 19th century. In the early 1880s, when nearby Victor Harbor was making a bid to become South Australia's capital city, it became the site of a major port and it was joined to the mainland by a wooden causeway in 1882. Goods were shipped down the Murray River, then brought here by train and tram to be loaded onto ships. The ships are long gone, and the island is now a nature reserve, but you can still walk or take a horsedrawn tram across the causeway. Once on the island, you can follow the Kaiki Walk (1.5 km) around the rocky, boulder-strewn shores, walk along the old jetty and then drop into the penguin centre to view and learn about the island's most famous residents, little penguins. Tours to view these charming creatures returning to their nests at dusk can be booked here.

▶ *Victor Harbor.*

4 Deep Creek Conservation Park

Pristine pockets of forest and stunning coastal scenery

Deep Creek protects the largest tract of natural vegetation on the Fleurieu Peninsula. Tall trees line the coastal cliffs and steep-sided valleys. Moist gullies, fed by permanent creeks, shelter ferns and orchids. Peregrine falcons and sea eagles soar above headlands and beaches, while rare birds such as the southern emu wren and elegant parrot are sometimes spotted inland; the park also supports the state's largest population of endangered short-nosed bandicoots. Among the easiest of the many walks are the half-hour Stringybark Loop Walk, which winds through stringybark forest and over burbling creeks, and the 5-km-return Spring Wildflower Walk, which follows a fire trail through undulating scrubland known for its colourful springtime blooms. Tapanappa Lookout offers marvellous views of the coast.

▶ *40 km west of Victor Harbor via Range Rd.*

Visitor information

Flinders Chase National Park 08 8559 7235
Goolwa 1300 466 592
McLaren Vale 08 8323 9944
Penneshaw 08 8553 1185
Strathalbyn 1300 007 842
Victor Harbor 08 8551 0777

Island ark

Isolation and an absence of predators have allowed wildlife – native and introduced – to flourish on Kangaroo Island.

Dingoes never made it to Kangaroo Island. Nor have introduced species such as the red fox and rabbit, which have caused such havoc elsewhere in Australia. Consequently, the island's land-dwelling creatures, ranging from possums and goannas to Kangaroo Island kangaroos (a subspecies of the eastern grey) and Tammar wallabies, have lived on here relatively undisturbed, enduring in abundance while mainland populations have dwindled.

The island's marine mammals had a harder time, being hunted ruthlessly by sealers and whalers in the 19th century, but have since made a remarkable come-back. Sea lions and fur seals throng the shores and there are sizeable little penguin colonies at Penneshaw and Kingscote (guided tours available). Birdlife is also prolific, and this is the last refuge of the South Australian glossy black cockatoo.

Several mainland species were introduced here to ensure their preservation, notably the Cape Barren goose, platypus and koala. The koalas arrived in the 1920s and are now so numerous that they have defoliated large areas of forest. In 1881, August Fiebig brought 12 hives of bees from Liguria in Italy and set up an apiary near Penneshaw. The island's Ligurian bees are now believed to be the only pure stock of this species left anywhere in the world.

5 Admirals Arch

Where seals make a grand entrance

Hordes of New Zealand fur seals haul themselves out of the surf and lumber up the rocks around and beneath this majestic, stalactite-encrusted natural archway. It was hollowed out of the limestone promontory by wave action that initially formed a giant cave before breaking right through. The seals were once hunted close to extinction for their pelts, but are now abundant and the colony here numbers up to 7000. Nearby, the tip of Cape du Couedic is crowned by a lighthouse first lit in 1909, sited 105 m above the sea.

► *Flinders Chase National Park, 146 km west of Penneshaw.*

6 Remarkable Rocks

Sculpted stones crown granite dome

Aptly named, these magnificent boulders sit atop the great granite mass of Kilpatrick Point, a prominent vantage point with sweeping views of the Southern Ocean. The granite formed 500 million years ago as a subterranean flow of magma that intruded into surrounding rocks. Weathering exposed the rock and cracked its surface, isolating smaller blocks on the summit. The blocks were then whittled and honeycombed by water and salt-laden winds, leaving these strange formations, made yet more fantastic by mineral stains and a coating of orange lichen. The arches, nooks and holes provide plentiful opportunities for artistic and fun photographs, but visitors must take care as the rocks can be slippery and winds tempestuous.

► *Flinders Chase National Park, 150 km west of Penneshaw.*

7 Kelly Hill Caves

Extensive subterranean system, stumbled upon by an unfortunate horse

In the 1880s, a stockman named Kelsey was riding his horse through the thick scrub here when it suddenly fell into and became trapped in a sinkhole. Kelsey went for help, but by the time he came back the horse had disappeared. Later investigations revealed the sinkhole to be part of an extensive and mysterious underground realm of tunnels and chambers, many adorned with ornate calcite formations. Guided tours explore some of the caves, highlighting beautiful stalagmites, stalactites, shawls and straws, and adventure-caving expeditions can be organised for those who want to delve deeper.

▶ *Kelly Hill Conservation Park, 113 km south-west of Penneshaw.*

8 Seal Bay

Ranger-guided rendezvous with sea lions

It's a slightly unnerving experience, wandering through a colony of up to 100 Australian sea lions, with the huge bulls – measuring up to 2.5 m long and 220 kg, and displaying powerful teeth and jaws – eyeing you up as you pass. But the rangers who lead these thrilling tours along the sands of Seal Bay are alert to the slightest sign of aggression and adept at keeping their charges at just the right distance. So you can relax and just marvel at the scenes around you – sea lions lolloping out of the surf, territorial males sizing up their rivals, pups snuggling up to their mothers, and the waves rolling in endlessly on the pristine white sands. And count your blessings: this is one of the few places in the world where sea lions tolerate human visitors. And if you prefer to keep your distance, you can still peer down on the colony from the 800-m boardwalk just above the beach.

▶ *Seal Bay Conservation Park, 87 km south-west of Penneshaw.*

YOUNG AND FEMALE SEA LIONS ON THE SANDS AT SEAL BAY

Limestone Coast

Subterranean passageways and fossil-filled chambers honeycomb this low-lying limestone plain, and old seaports and lagoons thronging with birds line its shoreline. Volcanic craters loom above the southern plains, and fabled vineyards flank charming villages in the interior.

1 Old Tailem Town

Turn a corner and turn back time

This is Australia's largest pioneer village re-creation, incorporating more than 110 re-located heritage buildings arranged in 12 streets. Most are at least a century old, though they date from between 1870 and 1960, and all are furnished with fittings, artefacts, equipment and tools from the relevant era. Among them are more than 30 shops, a school, a picture theatre, a stable housing Clydesdale horses, a railway with 1 km of track and 19 carriages, and a hall where visitors can dance to old-time music. There's even a collection of early speedboats, including the world's first hydroplane.

▶ *South Eastern Fwy, 5 km north of Tailem Bend.*

2 Jacks Point

Top spot for viewing Coorong birdlife

The Coorong (see opposite) is one of the country's most important wetland reserves and a vital breeding place for a wide range of bird species. The short walk to Jacks Point (1.2 km, 20 minutes return) provides an introduction to the dune and wetland ecosystems and some of the best and most easily accessible views of the lagoons and birdlife. In particular, the waters beneath the viewing shelter are among the Coorong's most important pelican breeding grounds and you can normally observe large numbers of these very large birds. En route to the lookout, interpretive signs identify plants and explain their use by the local Ngarrindjeri people for food and medicine and to weave baskets and hats.

▶ *Princes Hwy, 43 km south of Tailem Bend.*

3 Bordertown Wildlife Park

Have a peek at a mob of white kangaroos

They're there, in among the reds and greys, and red-neck and Tammar wallabies, though you'll have to peer through the perimeter fence to see them, as public access is not permitted: a group of about 15 white kangaroos. And they really are white. All are the progeny or descendants of a large male white kangaroo that was captured near the NSW border and brought here in 1980. More than 50 have been bred since, with many having been placed in other reserves and zoos.

▶ *Dukes Hwy, Bordertown.*

4 Analemmatic Sundial

Cast a shadow to tell the time

An analemmatic sundial consists of a semicircle of 15 numbered hour markers facing inward towards a stone platform or analemma. Stand at the appropriate point on the platform for the time of year, and your shadow will indicate the time of day on the markers. Located on a small island in Maria Creek, this is one of only a few such sundials in the world.

▶ *Apex Park, East Tce, Kingston SE.*

Visitor information

Beachport 08 8735 8029
Bordertown 08 8752 0700
Millicent 08 8733 0904
Mount Gambier 08 8724 9750
Naracoorte 08 8762 1399
Penola 08 8737 2855

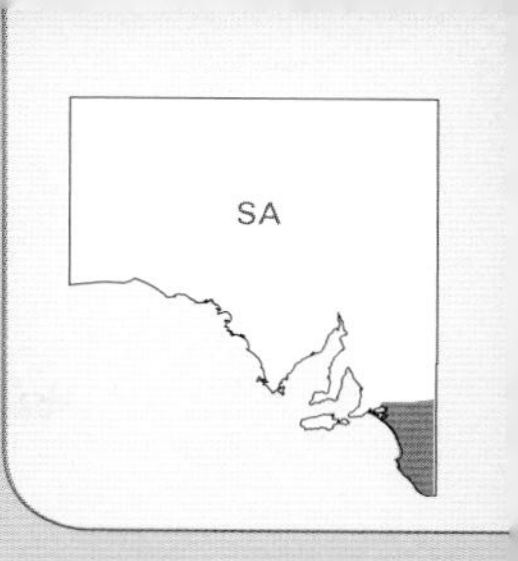

The magic of the Coorong

Sheltered from the sea by the sand dunes of the Younghusband Peninsula, these shallow saline lagoons brim with birdlife.

Only a couple of kilometres wide on average, but more than 130 km long, the Coorong's waterways arc along the Limestone Coast from Lake Alexandrina to Lacepede Bay. Considered wetlands of international significance, they are a refuge for vast numbers of resident and migratory birds belonging to more than 200 species, including ducks, swans, terns, grebes and cormorants, and a vital breeding ground for Australian pelicans – more gather here than anywhere else in Australia.

The Coorong's waterways are fed by the Murray River via Lakes Alexandrina and Albert. The lakes are classified as freshwater, but the lagoons become progressively narrower and more silted and salty, until at the southern end, they have a much higher salt content than the sea. In recent years, however, heavier than normal rains in south-eastern Australia have reduced salinity levels to some extent and boosted fish and, consequently, bird breeding levels.

For the Ngarrindjeri people, food was plentiful enough here to sustain semi-permanent settlement for thousands of years; middens of discarded shells still mark their camp sites. In the 1850s, many Chinese gold prospectors disembarked in this region and the ruins of a circular well they built can be seen at Chinamans Well. There are good lagoon viewing points at Pelican Point, Jacks Point (see entry) and Salt Creek, and the best 2WD access to the shore is at 42 Mile Crossing.

PELICANS AND SEAGULLS GATHER ON THE COORONG

CAPE DOMBEY OBELISK, ROBE

5 Cape Dombey Obelisk

Lifesaving landmark

In the mid-1800s Robe became one of South Australia's busiest ports, especially after the start of the Victorian gold rush, when thousands of prospectors, including 16,000 Chinese miners and their families, were landed here by shipping companies in order to avoid paying the Victorian government's poll tax. The entrance to Guichen Bay was consequently a busy shipping lane, and not without its risks. This distinctive 12-m-high red-and-white structure was erected in 1852 to help guide ships into the bay. In addition, it was used to store rockets and rescue equipment. The rockets were used to fire ropes and other aids to ships in distress, and saved many lives.

▶ *Cape Dombey, Robe, 43 km south of Princes Hwy at Kingston SE.*

6 Naracoorte Caves

Go underground to see one of the world's richest fossil deposits

This extraordinary subterranean realm of 26 caves has revealed much about the geological and natural history of the Limestone Coast region. Geologists have established that the limestone itself formed beneath the ocean before being uplifted about 26 million years ago. Water percolating down through cracks then slowly created Naracoorte's network of chambers and passages. Hundreds of fossils have been found in rock layers and cavities, dating back up to half a million years and painting a remarkably detailed picture of the region's ancient fauna – skeletons show, for example, that no fewer than 20 kangaroo species roamed the plains then. Tours take in several caves, including Alexandra Cave, with its exquisite calcite formations; Bat Cave, a seasonal nursery for a colony of 300,000 bentwing bats; and Victoria Fossil Cave, which has yielded the country's largest and best-preserved animal fossils.

▶ *Hynam–Caves Rd, 10 km south of Naracoorte.*

7 Bool Lagoon Game Reserve

Home away from home for East Asian migrants

Recognised as a wetland of international importance under the Ramsar Convention, Bool Lagoon is home to more than 150 species of waterbirds, many of them rare and endangered. Twenty-seven species, including sandpipers and plovers, migrate here annually from Japan, China and Siberia, seeking refuge from the Northern-Hemisphere winter. In spring, breeding colonies of egrets and spoonbills nest noisily in the tea-trees that grow around the lagoon's south-eastern basin. You can watch all these comings and goings from a boardwalk and bird hide. The adjacent but smaller Hacks Lagoon Reserve attracts similar birdlife and has camping.

▶ *Bool Lagoon Rd, 24 km south of Naracoorte.*

8 Wynns Coonawarra

Iconic *terra rossa* winery

Three essential ingredients for the production of top-quality red wines converge in the Coonawarra district: a long, cool ripening season, pure underground water and a layer of rich, well-drained soil – in this case a strip of distinctive red earth, or *terra rossa*, about 15 km long and 1 km wide running south to Penola. Substantial vineyards were first planted here in 1890 by John Riddoch, who subsequently built this grand winery, taken over by the Wynn family in 1951. Since then it has produced some of Australia's most highly regarded red wines. You can sample them at the cellar door in the distinctive triple-gabled 1891 building, which Riddoch called Chateau Comaum, and even join a 'Make Your Own Blend' tour to concoct your preferred mix of shiraz, cabernet sauvignon and merlot to take away.

▶ *Memorial Dr, Coonawarra, 40 km south of Naracoorte.*

9 Penola

Where a saint taught school

The oldest town in the south-east, Penola has a delightful main street lined with awnings – some festooned with grapevines – and a historic precinct, Petticoat Lane, incorporating early slab timber and stone cottages. The oldest, Sharam Cottage, dates from the 1850s. Nearby is the 1867 schoolhouse built by the founders of the religious order of the Sisters of St Joseph, Father Julian Tenison Woods and Sister Mary McKillop – who was canonised in 2010. Displays in here and at the Mary McKillop Interpretive Centre chronicle the saint's life and work. The wider history of the region is recounted in the John Riddoch Centre.

▶ *51 km south of Naracoorte.*

10 Yallum Park

Perhaps the best-preserved Victorian-era house in Australia

This grand, gracious homestead was built for John Riddoch (see Wynns Coonawarra) between 1878 and 1880. Designed in Italianate style, the two-storey structure is surrounded by exquisite formal gardens planted with trees from every corner of the globe. Inside, most of the original furnishings and fittings have been preserved, including stained-glass and etched windows, William Morris wallpapers, marble mantlepieces and ornate glass and silverware. Visits are by appointment, though tours take place every so often – contact the Penola visitor centre for details.

▶ *Millicent Rd, Penola, 59 km south of Naracoorte.*

11 Woakwine Cutting

Said to be Australia's largest two-man engineering project

It may not look like much in these days of gargantuan construction projects, but this roadside oddity is testimony to an individual's extraordinary determination. In 1957, Murray McCourt, seeking an effective way to drain his land, decided that the best solution was to cut a channel through adjacent ranges to Lake George. Assisted by just one worker, Dick McIntyre, he began excavating a sheer-walled trench. Three years later, they had finished. Running for 1 km, the cutting is 3 m wide at the base and reaches a depth of 28.34 m. A viewing platform overlooks McCourt's handiwork and also provides fine views of Lake George and coastal dunes.

▶ *Southern Ports Hwy, 12 km north of Beachport.*

12 Tantanoola Caves

Show cave inside an ancient sea cliff

Set amid pine plantations, this network of chambers has formed inside a line of dolomite cliffs that were part of an ancient coastline. Guided tours visit the main chamber, which has an amazing array of fluted pipes and filigreed stalactites and stalagmites. After touring the cave, picnic under the trees or stroll along the walking trail around the Up and Down Rocks to enjoy views of the surrounding forests, volcanic peaks and distant coastline.

▶ *Tantanoola Caves Conservation Park, Princes Hwy, 26 km north-west of Mount Gambier.*

13 Blue Lake

Volcano plays the blues

The precise shade shifts with the season, but the lake always lives up to its name: in winter the waters are a steely blue-grey, in summer a startling sapphire. Blue Lake occupies one of the three craters that crown Mount Gambier, the continent's youngest volcano at a spritely 4500 years

MOUNT GAMBIER'S BLUE LAKE LIVING UP TO ITS NAME

old. A road encircles the 3.6-km circumference and there are several lookouts. More than 80 m deep, the lake supplies the city with drinking water; an interpretive centre within the Blue Lake Pumping Station explains the process. The Adam Lindsay Gordon Obelisk marks the spot where the daredevil poet (see Dingley Dell) is said to have jumped a guardrail on horseback, turning the animal in mid-air to land centimetres from the edge of a narrow ledge, 70 m above the water.

▶ *John Watson Dr, Mount Gambier.*

14 Mount Schanck

Climb into the crater of a young but extinct volcano

The same volcanic eruptions that formed Mount Gambier (see Blue Lake) 4500 years ago also gave rise to Mount Schanck, whose prominent cone rises 100 m above the surrounding plains. From the car park, a walking track (2–3 hours return) with interpretive signs climbs fairly steeply to a lookout on the rim of the main crater, from where you can peer into its depths and north to Mount Gambier. From here, you can continue around the edge of the crater, which measures 300 m in diameter, or descend to its floor via a steep path. The volcano was named in 1800 by mariner James Grant after the designer of his ship, Admiral John Schanck.

▶ *Mount Schanck State Heritage Area, Port MacDonnell Rd, 16 km south of Mount Gambier.*

15 Dingley Dell

A poet's home and inspiration

Between 1864 and 1867, the poet and horseman Adam Lindsay Gordon made this charming colonial cottage his coastal retreat. It was here that he wrote much of his work – notably most of the books *Sea Spray* and *Drift Smoke and Bush Ballads* – and spent his happiest times. Today, filled with Gordon's belongings and other mementos of his era, the cottage provides insights into both the poet's character and everyday life in this district in the 1860s. Outside, a trail meanders through eucalypts and wattles and along elevated ridges, revealing fine vistas of the volcanic humps of Mounts Schanck and Gambier.

▶ *Port MacDonnell Rd, 29 km south of Mount Gambier.*

Index

Page numbers in *italics* refer to photographs

A

B

C

G

H

I

N

O

P

T

U

V

W

Picture credits

Front cover *left to right* Alamy, Shutterstock, Tourism Victoria **Spine** Alamy **Back cover** *main* Getty Images *top left to right* Dreamstime, Auscape, Auscape, Alamy, Photolibrary, Auscape **1** Tourism Victoria **2–3** OzStock Images **4–5** Photolibrary **6** Alamy **8–9** iStockphoto **10–11** Shutterstock **12** Wildlight **14–15** Photolibrary **17** Auscape **18** Alamy **22** Photolibrary **25** Corbis **27** Tourism Western Australia **29** Tourism Western Australia **31** Photolibrary **34–35** Photolibrary **39** Photolibrary **40** Auscape **42–43** Photolibrary **45** Corbis **46–47** Tourism Western Australia **48–49** Photolibrary **52** Auscape **55** Tourism Western Australia **57** Getty Images **59** Corbis **64–65** Photolibrary **66–67** Photolibrary **68–69** Wildlight **70–71** Photolibrary **72** Shutterstock **73** Shutterstock **74** Wikipedia Commons **77** Tourism Queensland **78–79** Getty Images **83** Shutterstock **86** The Heritage Hotel, Rockhampton **88–89** Tourism Queensland **90** Alamy **93** Photolibrary **94** Tourism Queensland **96–97** Shutterstock **99** Tourism Queensland **100–101** Tourism Queensland **103** Abbey Museum of Art and Archaeology **104–105** Tourism Queensland **109** Alamy **111** Tourism Queensland **112–113** Shutterstock **116** OzStock Images **118–119** Photolibrary **121** Tourism New South Wales **123** University of New England **125** Bob King **126–127** Shutterstock **129** Auscape **130–131** Shutterstock **132** Tourism New South Wales **134** Getty Images **137** iStockphoto **138** Alamy **140–141** Tourism New South Wales **143** Photolibrary **145** Tourism New South Wales **146** Tourism New South Wales **148** Donna Heldon **151** Lonely Planet **154** Shutterstock **155** Alamy **156–157** Tourism New South Wales **161** Photolibrary **162** Tourism New South Wales **165** Alamy **168–169** Photolibrary **171** Auscape **172–173** Wildlight **174** Tourism New South Wales **178–179** Photolibrary **180** Tourism New South Wales **183** Photolibrary **184** Wildlight **186–187** Shutterstock **188–189** Corbis **191** Australian Capital Tourism **192** Alamy **194–195** Shutterstock **197** Wildlight **198–199** Tourism Victoria **201** Photolibrary **202** Alamy **205** Tourism Victoria **206** Sovereign Hill **209** Tourism Victoria **210–211** Tourism Victoria **212** Tourism Victoria **215** Wildlight **218–219** OzStock Images **221** Tourism Victoria **223–224** Dreamstime **224** Auscape **227** Tourism Victoria **230** Photolibrary **233** Photolibrary **234** Photolibrary **237** Tourism Victoria **238–239** Auscape **241** Tourism Victoria **242** Photolibrary **244–245** Tourism Victoria **246–247** Photolibrary **248–248** Photolibrary **251** Photolibrary **253** Dreamstime **255** Photolibrary **256** Tourism Tasmania **258–259** Getty Images **260–261** Leigh Carmichael/MONA Museum of Old and New Art **265** Getty Images **266–267** Tourism Tasmania **268** Tourism Tasmania **269–270** Shutterstock **272–273** Photolibrary **274** Auscape **275** Tourism South Australia **277** Photolibrary **278** Steamtown Heritage Rail Centre **280–281** Photolibrary **285** Photolibrary **287** Photolibrary **288** The Château Tanunda Estate **290** Banrock Station **292–293** Photolibrary **295** iStockphoto **296** Tourism South Australia **299** Photolibrary **300** Photolibrary **303** Dreamstime **305** Photolibrary **307** Shutterstock **308–309** Dreamstime

AUSTRALIA'S MOST AMAZING PLACES

Project Editor Scott Forbes

Senior Editor Samantha Kent

Writers Scott Forbes, Margaret McPhee

Concept Design Donna Heldon and Kylie Mulquin

Project Designer Stan Lamond

Senior Designer Donna Heldon

Cartography John Frith, Flat Earth Mapping

Photographic Coordinator Natalie Zizic

Picture Researchers Natalie Zizic, Clare Forte, Helen Flint

Proofreader Kevin Diletti

Index Diane Harriman

Senior Production Controller Monique Tesoriero

READER'S DIGEST GENERAL BOOKS

Editorial Director Lynn Lewis

Managing Editor Rosemary McDonald

Art Director Carole Orbell

Front cover *left to right* Elephant Rocks, near Greens Pool, William Bay National Park, Western Australia; Dorrigo National Park, New South Wales; Princess Margaret Rose Cave, Lower Glenelg National Park, Victoria
Spine Dandenong Ranges National Park, Victoria
Back cover *main image* Wallaman Falls, Girringun National Park, Queensland; *top left to top right* Seal Bay Conservation Park, Kangaroo Island, South Australia; rock art at Ubirr, Northern Territory; Black Lighthouse, Queenscliff, Victoria; Main shrine, Nan Tien Temple, Wollongong, New South Wales; Bridestowe Estate Lavender Farm, Nabola, Tasmania; sculpture by Antony Gormley, Lake Ballard, Western Australia
Page 1 Great Hall, NGV International, Melbourne, Victoria
Pages 2–3 The Lost City, Cape Crawford, Northern Territory
Pages 4–5 Heart Reef, Great Barrier Reef, Queensland
Page 6 Dandenong Ranges National Park, Victoria

Australia's Most Amazing Places is published by
Reader's Digest (Australia) Pty Limited
80 Bay Street, Ultimo, NSW, 2007
www.readersdigest.com.au
www.readersdigest.co.nz

First published in 2011. Reprinted 2012 (pbk.)

National Library of Australia
Cataloguing-in-Publication entry
Title: Australia's most amazing places.
ISBN: 978-1-921743-97-9 (hbk.)
978-1-921744-10-5 (pbk.)
Notes: Includes index.
Subjects: Historic sites – Australia. Australia – Geography. Australia – Description and travel.
Other Authors/Contributors: Reader's Digest (Australia)
Dewey Number: 919.4

Prepress by Sinnott Bros, Sydney
Printed and bound by Leo Paper Products, China

We are interested in receiving your comments on the content of this book. Write to:
The Editor, General Books Editorial,
Reader's Digest (Australia) Pty Limited,
GPO Box 4353, Sydney, NSW 2001
or email us at: bookeditors.au@readersdigest.com

To order additional copies of *Australia's Most Amazing Places,* please contact us at:
www.readersdigest.com.au or phone 1300 300 030 (Australia); www.readersdigest.co.nz; or phone 0800 400 060 (New Zealand) or email us at customerservice@readersdigest.com.au

Concept code: AU 0837
Product code: 041 4502 (hbk)
041 4503 (pbk)

Key to regions

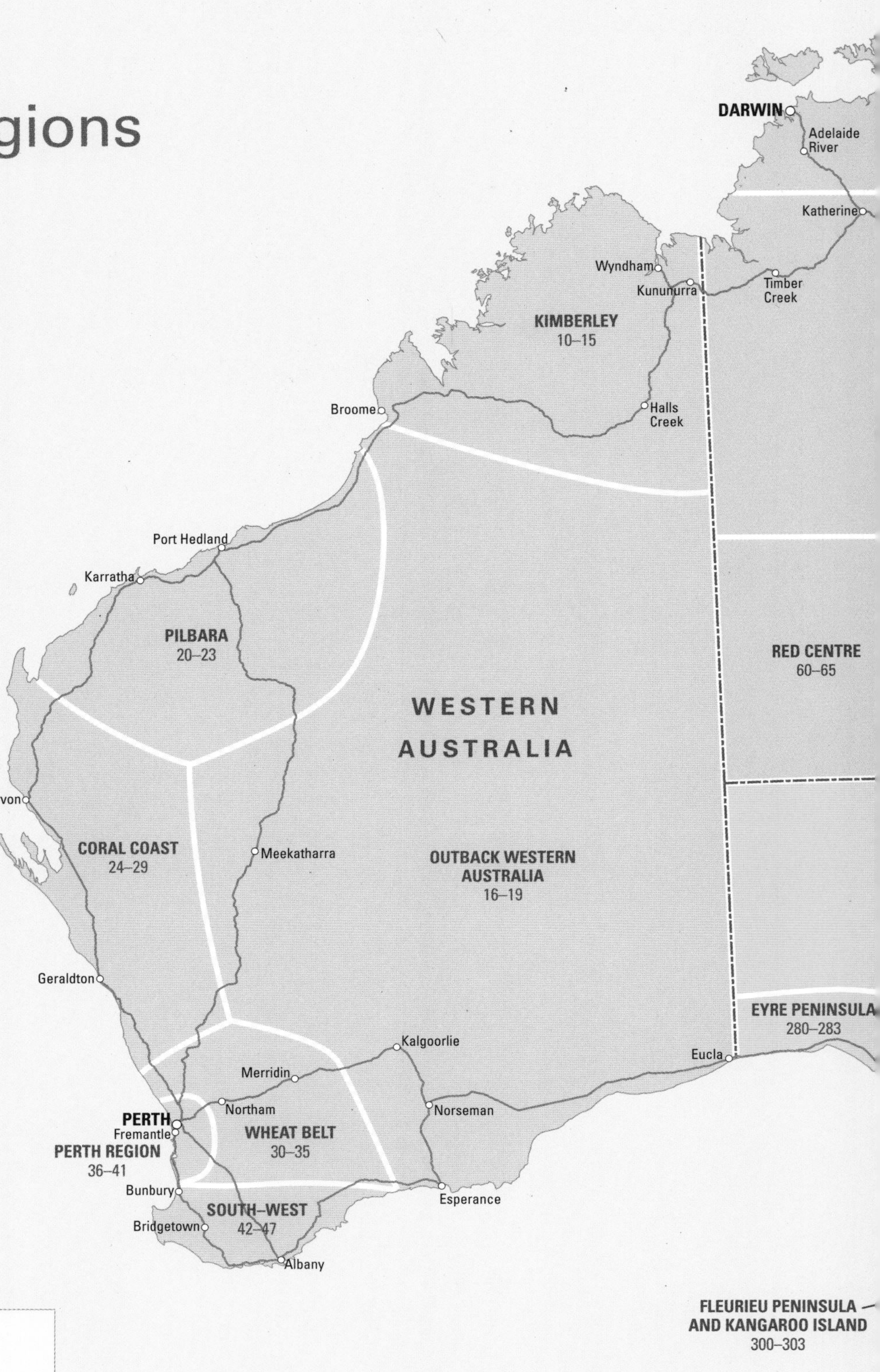
DARWIN
Adelaide River
Katherine
Wyndham
Kununurra
Timber Creek
KIMBERLEY
10–15
Broome
Halls Creek
Port Hedland
Karratha
PILBARA
20–23
RED CENTRE
60–65
WESTERN AUSTRALIA
Carnarvon
CORAL COAST
24–29
Meekatharra
OUTBACK WESTERN AUSTRALIA
16–19
Geraldton
EYRE PENINSULA
280–283
Kalgoorlie
Eucla
Merridin
Northam
Norseman
PERTH
Fremantle
PERTH REGION
36–41
WHEAT BELT
30–35
Bunbury
SOUTH-WEST
42–47
Esperance
Bridgetown
Albany
FLEURIEU PENINSULA AND KANGAROO ISLAND
300–303

City centre maps